THE COMPLETE NEWSPAPER

Wallace & Gromit

COMIC STRIPS COLLECTION

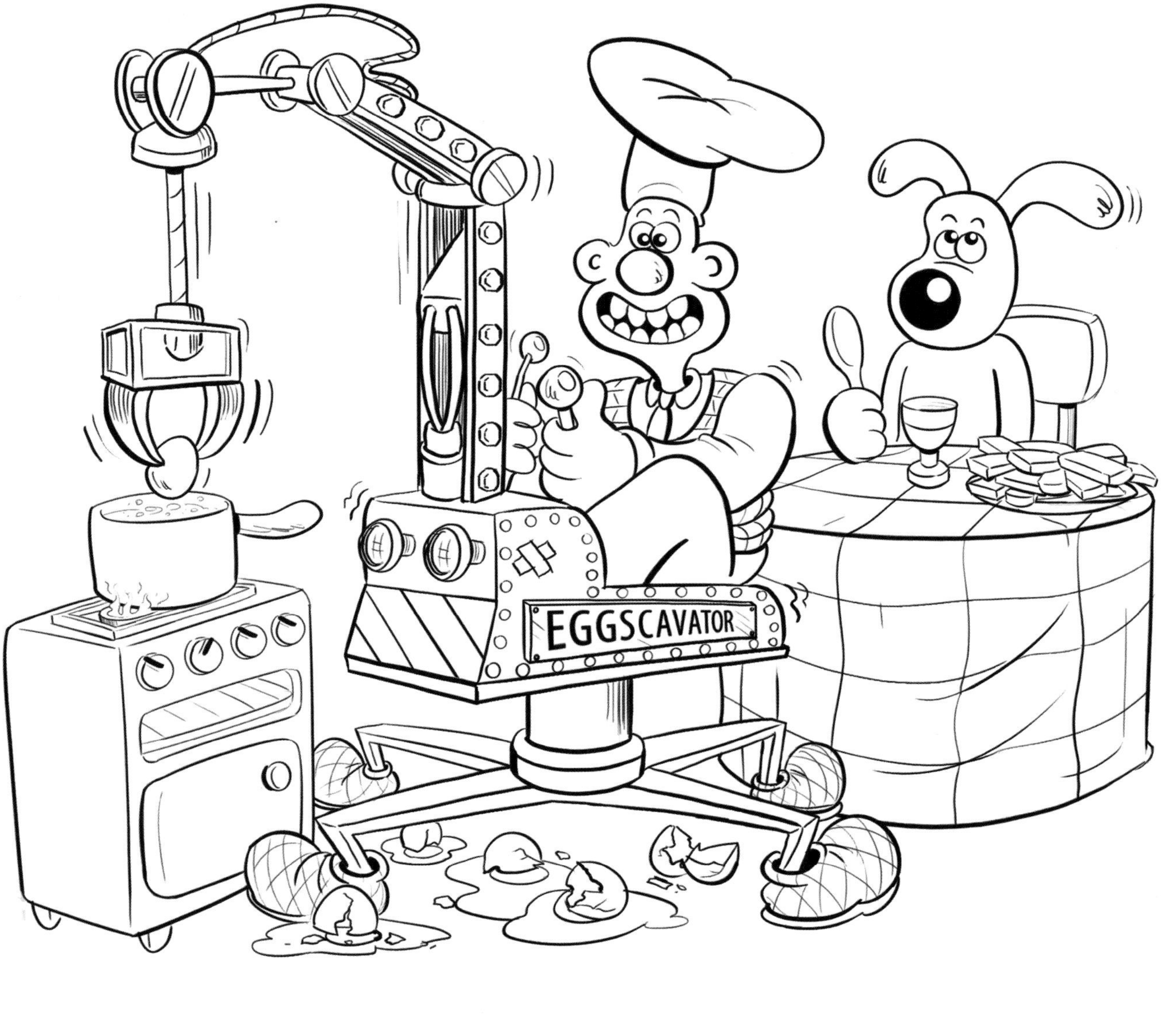
EGGSCAVATOR

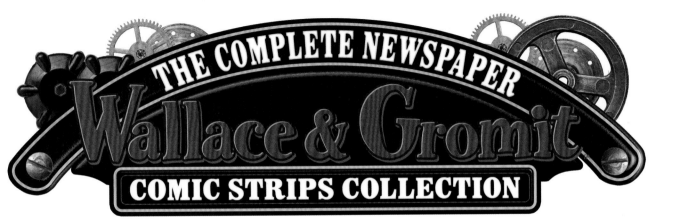

Wallace & Gromit:

The Complete Newspaper Comic Strips Collection.
Volume 3: 2012 - 2013

ISBN: 9781782762041

Published by Titan Comics, a division of Titan Publishing Group Ltd.,
144 Southwark St., London, SE1 0UP.

Wallace & Gromit newspaper comic strips originally published in The Sun newspaper.

A CIP catalogue record for this title is available from the British Library.

This edition first published: April 2015

Printed in China

10 9 8 7 6 5 4 3 2 1

EDITOR - David Manley-Leach DESIGNER - Donna Askem

TITAN COMICS - *Senior Comics Editor:* Martin Eden *Art Director:* Oz Browne *Studio Manager:* Emma Smith
Production Manager: Obi Onuora *Production Supervisors:* Maria Pearson, Jackie Flook *Production Assistant:* Peter James
Circulation Manager: Steve Tothill *Marketing Manager:* Ricky Claydon *Advertising Manager:* Michelle Fairlamb
Publishing Manager: Darryl Tothill *Publishing Director:* Chris Teather *Operations Director:* Leigh Baulch
Executive Director: Vivian Cheung *Publisher:* Nick Landau

Volume 3: 2012 - 2013

TITAN COMICS

Foreword by Peter Lord CBE

I've always loved comics, all my life. Can't get enough of them. In fact my only complaint is that there aren't enough of the really comic ones around these days. Oh yes, there are plenty of super-heroes and cool manga and there's no shortage of gloomy urban realism – but the classic British comic – the one that actually makes you laugh – is getting harder to find.

I know that when Nick Park first created Wallace and Gromit, a lot of the ideas and the images came out of the world of comic books. It's the sort of world where wonderful things come out of ordinary situations, where a man can build a rocket in his cellar and fly it to the moon in the distant hope that he'll find some cheese there. Or where a penguin can turn up at the front door and get taken in as a lodger – no questions asked.

And the terrific cartoons in this book carry on the grand old tradition of Wallace and Gromit stories. Including everything you'd want to see from the dynamic duo of West Wallaby Street. It's got inventions, as Wallace continues to build incredible machines to make life simpler – in the most complicated way possible. It's got cheese, of course – where would Wallace be without his Wensleydale? And it's got some really terrible puns – always a big part of their lives.

So welcome to the cosy, familiar and yet utterly barmy world of Wallace and Gromit. Put on the kettle, settle down with a plate of cheese and crackers and celebrate the collected adventures of these two most British cartoon characters.

Peter Lord CBE
Co-Founder Aardman Animations

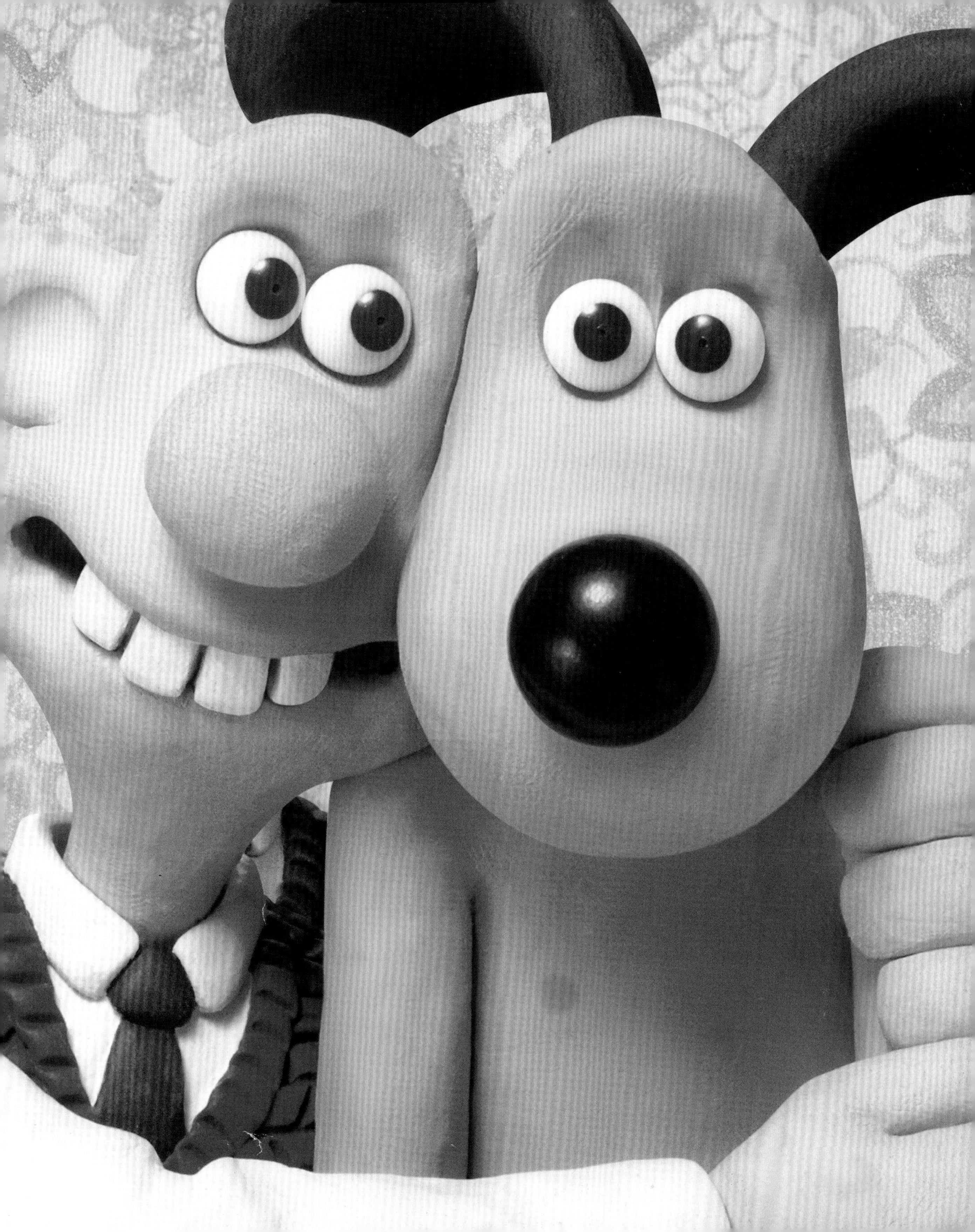

Wallace & Gromit - Lovely Jubilee

by Aardman & Titan Comics

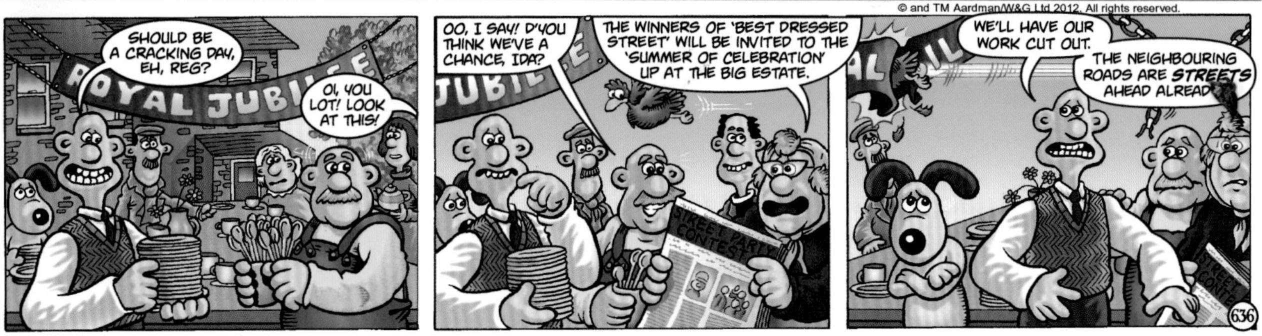
SHOULD BE A CRACKING DAY, EH, REG?
ROYAL JUBILEE
OI, YOU LOT! LOOK AT THIS!
OO, I SAY! D'YOU THINK WE'VE A CHANCE, IDA?
THE WINNERS OF 'BEST DRESSED STREET' WILL BE INVITED TO THE 'SUMMER OF CELEBRATION' UP AT THE BIG ESTATE.
STREET PARTY CONTEST
WE'LL HAVE OUR WORK CUT OUT.
THE NEIGHBOURING ROADS ARE ***STREETS*** AHEAD ALREAD
636

Wallace & Gromit - Lovely Jubilee

by Aardman & Titan Comics

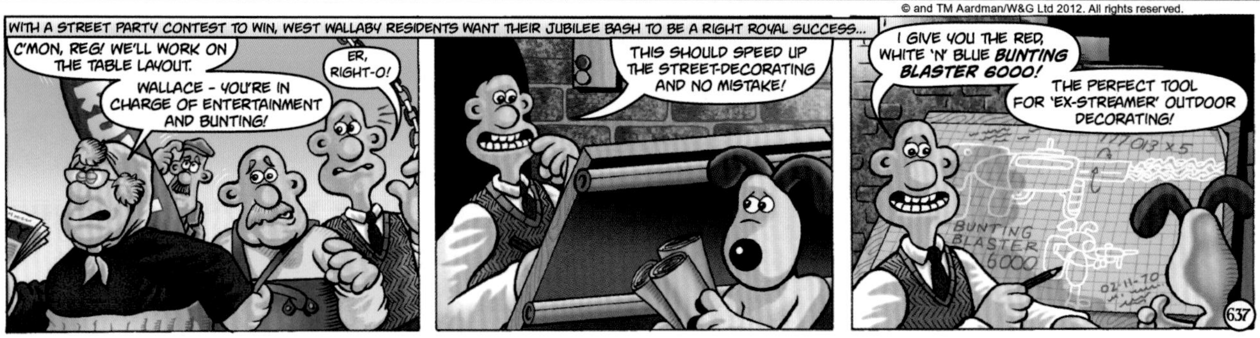
WITH A STREET PARTY CONTEST TO WIN, WEST WALLABY RESIDENTS WANT THEIR JUBILEE BASH TO BE A RIGHT ROYAL SUCCESS...
C'MON, REG! WE'LL WORK ON THE TABLE LAYOUT.
WALLACE - YOU'RE IN CHARGE OF ENTERTAINMENT AND BUNTING!
ER, RIGHT-O!
THIS SHOULD SPEED UP THE STREET-DECORATING AND NO MISTAKE!
I GIVE YOU THE RED, WHITE 'N' BLUE ***BUNTING BLASTER 6000!***
THE PERFECT TOOL FOR 'EX-STREAMER' OUTDOOR DECORATING!
BUNTING BLASTER 6000
637

Wallace & Gromit - Lovely Jubilee

by Aardman & Titan Comics

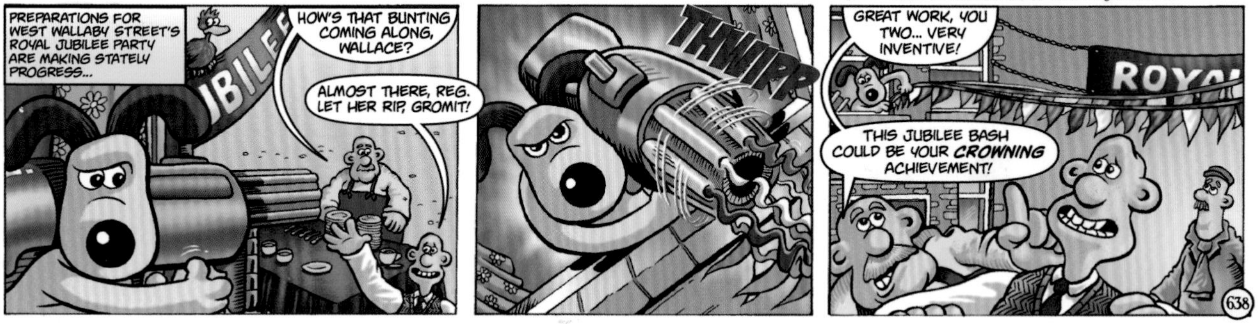
PREPARATIONS FOR WEST WALLABY STREET'S ROYAL JUBILEE PARTY ARE MAKING STATELY PROGRESS...
HOW'S THAT BUNTING COMING ALONG, WALLACE?
ALMOST THERE, REG. LET HER RIP, GROMIT!
THWIPP
GREAT WORK, YOU TWO... VERY INVENTIVE!
THIS JUBILEE BASH COULD BE YOUR ***CROWNING*** ACHIEVEMENT!
638

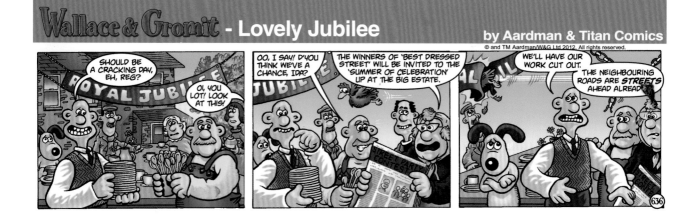

Wallace & Gromit - Lovely Jubilee

by Aardman & Titan Comics

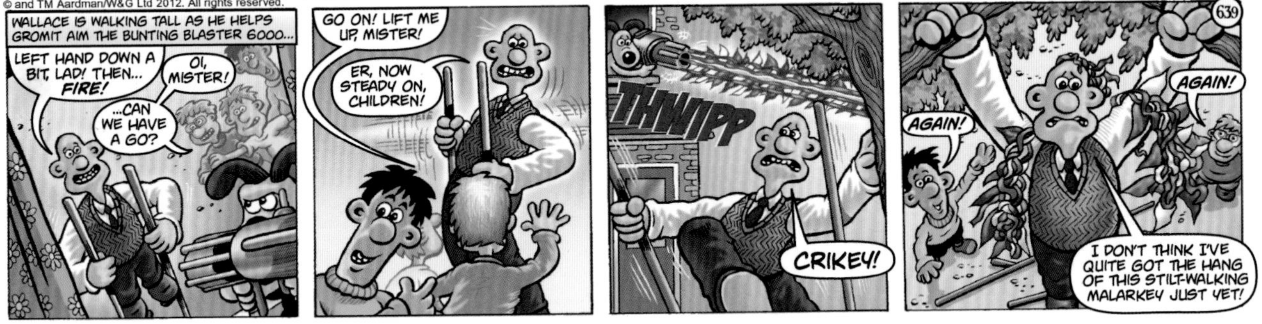

639
WALLACE IS WALKING TALL AS HE HELPS GROMIT AIM THE BUNTING BLASTER 6000...
LEFT HAND DOWN A BIT, LAD! THEN... FIRE!
OI, MISTER!
...CAN WE HAVE A GO?
GO ON! LIFT ME UP, MISTER!
ER, NOW STEADY ON, CHILDREN!
THWIPP
CRIKEY!
AGAIN!
AGAIN!
I DON'T THINK I'VE QUITE GOT THE HANG OF THIS STILT-WALKING MALARKEY JUST YET!

Wallace & Gromit - Lovely Jubilee

by Aardman & Titan Comics

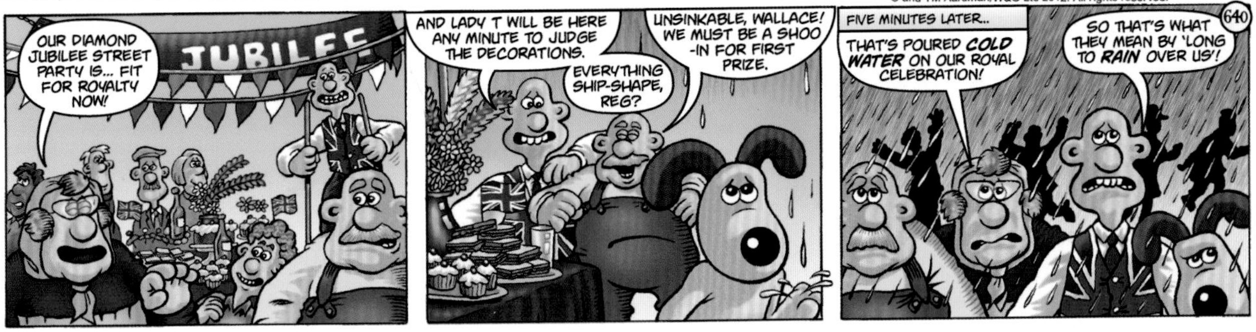

JUBILEE
OUR DIAMOND JUBILEE STREET PARTY IS... FIT FOR ROYALTY NOW!
AND LADY T WILL BE HERE ANY MINUTE TO JUDGE THE DECORATIONS.
EVERYTHING SHIP-SHAPE, REG?
UNSINKABLE, WALLACE! WE MUST BE A SHOO -IN FOR FIRST PRIZE.
640
FIVE MINUTES LATER...
THAT'S POURED COLD WATER ON OUR ROYAL CELEBRATION!
SO THAT'S WHAT THEY MEAN BY 'LONG TO RAIN OVER US'!

Wallace & Gromit - Lovely Jubilee

by Aardman & Titan Comics

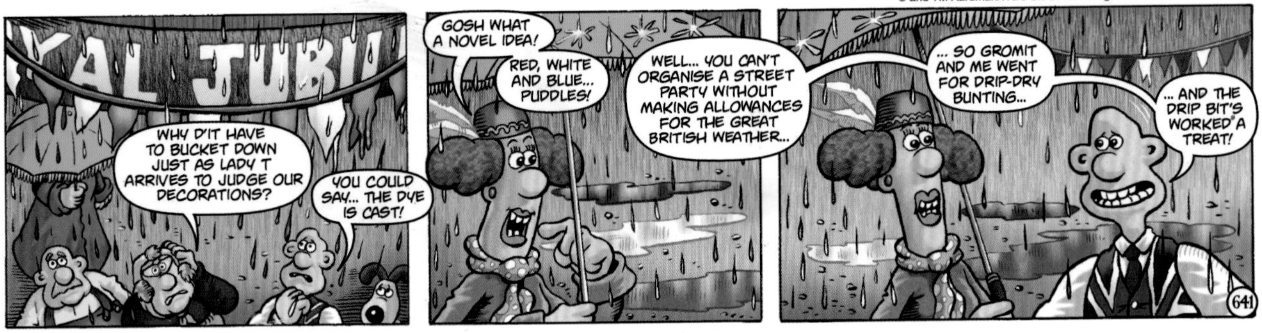

YAL JUBI
WHY D'IT HAVE TO BUCKET DOWN JUST AS LADY T ARRIVES TO JUDGE OUR DECORATIONS?
YOU COULD SAY... THE DYE IS CAST!
GOSH WHAT A NOVEL IDEA!
RED, WHITE AND BLUE... PUDDLES!
WELL... YOU CAN'T ORGANISE A STREET PARTY WITHOUT MAKING ALLOWANCES FOR THE GREAT BRITISH WEATHER...
... SO GROMIT AND ME WENT FOR DRIP-DRY BUNTING...
... AND THE DRIP BIT'S WORKED A TREAT!
641

Wallace & Gromit - Lovely Jubilee

by Aardman & Titan Comics

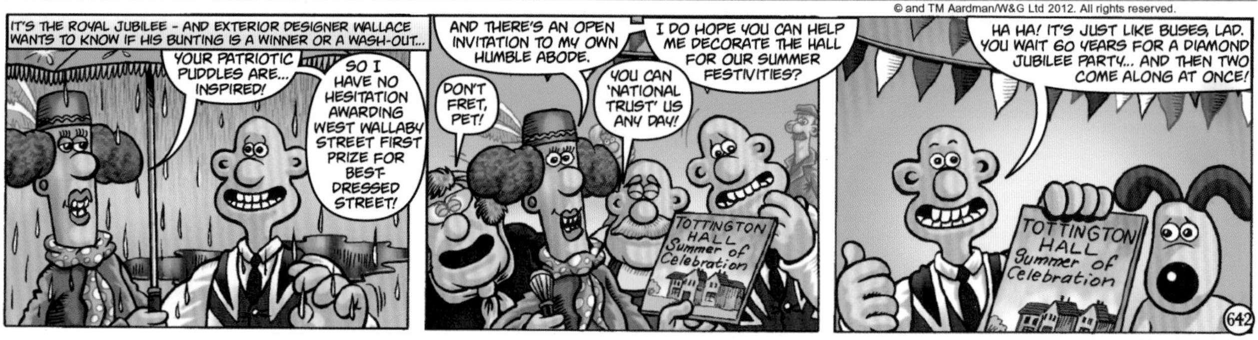
IT'S THE ROYAL JUBILEE - AND EXTERIOR DESIGNER WALLACE WANTS TO KNOW IF HIS BUNTING IS A WINNER OR A WASH-OUT...
YOUR PATRIOTIC PUDDLES ARE... INSPIRED!
SO I HAVE NO HESITATION AWARDING WEST WALLABY STREET FIRST PRIZE FOR BEST-DRESSED STREET!
AND THERE'S AN OPEN INVITATION TO MY OWN HUMBLE ABODE.
DON'T FRET, PET!
YOU CAN 'NATIONAL TRUST' US ANY DAY!
I DO HOPE YOU CAN HELP ME DECORATE THE HALL FOR OUR SUMMER FESTIVITIES?
TOTTINGTON HALL Summer of Celebration
HA HA! IT'S JUST LIKE BUSES, LAD. YOU WAIT 60 YEARS FOR A DIAMOND JUBILEE PARTY... AND THEN TWO COME ALONG AT ONCE!
TOTTINGTON HALL Summer of Celebration
642

The End

Wallace & Gromit - Hunt for Red Dog Collar

by Aardman & Titan Comics

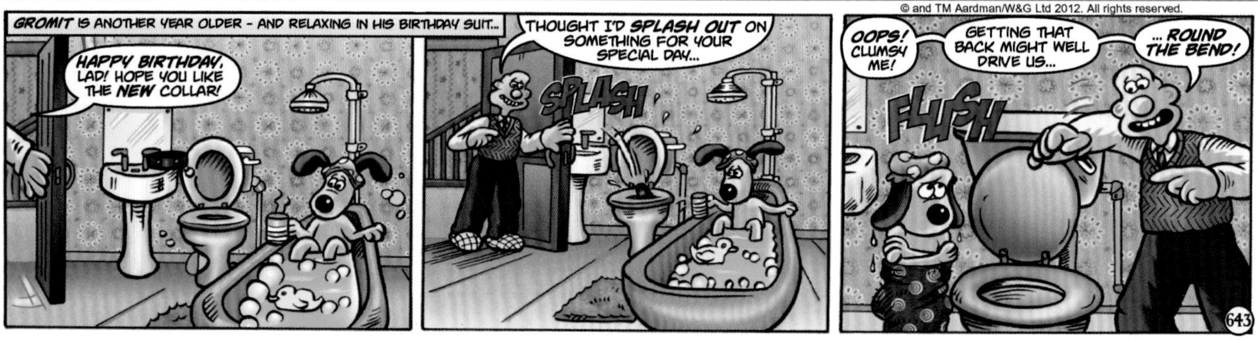
GROMIT IS ANOTHER YEAR OLDER - AND RELAXING IN HIS BIRTHDAY SUIT...
HAPPY BIRTHDAY, LAD! HOPE YOU LIKE THE NEW COLLAR!
THOUGHT I'D SPLASH OUT ON SOMETHING FOR YOUR SPECIAL DAY...
SPLASH
OOPS! CLUMSY ME!
GETTING THAT BACK MIGHT WELL DRIVE US...
... ROUND THE BEND!
FLUSH
643

Wallace & Gromit - Hunt for Red Dog Collar

by Aardman & Titan Comics

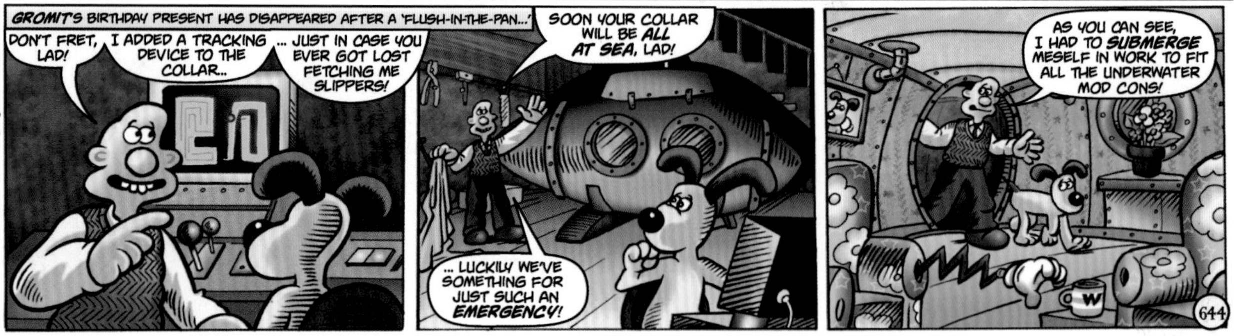
GROMIT'S BIRTHDAY PRESENT HAS DISAPPEARED AFTER A 'FLUSH-IN-THE-PAN...'
DON'T FRET, LAD!
I ADDED A TRACKING DEVICE TO THE COLLAR...
... JUST IN CASE YOU EVER GOT LOST FETCHING ME SLIPPERS!
SOON YOUR COLLAR WILL BE ALL AT SEA, LAD!
... LUCKILY WE'VE SOMETHING FOR JUST SUCH AN EMERGENCY!
AS YOU CAN SEE, I HAD TO SUBMERGE MESELF IN WORK TO FIT ALL THE UNDERWATER MOD CONS!
644

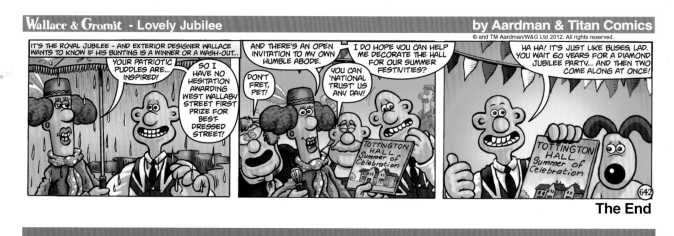

Wallace & Gromit - Hunt for Red Dog Collar
by Aardman & Titan Comics

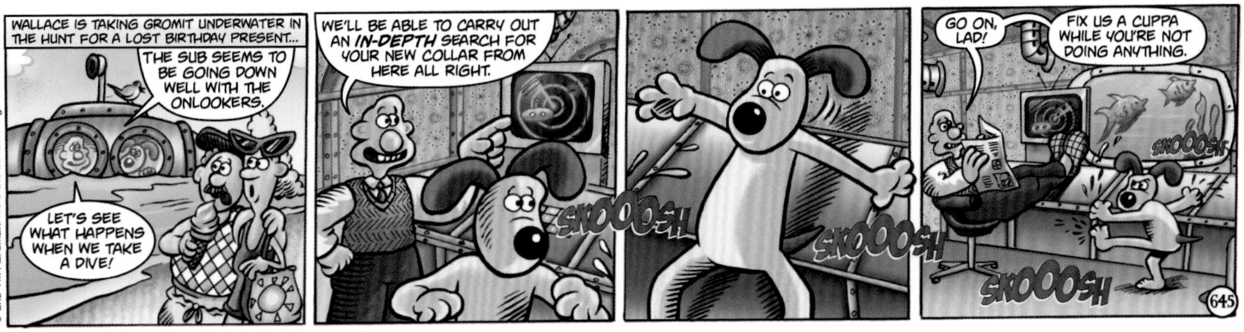

WALLACE IS TAKING GROMIT UNDERWATER IN THE HUNT FOR A LOST BIRTHDAY PRESENT...
THE SUB SEEMS TO BE GOING DOWN WELL WITH THE ONLOOKERS.
LET'S SEE WHAT HAPPENS WHEN WE TAKE A DIVE!
WE'LL BE ABLE TO CARRY OUT AN *IN-DEPTH* SEARCH FOR YOUR NEW COLLAR FROM HERE ALL RIGHT.
SKOOOSH
SKOOOSH
GO ON, LAD!
FIX US A CUPPA WHILE YOU'RE NOT DOING ANYTHING.
SKOOOSH
SKOOOSH
645

Wallace & Gromit - Hunt for Red Dog Collar
by Aardman & Titan Comics

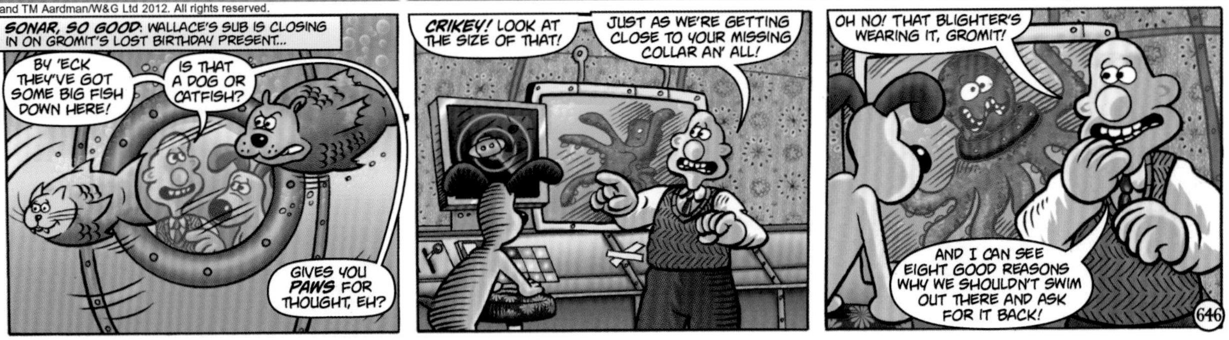

SONAR, SO GOOD: WALLACE'S SUB IS CLOSING IN ON GROMIT'S LOST BIRTHDAY PRESENT...
BY 'ECK THEY'VE GOT SOME BIG FISH DOWN HERE!
IS THAT A DOG OR CATFISH?
GIVES YOU *PAWS* FOR THOUGHT, EH?
CRIKEY! LOOK AT THE SIZE OF THAT!
JUST AS WE'RE GETTING CLOSE TO YOUR MISSING COLLAR AN' ALL!
OH NO! THAT BLIGHTER'S WEARING IT, GROMIT!
AND I CAN SEE EIGHT GOOD REASONS WHY WE SHOULDN'T SWIM OUT THERE AND ASK FOR IT BACK!
646

Wallace & Gromit - Hunt for Red Dog Collar
by Aardman & Titan Comics

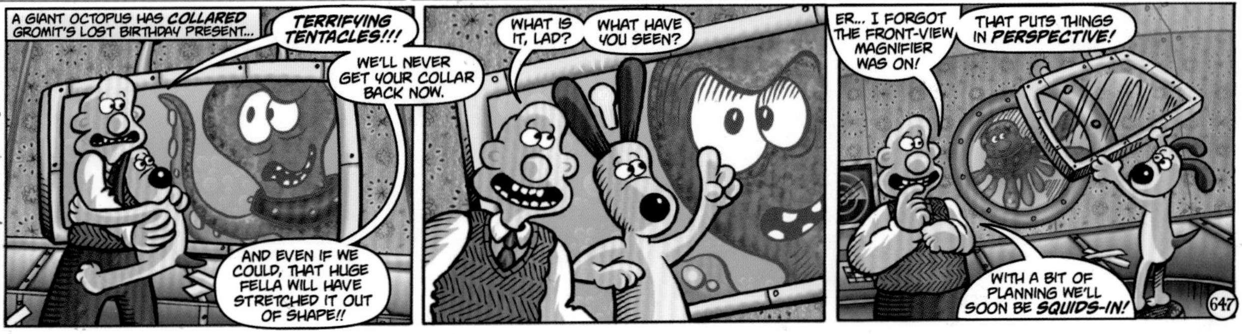

A GIANT OCTOPUS HAS *COLLARED* GROMIT'S LOST BIRTHDAY PRESENT...
TERRIFYING TENTACLES!!!
WE'LL NEVER GET YOUR COLLAR BACK NOW.
AND EVEN IF WE COULD, THAT HUGE FELLA WILL HAVE STRETCHED IT OUT OF SHAPE!!
WHAT IS IT, LAD?
WHAT HAVE YOU SEEN?
ER... I FORGOT THE FRONT-VIEW MAGNIFIER WAS ON!
THAT PUTS THINGS IN *PERSPECTIVE!*
WITH A BIT OF PLANNING WE'LL SOON BE *SQUIDS-IN!*
647

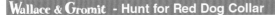

Wallace & Gromit - Hunt for Red Dog Collar

by Aardman & Titan Comics

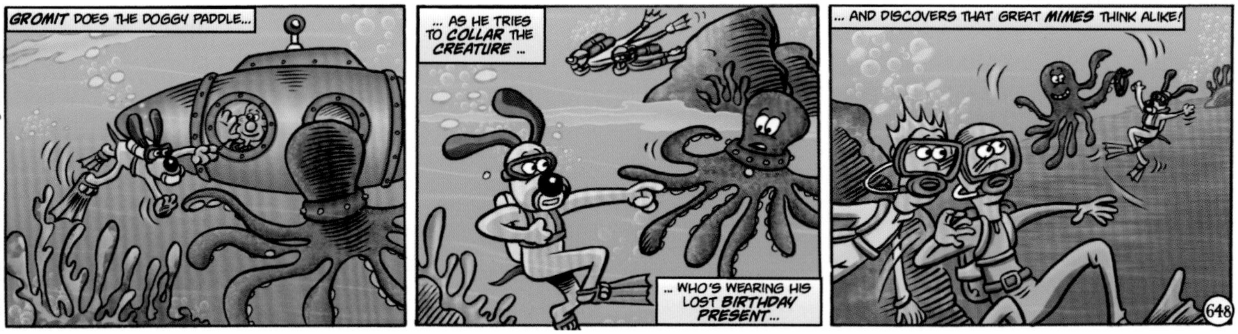

GROMIT DOES THE DOGGY PADDLE...
... AS HE TRIES TO COLLAR THE CREATURE ...
... WHO'S WEARING HIS LOST BIRTHDAY PRESENT...
... AND DISCOVERS THAT GREAT MIMES THINK ALIKE!
648

Wallace & Gromit - Hunt for Red Dog Collar

by Aardman & Titan Comics

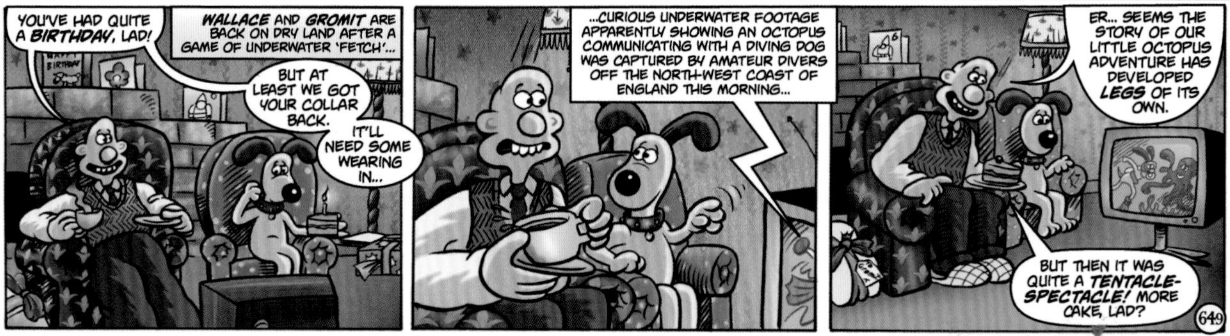

YOU'VE HAD QUITE A BIRTHDAY, LAD!
WALLACE AND GROMIT ARE BACK ON DRY LAND AFTER A GAME OF UNDERWATER 'FETCH'...
BUT AT LEAST WE GOT YOUR COLLAR BACK.
IT'LL NEED SOME WEARING IN...
...CURIOUS UNDERWATER FOOTAGE APPARENTLY SHOWING AN OCTOPUS COMMUNICATING WITH A DIVING DOG WAS CAPTURED BY AMATEUR DIVERS OFF THE NORTH-WEST COAST OF ENGLAND THIS MORNING...
ER... SEEMS THE STORY OF OUR LITTLE OCTOPUS ADVENTURE HAS DEVELOPED LEGS OF ITS OWN.
BUT THEN IT WAS QUITE A TENTACLE-SPECTACLE! MORE CAKE, LAD?
649

The End

Wallace & Gromit - We shine! You shine! Shoe shine!

by Aardman & Titan Comics

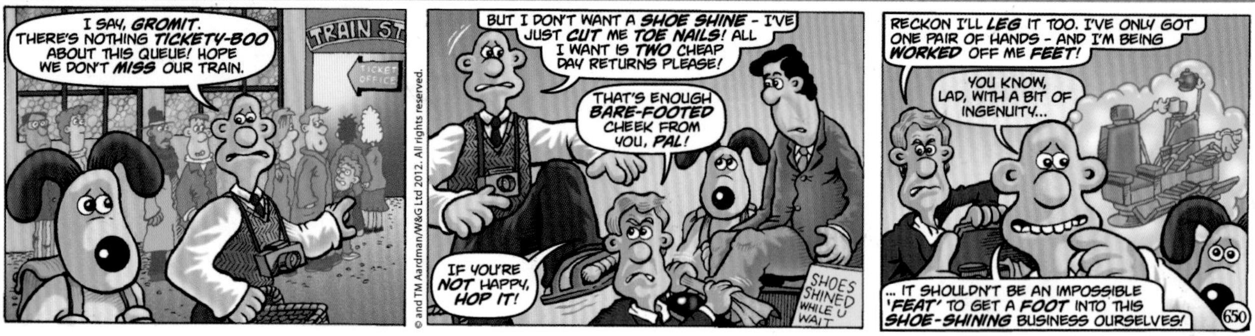

I SAY, GROMIT. THERE'S NOTHING TICKETY-BOO ABOUT THIS QUEUE! HOPE WE DON'T MISS OUR TRAIN.
TRAIN ST
TICKET OFFICE
BUT I DON'T WANT A SHOE SHINE - I'VE JUST CUT ME TOE NAILS! ALL I WANT IS TWO CHEAP DAY RETURNS PLEASE!
THAT'S ENOUGH BARE-FOOTED CHEEK FROM YOU, PAL!
IF YOU'RE NOT HAPPY, HOP IT!
SHOES SHINED WHILE U WAIT
RECKON I'LL LEG IT TOO. I'VE ONLY GOT ONE PAIR OF HANDS - AND I'M BEING WORKED OFF ME FEET!
YOU KNOW, LAD, WITH A BIT OF INGENUITY...
... IT SHOULDN'T BE AN IMPOSSIBLE 'FEAT' TO GET A FOOT INTO THIS SHOE-SHINING BUSINESS OURSELVES!
650

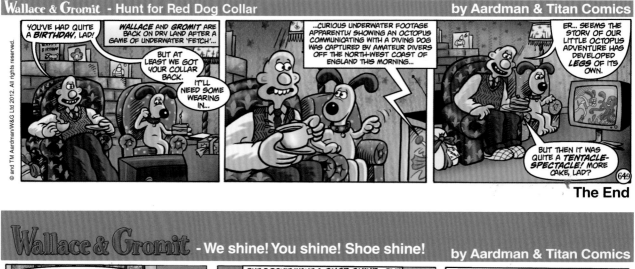

Wallace & Gromit - We shine! You shine! Shoe shine! by Aardman & Titan Comics

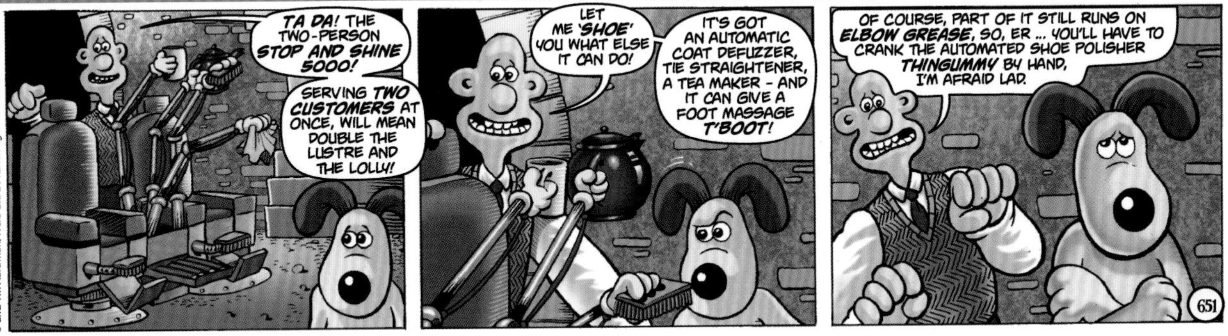
TA DA! THE TWO-PERSON STOP AND SHINE 5000!
SERVING TWO CUSTOMERS AT ONCE, WILL MEAN DOUBLE THE LUSTRE AND THE LOLLY!
LET ME 'SHOE' YOU WHAT ELSE IT CAN DO!
IT'S GOT AN AUTOMATIC COAT DEFUZZER, TIE STRAIGHTENER, A TEA MAKER - AND IT CAN GIVE A FOOT MASSAGE T'BOOT!
OF COURSE, PART OF IT STILL RUNS ON ELBOW GREASE, SO, ER ... YOU'LL HAVE TO CRANK THE AUTOMATED SHOE POLISHER THINGUMMY BY HAND, I'M AFRAID LAD.
651

Wallace & Gromit - We shine! You shine! Shoe shine! by Aardman & Titan Comics

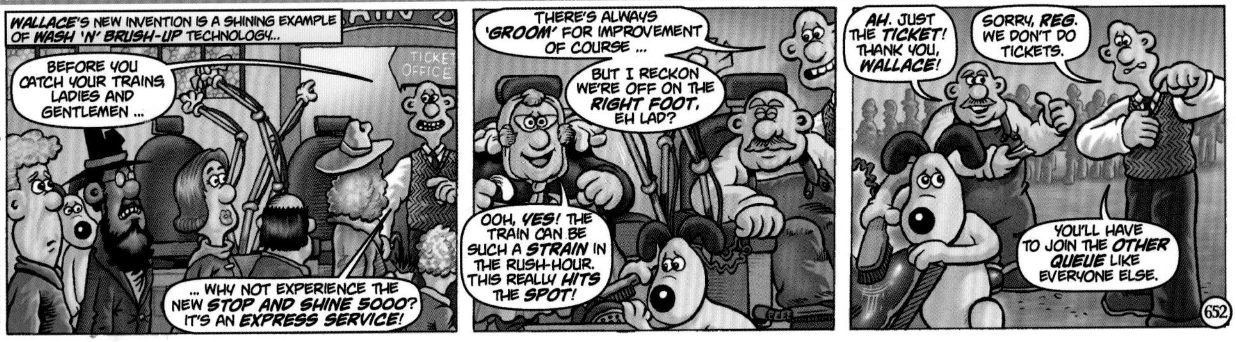
WALLACE'S NEW INVENTION IS A SHINING EXAMPLE OF WASH 'N' BRUSH-UP TECHNOLOGY...
BEFORE YOU CATCH YOUR TRAINS, LADIES AND GENTLEMEN ...
TICKET OFFICE
... WHY NOT EXPERIENCE THE NEW STOP AND SHINE 5000? IT'S AN EXPRESS SERVICE!
THERE'S ALWAYS 'GROOM' FOR IMPROVEMENT OF COURSE ...
BUT I RECKON WE'RE OFF ON THE RIGHT FOOT, EH LAD?
OOH, YES! THE TRAIN CAN BE SUCH A STRAIN IN THE RUSH-HOUR. THIS REALLY HITS THE SPOT!
AH. JUST THE TICKET! THANK YOU, WALLACE!
SORRY, REG. WE DON'T DO TICKETS.
YOU'LL HAVE TO JOIN THE OTHER QUEUE LIKE EVERYONE ELSE.
652

Wallace & Gromit - We shine! You shine! Shoe shine! by Aardman & Titan Comics

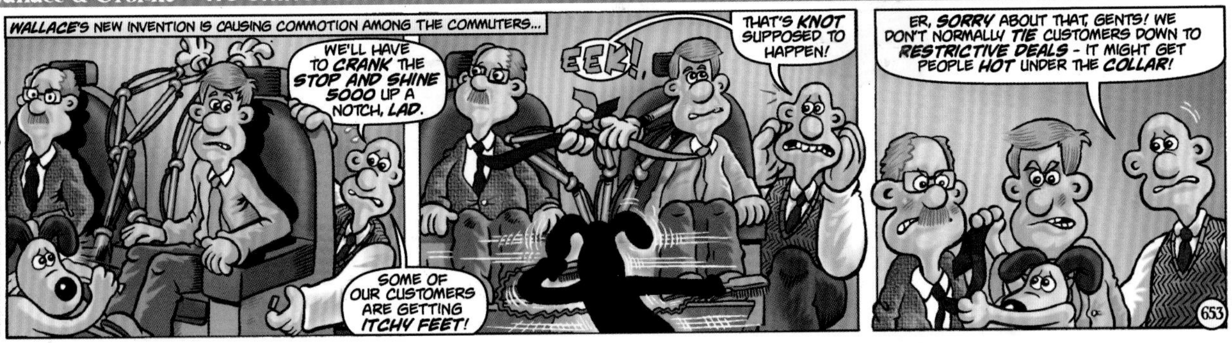
WALLACE'S NEW INVENTION IS CAUSING COMMOTION AMONG THE COMMUTERS...
WE'LL HAVE TO CRANK THE STOP AND SHINE 5000 UP A NOTCH, LAD.
SOME OF OUR CUSTOMERS ARE GETTING ITCHY FEET!
EEK!
THAT'S KNOT SUPPOSED TO HAPPEN!
ER, SORRY ABOUT THAT, GENTS! WE DON'T NORMALLY TIE CUSTOMERS DOWN TO RESTRICTIVE DEALS - IT MIGHT GET PEOPLE HOT UNDER THE COLLAR!
653

Wallace & Gromit - We shine! You shine! Shoe shine! by Aardman & Titan Comics

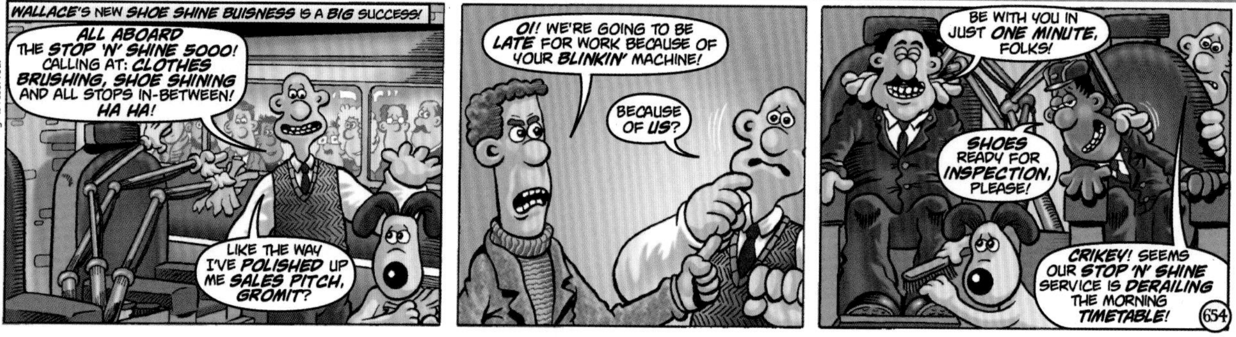

WALLACE'S NEW SHOE SHINE BUISNESS IS A BIG SUCCESS!
ALL ABOARD THE STOP 'N' SHINE 5000! CALLING AT: CLOTHES BRUSHING, SHOE SHINING AND ALL STOPS IN-BETWEEN! HA HA!
LIKE THE WAY I'VE POLISHED UP ME SALES PITCH, GROMIT?
OI! WE'RE GOING TO BE LATE FOR WORK BECAUSE OF YOUR BLINKIN' MACHINE!
BECAUSE OF US?
BE WITH YOU IN JUST ONE MINUTE, FOLKS!
SHOES READY FOR INSPECTION, PLEASE!
CRIKEY! SEEMS OUR STOP 'N' SHINE SERVICE IS DERAILING THE MORNING TIMETABLE!
654

Wallace & Gromit - We shine! You shine! Shoe shine! by Aardman & Titan Comics

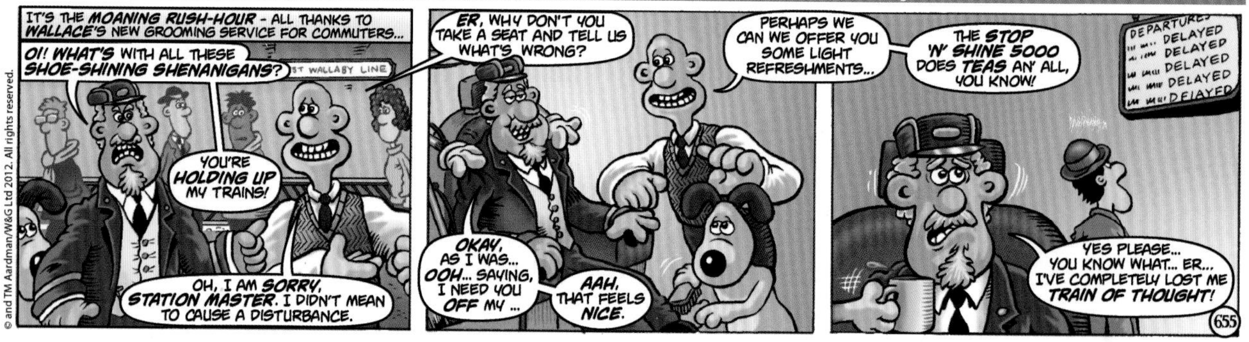

IT'S THE MOANING RUSH-HOUR – ALL THANKS TO WALLACE'S NEW GROOMING SERVICE FOR COMMUTERS...
OI! WHAT'S WITH ALL THESE SHOE-SHINING SHENANIGANS?
ST WALLABY LINE
YOU'RE HOLDING UP MY TRAINS!
OH, I AM SORRY, STATION MASTER. I DIDN'T MEAN TO CAUSE A DISTURBANCE.
ER, WHY DON'T YOU TAKE A SEAT AND TELL US WHAT'S WRONG?
OKAY, AS I WAS... OOH... SAYING, I NEED YOU OFF MY ...
AAH, THAT FEELS NICE.
PERHAPS WE CAN WE OFFER YOU SOME LIGHT REFRESHMENTS...
THE STOP 'N' SHINE 5000 DOES TEAS AN' ALL, YOU KNOW!
DEPARTURES
DELAYED
DELAYED
DELAYED
DELAYED
DELAYED
YES PLEASE... YOU KNOW WHAT... ER... I'VE COMPLETELY LOST ME TRAIN OF THOUGHT!
655

Wallace & Gromit - We shine! You shine! Shoe shine! by Aardman & Titan Comics

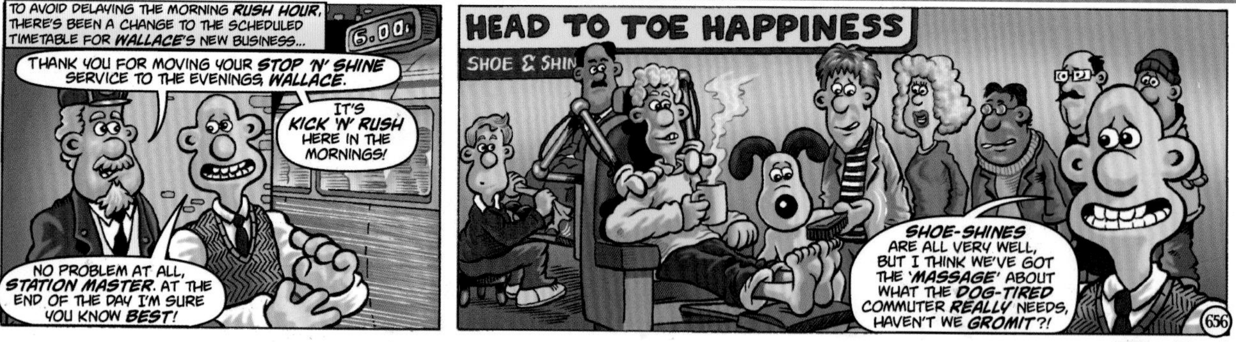

TO AVOID DELAYING THE MORNING RUSH HOUR, THERE'S BEEN A CHANGE TO THE SCHEDULED TIMETABLE FOR WALLACE'S NEW BUSINESS...
5.00
THANK YOU FOR MOVING YOUR STOP 'N' SHINE SERVICE TO THE EVENINGS, WALLACE.
IT'S KICK 'N' RUSH HERE IN THE MORNINGS!
NO PROBLEM AT ALL, STATION MASTER. AT THE END OF THE DAY I'M SURE YOU KNOW BEST!
HEAD TO TOE HAPPINESS
SHOE & SHIN
SHOE-SHINES ARE ALL VERY WELL, BUT I THINK WE'VE GOT THE 'MASSAGE' ABOUT WHAT THE DOG-TIRED COMMUTER REALLY NEEDS, HAVEN'T WE GROMIT?!
656

The End

Wallace & Gromit - West Wallaby Street Games by Aardman & Titan Comics

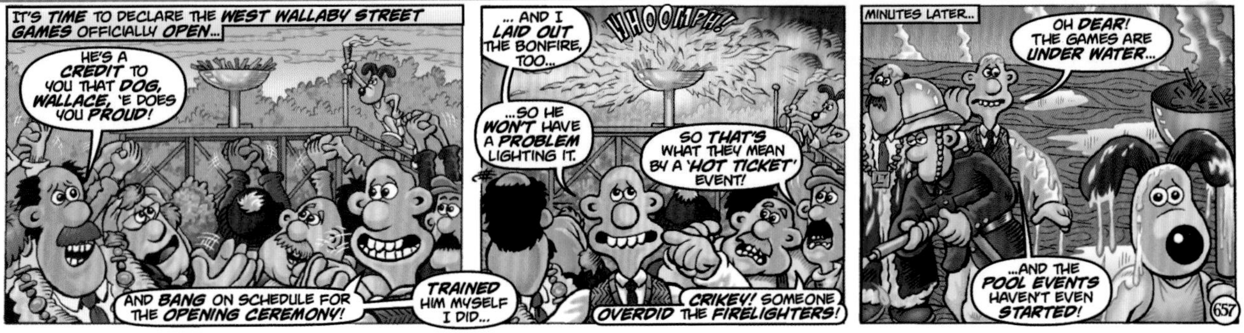
IT'S TIME TO DECLARE THE WEST WALLABY STREET GAMES OFFICIALLY OPEN...
HE'S A CREDIT TO YOU THAT DOG, WALLACE, 'E DOES YOU PROUD!
TRAINED HIM MYSELF I DID...
AND BANG ON SCHEDULE FOR THE OPENING CEREMONY!
... AND I LAID OUT THE BONFIRE, TOO...
...SO HE WON'T HAVE A PROBLEM LIGHTING IT.
WHOOMPH!
SO THAT'S WHAT THEY MEAN BY A 'HOT TICKET' EVENT!
CRIKEY! SOMEONE OVERDID THE FIRELIGHTERS!
MINUTES LATER..
OH DEAR! THE GAMES ARE UNDER WATER...
...AND THE POOL EVENTS HAVEN'T EVEN STARTED!
657

Wallace & Gromit - West Wallaby Street Games by Aardman & Titan Comics

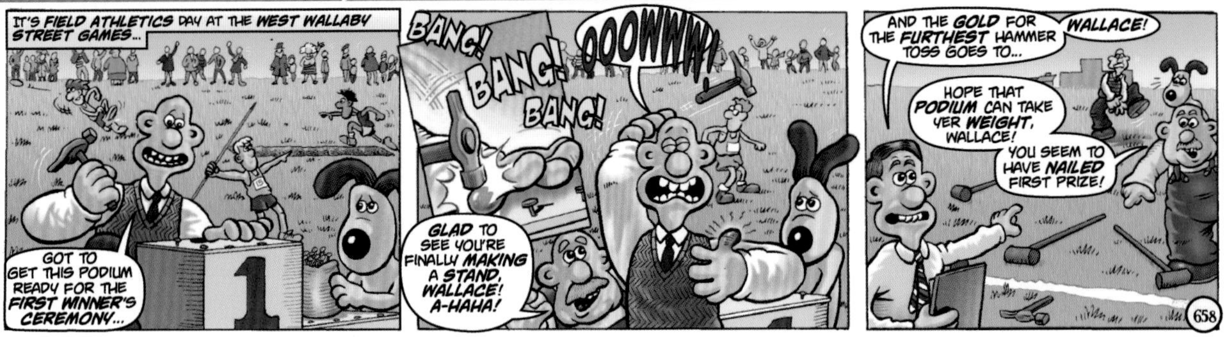
IT'S FIELD ATHLETICS DAY AT THE WEST WALLABY STREET GAMES...
GOT TO GET THIS PODIUM READY FOR THE FIRST WINNER'S CEREMONY...
1
BANG! BANG! BANG!
OOOWWW!
GLAD TO SEE YOU'RE FINALLY MAKING A STAND, WALLACE! A-HAHA!
AND THE GOLD FOR THE FURTHEST HAMMER TOSS GOES TO...
WALLACE!
HOPE THAT PODIUM CAN TAKE YER WEIGHT, WALLACE!
YOU SEEM TO HAVE NAILED FIRST PRIZE!
658

Wallace & Gromit - West Wallaby Street Games by Aardman & Titan Comics

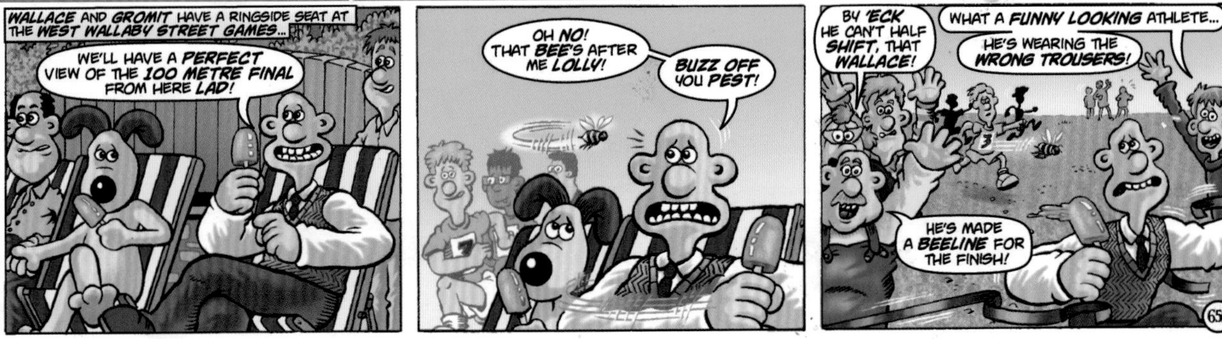
WALLACE AND GROMIT HAVE A RINGSIDE SEAT AT THE WEST WALLABY STREET GAMES...
WE'LL HAVE A PERFECT VIEW OF THE 100 METRE FINAL FROM HERE LAD!
OH NO! THAT BEE'S AFTER ME LOLLY!
BUZZ OFF YOU PEST!
BY 'ECK HE CAN'T HALF SHIFT, THAT WALLACE!
WHAT A FUNNY LOOKING ATHLETE...
HE'S WEARING THE WRONG TROUSERS!
HE'S MADE A BEELINE FOR THE FINISH!
659

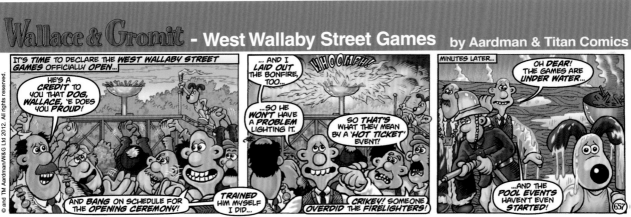

Wallace & Gromit - West Wallaby Street Games by Aardman & Titan Comics

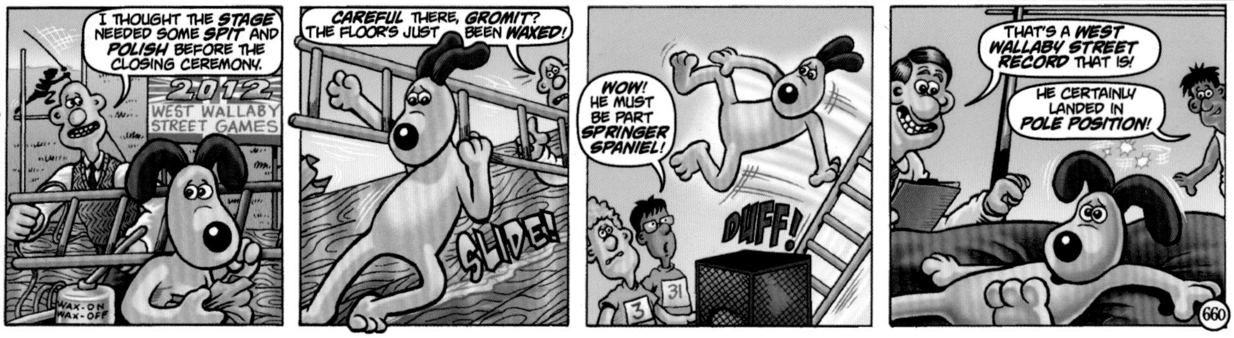

I THOUGHT THE STAGE NEEDED SOME SPIT AND POLISH BEFORE THE CLOSING CEREMONY.
2012 WEST WALLABY STREET GAMES
WAX-ON WAX-OFF
CAREFUL THERE, GROMIT? THE FLOOR'S JUST BEEN WAXED!
SLIDE!
WOW! HE MUST BE PART SPRINGER SPANIEL!
DUFF!
THAT'S A WEST WALLABY STREET RECORD THAT IS!
HE CERTAINLY LANDED IN POLE POSITION!
660

Wallace & Gromit - West Wallaby Street Games by Aardman & Titan Comics

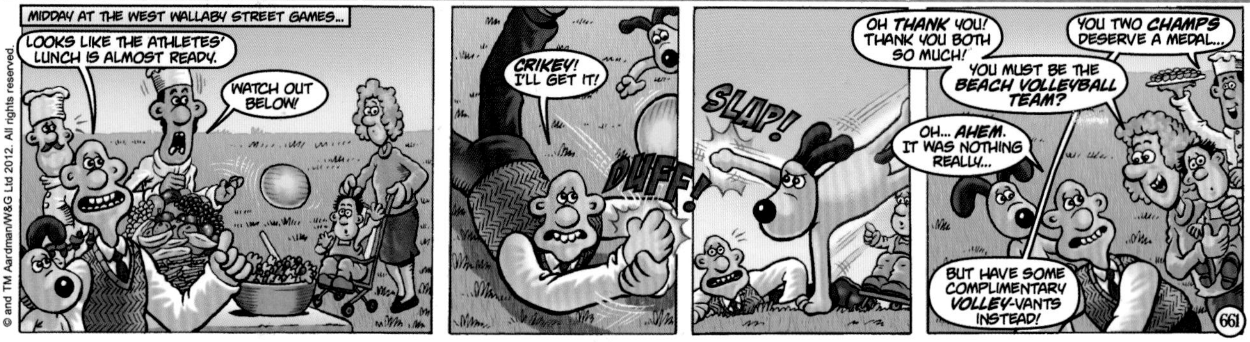

MIDDAY AT THE WEST WALLABY STREET GAMES...
LOOKS LIKE THE ATHLETES' LUNCH IS ALMOST READY.
WATCH OUT BELOW!
CRIKEY! I'LL GET IT!
DUFF!
SLAP!
OH THANK YOU! THANK YOU BOTH SO MUCH!
YOU TWO CHAMPS DESERVE A MEDAL...
YOU MUST BE THE BEACH VOLLEYBALL TEAM?
OH... AHEM. IT WAS NOTHING REALLY...
BUT HAVE SOME COMPLIMENTARY VOLLEY-VANTS INSTEAD!
661

Wallace & Gromit - West Wallaby Street Games by Aardman & Titan Comics

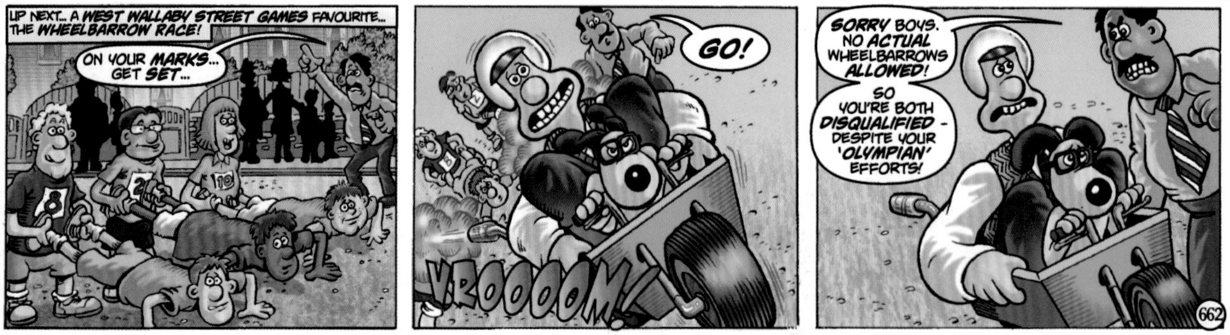

UP NEXT... A WEST WALLABY STREET GAMES FAVOURITE... THE WHEELBARROW RACE!
ON YOUR MARKS... GET SET...
GO!
VROOOOM!
SORRY BOYS. NO ACTUAL WHEELBARROWS ALLOWED!
SO YOU'RE BOTH DISQUALIFIED - DESPITE YOUR 'OLYMPIAN' EFFORTS!
662

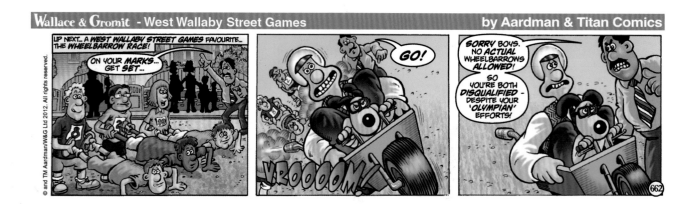

Wallace & Gromit - West Wallaby Street Games — by Aardman & Titan Comics

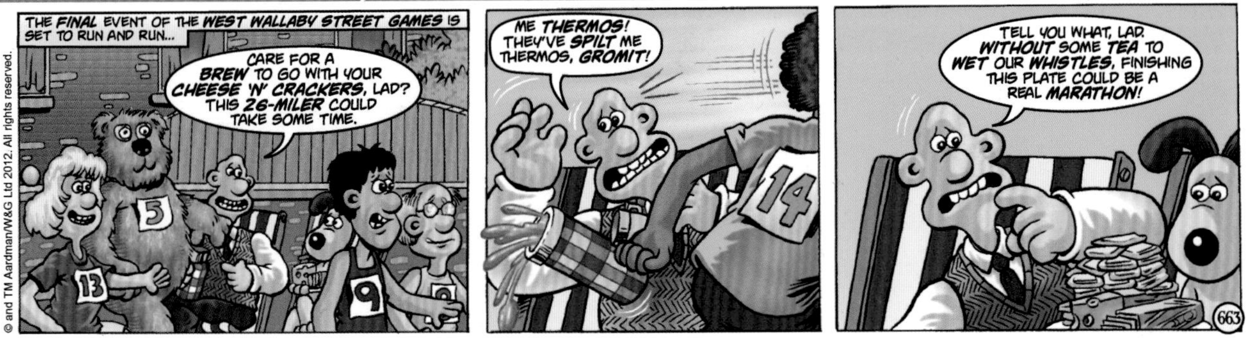
THE FINAL EVENT OF THE WEST WALLABY STREET GAMES IS SET TO RUN AND RUN...
CARE FOR A BREW TO GO WITH YOUR CHEESE 'N' CRACKERS, LAD? THIS 26-MILER COULD TAKE SOME TIME.
ME THERMOS! THEY'VE SPILT ME THERMOS, GROMIT!
TELL YOU WHAT, LAD. WITHOUT SOME TEA TO WET OUR WHISTLES, FINISHING THIS PLATE COULD BE A REAL MARATHON!
663

The End

Wallace & Gromit - Crop Circles

by Aardman & Titan Comics

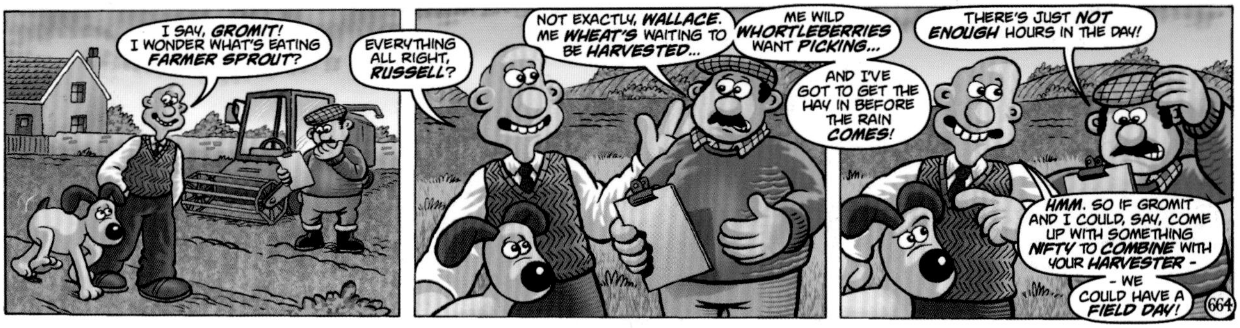
I SAY, GROMIT! I WONDER WHAT'S EATING FARMER SPROUT?
EVERYTHING ALL RIGHT, RUSSELL?
NOT EXACTLY, WALLACE. ME WHEAT'S WAITING TO BE HARVESTED...
ME WILD WHORTLEBERRIES WANT PICKING...
AND I'VE GOT TO GET THE HAY IN BEFORE THE RAIN COMES!
THERE'S JUST NOT ENOUGH HOURS IN THE DAY!
HMM. SO IF GROMIT AND I COULD, SAY, COME UP WITH SOMETHING NIFTY TO COMBINE WITH YOUR HARVESTER -
- WE COULD HAVE A FIELD DAY!
664

Wallace & Gromit - Crop Circles — by Aardman & Titan Comics

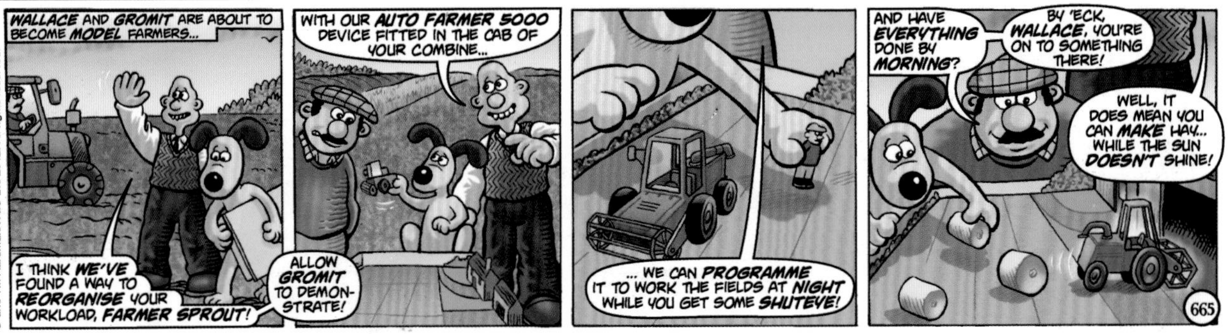
WALLACE AND GROMIT ARE ABOUT TO BECOME MODEL FARMERS...
I THINK WE'VE FOUND A WAY TO REORGANISE YOUR WORKLOAD, FARMER SPROUT!
ALLOW GROMIT TO DEMON-STRATE!
WITH OUR AUTO FARMER 5000 DEVICE FITTED IN THE CAB OF YOUR COMBINE...
... WE CAN PROGRAMME IT TO WORK THE FIELDS AT NIGHT WHILE YOU GET SOME SHUTEYE!
AND HAVE EVERYTHING DONE BY MORNING?
BY 'ECK, WALLACE, YOU'RE ON TO SOMETHING THERE!
WELL, IT DOES MEAN YOU CAN MAKE HAY... WHILE THE SUN DOESN'T SHINE!
665

Wallace & Gromit - Crop Circles by Aardman & Titan Comics

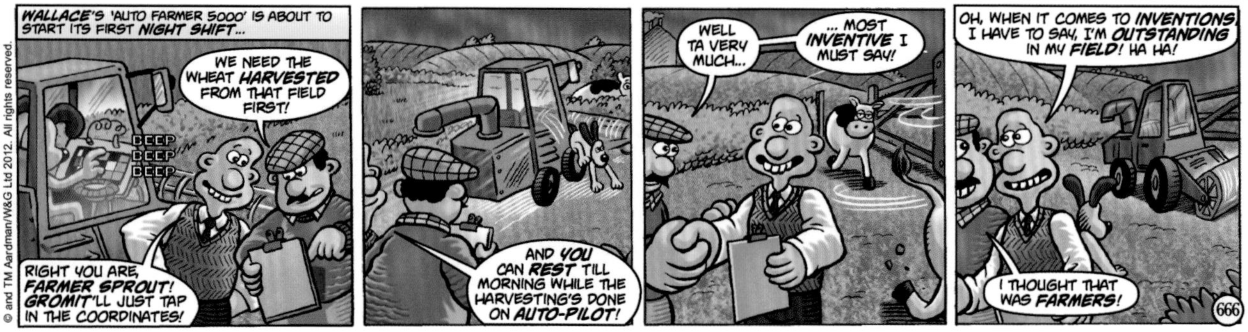
WALLACE'S 'AUTO FARMER 5000' IS ABOUT TO START ITS FIRST NIGHT SHIFT...
WE NEED THE WHEAT HARVESTED FROM THAT FIELD FIRST!
BEEP
BEEP
BEEP
RIGHT YOU ARE, FARMER SPROUT! GROMIT'LL JUST TAP IN THE COORDINATES!
AND YOU CAN REST TILL MORNING WHILE THE HARVESTING'S DONE ON AUTO-PILOT!
WELL TA VERY MUCH...
... MOST INVENTIVE I MUST SAY!
OH, WHEN IT COMES TO INVENTIONS, I HAVE TO SAY, I'M OUTSTANDING IN MY FIELD! HA HA!
I THOUGHT THAT WAS FARMERS!
666

Wallace & Gromit - Crop Circles by Aardman & Titan Comics

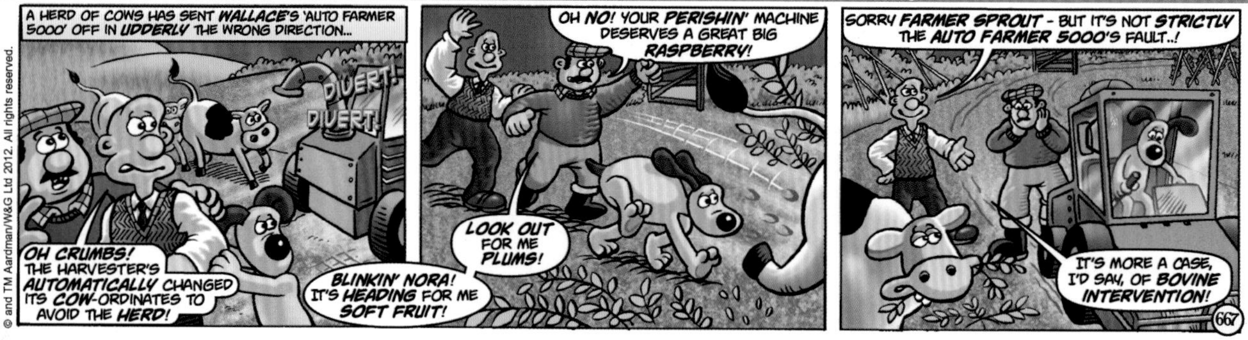
A HERD OF COWS HAS SENT WALLACE'S 'AUTO FARMER 5000' OFF IN UDDERLY THE WRONG DIRECTION...
DIVERT!
DIVERT!
OH CRUMBS! THE HARVESTER'S AUTOMATICALLY CHANGED ITS COW-ORDINATES TO AVOID THE HERD!
OH NO! YOUR PERISHIN' MACHINE DESERVES A GREAT BIG RASPBERRY!
LOOK OUT FOR ME PLUMS!
BLINKIN' NORA! IT'S HEADING FOR ME SOFT FRUIT!
SORRY FARMER SPROUT - BUT IT'S NOT STRICTLY THE AUTO FARMER 5000'S FAULT..!
IT'S MORE A CASE, I'D SAY, OF BOVINE INTERVENTION!
667

Wallace & Gromit - Crop Circles by Aardman & Titan Comics

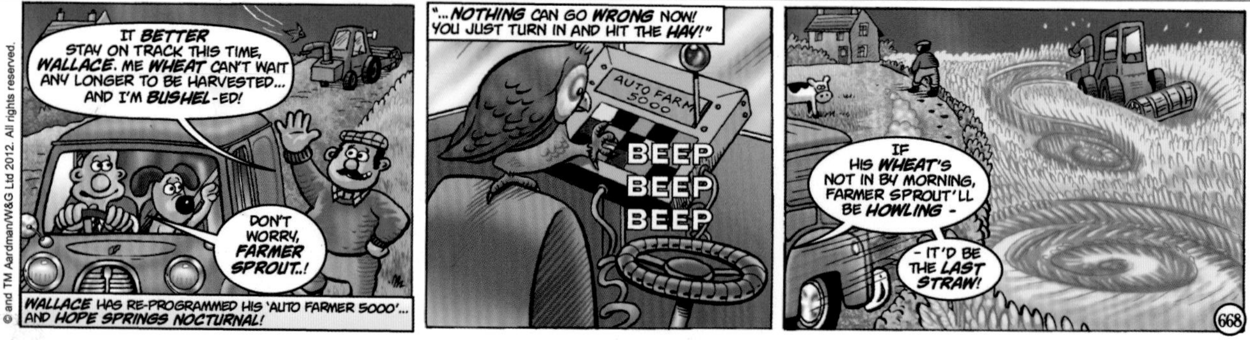
IT BETTER STAY ON TRACK THIS TIME, WALLACE. ME WHEAT CAN'T WAIT ANY LONGER TO BE HARVESTED... AND I'M BUSHEL-ED!
DON'T WORRY, FARMER SPROUT..!
WALLACE HAS RE-PROGRAMMED HIS 'AUTO FARMER 5000'... AND HOPE SPRINGS NOCTURNAL!
"...NOTHING CAN GO WRONG NOW! YOU JUST TURN IN AND HIT THE HAY!"
AUTO FARM 5000
BEEP
BEEP
BEEP
IF HIS WHEAT'S NOT IN BY MORNING, FARMER SPROUT'LL BE HOWLING -
- IT'D BE THE LAST STRAW!
668

Wallace & Gromit - Crop Circles
by Aardman & Titan Comics

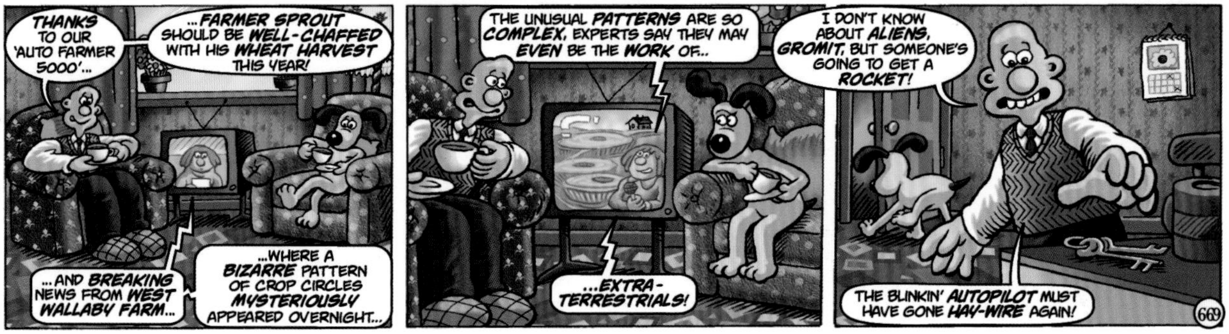
THANKS TO OUR 'AUTO FARMER 5000'...
...FARMER SPROUT SHOULD BE WELL-CHAFFED WITH HIS WHEAT HARVEST THIS YEAR!
...AND BREAKING NEWS FROM WEST WALLABY FARM...
...WHERE A BIZARRE PATTERN OF CROP CIRCLES MYSTERIOUSLY APPEARED OVERNIGHT...
THE UNUSUAL PATTERNS ARE SO COMPLEX, EXPERTS SAY THEY MAY EVEN BE THE WORK OF...
...EXTRA-TERRESTRIALS!
I DON'T KNOW ABOUT ALIENS, GROMIT, BUT SOMEONE'S GOING TO GET A ROCKET!
THE BLINKIN' AUTOPILOT MUST HAVE GONE HAY-WIRE AGAIN!
669

Wallace & Gromit - Crop Circles
by Aardman & Titan Comics

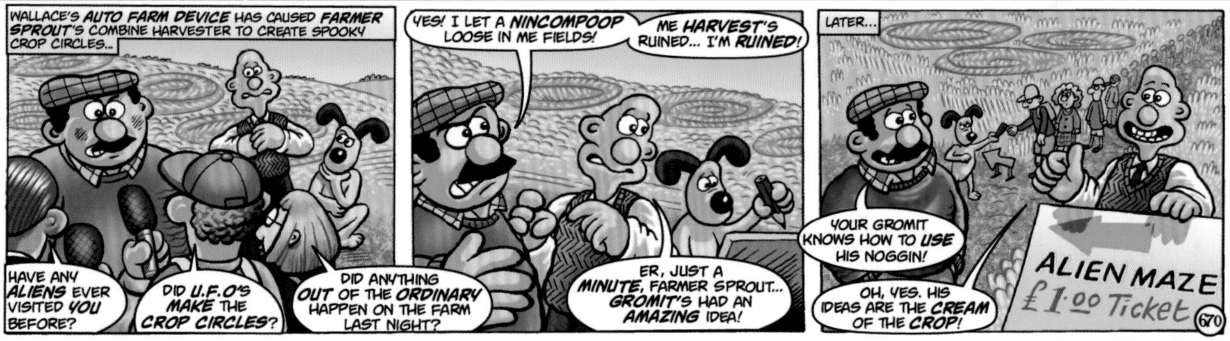
WALLACE'S AUTO FARM DEVICE HAS CAUSED FARMER SPROUT'S COMBINE HARVESTER TO CREATE SPOOKY CROP CIRCLES...
HAVE ANY ALIENS EVER VISITED YOU BEFORE?
DID U.F.O'S MAKE THE CROP CIRCLES?
DID ANYTHING OUT OF THE ORDINARY HAPPEN ON THE FARM LAST NIGHT?
YES! I LET A NINCOMPOOP LOOSE IN ME FIELDS!
ME HARVEST'S RUINED... I'M RUINED!
ER, JUST A MINUTE, FARMER SPROUT... GROMIT'S HAD AN AMAZING IDEA!
LATER...
YOUR GROMIT KNOWS HOW TO USE HIS NOGGIN!
OH, YES. HIS IDEAS ARE THE CREAM OF THE CROP!
ALIEN MAZE
£1.00 Ticket
670

The End

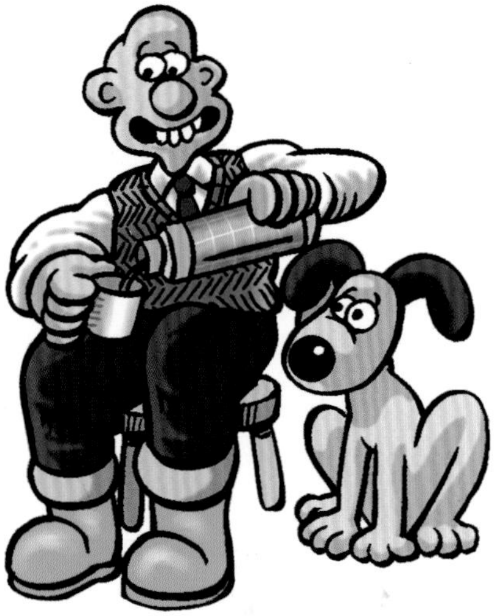

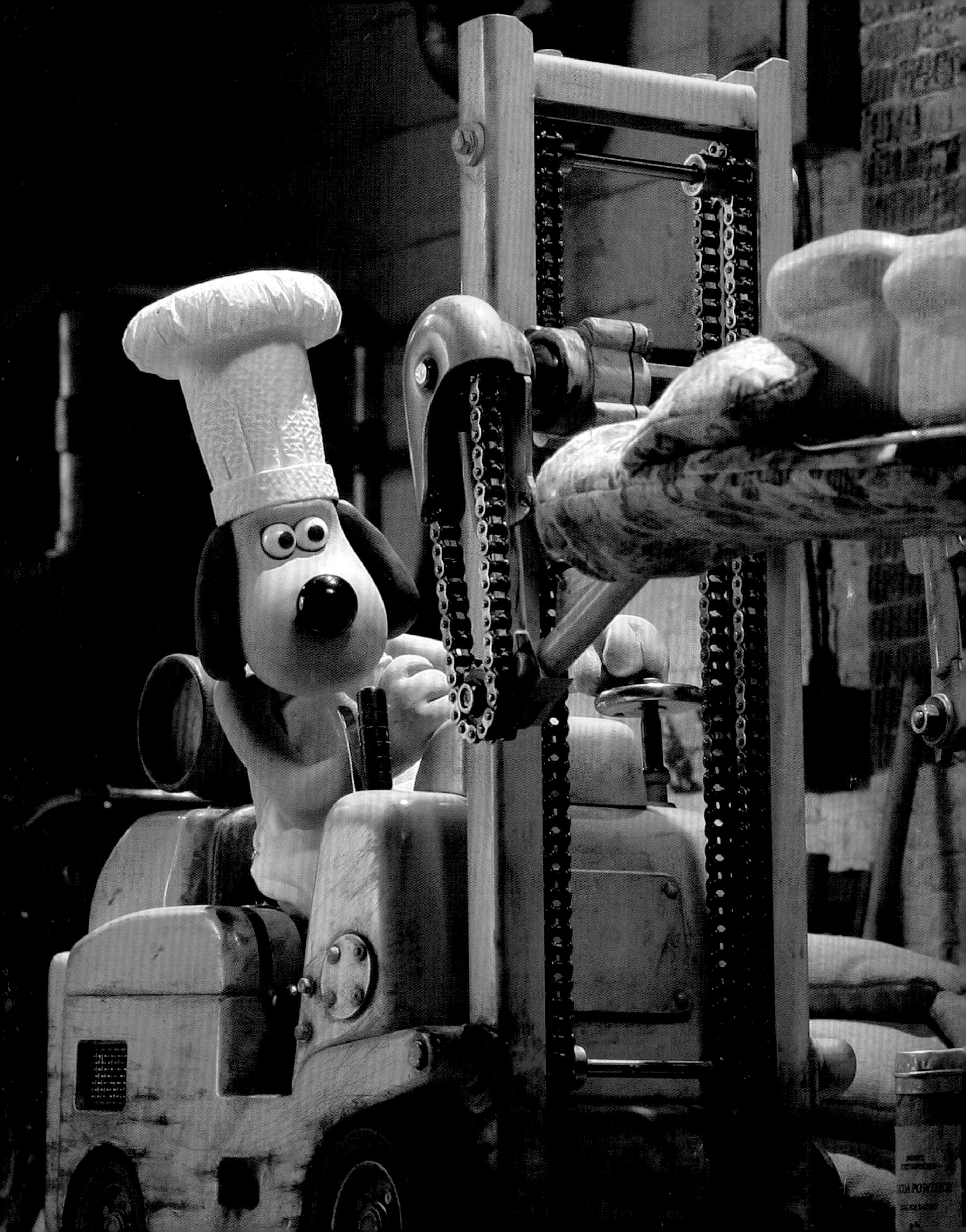

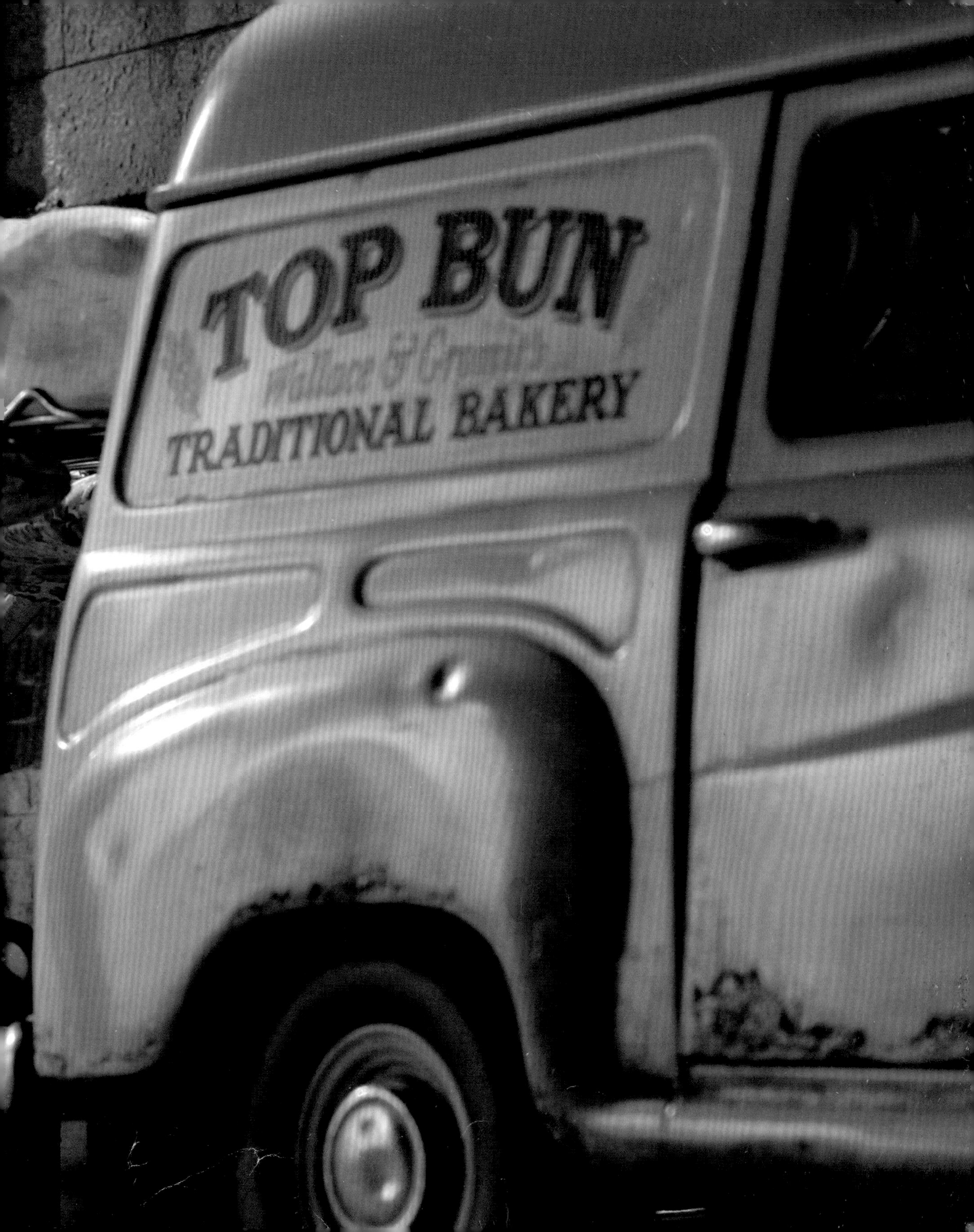
TOP BUN
TRADITIONAL BAKERY

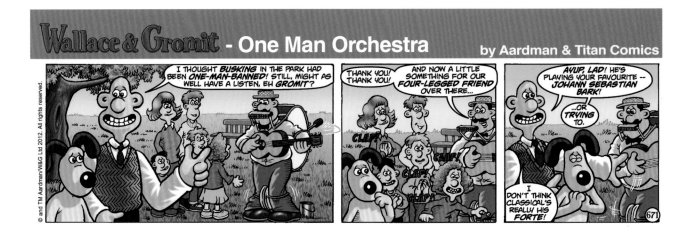

Wallace & Gromit - One Man Orchestra

by Aardman & Titan Comics

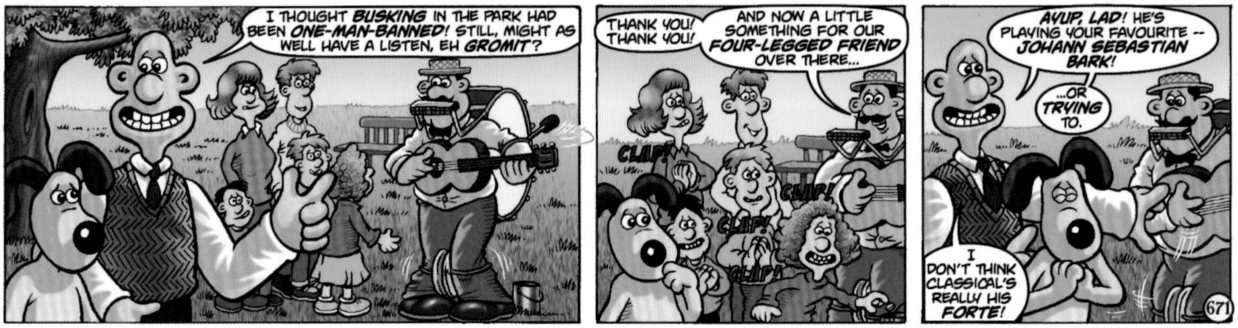
I THOUGHT BUSKING IN THE PARK HAD BEEN ONE-MAN-BANNED! STILL, MIGHT AS WELL HAVE A LISTEN, EH GROMIT?
THANK YOU! THANK YOU!
AND NOW A LITTLE SOMETHING FOR OUR FOUR-LEGGED FRIEND OVER THERE...
CLAP!
CLAP!
CLAP!
CLAP!
AYUP, LAD! HE'S PLAYING YOUR FAVOURITE -- JOHANN SEBASTIAN BARK!
...OR TRYING TO.
I DON'T THINK CLASSICAL'S REALLY HIS FORTE!
671

Wallace & Gromit - One Man Orchestra

by Aardman & Titan Comics

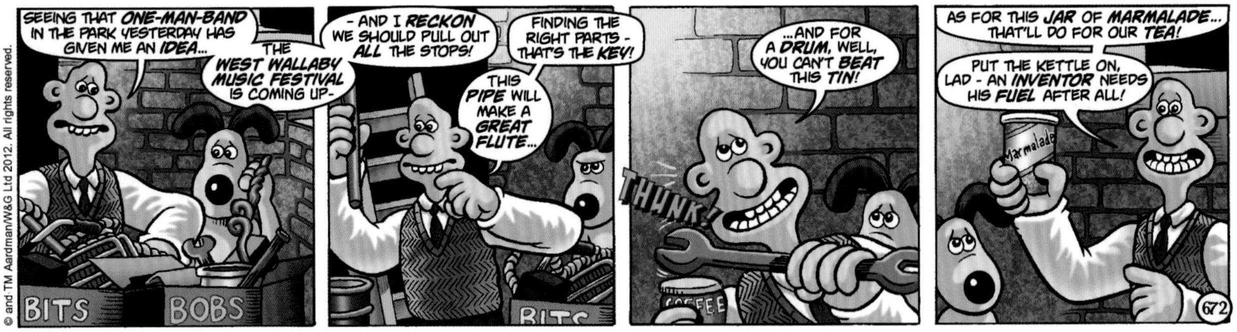
SEEING THAT ONE-MAN-BAND IN THE PARK YESTERDAY HAS GIVEN ME AN IDEA...
THE WEST WALLABY MUSIC FESTIVAL IS COMING UP-
BITS
BOBS
- AND I RECKON WE SHOULD PULL OUT ALL THE STOPS!
FINDING THE RIGHT PARTS - THAT'S THE KEY!
THIS PIPE WILL MAKE A GREAT FLUTE...
BITS
...AND FOR A DRUM, WELL, YOU CAN'T BEAT THIS TIN!
THUNK!
COFFEE
AS FOR THIS JAR OF MARMALADE... THAT'LL DO FOR OUR TEA!
PUT THE KETTLE ON, LAD - AN INVENTOR NEEDS HIS FUEL AFTER ALL!
Marmalade
672

Wallace & Gromit - One Man Orchestra

by Aardman & Titan Comics

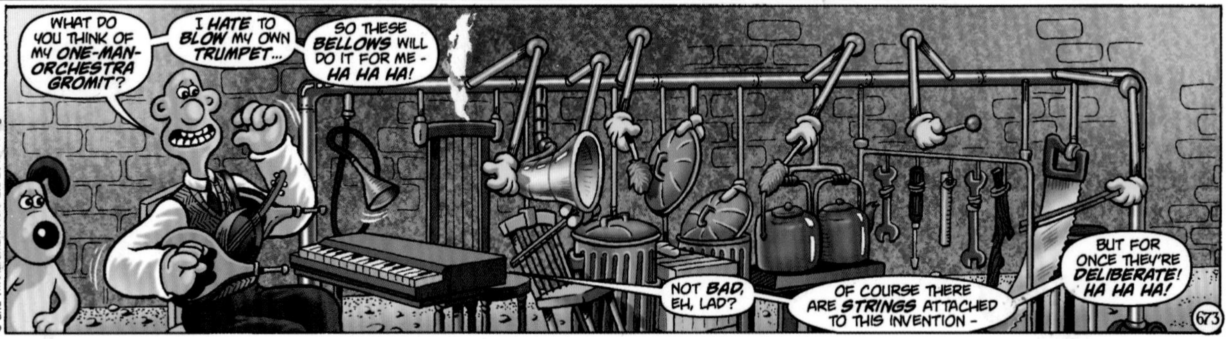
WHAT DO YOU THINK OF MY ONE-MAN-ORCHESTRA GROMIT?
I HATE TO BLOW MY OWN TRUMPET...
SO THESE BELLOWS WILL DO IT FOR ME - HA HA HA!
NOT BAD, EH, LAD?
OF COURSE THERE ARE STRINGS ATTACHED TO THIS INVENTION -
BUT FOR ONCE THEY'RE DELIBERATE! HA HA HA!
673

Wallace & Gromit - One Man Orchestra by Aardman & Titan Comics

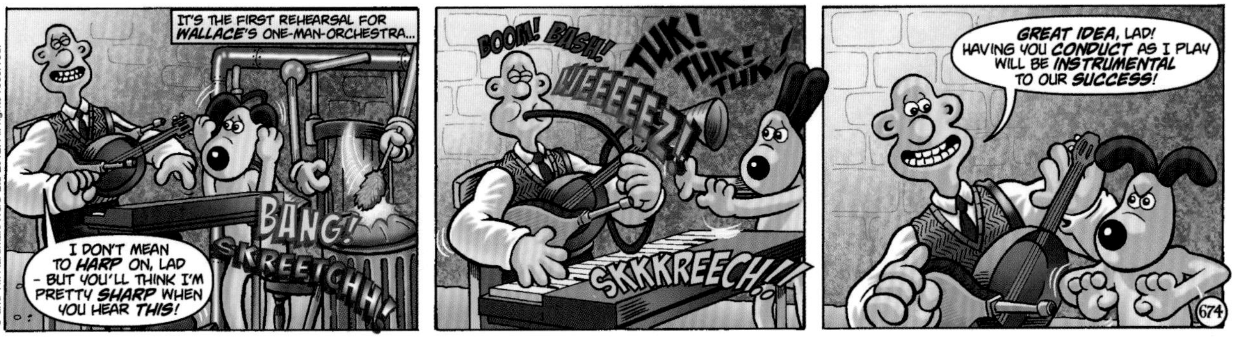
IT'S THE FIRST REHEARSAL FOR WALLACE'S ONE-MAN-ORCHESTRA...
I DON'T MEAN TO HARP ON, LAD - BUT YOU'LL THINK I'M PRETTY SHARP WHEN YOU HEAR THIS!
BANG!
SKREETCHH!
BOOM! BASH!
TUK! TUK! TUK!
WEEEEEEZ!!
SKKKREECH!!!
GREAT IDEA, LAD! HAVING YOU CONDUCT AS I PLAY WILL BE INSTRUMENTAL TO OUR SUCCESS!
674

Wallace & Gromit - One Man Orchestra by Aardman & Titan Comics

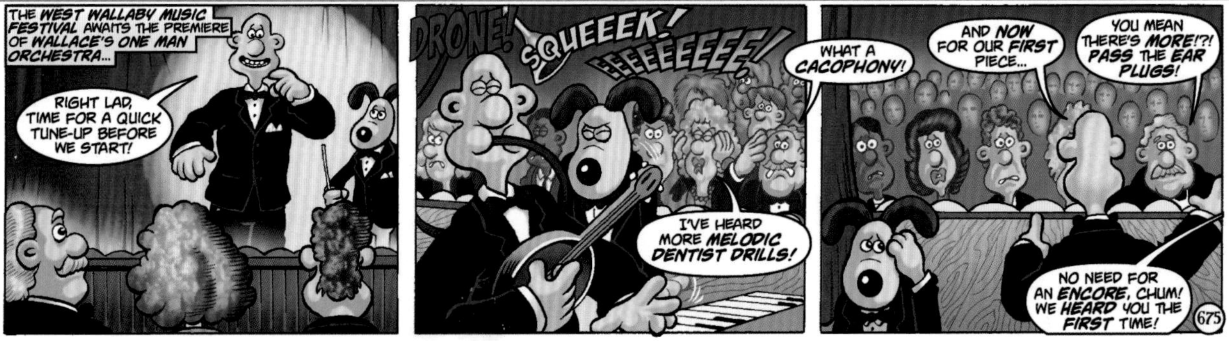
THE WEST WALLABY MUSIC FESTIVAL AWAITS THE PREMIERE OF WALLACE'S ONE MAN ORCHESTRA...
RIGHT LAD, TIME FOR A QUICK TUNE-UP BEFORE WE START!
DRONE!
SQUEEEK!
EEEEEEEEE!
WHAT A CACOPHONY!
I'VE HEARD MORE MELODIC DENTIST DRILLS!
AND NOW FOR OUR FIRST PIECE...
YOU MEAN THERE'S MORE!?! PASS THE EAR PLUGS!
NO NEED FOR AN ENCORE, CHUM! WE HEARD YOU THE FIRST TIME!
675

Wallace & Gromit - One Man Orchestra by Aardman & Titan Comics

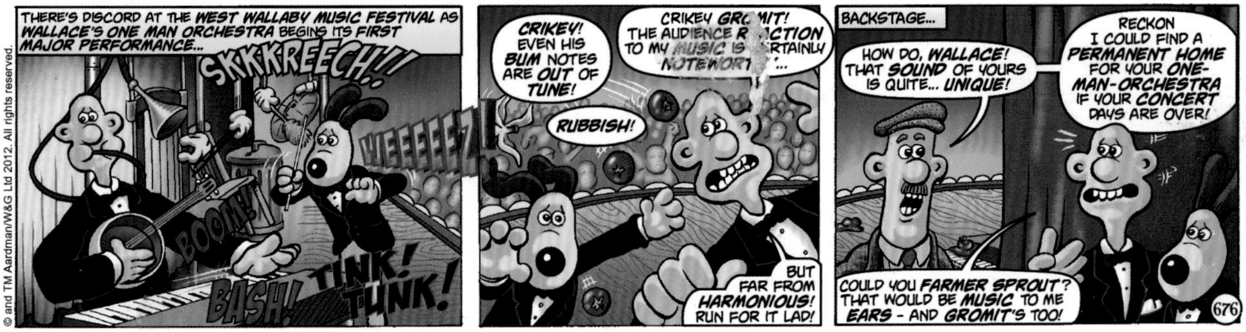
THERE'S DISCORD AT THE WEST WALLABY MUSIC FESTIVAL AS WALLACE'S ONE MAN ORCHESTRA BEGINS ITS FIRST MAJOR PERFORMANCE...
SKKKREECH!!!
WEEEEEZ!!
BOOM!
BASH!
TINK! TUNK!
CRIKEY! EVEN HIS BUM NOTES ARE OUT OF TUNE!
RUBBISH!
CRIKEY GROMIT! THE AUDIENCE REACTION TO MY MUSIC IS CERTAINLY NOTEWORTHY...
BUT FAR FROM HARMONIOUS! RUN FOR IT LAD!
BACKSTAGE...
HOW DO, WALLACE! THAT SOUND OF YOURS IS QUITE... UNIQUE!
RECKON I COULD FIND A PERMANENT HOME FOR YOUR ONE-MAN-ORCHESTRA IF YOUR CONCERT DAYS ARE OVER!
COULD YOU FARMER SPROUT? THAT WOULD BE MUSIC TO ME EARS - AND GROMIT'S TOO!
676

Wallace & Gromit - One Man Orchestra

by Aardman & Titan Comics

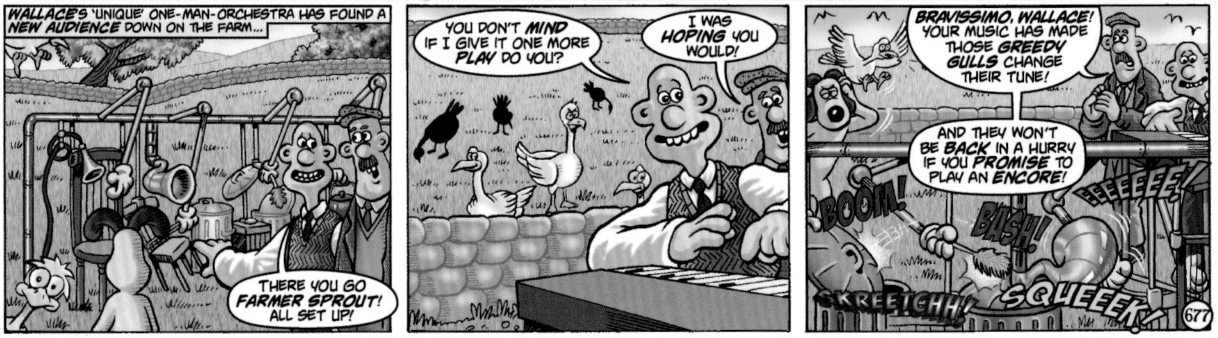
WALLACE'S 'UNIQUE' ONE-MAN-ORCHESTRA HAS FOUND A NEW AUDIENCE DOWN ON THE FARM...
THERE YOU GO FARMER SPROUT! ALL SET UP!
YOU DON'T MIND IF I GIVE IT ONE MORE PLAY DO YOU?
I WAS HOPING YOU WOULD!
BRAVISSIMO, WALLACE! YOUR MUSIC HAS MADE THOSE GREEDY GULLS CHANGE THEIR TUNE!
AND THEY WON'T BE BACK IN A HURRY IF YOU PROMISE TO PLAY AN ENCORE!
BOOM!
BASH!
EEEEEEE!
SKREEEICHH!
SQUEEEK!
677

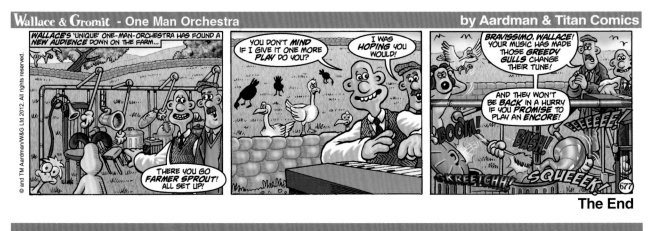

The End

Wallace & Gromit - An Inspector Calls

by Aardman & Titan Comics

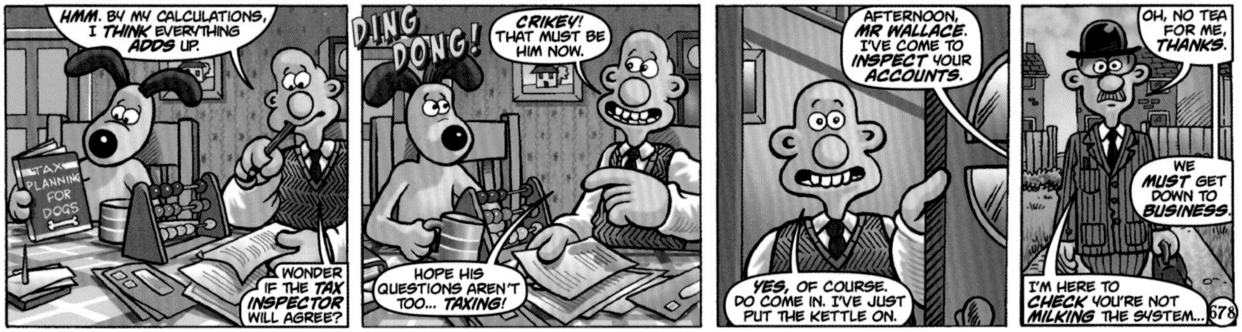
HMM. BY MY CALCULATIONS, I THINK EVERYTHING ADDS UP.
TAX PLANNING FOR DOGS
WONDER IF THE TAX INSPECTOR WILL AGREE?
DING DONG!
CRIKEY! THAT MUST BE HIM NOW.
HOPE HIS QUESTIONS AREN'T TOO... TAXING!
AFTERNOON, MR WALLACE. I'VE COME TO INSPECT YOUR ACCOUNTS.
YES, OF COURSE. DO COME IN. I'VE JUST PUT THE KETTLE ON.
OH, NO TEA FOR ME, THANKS.
WE MUST GET DOWN TO BUSINESS.
I'M HERE TO CHECK YOU'RE NOT MILKING THE SYSTEM...
678

Wallace & Gromit - An Inspector Calls

by Aardman & Titan Comics

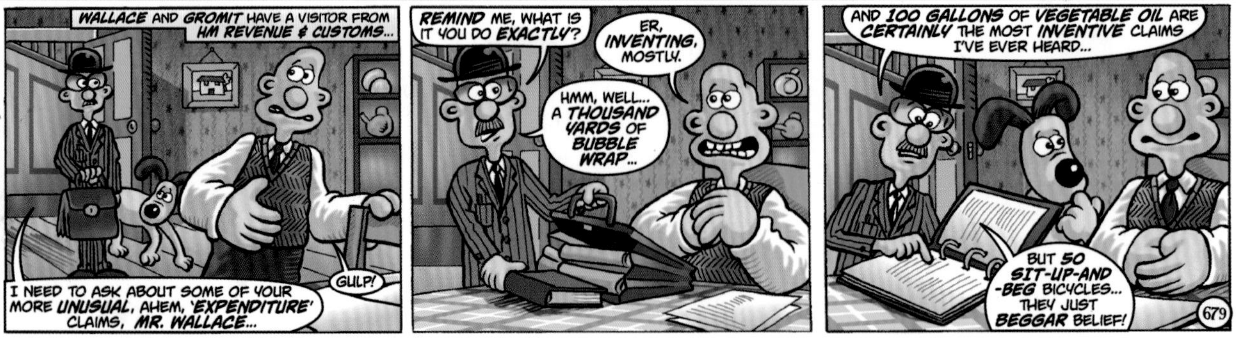
WALLACE AND GROMIT HAVE A VISITOR FROM HM REVENUE & CUSTOMS...
I NEED TO ASK ABOUT SOME OF YOUR MORE UNUSUAL, AHEM, 'EXPENDITURE' CLAIMS, MR. WALLACE...
GULP!
REMIND ME, WHAT IS IT YOU DO EXACTLY?
ER, INVENTING, MOSTLY.
HMM, WELL... A THOUSAND YARDS OF BUBBLE WRAP...
AND 100 GALLONS OF VEGETABLE OIL ARE CERTAINLY THE MOST INVENTIVE CLAIMS I'VE EVER HEARD...
BUT 50 SIT-UP-AND -BEG BICYCLES... THEY JUST BEGGAR BELIEF!
679

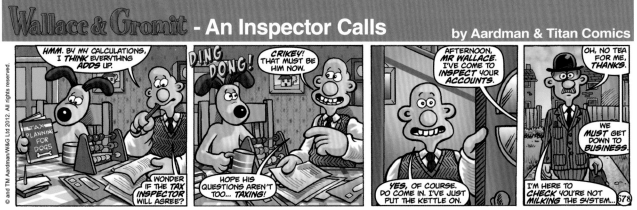

Wallace & Gromit - An Inspector Calls

by Aardman & Titan Comics

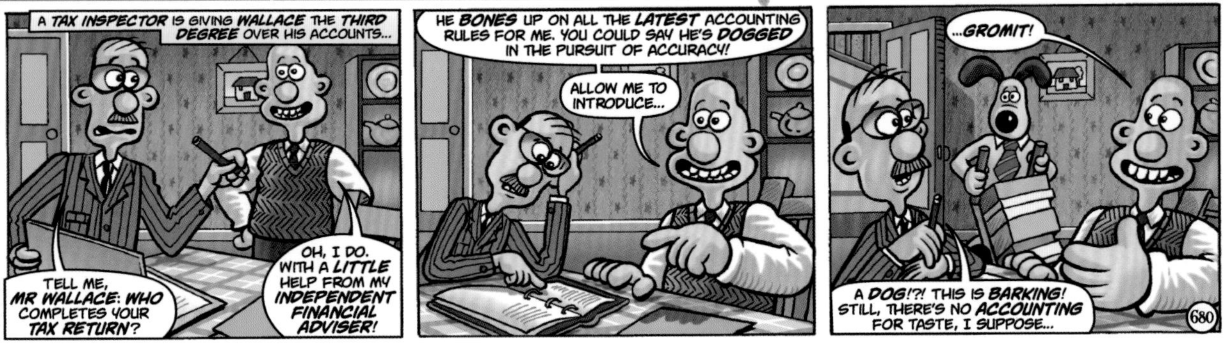

A TAX INSPECTOR IS GIVING WALLACE THE THIRD DEGREE OVER HIS ACCOUNTS...
TELL ME, MR WALLACE: WHO COMPLETES YOUR TAX RETURN?
OH, I DO. WITH A LITTLE HELP FROM MY INDEPENDENT FINANCIAL ADVISER!
HE BONES UP ON ALL THE LATEST ACCOUNTING RULES FOR ME. YOU COULD SAY HE'S DOGGED IN THE PURSUIT OF ACCURACY!
ALLOW ME TO INTRODUCE...
...GROMIT!
A DOG!?! THIS IS BARKING! STILL, THERE'S NO ACCOUNTING FOR TASTE, I SUPPOSE...
680

Wallace & Gromit - An Inspector Calls

by Aardman & Titan Comics

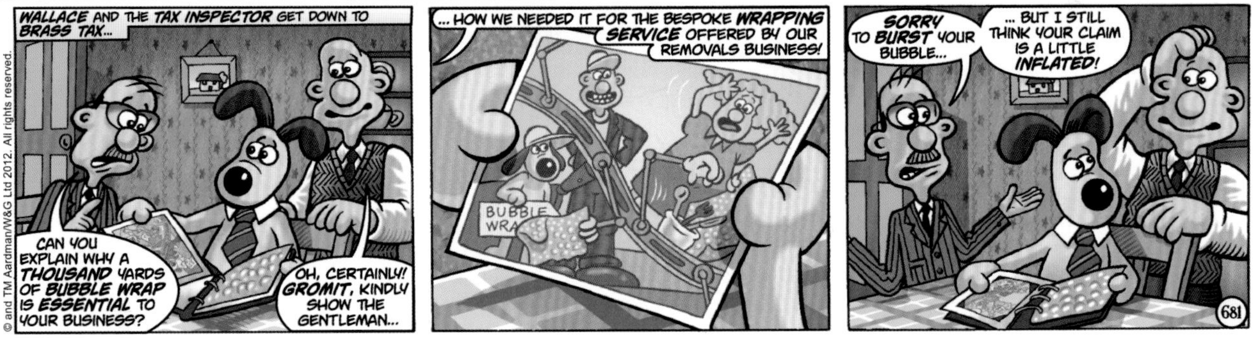

WALLACE AND THE TAX INSPECTOR GET DOWN TO BRASS TAX...
CAN YOU EXPLAIN WHY A THOUSAND YARDS OF BUBBLE WRAP IS ESSENTIAL TO YOUR BUSINESS?
OH, CERTAINLY! GROMIT, KINDLY SHOW THE GENTLEMAN...
... HOW WE NEEDED IT FOR THE BESPOKE WRAPPING SERVICE OFFERED BY OUR REMOVALS BUSINESS!
BUBBLE WRA
SORRY TO BURST YOUR BUBBLE...
... BUT I STILL THINK YOUR CLAIM IS A LITTLE INFLATED!
681

Wallace & Gromit - An Inspector Calls

by Aardman & Titan Comics

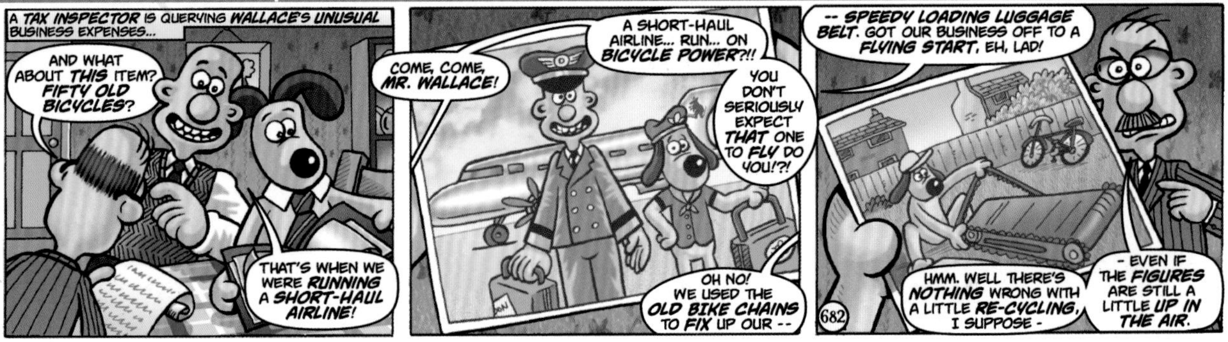

A TAX INSPECTOR IS QUERYING WALLACE'S UNUSUAL BUSINESS EXPENSES...
AND WHAT ABOUT THIS ITEM? FIFTY OLD BICYCLES?
THAT'S WHEN WE WERE RUNNING A SHORT-HAUL AIRLINE!
COME, COME, MR. WALLACE!
A SHORT-HAUL AIRLINE... RUN... ON BICYCLE POWER?!!
YOU DON'T SERIOUSLY EXPECT THAT ONE TO FLY DO YOU!?!
OH NO! WE USED THE OLD BIKE CHAINS TO FIX UP OUR --
682
-- SPEEDY LOADING LUGGAGE BELT. GOT OUR BUSINESS OFF TO A FLYING START, EH, LAD!
HMM. WELL THERE'S NOTHING WRONG WITH A LITTLE RE-CYCLING, I SUPPOSE -
- EVEN IF THE FIGURES ARE STILL A LITTLE UP IN THE AIR.

Wallace & Gromit - An Inspector Calls

by Aardman & Titan Comics

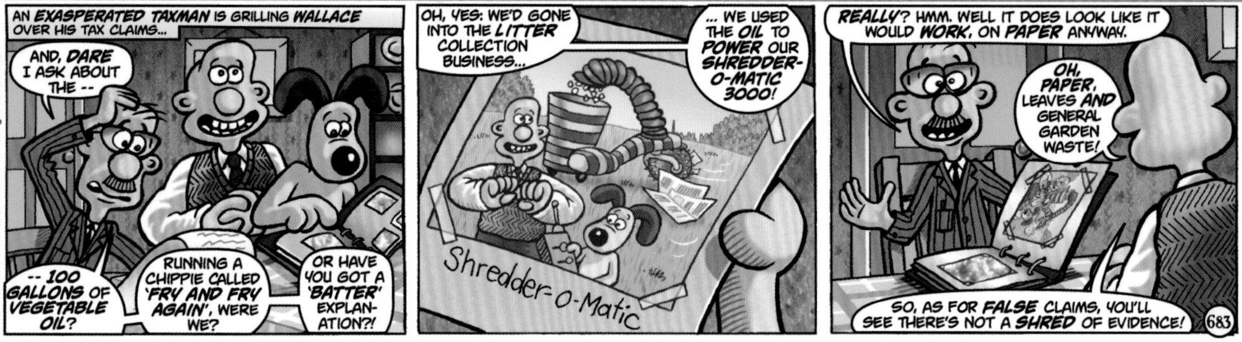
AN EXASPERATED TAXMAN IS GRILLING WALLACE OVER HIS TAX CLAIMS...
AND, DARE I ASK ABOUT THE --
-- 100 GALLONS OF VEGETABLE OIL?
RUNNING A CHIPPIE CALLED 'FRY AND FRY AGAIN', WERE WE?
OR HAVE YOU GOT A 'BATTER' EXPLANATION?!
OH, YES: WE'D GONE INTO THE LITTER COLLECTION BUSINESS...
... WE USED THE OIL TO POWER OUR SHREDDER-O-MATIC 3000!
Shredder-O-Matic
REALLY? HMM. WELL IT DOES LOOK LIKE IT WOULD WORK, ON PAPER ANYWAY.
OH, PAPER, LEAVES AND GENERAL GARDEN WASTE!
SO, AS FOR FALSE CLAIMS, YOU'LL SEE THERE'S NOT A SHRED OF EVIDENCE!
683

Wallace & Gromit - An Inspector Calls

by Aardman & Titan Comics

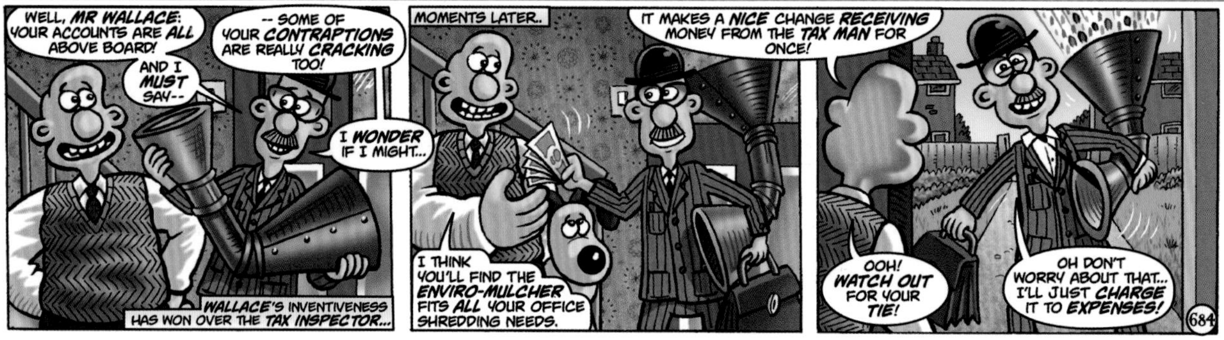
WELL, MR WALLACE: YOUR ACCOUNTS ARE ALL ABOVE BOARD!
AND I MUST SAY--
-- SOME OF YOUR CONTRAPTIONS ARE REALLY CRACKING TOO!
I WONDER IF I MIGHT...
WALLACE'S INVENTIVENESS HAS WON OVER THE TAX INSPECTOR...
MOMENTS LATER..
IT MAKES A NICE CHANGE RECEIVING MONEY FROM THE TAX MAN FOR ONCE!
I THINK YOU'LL FIND THE ENVIRO-MULCHER FITS ALL YOUR OFFICE SHREDDING NEEDS.
OOH! WATCH OUT FOR YOUR TIE!
OH DON'T WORRY ABOUT THAT... I'LL JUST CHARGE IT TO EXPENSES!
684

The End

Wallace & Gromit - I Drought It

by Aardman & Titan Comics

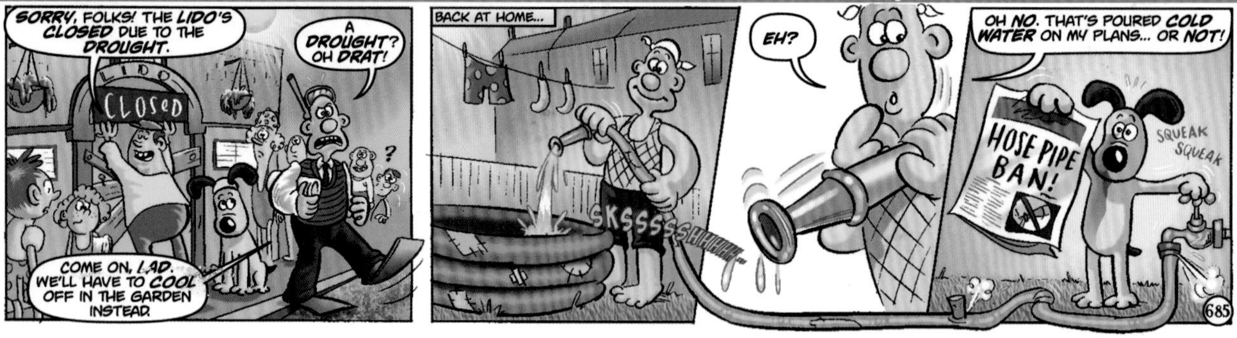
SORRY, FOLKS! THE LIDO'S CLOSED DUE TO THE DROUGHT.
A DROUGHT? OH DRAT!
CLOSED
COME ON, LAD. WE'LL HAVE TO COOL OFF IN THE GARDEN INSTEAD.
BACK AT HOME...
SKSSSSSHHHHH
EH?
OH NO. THAT'S POURED COLD WATER ON MY PLANS... OR NOT!
HOSE PIPE BAN!
SQUEAK SQUEAK
685

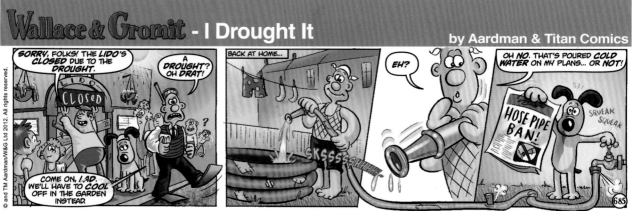

Wallace & Gromit - I Drought It

by Aardman & Titan Comics

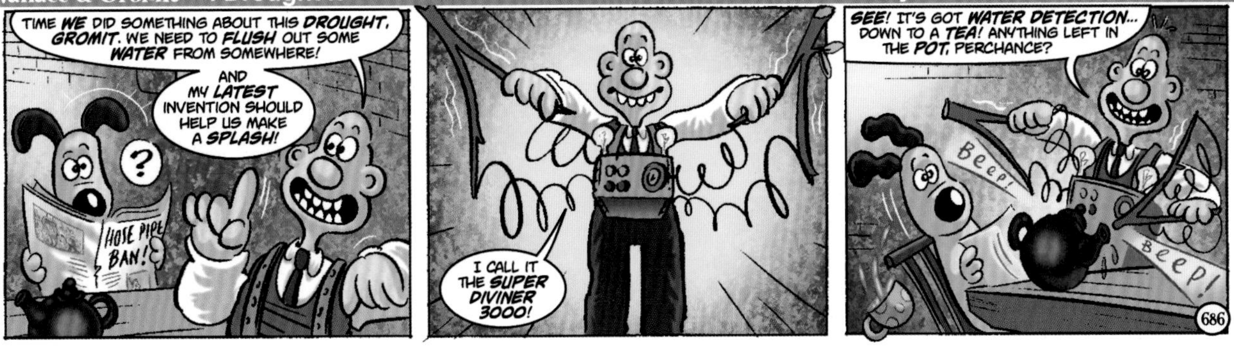
TIME WE DID SOMETHING ABOUT THIS DROUGHT, GROMIT. WE NEED TO FLUSH OUT SOME WATER FROM SOMEWHERE!
?
HOSE PIPE BAN!
AND MY LATEST INVENTION SHOULD HELP US MAKE A SPLASH!
I CALL IT THE SUPER DIVINER 3000!
SEE! IT'S GOT WATER DETECTION... DOWN TO A TEA! ANYTHING LEFT IN THE POT, PERCHANCE?
Beep!
Beep!
686

Wallace & Gromit - I Drought It

by Aardman & Titan Comics

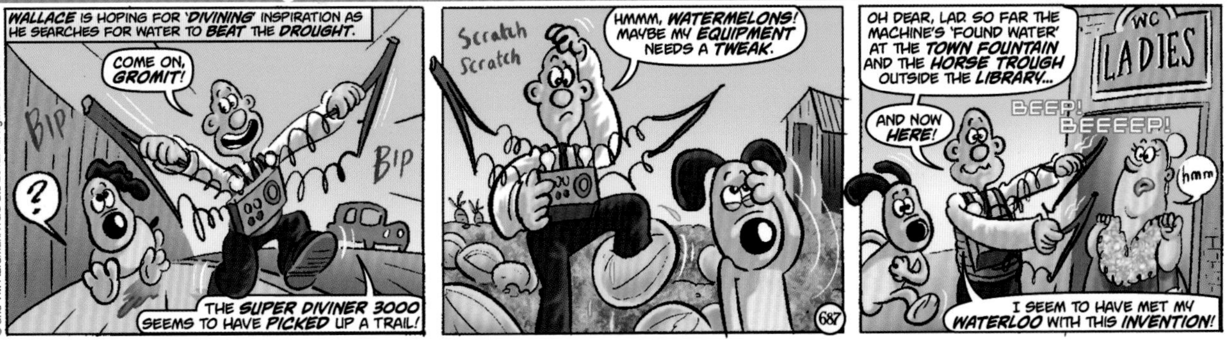
WALLACE IS HOPING FOR 'DIVINING' INSPIRATION AS HE SEARCHES FOR WATER TO BEAT THE DROUGHT.
COME ON, GROMIT!
BIP
BIP
?
THE SUPER DIVINER 3000 SEEMS TO HAVE PICKED UP A TRAIL!
Scratch
Scratch
HMMM, WATERMELONS! MAYBE MY EQUIPMENT NEEDS A TWEAK.
687
OH DEAR, LAD. SO FAR THE MACHINE'S 'FOUND WATER' AT THE TOWN FOUNTAIN AND THE HORSE TROUGH OUTSIDE THE LIBRARY...
WC
LADIES
AND NOW HERE!
BEEP!
BEEEEP!
hmm
I SEEM TO HAVE MET MY WATERLOO WITH THIS INVENTION!

Wallace & Gromit - I Drought It

by Aardman & Titan Comics

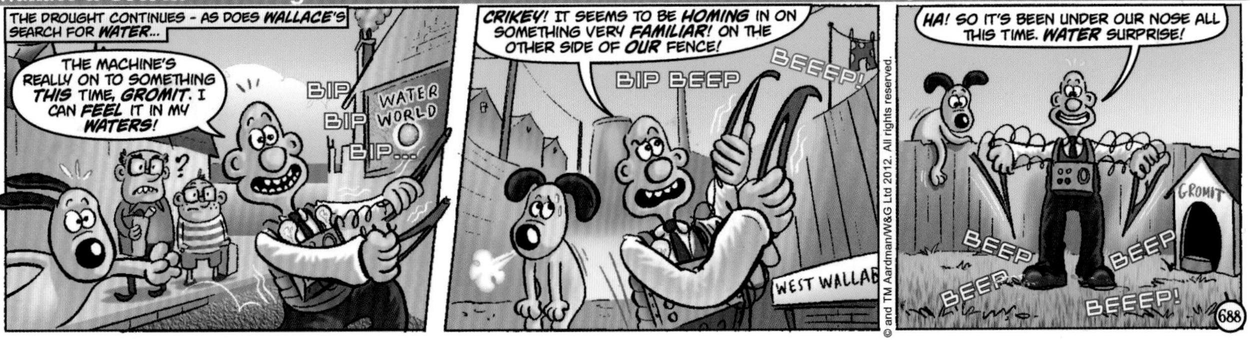
THE DROUGHT CONTINUES - AS DOES WALLACE'S SEARCH FOR WATER...
THE MACHINE'S REALLY ON TO SOMETHING THIS TIME, GROMIT. I CAN FEEL IT IN MY WATERS!
?
BIP
BIP
BIP...
WATER WORLD
CRIKEY! IT SEEMS TO BE HOMING IN ON SOMETHING VERY FAMILIAR! ON THE OTHER SIDE OF OUR FENCE!
BIP BEEP
BEEEP!
WEST WALLAB
HA! SO IT'S BEEN UNDER OUR NOSE ALL THIS TIME. WATER SURPRISE!
GROMIT
BEEP
BEEP
BEEP
BEEEP!
688

Wallace & Gromit - I Drought It
by Aardman & Titan Comics

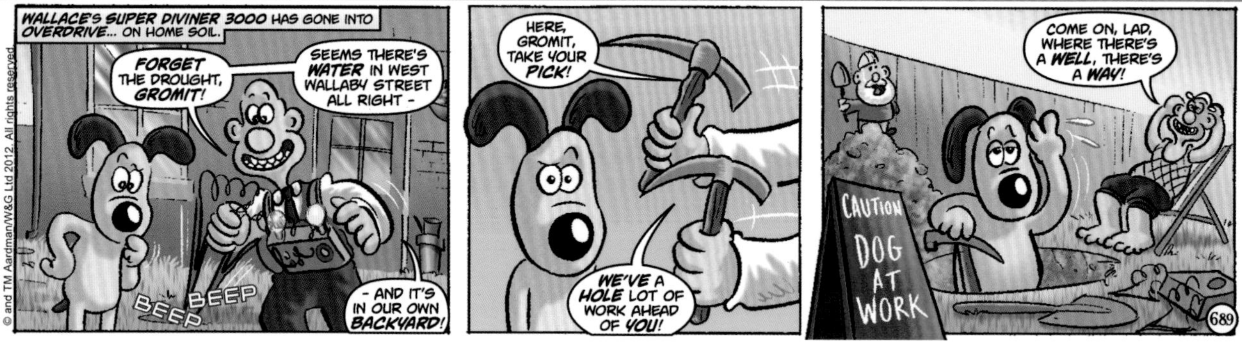
WALLACE'S SUPER DIVINER 3000 HAS GONE INTO OVERDRIVE... ON HOME SOIL.
FORGET THE DROUGHT, GROMIT!
SEEMS THERE'S WATER IN WEST WALLABY STREET ALL RIGHT -
BEEP
BEEP
- AND IT'S IN OUR OWN BACKYARD!
HERE, GROMIT, TAKE YOUR PICK!
WE'VE A HOLE LOT OF WORK AHEAD OF YOU!
COME ON, LAD, WHERE THERE'S A WELL, THERE'S A WAY!
CAUTION
DOG AT WORK
689

Wallace & Gromit - I Drought It
by Aardman & Titan Comics

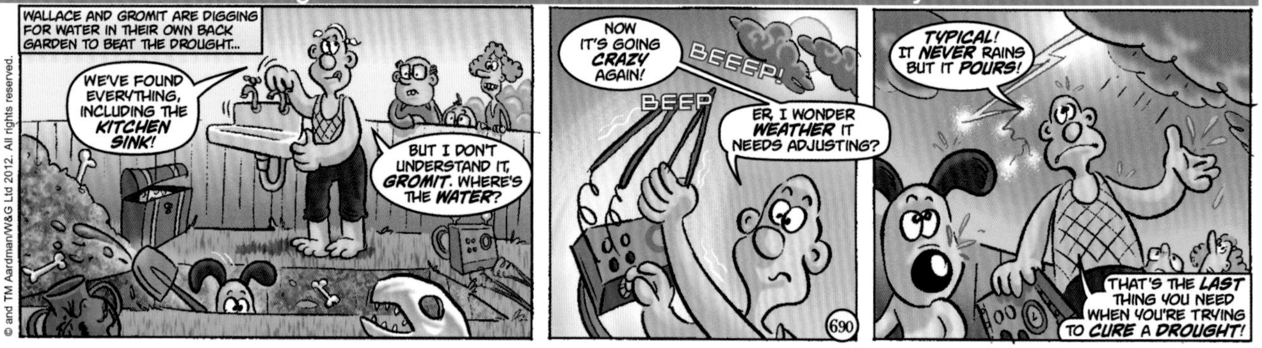
WALLACE AND GROMIT ARE DIGGING FOR WATER IN THEIR OWN BACK GARDEN TO BEAT THE DROUGHT...
WE'VE FOUND EVERYTHING, INCLUDING THE KITCHEN SINK!
BUT I DON'T UNDERSTAND IT, GROMIT. WHERE'S THE WATER?
NOW IT'S GOING CRAZY AGAIN!
BEEEP!
BEEP
ER, I WONDER WEATHER IT NEEDS ADJUSTING?
690
TYPICAL! IT NEVER RAINS BUT IT POURS!
THAT'S THE LAST THING YOU NEED WHEN YOU'RE TRYING TO CURE A DROUGHT!

Wallace & Gromit - I Drought It
by Aardman & Titan Comics

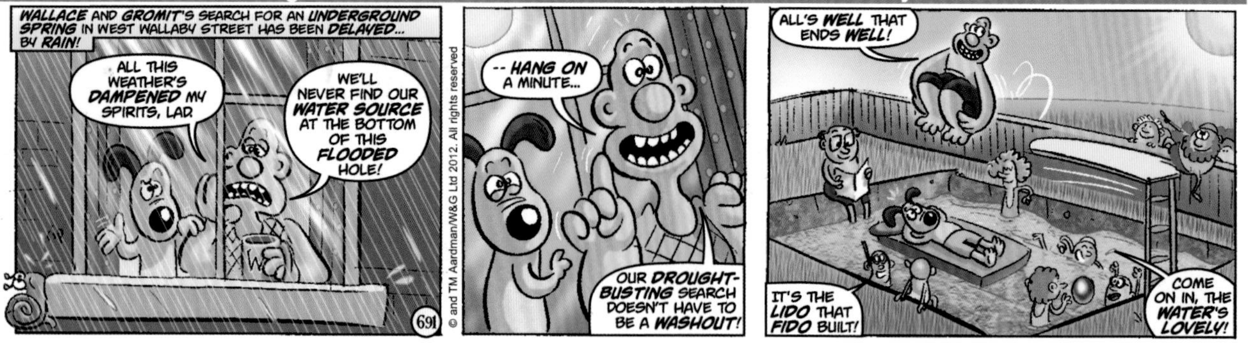
WALLACE AND GROMIT'S SEARCH FOR AN UNDERGROUND SPRING IN WEST WALLABY STREET HAS BEEN DELAYED... BY RAIN!
ALL THIS WEATHER'S DAMPENED MY SPIRITS, LAD.
WE'LL NEVER FIND OUR WATER SOURCE AT THE BOTTOM OF THIS FLOODED HOLE!
691
-- HANG ON A MINUTE...
OUR DROUGHT-BUSTING SEARCH DOESN'T HAVE TO BE A WASHOUT!
ALL'S WELL THAT ENDS WELL!
IT'S THE LIDO THAT FIDO BUILT!
COME ON IN, THE WATER'S LOVELY!

The End

Wallace & Gromit - Hedge Your Bets

by Aardman & Titan Comics

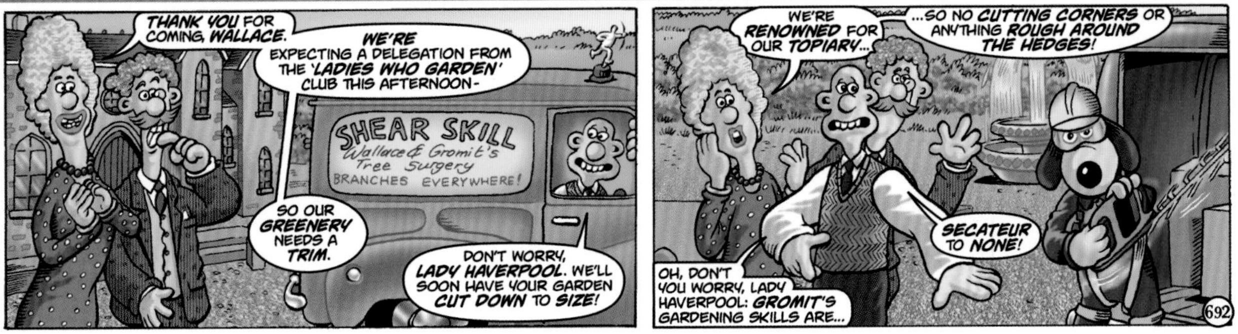
THANK YOU FOR COMING, WALLACE.
WE'RE EXPECTING A DELEGATION FROM THE 'LADIES WHO GARDEN' CLUB THIS AFTERNOON-
SHEAR SKILL
Wallace & Gromit's Tree Surgery
BRANCHES EVERYWHERE!
SO OUR GREENERY NEEDS A TRIM.
DON'T WORRY, LADY HAVERPOOL. WE'LL SOON HAVE YOUR GARDEN CUT DOWN TO SIZE!
WE'RE RENOWNED FOR OUR TOPIARY...
...SO NO CUTTING CORNERS OR ANYTHING ROUGH AROUND THE HEDGES!
SECATEUR TO NONE!
OH, DON'T YOU WORRY, LADY HAVERPOOL: GROMIT'S GARDENING SKILLS ARE...
692

Wallace & Gromit - Hedge Your Bets

by Aardman & Titan Comics

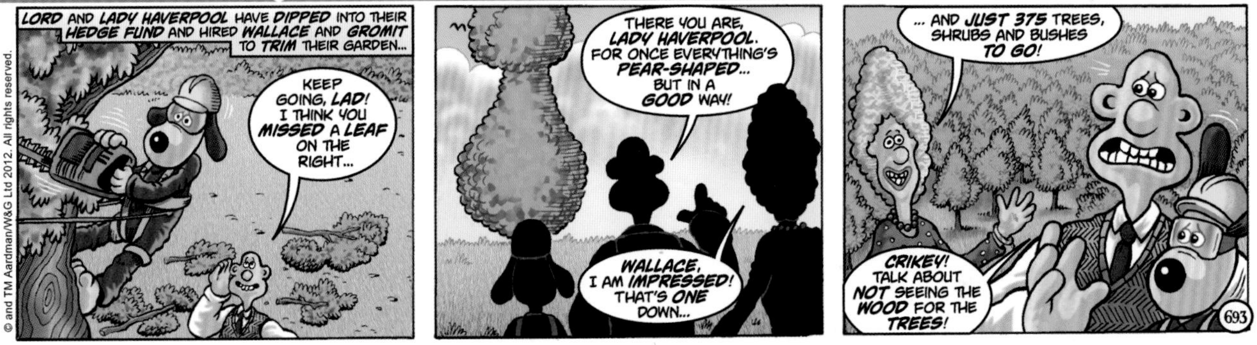
LORD AND LADY HAVERPOOL HAVE DIPPED INTO THEIR HEDGE FUND AND HIRED WALLACE AND GROMIT TO TRIM THEIR GARDEN...
KEEP GOING, LAD! I THINK YOU MISSED A LEAF ON THE RIGHT...
THERE YOU ARE, LADY HAVERPOOL. FOR ONCE EVERYTHING'S PEAR-SHAPED... BUT IN A GOOD WAY!
WALLACE, I AM IMPRESSED! THAT'S ONE DOWN...
... AND JUST 375 TREES, SHRUBS AND BUSHES TO GO!
CRIKEY! TALK ABOUT NOT SEEING THE WOOD FOR THE TREES!
693

Wallace & Gromit - Hedge Your Bets

by Aardman & Titan Comics

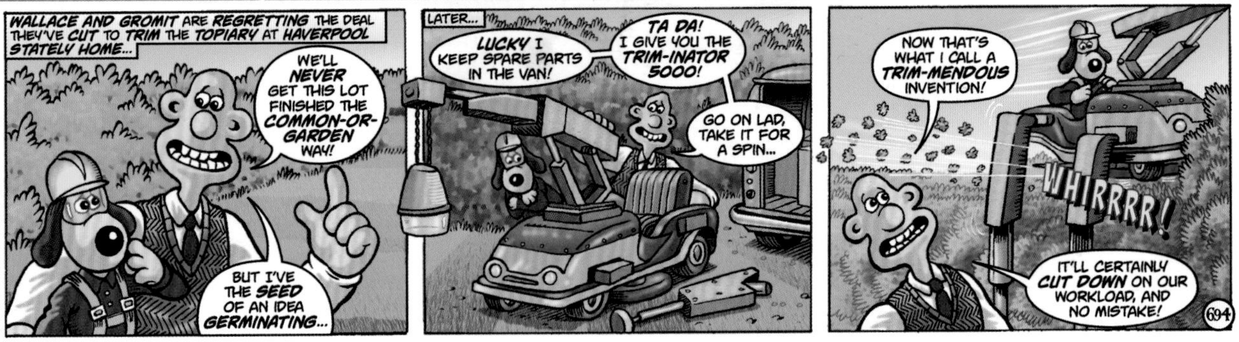
WALLACE AND GROMIT ARE REGRETTING THE DEAL THEY'VE CUT TO TRIM THE TOPIARY AT HAVERPOOL STATELY HOME...
WE'LL NEVER GET THIS LOT FINISHED THE COMMON-OR-GARDEN WAY!
BUT I'VE THE SEED OF AN IDEA GERMINATING...
LATER...
LUCKY I KEEP SPARE PARTS IN THE VAN!
TA DA! I GIVE YOU THE TRIM-INATOR 5000!
GO ON LAD, TAKE IT FOR A SPIN...
NOW THAT'S WHAT I CALL A TRIM-MENDOUS INVENTION!
WHIRRRR!
IT'LL CERTAINLY CUT DOWN ON OUR WORKLOAD, AND NO MISTAKE!
694

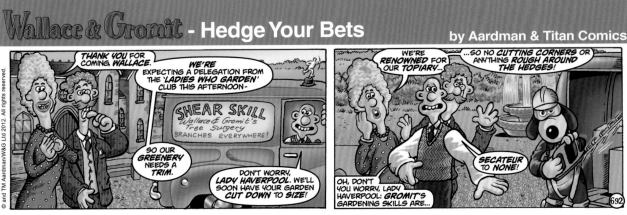

Wallace & Gromit - Hedge Your Bets by Aardman & Titan Comics

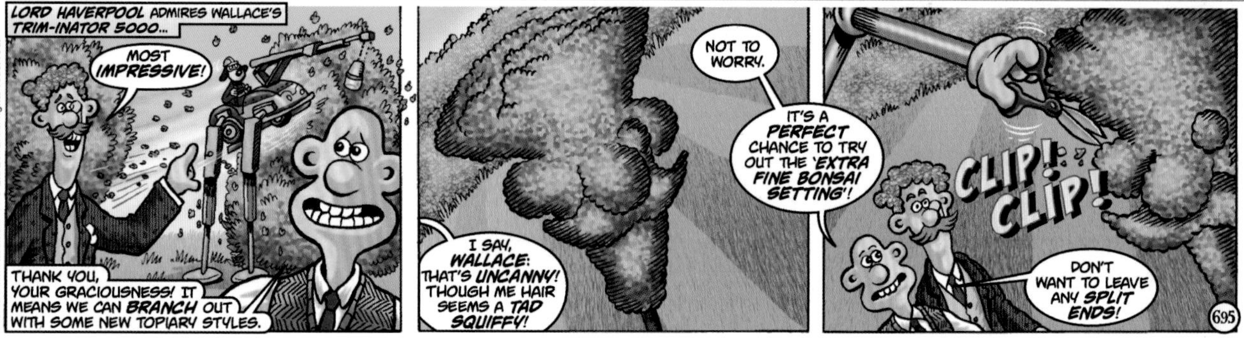

LORD HAVERPOOL ADMIRES WALLACE'S TRIM-INATOR 5000...
MOST IMPRESSIVE!
THANK YOU, YOUR GRACIOUSNESS! IT MEANS WE CAN BRANCH OUT WITH SOME NEW TOPIARY STYLES.
NOT TO WORRY.
IT'S A PERFECT CHANCE TO TRY OUT THE 'EXTRA FINE BONSAI SETTING'!
I SAY, WALLACE: THAT'S UNCANNY! THOUGH ME HAIR SEEMS A TAD SQUIFFY!
CLIP! CLIP!
DON'T WANT TO LEAVE ANY SPLIT ENDS!
695

Wallace & Gromit - Hedge Your Bets by Aardman & Titan Comics

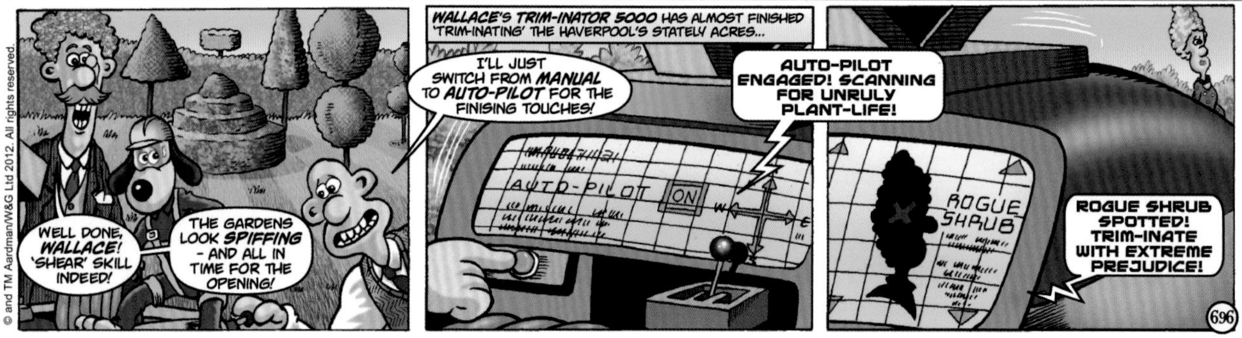

WELL DONE, WALLACE! 'SHEAR' SKILL INDEED!
THE GARDENS LOOK SPIFFING - AND ALL IN TIME FOR THE OPENING!
WALLACE'S TRIM-INATOR 5000 HAS ALMOST FINISHED 'TRIM-INATING' THE HAVERPOOL'S STATELY ACRES...
I'LL JUST SWITCH FROM MANUAL TO AUTO-PILOT FOR THE FINISING TOUCHES!
AUTO-PILOT ENGAGED! SCANNING FOR UNRULY PLANT-LIFE!
AUTO-PILOT ON
ROGUE SHRUB
ROGUE SHRUB SPOTTED! TRIM-INATE WITH EXTREME PREJUDICE!
696

© and TM Aardman/W&G Ltd 2012. All rights reserved.

Wallace & Gromit - Hedge Your Bets by Aardman & Titan Comics

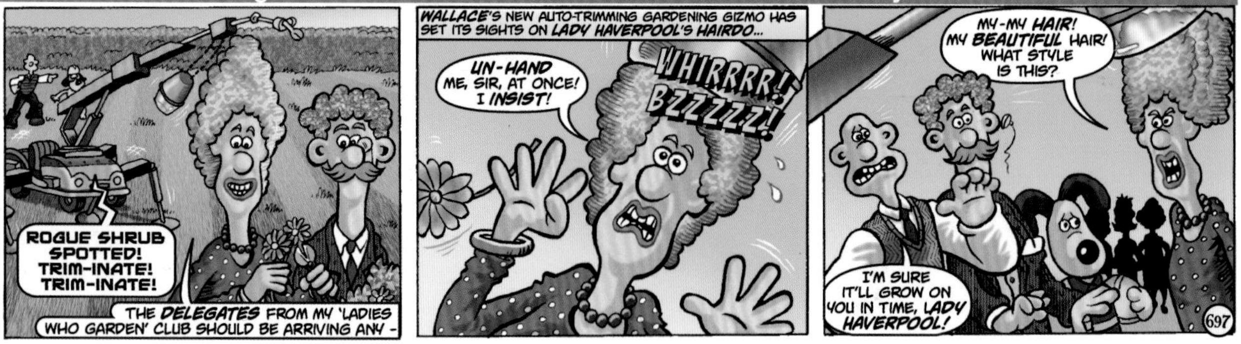

ROGUE SHRUB SPOTTED! TRIM-INATE! TRIM-INATE!
THE DELEGATES FROM MY 'LADIES WHO GARDEN' CLUB SHOULD BE ARRIVING ANY -
WALLACE'S NEW AUTO-TRIMMING GARDENING GIZMO HAS SET ITS SIGHTS ON LADY HAVERPOOL'S HAIRDO...
UN-HAND ME, SIR, AT ONCE! I INSIST!
WHIRRRR! BZZZZZ!
MY-MY HAIR! MY BEAUTIFUL HAIR! WHAT STYLE IS THIS?
I'M SURE IT'LL GROW ON YOU IN TIME, LADY HAVERPOOL!
697

© and TM Aardman/W&G Ltd 2012. All rights reserved.

Wallace & Gromit - Hedge Your Bets

by Aardman & Titan Comics

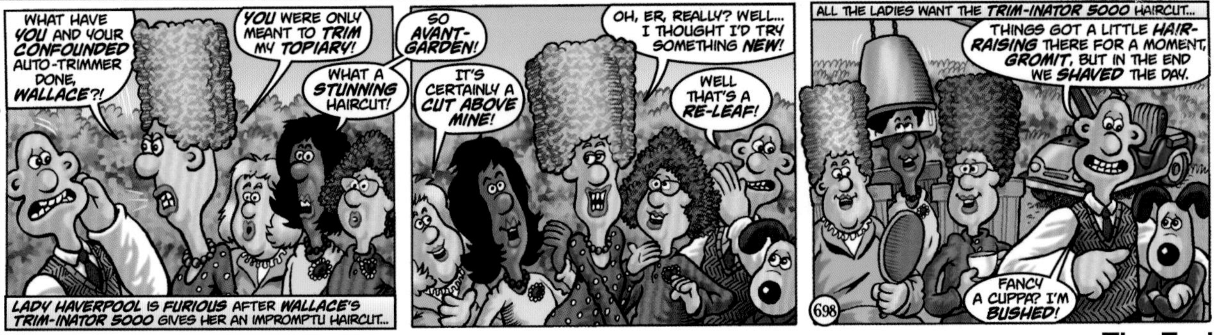
WHAT HAVE YOU AND YOUR CONFOUNDED AUTO-TRIMMER DONE, WALLACE?!
YOU WERE ONLY MEANT TO TRIM MY TOPIARY!
WHAT A STUNNING HAIRCUT!
SO AVANT-GARDEN!
LADY HAVERPOOL IS FURIOUS AFTER WALLACE'S TRIM-INATOR 5000 GIVES HER AN IMPROMPTU HAIRCUT...
IT'S CERTAINLY A CUT ABOVE MINE!
OH, ER, REALLY? WELL... I THOUGHT I'D TRY SOMETHING NEW!
WELL THAT'S A RE-LEAF!
ALL THE LADIES WANT THE TRIM-INATOR 5000 HAIRCUT...
THINGS GOT A LITTLE HAIR-RAISING THERE FOR A MOMENT, GROMIT, BUT IN THE END WE SHAVED THE DAY.
FANCY A CUPPA? I'M BUSHED!
698

The End

Wallace & Gromit - Joust Good Friends

by Aardman & Titan Comics

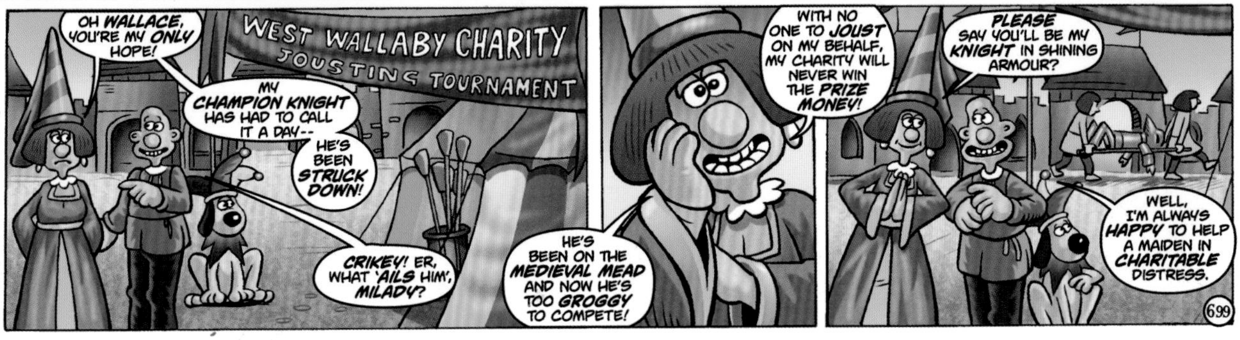
WEST WALLABY CHARITY JOUSTING TOURNAMENT
OH WALLACE, YOU'RE MY ONLY HOPE!
MY CHAMPION KNIGHT HAS HAD TO CALL IT A DAY--
HE'S BEEN STRUCK DOWN!
CRIKEY! ER, WHAT 'AILS HIM', MILADY?
HE'S BEEN ON THE MEDIEVAL MEAD AND NOW HE'S TOO GROGGY TO COMPETE!
WITH NO ONE TO JOUST ON MY BEHALF, MY CHARITY WILL NEVER WIN THE PRIZE MONEY!
PLEASE SAY YOU'LL BE MY KNIGHT IN SHINING ARMOUR?
WELL, I'M ALWAYS HAPPY TO HELP A MAIDEN IN CHARITABLE DISTRESS.
699

Wallace & Gromit - Joust Good Friends

by Aardman & Titan Comics

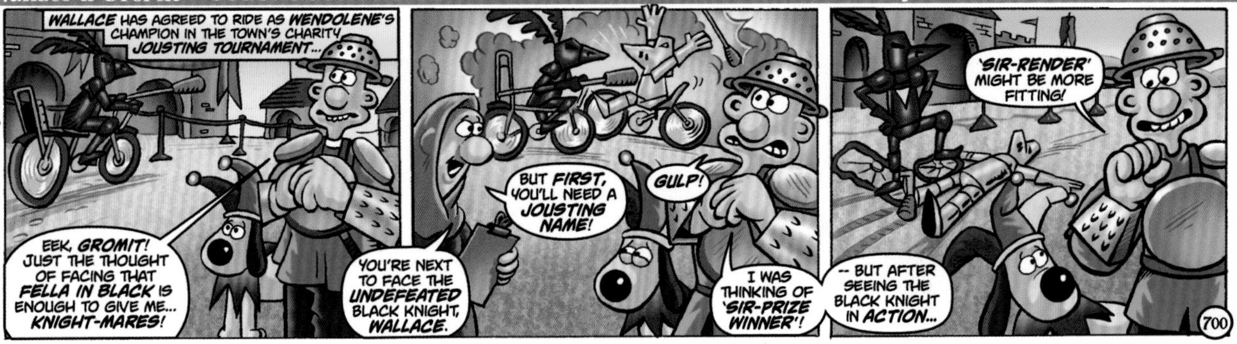
WALLACE HAS AGREED TO RIDE AS WENDOLENE'S CHAMPION IN THE TOWN'S CHARITY JOUSTING TOURNAMENT...
EEK, GROMIT! JUST THE THOUGHT OF FACING THAT FELLA IN BLACK IS ENOUGH TO GIVE ME... KNIGHT-MARES!
YOU'RE NEXT TO FACE THE UNDEFEATED BLACK KNIGHT, WALLACE.
BUT FIRST, YOU'LL NEED A JOUSTING NAME!
GULP!
I WAS THINKING OF 'SIR-PRIZE WINNER'!
-- BUT AFTER SEEING THE BLACK KNIGHT IN ACTION...
'SIR-RENDER' MIGHT BE MORE FITTING!
700

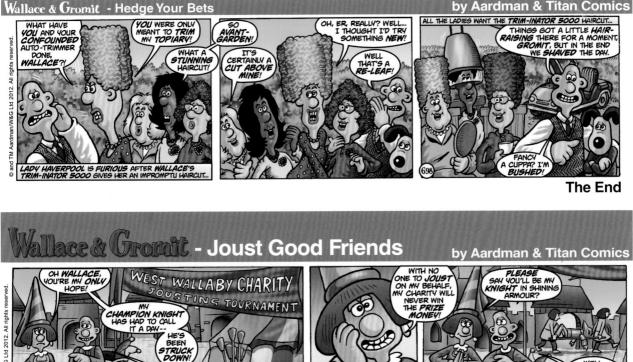

Wallace & Gromit - Joust Good Friends by Aardman & Titan Comics

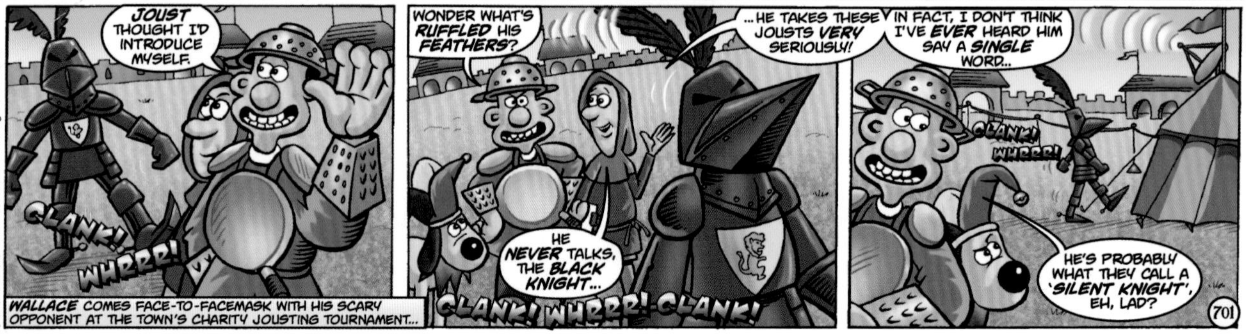
JOUST THOUGHT I'D INTRODUCE MYSELF.
CLANK!
WHRRR!
WALLACE COMES FACE-TO-FACEMASK WITH HIS SCARY OPPONENT AT THE TOWN'S CHARITY JOUSTING TOURNAMENT...
WONDER WHAT'S RUFFLED HIS FEATHERS?
HE NEVER TALKS, THE BLACK KNIGHT...
...HE TAKES THESE JOUSTS VERY SERIOUSLY!
CLANK! WHRRR! CLANK!
IN FACT, I DON'T THINK I'VE EVER HEARD HIM SAY A SINGLE WORD...
CLANK!
WHRRR!
HE'S PROBABLY WHAT THEY CALL A 'SILENT KNIGHT', EH, LAD?
701

Wallace & Gromit - Joust Good Friends by Aardman & Titan Comics

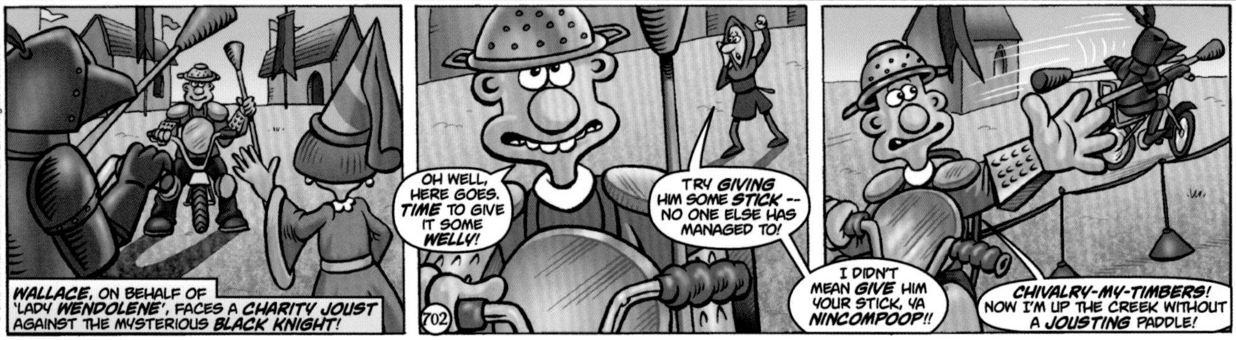
WALLACE, ON BEHALF OF 'LADY WENDOLENE', FACES A CHARITY JOUST AGAINST THE MYSTERIOUS BLACK KNIGHT!
OH WELL, HERE GOES. TIME TO GIVE IT SOME WELLY!
TRY GIVING HIM SOME STICK -- NO ONE ELSE HAS MANAGED TO!
I DIDN'T MEAN GIVE HIM YOUR STICK, YA NINCOMPOOP!!
702
CHIVALRY-MY-TIMBERS! NOW I'M UP THE CREEK WITHOUT A JOUSTING PADDLE!

Wallace & Gromit - Joust Good Friends by Aardman & Titan Comics

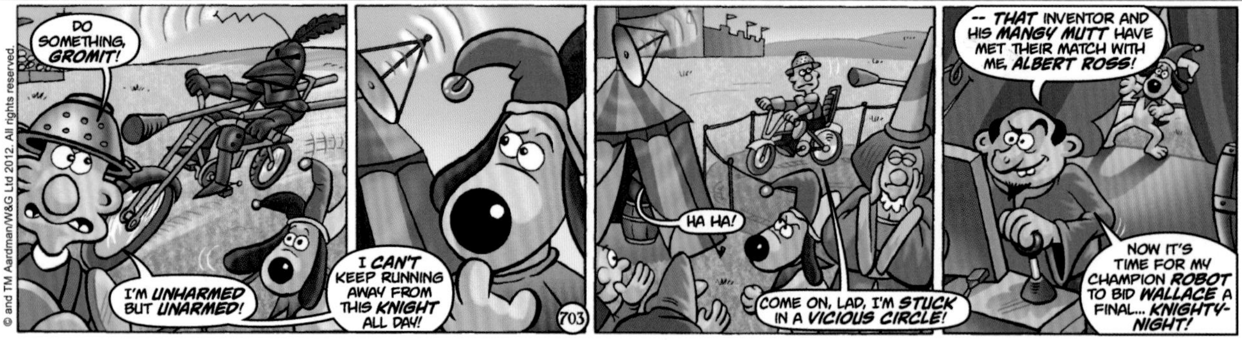
DO SOMETHING, GROMIT!
I'M UNHARMED BUT UNARMED!
I CAN'T KEEP RUNNING AWAY FROM THIS KNIGHT ALL DAY!
703
HA HA!
COME ON, LAD, I'M STUCK IN A VICIOUS CIRCLE!
-- THAT INVENTOR AND HIS MANGY MUTT HAVE MET THEIR MATCH WITH ME, ALBERT ROSS!
NOW IT'S TIME FOR MY CHAMPION ROBOT TO BID WALLACE A FINAL... KNIGHTY-NIGHT!

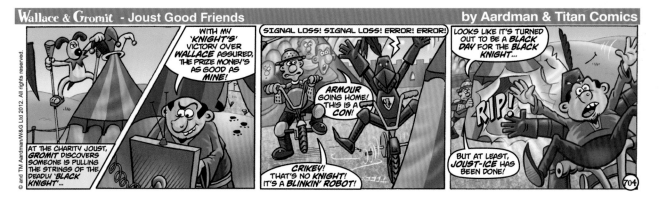

Wallace & Gromit - Joust Good Friends — by Aardman & Titan Comics

© and TM Aardman/W&G Ltd 2012. All rights reserved.
AT THE CHARITY JOUST, GROMIT DISCOVERS SOMEONE IS PULLING THE STRINGS OF THE DEADLY 'BLACK KNIGHT'...
WITH MY 'KNIGHT'S' VICTORY OVER WALLACE ASSURED, THE PRIZE MONEY'S AS GOOD AS MINE!
SIGNAL LOSS! SIGNAL LOSS! ERROR! ERROR!
ARMOUR GOING HOME! THIS IS A CON!
CRIKEY! THAT'S NO KNIGHT! IT'S A BLINKIN' ROBOT!
LOOKS LIKE IT'S TURNED OUT TO BE A BLACK DAY FOR THE BLACK KNIGHT...
RIP!
BUT AT LEAST, JOUST-ICE HAS BEEN DONE!
704

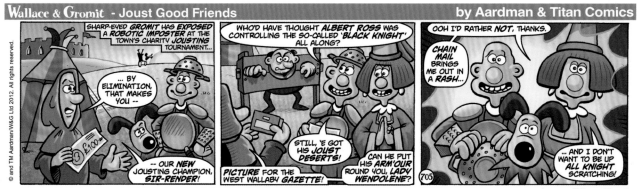

Wallace & Gromit - Joust Good Friends — by Aardman & Titan Comics

© and TM Aardman/W&G Ltd 2012. All rights reserved.
SHARP-EYED GROMIT HAS EXPOSED A ROBOTIC IMPOSTER AT THE TOWN'S CHARITY JOUSTING TOURNAMENT...
... BY ELIMINATION, THAT MAKES YOU --
-- OUR NEW JOUSTING CHAMPION, SIR-RENDER!
£100
WHO'D HAVE THOUGHT ALBERT ROSS WAS CONTROLLING THE SO-CALLED 'BLACK KNIGHT' ALL ALONG?
STILL, 'E GOT HIS JOUST DESERTS!
PICTURE FOR THE WEST WALLABY GAZETTE!
CAN HE PUT HIS ARM'OUR ROUND YOU, LADY WENDOLENE?
705
OOH I'D RATHER NOT, THANKS.
CHAIN MAIL BRINGS ME OUT IN A RASH...
... AND I DON'T WANT TO BE UP ALL KNIGHT SCRATCHING!

The End

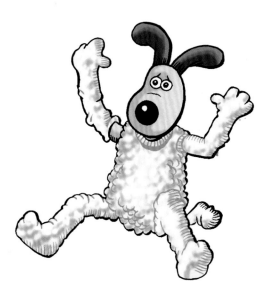

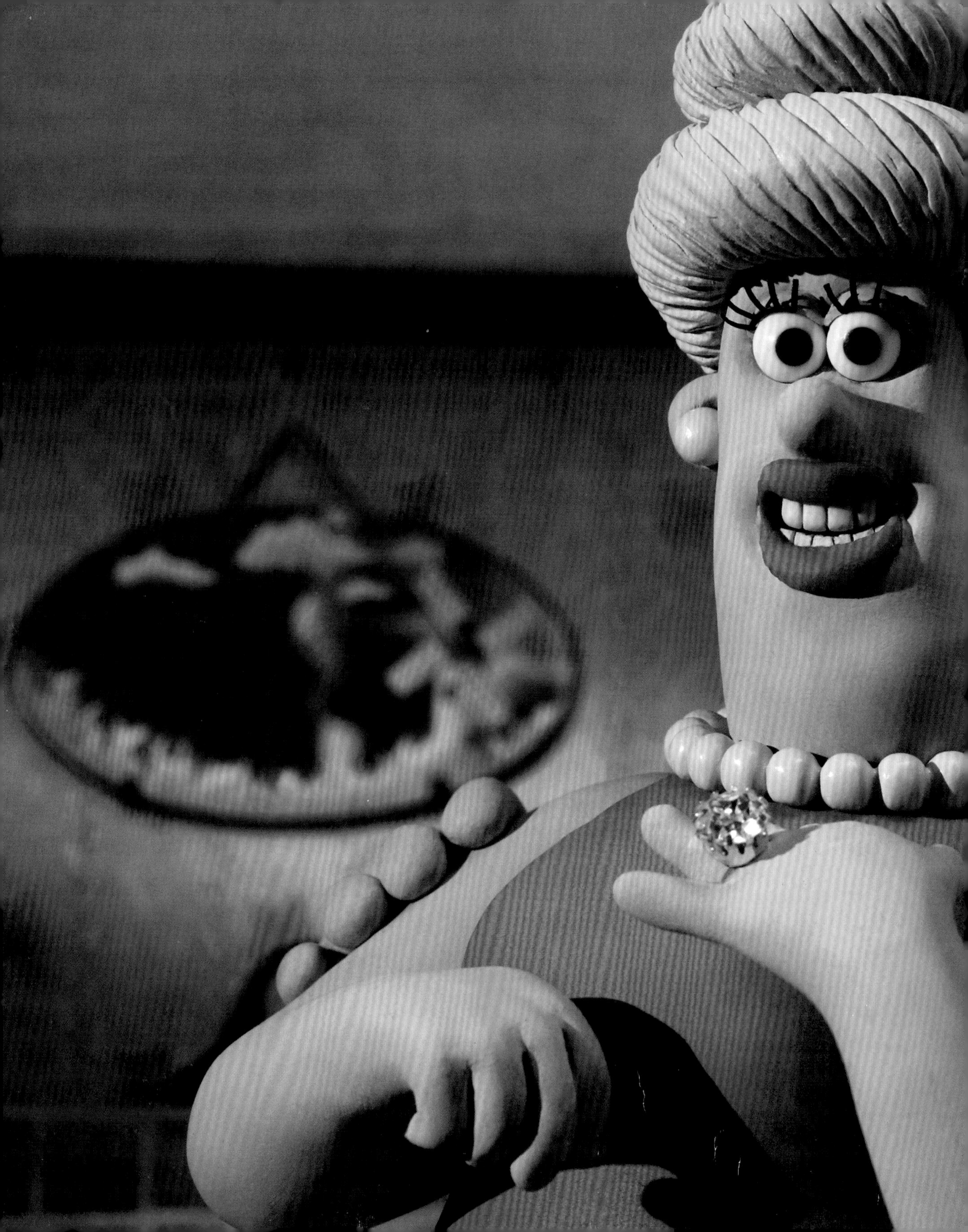

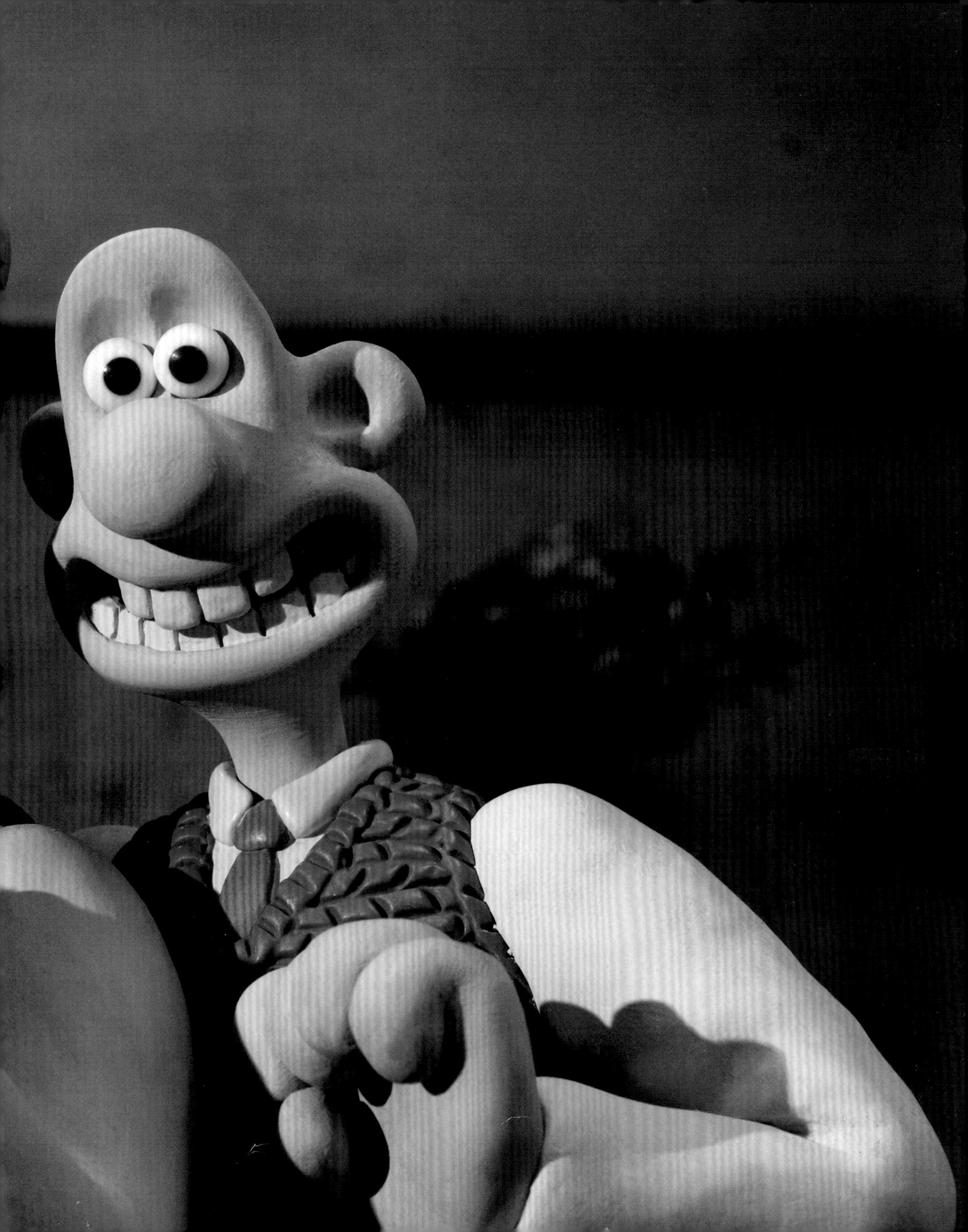

Wallace & Gromit - Beauty and the Beast of Wallaby Moor by Aardman & Titan Comics

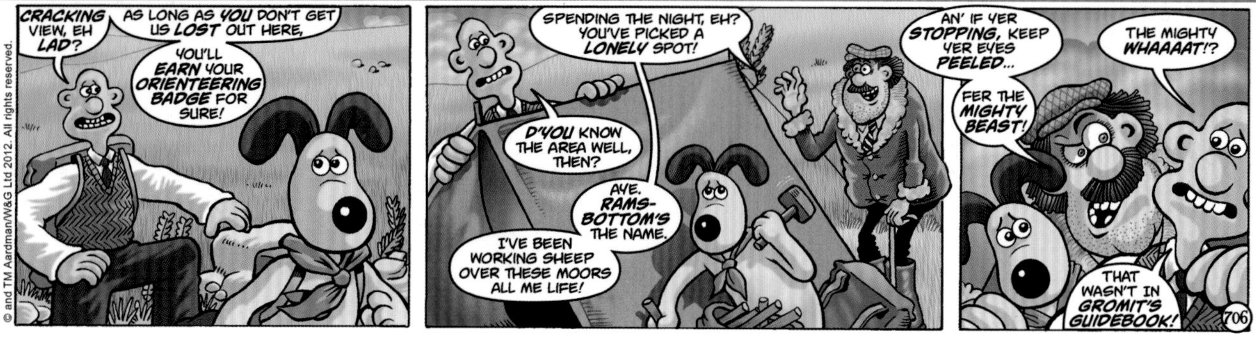
CRACKING VIEW, EH LAD?
AS LONG AS YOU DON'T GET US LOST OUT HERE,
YOU'LL EARN YOUR ORIENTEERING BADGE FOR SURE!
SPENDING THE NIGHT, EH? YOU'VE PICKED A LONELY SPOT!
D'YOU KNOW THE AREA WELL, THEN?
AYE. RAMS-BOTTOM'S THE NAME.
I'VE BEEN WORKING SHEEP OVER THESE MOORS ALL ME LIFE!
AN' IF YER STOPPING, KEEP YER EYES PEELED...
FER THE MIGHTY BEAST!
THE MIGHTY WHAAAAT!?
THAT WASN'T IN GROMIT'S GUIDEBOOK!
706

Wallace & Gromit - Beauty and the Beast of Wallaby Moor by Aardman & Titan Comics

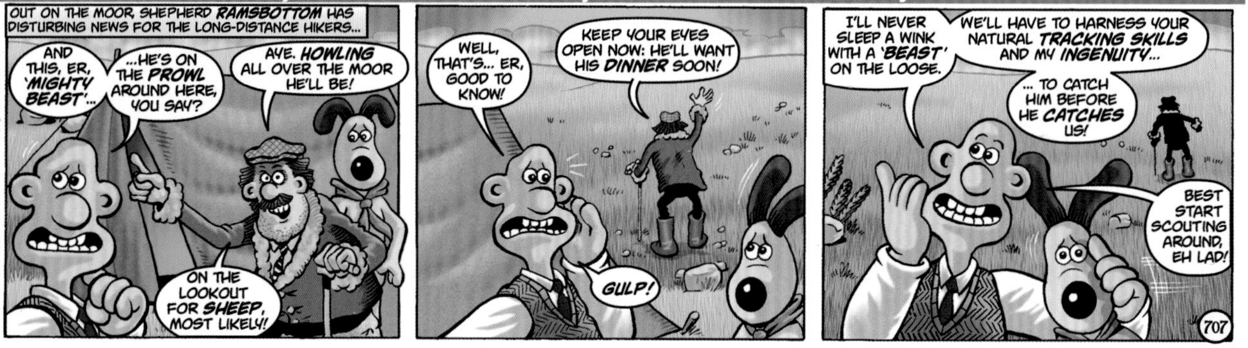
OUT ON THE MOOR, SHEPHERD RAMSBOTTOM HAS DISTURBING NEWS FOR THE LONG-DISTANCE HIKERS...
AND THIS, ER, 'MIGHTY BEAST'...
...HE'S ON THE PROWL AROUND HERE, YOU SAY?
AYE. HOWLING ALL OVER THE MOOR HE'LL BE!
ON THE LOOKOUT FOR SHEEP, MOST LIKELY!
WELL, THAT'S... ER, GOOD TO KNOW!
KEEP YOUR EYES OPEN NOW: HE'LL WANT HIS DINNER SOON!
GULP!
I'LL NEVER SLEEP A WINK WITH A 'BEAST' ON THE LOOSE.
WE'LL HAVE TO HARNESS YOUR NATURAL TRACKING SKILLS AND MY INGENUITY...
... TO CATCH HIM BEFORE HE CATCHES US!
BEST START SCOUTING AROUND, EH LAD!
707

Wallace & Gromit - Beauty and the Beast of Wallaby Moor by Aardman & Titan Comics

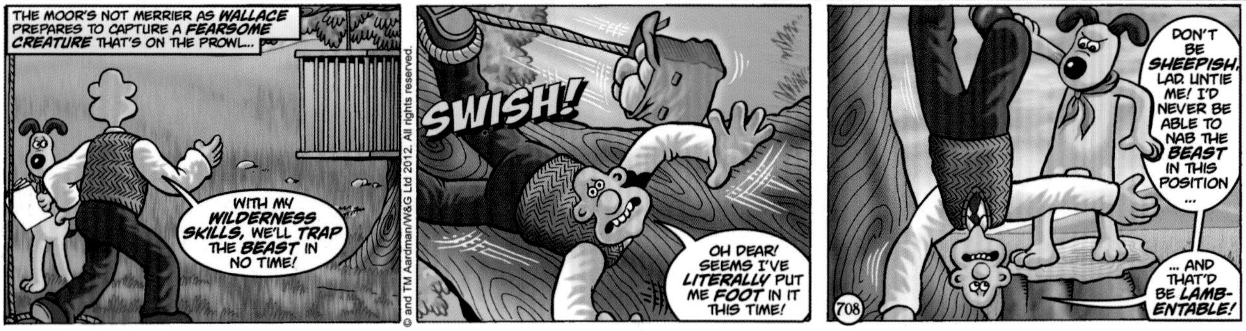
THE MOOR'S NOT MERRIER AS WALLACE PREPARES TO CAPTURE A FEARSOME CREATURE THAT'S ON THE PROWL...
WITH MY WILDERNESS SKILLS, WE'LL TRAP THE BEAST IN NO TIME!
SWISH!
OH DEAR! SEEMS I'VE LITERALLY PUT ME FOOT IN IT THIS TIME!
708
DON'T BE SHEEPISH, LAD. UNTIE ME! I'D NEVER BE ABLE TO NAB THE BEAST IN THIS POSITION ...
... AND THAT'D BE LAMB-ENTABLE!

Wallace & Gromit - Beauty and the Beast of Wallaby Moor | by Aardman & Titan Comics

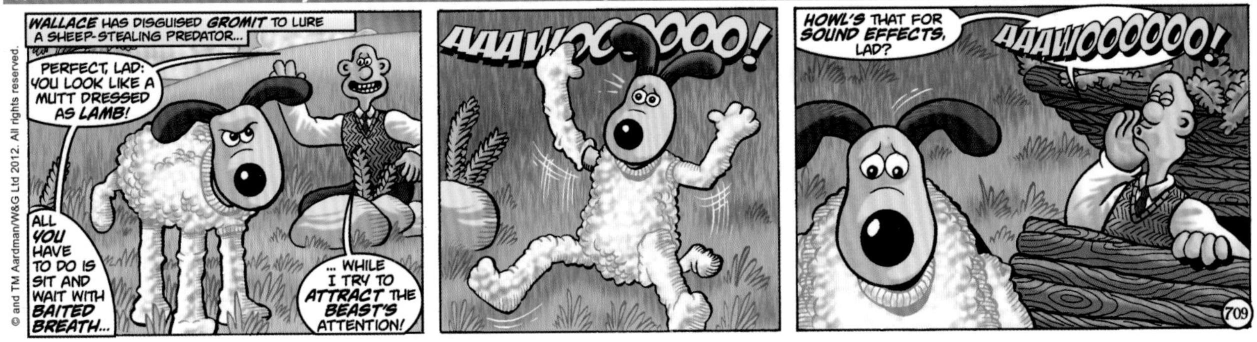
WALLACE HAS DISGUISED GROMIT TO LURE A SHEEP-STEALING PREDATOR...
PERFECT, LAD: YOU LOOK LIKE A MUTT DRESSED AS LAMB!
ALL YOU HAVE TO DO IS SIT AND WAIT WITH BAITED BREATH...
... WHILE I TRY TO ATTRACT THE BEAST'S ATTENTION!
AAAWOOOOOO!
HOWL'S THAT FOR SOUND EFFECTS, LAD?
AAAWOOOOOOO!
709

Wallace & Gromit - Beauty and the Beast of Wallaby Moor | by Aardman & Titan Comics

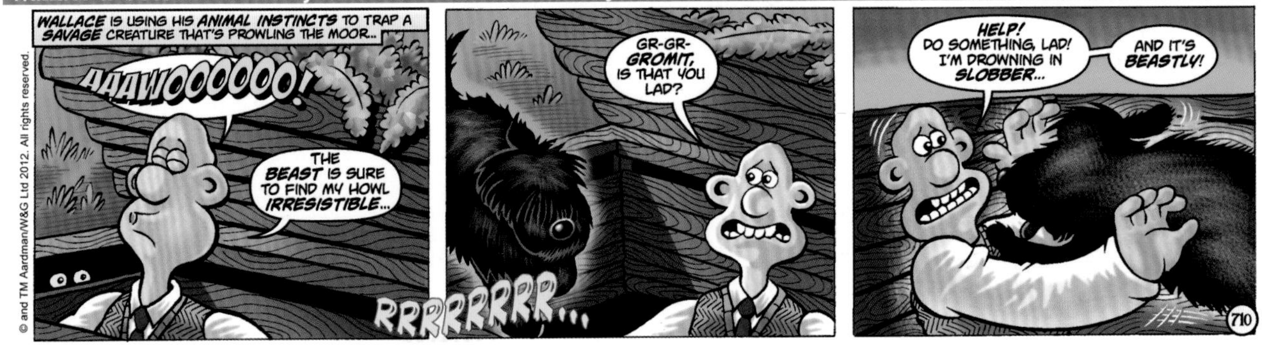
WALLACE IS USING HIS ANIMAL INSTINCTS TO TRAP A SAVAGE CREATURE THAT'S PROWLING THE MOOR...
AAAWOOOOOOO!
THE BEAST IS SURE TO FIND MY HOWL IRRESISTIBLE...
GR-GR-GROMIT, IS THAT YOU LAD?
RRRRRRRR...
HELP! DO SOMETHING, LAD! I'M DROWNING IN SLOBBER...
AND IT'S BEASTLY!
710

Wallace & Gromit - Beauty and the Beast of Wallaby Moor | by Aardman & Titan Comics

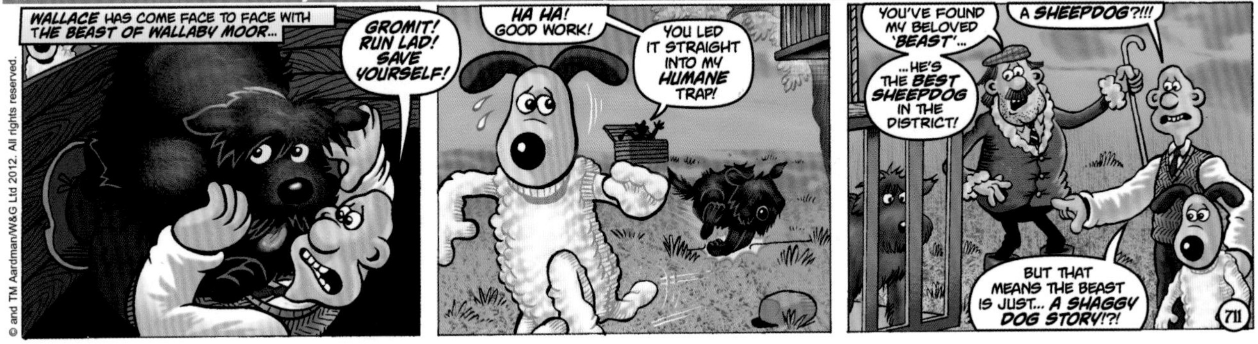
WALLACE HAS COME FACE TO FACE WITH THE BEAST OF WALLABY MOOR...
GROMIT! RUN LAD! SAVE YOURSELF!
HA HA! GOOD WORK!
YOU LED IT STRAIGHT INTO MY HUMANE TRAP!
YOU'VE FOUND MY BELOVED 'BEAST'...
...HE'S THE BEST SHEEPDOG IN THE DISTRICT!
A SHEEPDOG?!!!
BUT THAT MEANS THE BEAST IS JUST... A SHAGGY DOG STORY!?!
711

Wallace & Gromit - Beauty and the Beast of Wallaby Moor

by Aardman & Titan Comics

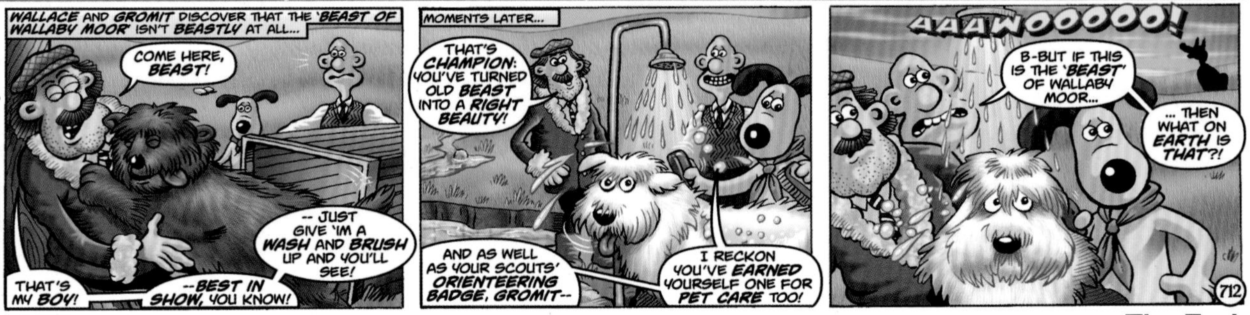

WALLACE AND GROMIT DISCOVER THAT THE 'BEAST OF WALLABY MOOR' ISN'T BEASTLY AT ALL...
COME HERE, BEAST!
THAT'S MY BOY!
--BEST IN SHOW, YOU KNOW!
-- JUST GIVE 'IM A WASH AND BRUSH UP AND YOU'LL SEE!
MOMENTS LATER...
THAT'S CHAMPION: YOU'VE TURNED OLD BEAST INTO A RIGHT BEAUTY!
AND AS WELL AS YOUR SCOUTS' ORIENTEERING BADGE, GROMIT--
I RECKON YOU'VE EARNED YOURSELF ONE FOR PET CARE TOO!
AAAWOOOOO!
B-BUT IF THIS IS THE 'BEAST' OF WALLABY MOOR...
... THEN WHAT ON EARTH IS THAT?!
712

The End

Wallace & Gromit - The Pies Have It

by Aardman & Titan Comics

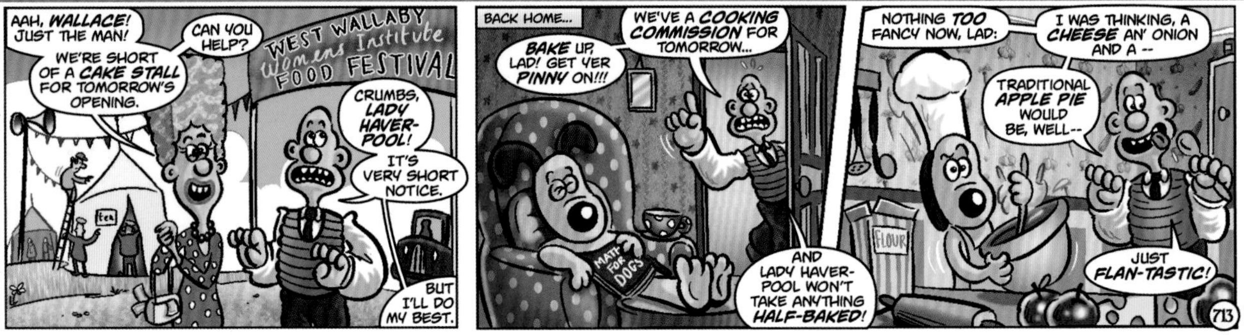

AAH, WALLACE! JUST THE MAN!
WE'RE SHORT OF A CAKE STALL FOR TOMORROW'S OPENING.
CAN YOU HELP?
WEST WALLABY Womens Institute FOOD FESTIVAL
Tea
CRUMBS, LADY HAVERPOOL!
IT'S VERY SHORT NOTICE.
BUT I'LL DO MY BEST.
BACK HOME...
WE'VE A COOKING COMMISSION FOR TOMORROW...
BAKE UP, LAD! GET YER PINNY ON!!!
MATHS FOR DOGS
AND LADY HAVERPOOL WON'T TAKE ANYTHING HALF-BAKED!
NOTHING TOO FANCY NOW, LAD:
I WAS THINKING, A CHEESE AN' ONION AND A --
TRADITIONAL APPLE PIE WOULD BE, WELL--
JUST FLAN-TASTIC!
FLOUR
713

Wallace & Gromit - The Pies Have It

by Aardman & Titan Comics

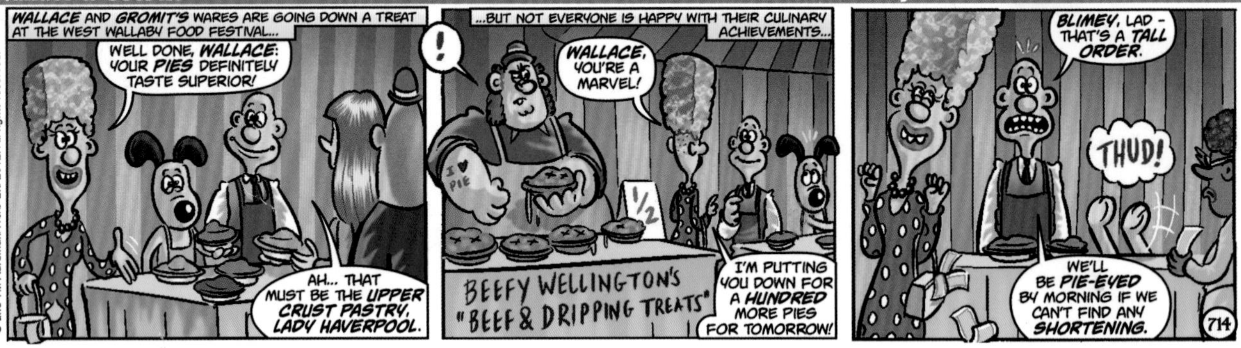

WALLACE AND GROMIT'S WARES ARE GOING DOWN A TREAT AT THE WEST WALLABY FOOD FESTIVAL...
WELL DONE, WALLACE: YOUR PIES DEFINITELY TASTE SUPERIOR!
AH... THAT MUST BE THE UPPER CRUST PASTRY, LADY HAVERPOOL.
...BUT NOT EVERYONE IS HAPPY WITH THEIR CULINARY ACHIEVEMENTS...
!
I ♥ PIE
WALLACE, YOU'RE A MARVEL!
1/2
BEEFY WELLINGTON'S "BEEF & DRIPPING TREATS"
I'M PUTTING YOU DOWN FOR A HUNDRED MORE PIES FOR TOMORROW!
BLIMEY, LAD - THAT'S A TALL ORDER.
THUD!
WE'LL BE PIE-EYED BY MORNING IF WE CAN'T FIND ANY SHORTENING.
714

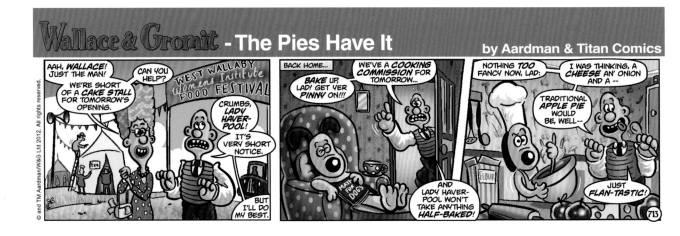

Wallace & Gromit - The Pies Have It
by Aardman & Titan Comics

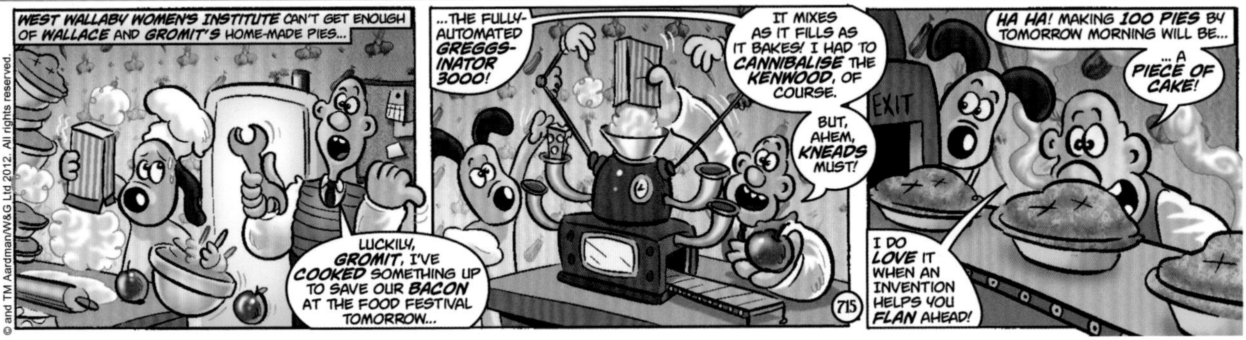
WEST WALLABY WOMEN'S INSTITUTE CAN'T GET ENOUGH OF WALLACE AND GROMIT'S HOME-MADE PIES...
LUCKILY, GROMIT, I'VE COOKED SOMETHING UP TO SAVE OUR BACON AT THE FOOD FESTIVAL TOMORROW...
...THE FULLY-AUTOMATED GREGGS-INATOR 3000!
IT MIXES AS IT FILLS AS IT BAKES! I HAD TO CANNIBALISE THE KENWOOD, OF COURSE.
BUT, AHEM, KNEADS MUST!
715
EXIT
HA HA! MAKING 100 PIES BY TOMORROW MORNING WILL BE...
... A PIECE OF CAKE!
I DO LOVE IT WHEN AN INVENTION HELPS YOU FLAN AHEAD!

Wallace & Gromit - The Pies Have It
by Aardman & Titan Comics

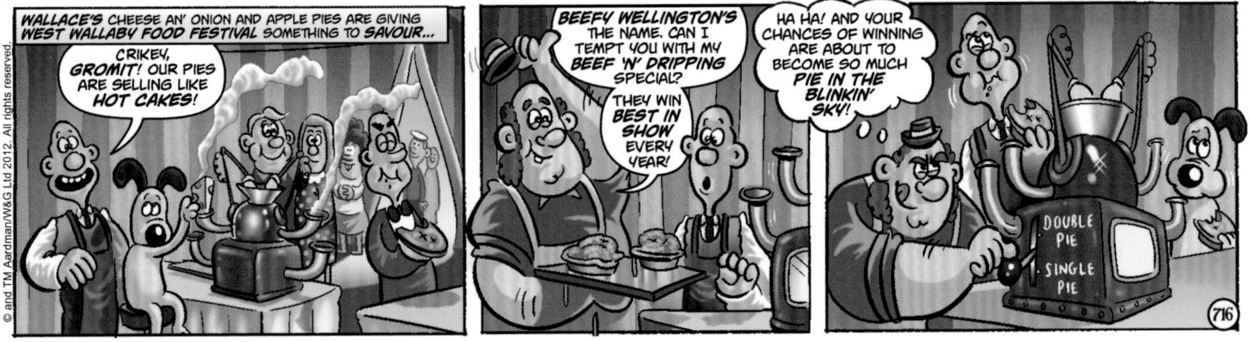
WALLACE'S CHEESE AN' ONION AND APPLE PIES ARE GIVING WEST WALLABY FOOD FESTIVAL SOMETHING TO SAVOUR...
CRIKEY, GROMIT! OUR PIES ARE SELLING LIKE HOT CAKES!
BEEFY WELLINGTON'S THE NAME. CAN I TEMPT YOU WITH MY BEEF 'N' DRIPPING SPECIAL?
THEY WIN BEST IN SHOW EVERY YEAR!
HA HA! AND YOUR CHANCES OF WINNING ARE ABOUT TO BECOME SO MUCH PIE IN THE BLINKIN' SKY!
DOUBLE PIE
SINGLE PIE
716

Wallace & Gromit - The Pies Have It
by Aardman & Titan Comics

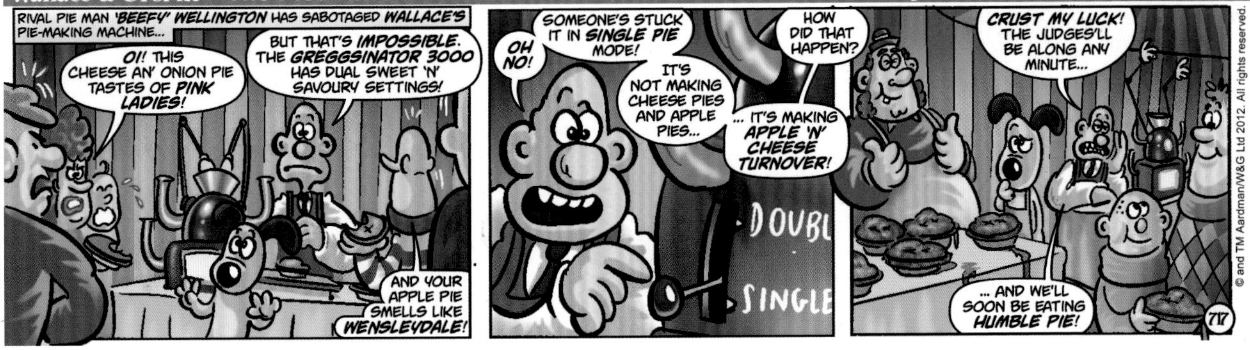
RIVAL PIE MAN 'BEEFY' WELLINGTON HAS SABOTAGED WALLACE'S PIE-MAKING MACHINE...
OI! THIS CHEESE AN' ONION PIE TASTES OF PINK LADIES!
BUT THAT'S IMPOSSIBLE. THE GREGGSINATOR 3000 HAS DUAL SWEET 'N' SAVOURY SETTINGS!
AND YOUR APPLE PIE SMELLS LIKE WENSLEYDALE!
OH NO!
SOMEONE'S STUCK IT IN SINGLE PIE MODE!
IT'S NOT MAKING CHEESE PIES AND APPLE PIES...
HOW DID THAT HAPPEN?
... IT'S MAKING APPLE 'N' CHEESE TURNOVER!
DOUBL
SINGLE
CRUST MY LUCK! THE JUDGES'LL BE ALONG ANY MINUTE...
... AND WE'LL SOON BE EATING HUMBLE PIE!
717

Wallace & Gromit - The Pies Have It

by Aardman & Titan Comics

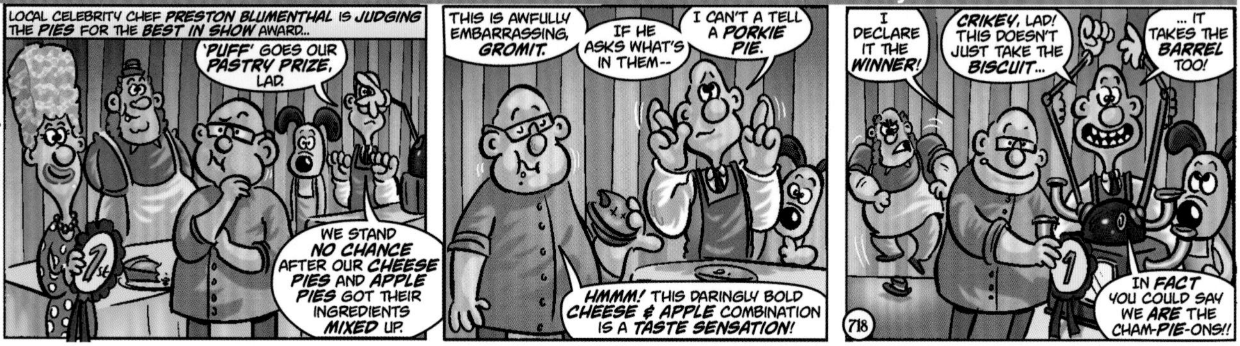
LOCAL CELEBRITY CHEF PRESTON BLUMENTHAL IS JUDGING THE PIES FOR THE BEST IN SHOW AWARD...
'PUFF' GOES OUR PASTRY PRIZE, LAD.
WE STAND NO CHANCE AFTER OUR CHEESE PIES AND APPLE PIES GOT THEIR INGREDIENTS MIXED UP.
THIS IS AWFULLY EMBARRASSING, GROMIT.
IF HE ASKS WHAT'S IN THEM--
I CAN'T A TELL A PORKIE PIE.
HMMM! THIS DARINGLY BOLD CHEESE & APPLE COMBINATION IS A TASTE SENSATION!
I DECLARE IT THE WINNER!
CRIKEY, LAD! THIS DOESN'T JUST TAKE THE BISCUIT...
... IT TAKES THE BARREL TOO!
IN FACT YOU COULD SAY WE ARE THE CHAM-PIE-ONS!!
718

Wallace & Gromit - The Pies Have It

by Aardman & Titan Comics

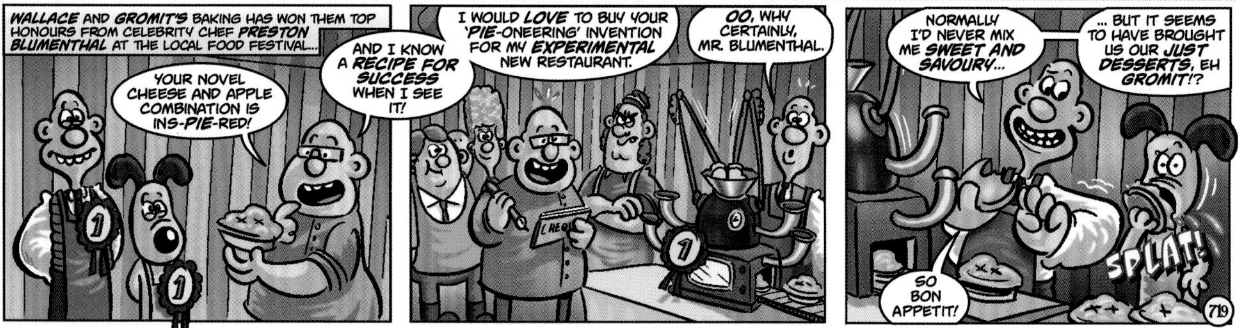
WALLACE AND GROMIT'S BAKING HAS WON THEM TOP HONOURS FROM CELEBRITY CHEF PRESTON BLUMENTHAL AT THE LOCAL FOOD FESTIVAL...
YOUR NOVEL CHEESE AND APPLE COMBINATION IS INS-PIE-RED!
AND I KNOW A RECIPE FOR SUCCESS WHEN I SEE IT!
I WOULD LOVE TO BUY YOUR 'PIE-ONEERING' INVENTION FOR MY EXPERIMENTAL NEW RESTAURANT.
OO, WHY CERTAINLY, MR. BLUMENTHAL.
NORMALLY I'D NEVER MIX ME SWEET AND SAVOURY...
... BUT IT SEEMS TO HAVE BROUGHT US OUR JUST DESSERTS, EH GROMIT!?
SO BON APPETIT!
SPLAT!
719

The End

Wallace & Gromit - Zoombaa Baa

by Aardman & Titan Comics

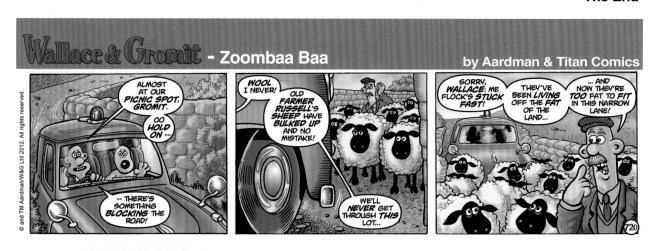

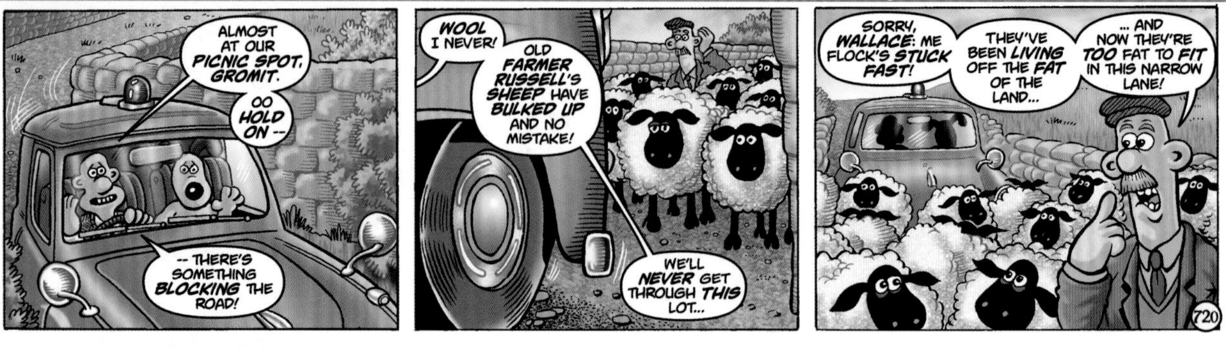
ALMOST AT OUR PICNIC SPOT, GROMIT.
OO HOLD ON --
-- THERE'S SOMETHING BLOCKING THE ROAD!
WOOL I NEVER!
OLD FARMER RUSSELL'S SHEEP HAVE BULKED UP AND NO MISTAKE!
WE'LL NEVER GET THROUGH THIS LOT...
SORRY, WALLACE: ME FLOCK'S STUCK FAST!
THEY'VE BEEN LIVING OFF THE FAT OF THE LAND...
... AND NOW THEY'RE TOO FAT TO FIT IN THIS NARROW LANE!
720

Wallace & Gromit - Zoombaa Baa by Aardman & Titan Comics

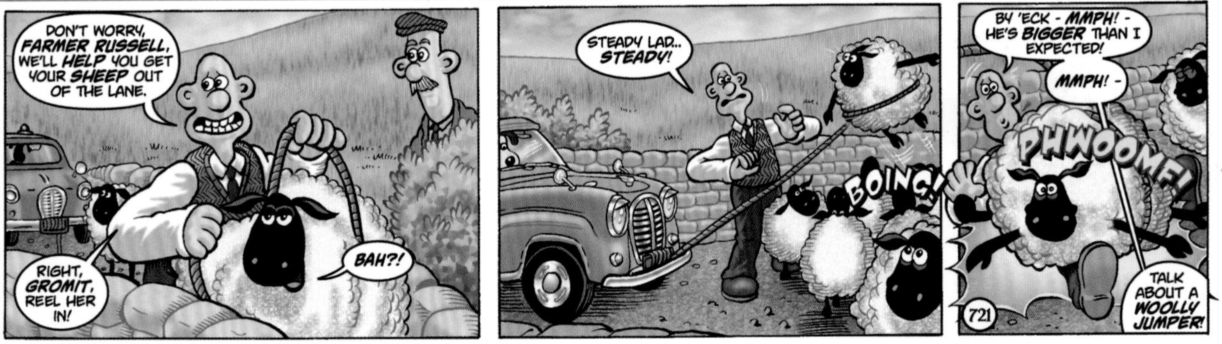

DON'T WORRY, FARMER RUSSELL, WE'LL HELP YOU GET YOUR SHEEP OUT OF THE LANE.
RIGHT, GROMIT, REEL HER IN!
BAH?!
STEADY LAD... STEADY!
BOING!
BY 'ECK - MMPH! - HE'S BIGGER THAN I EXPECTED!
MMPH! -
PHWOOMF!
TALK ABOUT A WOOLLY JUMPER!
721

Wallace & Gromit - Zoombaa Baa by Aardman & Titan Comics

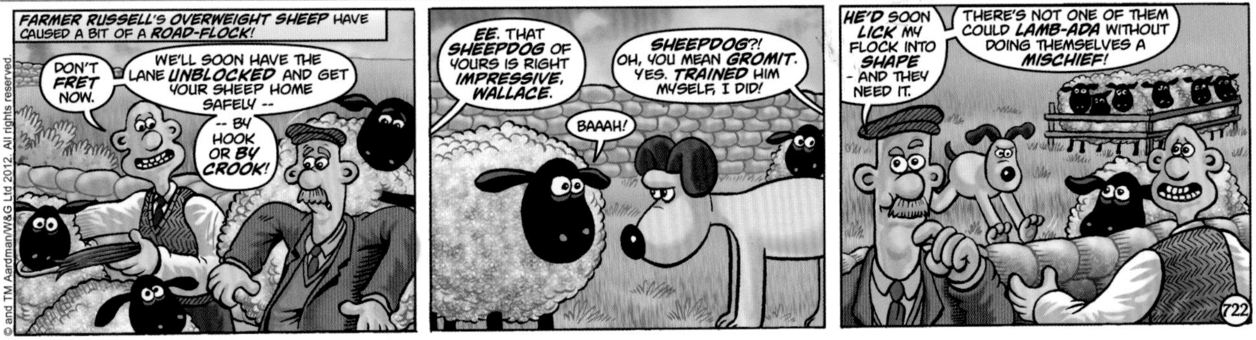

FARMER RUSSELL'S OVERWEIGHT SHEEP HAVE CAUSED A BIT OF A ROAD-FLOCK!
DON'T FRET NOW.
WE'LL SOON HAVE THE LANE UNBLOCKED AND GET YOUR SHEEP HOME SAFELY --
-- BY HOOK OR BY CROOK!
EE. THAT SHEEPDOG OF YOURS IS RIGHT IMPRESSIVE, WALLACE.
SHEEPDOG?! OH, YOU MEAN GROMIT. YES. TRAINED HIM MYSELF, I DID!
BAAAH!
HE'D SOON LICK MY FLOCK INTO SHAPE - AND THEY NEED IT.
THERE'S NOT ONE OF THEM COULD LAMB-ADA WITHOUT DOING THEMSELVES A MISCHIEF!
722

Wallace & Gromit - Zoombaa Baa by Aardman & Titan Comics

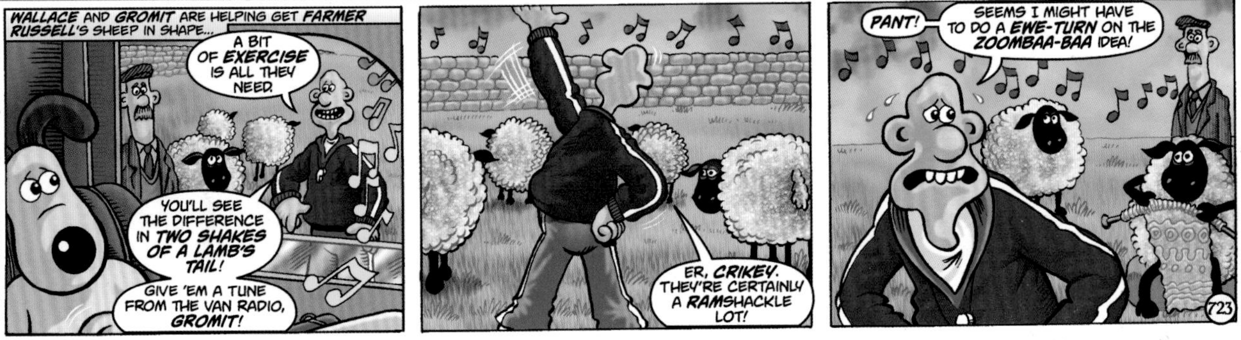

WALLACE AND GROMIT ARE HELPING GET FARMER RUSSELL'S SHEEP IN SHAPE...
A BIT OF EXERCISE IS ALL THEY NEED.
YOU'LL SEE THE DIFFERENCE IN TWO SHAKES OF A LAMB'S TAIL!
GIVE 'EM A TUNE FROM THE VAN RADIO, GROMIT!
ER, CRIKEY. THEY'RE CERTAINLY A RAMSHACKLE LOT!
PANT!
SEEMS I MIGHT HAVE TO DO A EWE-TURN ON THE ZOOMBAA-BAA IDEA!
723

Wallace & Gromit - Zoombaa Baa by Aardman & Titan Comics

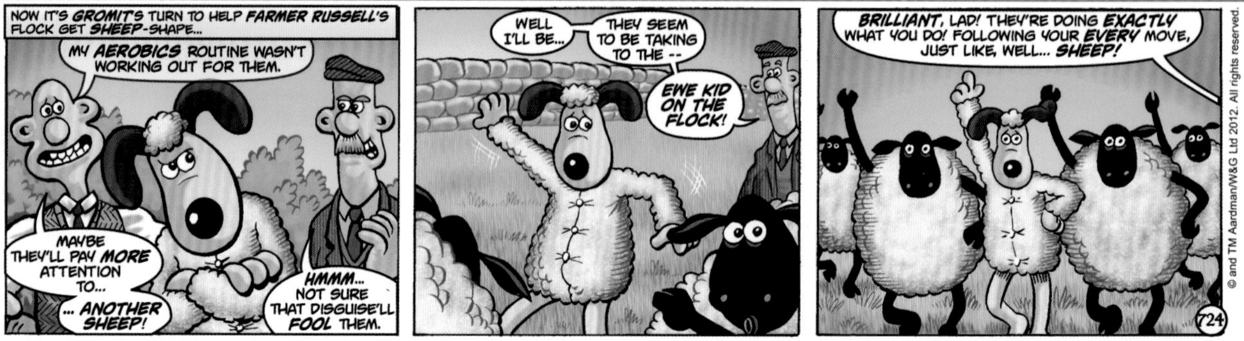

NOW IT'S GROMIT'S TURN TO HELP FARMER RUSSELL'S FLOCK GET SHEEP-SHAPE...
MY AEROBICS ROUTINE WASN'T WORKING OUT FOR THEM.
MAYBE THEY'LL PAY MORE ATTENTION TO...
... ANOTHER SHEEP!
HMMM... NOT SURE THAT DISGUISE'LL FOOL THEM.
WELL I'LL BE...
THEY SEEM TO BE TAKING TO THE --
EWE KID ON THE FLOCK!
BRILLIANT, LAD! THEY'RE DOING EXACTLY WHAT YOU DO! FOLLOWING YOUR EVERY MOVE, JUST LIKE, WELL... SHEEP!
724

Wallace & Gromit - Zoombaa Baa by Aardman & Titan Comics

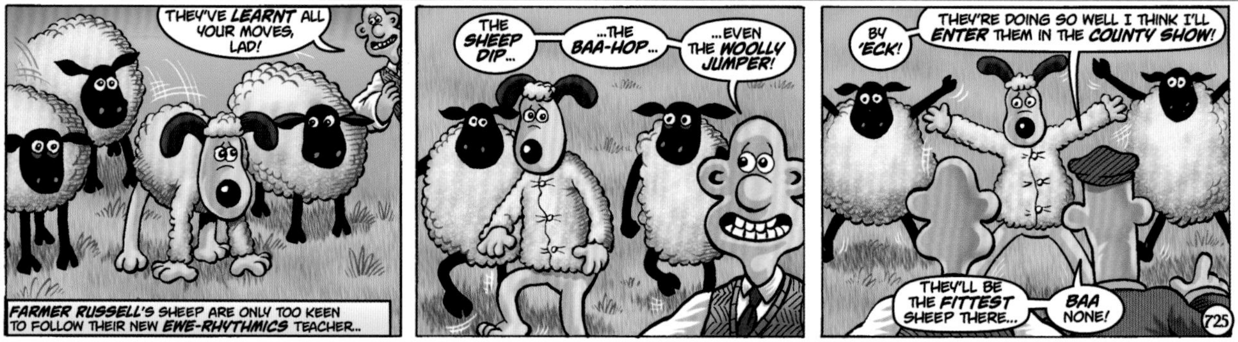

THEY'VE LEARNT ALL YOUR MOVES, LAD!
FARMER RUSSELL'S SHEEP ARE ONLY TOO KEEN TO FOLLOW THEIR NEW EWE-RHYTHMICS TEACHER..
THE SHEEP DIP...
...THE BAA-HOP...
...EVEN THE WOOLLY JUMPER!
BY 'ECK!
THEY'RE DOING SO WELL I THINK I'LL ENTER THEM IN THE COUNTY SHOW!
THEY'LL BE THE FITTEST SHEEP THERE...
BAA NONE!
725

Wallace & Gromit - Zoombaa Baa by Aardman & Titan Comics

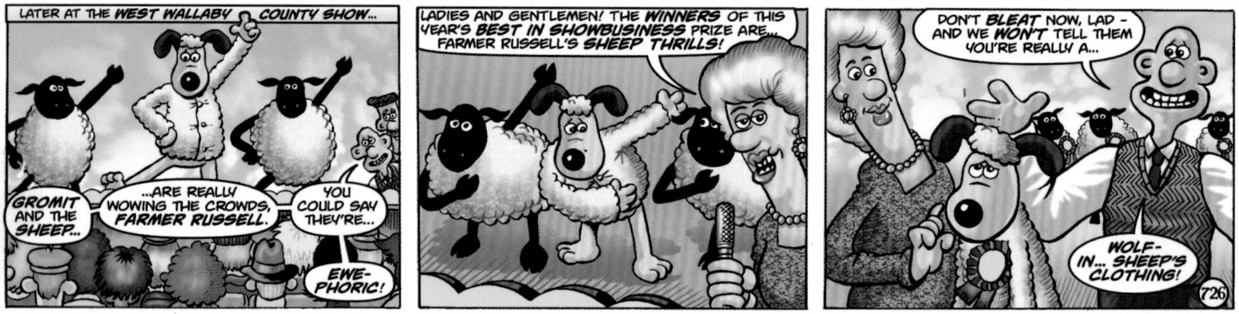

LATER AT THE WEST WALLABY COUNTY SHOW...
GROMIT AND THE SHEEP...
...ARE REALLY WOWING THE CROWDS, FARMER RUSSELL.
YOU COULD SAY THEY'RE...
EWE-PHORIC!
LADIES AND GENTLEMEN! THE WINNERS OF THIS YEAR'S BEST IN SHOWBUSINESS PRIZE ARE... FARMER RUSSELL'S SHEEP THRILLS!
DON'T BLEAT NOW, LAD - AND WE WON'T TELL THEM YOU'RE REALLY A...
WOLF- IN... SHEEP'S CLOTHING!
726

The End

Wallace & Gromit - Taken to the Cleaners

by Aardman & Titan Comics

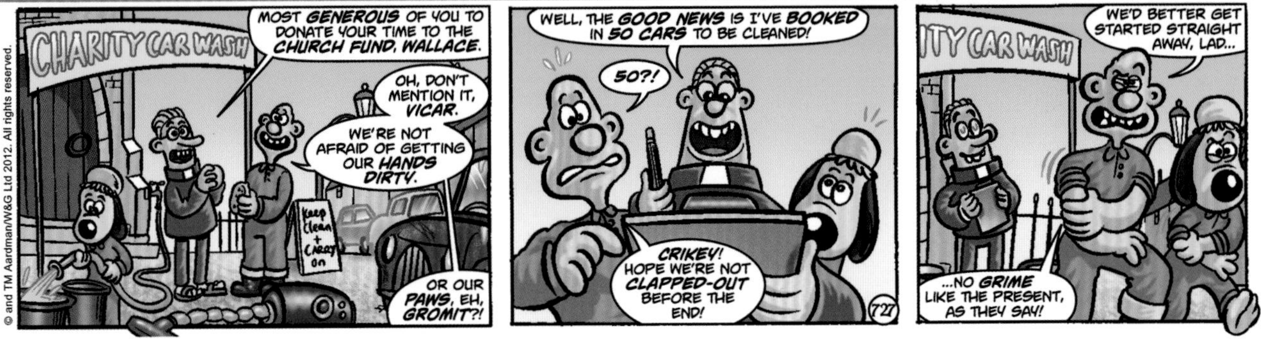

CHARITY CAR WASH
MOST GENEROUS OF YOU TO DONATE YOUR TIME TO THE CHURCH FUND, WALLACE.
OH, DON'T MENTION IT, VICAR.
WE'RE NOT AFRAID OF GETTING OUR HANDS DIRTY.
Keep Clean + Carry on
OR OUR PAWS, EH, GROMIT?!
WELL, THE GOOD NEWS IS I'VE BOOKED IN 50 CARS TO BE CLEANED!
50?!
CRIKEY! HOPE WE'RE NOT CLAPPED-OUT BEFORE THE END!
727
ITY CAR WASH
WE'D BETTER GET STARTED STRAIGHT AWAY, LAD...
...NO GRIME LIKE THE PRESENT, AS THEY SAY!

Wallace & Gromit - Taken to the Cleaners

by Aardman & Titan Comics

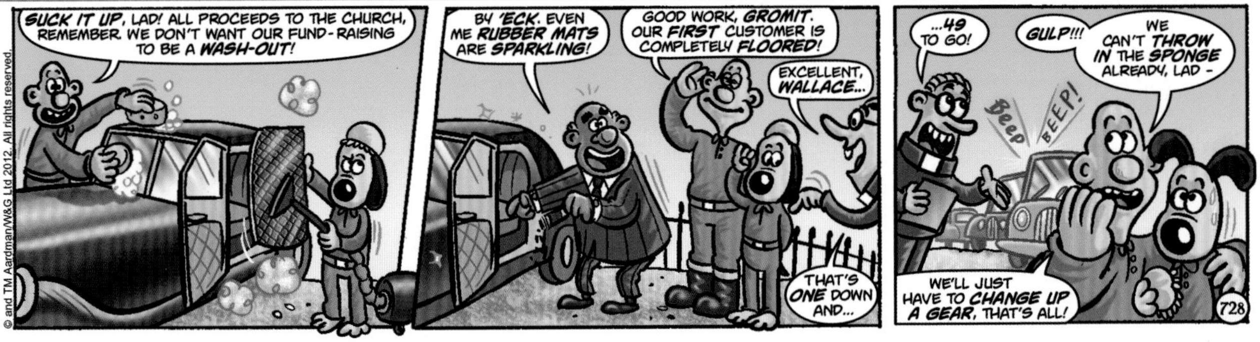

SUCK IT UP, LAD! ALL PROCEEDS TO THE CHURCH, REMEMBER. WE DON'T WANT OUR FUND-RAISING TO BE A WASH-OUT!
BY 'ECK. EVEN ME RUBBER MATS ARE SPARKLING!
GOOD WORK, GROMIT. OUR FIRST CUSTOMER IS COMPLETELY FLOORED!
EXCELLENT, WALLACE...
THAT'S ONE DOWN AND...
...49 TO GO!
GULP!!!
WE CAN'T THROW IN THE SPONGE ALREADY, LAD -
Beep
BEEP!
WE'LL JUST HAVE TO CHANGE UP A GEAR, THAT'S ALL!
728

Wallace & Gromit - Taken to the Cleaners

by Aardman & Titan Comics

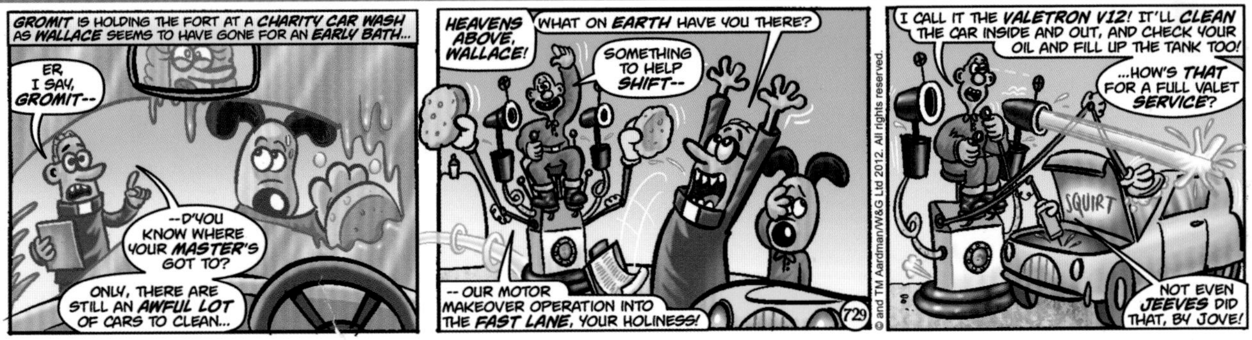

GROMIT IS HOLDING THE FORT AT A CHARITY CAR WASH AS WALLACE SEEMS TO HAVE GONE FOR AN EARLY BATH...
ER, I SAY, GROMIT--
--D'YOU KNOW WHERE YOUR MASTER'S GOT TO?
ONLY, THERE ARE STILL AN AWFUL LOT OF CARS TO CLEAN...
HEAVENS ABOVE, WALLACE!
WHAT ON EARTH HAVE YOU THERE?
SOMETHING TO HELP SHIFT--
--OUR MOTOR MAKEOVER OPERATION INTO THE FAST LANE, YOUR HOLINESS!
729
I CALL IT THE VALETRON V12! IT'LL CLEAN THE CAR INSIDE AND OUT, AND CHECK YOUR OIL AND FILL UP THE TANK TOO!
...HOW'S THAT FOR A FULL VALET SERVICE?
SQUIRT
NOT EVEN JEEVES DID THAT, BY JOVE!

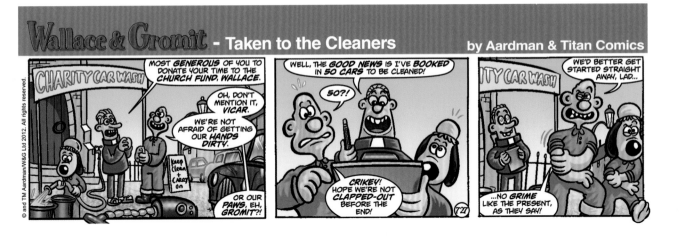

Wallace & Gromit - Taken to the Cleaners by Aardman & Titan Comics

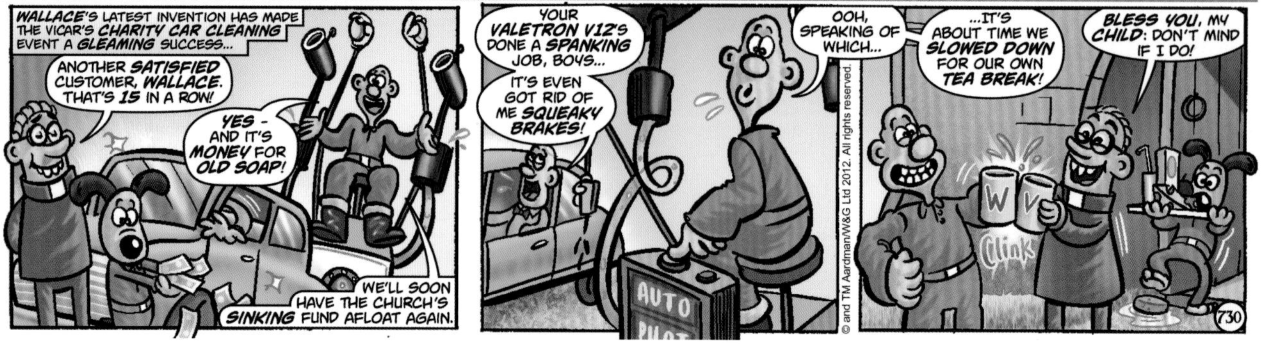

WALLACE'S LATEST INVENTION HAS MADE THE VICAR'S CHARITY CAR CLEANING EVENT A GLEAMING SUCCESS...
ANOTHER SATISFIED CUSTOMER, WALLACE. THAT'S 15 IN A ROW!
YES - AND IT'S MONEY FOR OLD SOAP!
WE'LL SOON HAVE THE CHURCH'S SINKING FUND AFLOAT AGAIN.
YOUR VALETRON V12'S DONE A SPANKING JOB, BOYS...
IT'S EVEN GOT RID OF ME SQUEAKY BRAKES!
AUTO
OOH, SPEAKING OF WHICH...
...IT'S ABOUT TIME WE SLOWED DOWN FOR OUR OWN TEA BREAK!
BLESS YOU, MY CHILD: DON'T MIND IF I DO!
W
W
Clink
730

Wallace & Gromit - Taken to the Cleaners by Aardman & Titan Comics

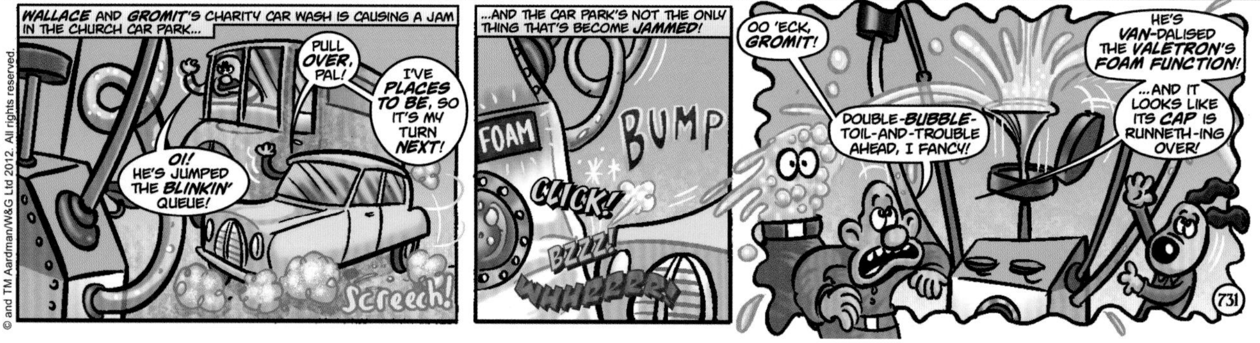

WALLACE AND GROMIT'S CHARITY CAR WASH IS CAUSING A JAM IN THE CHURCH CAR PARK...
PULL OVER, PAL!
I'VE PLACES TO BE, SO IT'S MY TURN NEXT!
OI! HE'S JUMPED THE BLINKIN' QUEUE!
Screech!
...AND THE CAR PARK'S NOT THE ONLY THING THAT'S BECOME JAMMED!
FOAM
BUMP
CLICK!
BZZZ!
WHHRRRR!
OO 'ECK, GROMIT!
DOUBLE-BUBBLE-TOIL-AND-TROUBLE AHEAD, I FANCY!
HE'S VAN-DALISED THE VALETRON'S FOAM FUNCTION!
...AND IT LOOKS LIKE ITS CAP IS RUNNETH-ING OVER!
731

Wallace & Gromit - Taken to the Cleaners by Aardman & Titan Comics

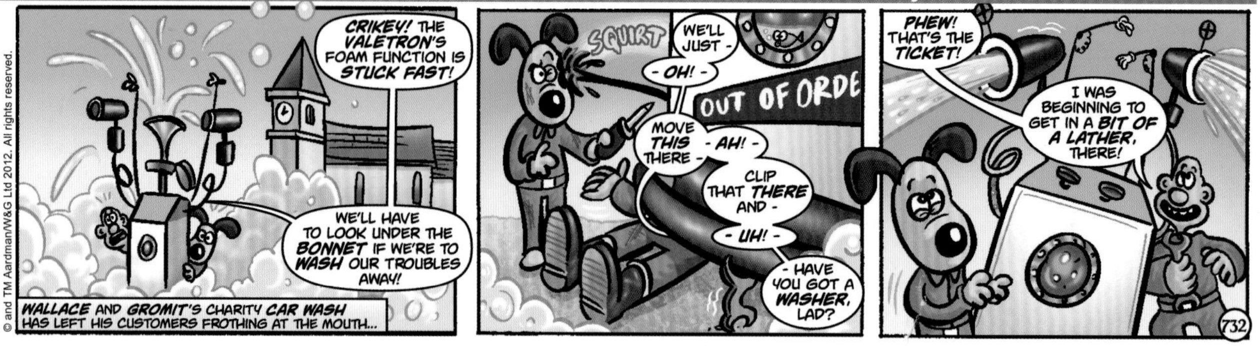

CRIKEY! THE VALETRON'S FOAM FUNCTION IS STUCK FAST!
WE'LL HAVE TO LOOK UNDER THE BONNET IF WE'RE TO WASH OUR TROUBLES AWAY!
WALLACE AND GROMIT'S CHARITY CAR WASH HAS LEFT HIS CUSTOMERS FROTHING AT THE MOUTH...
SQUIRT
WE'LL JUST -
- OH! -
OUT OF ORDE
MOVE THIS THERE -
- AH! -
CLIP THAT THERE AND -
- UH! -
- HAVE YOU GOT A WASHER, LAD?
PHEW! THAT'S THE TICKET!
I WAS BEGINNING TO GET IN A BIT OF A LATHER, THERE!
732

Wallace & Gromit - Taken to the Cleaners

by Aardman & Titan Comics

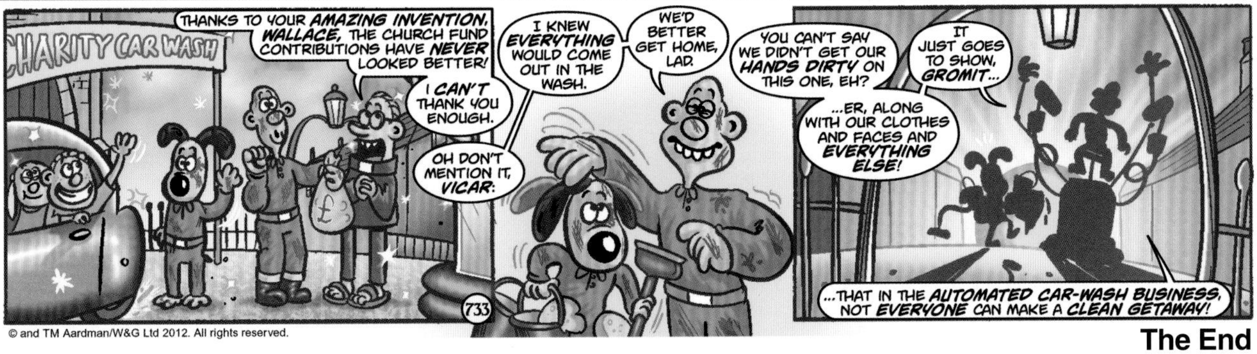

CHARITY CAR WASH
THANKS TO YOUR AMAZING INVENTION, WALLACE, THE CHURCH FUND CONTRIBUTIONS HAVE NEVER LOOKED BETTER!
I CAN'T THANK YOU ENOUGH.
OH DON'T MENTION IT, VICAR.
733
I KNEW EVERYTHING WOULD COME OUT IN THE WASH.
WE'D BETTER GET HOME, LAD.
YOU CAN'T SAY WE DIDN'T GET OUR HANDS DIRTY ON THIS ONE, EH?
...ER, ALONG WITH OUR CLOTHES AND FACES AND EVERYTHING ELSE!
IT JUST GOES TO SHOW, GROMIT...
...THAT IN THE AUTOMATED CAR-WASH BUSINESS, NOT EVERYONE CAN MAKE A CLEAN GETAWAY!

The End

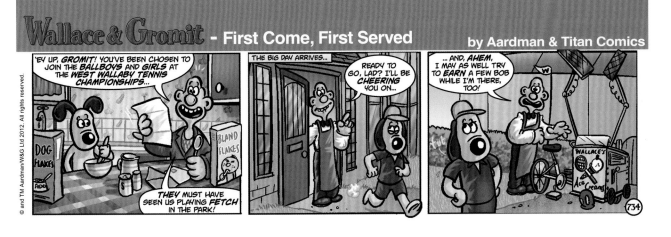

Wallace & Gromit - First Come, First Served

by Aardman & Titan Comics

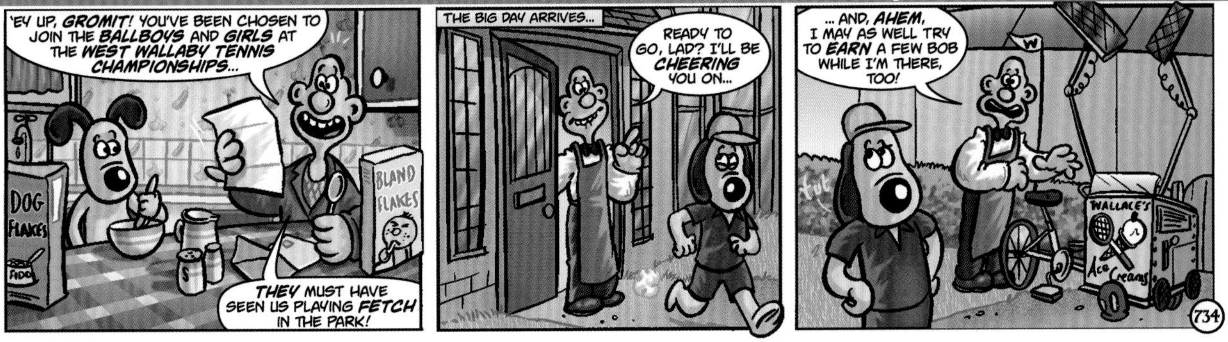

'EY UP, GROMIT! YOU'VE BEEN CHOSEN TO JOIN THE BALLBOYS AND GIRLS AT THE WEST WALLABY TENNIS CHAMPIONSHIPS...
DOG FLAKES
FIDO
BLAND FLAKES
THEY MUST HAVE SEEN US PLAYING FETCH IN THE PARK!
THE BIG DAY ARRIVES...
READY TO GO, LAD? I'LL BE CHEERING YOU ON...
... AND, AHEM, I MAY AS WELL TRY TO EARN A FEW BOB WHILE I'M THERE, TOO!
WALLACE'S Ace Creams
734

Wallace & Gromit - First Come, First Served

by Aardman & Titan Comics

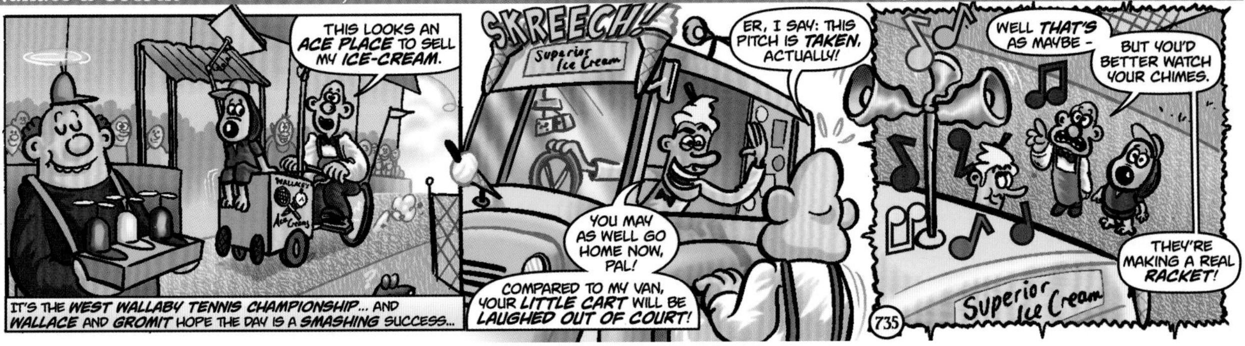

THIS LOOKS AN ACE PLACE TO SELL MY ICE-CREAM.
IT'S THE WEST WALLABY TENNIS CHAMPIONSHIP... AND WALLACE AND GROMIT HOPE THE DAY IS A SMASHING SUCCESS...
SKREECH!
Superior Ice Cream
ER, I SAY: THIS PITCH IS TAKEN, ACTUALLY!
YOU MAY AS WELL GO HOME NOW, PAL!
COMPARED TO MY VAN, YOUR LITTLE CART WILL BE LAUGHED OUT OF COURT!
WELL THAT'S AS MAYBE -
BUT YOU'D BETTER WATCH YOUR CHIMES.
THEY'RE MAKING A REAL RACKET!
Superior Ice Cream
735

Wallace & Gromit - First Come, First Served | by Aardman & Titan Comics

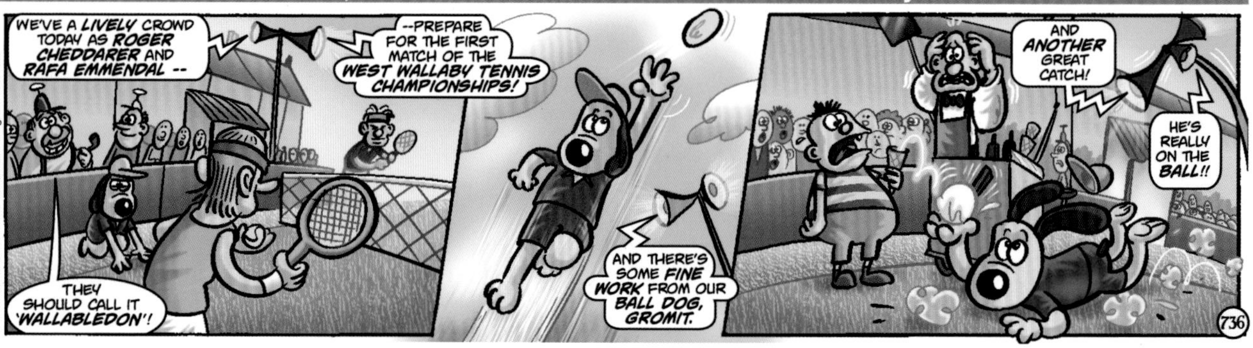
WE'VE A LIVELY CROWD TODAY AS ROGER CHEDDARER AND RAFA EMMENDAL --
--PREPARE FOR THE FIRST MATCH OF THE WEST WALLABY TENNIS CHAMPIONSHIPS!
THEY SHOULD CALL IT 'WALLABLEDON'!
AND THERE'S SOME FINE WORK FROM OUR BALL DOG, GROMIT.
AND ANOTHER GREAT CATCH!
HE'S REALLY ON THE BALL!!
736

Wallace & Gromit - First Come, First Served | by Aardman & Titan Comics

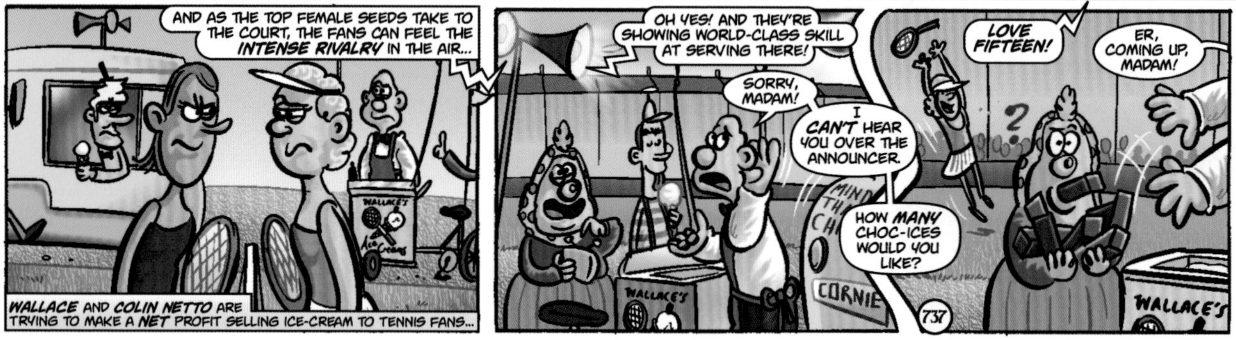
AND AS THE TOP FEMALE SEEDS TAKE TO THE COURT, THE FANS CAN FEEL THE INTENSE RIVALRY IN THE AIR...
WALLACE AND COLIN NETTO ARE TRYING TO MAKE A NET PROFIT SELLING ICE-CREAM TO TENNIS FANS...
OH YES! AND THEY'RE SHOWING WORLD-CLASS SKILL AT SERVING THERE!
SORRY, MADAM!
I CAN'T HEAR YOU OVER THE ANNOUNCER.
HOW MANY CHOC-ICES WOULD YOU LIKE?
CORNIE
LOVE FIFTEEN!
ER, COMING UP, MADAM!
WALLACE'S
737

Wallace & Gromit - First Come, First Served | by Aardman & Titan Comics

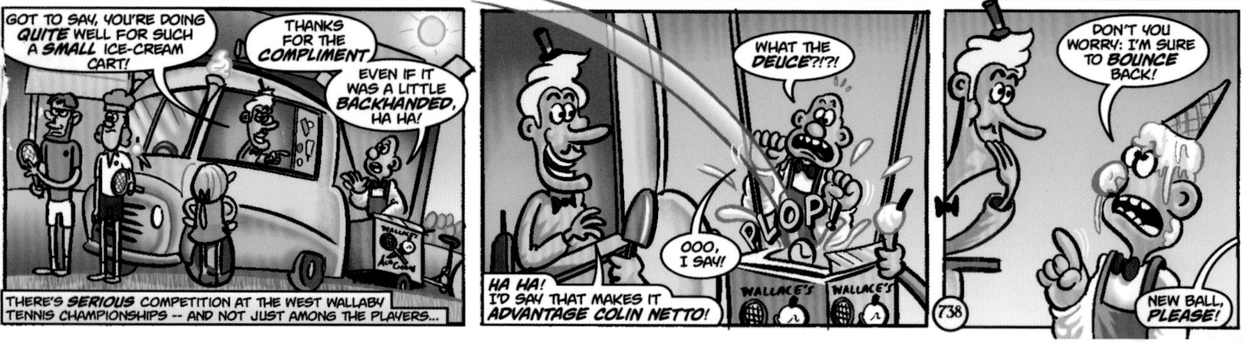
GOT TO SAY, YOU'RE DOING QUITE WELL FOR SUCH A SMALL ICE-CREAM CART!
THANKS FOR THE COMPLIMENT.
EVEN IF IT WAS A LITTLE BACKHANDED, HA HA!
THERE'S SERIOUS COMPETITION AT THE WEST WALLABY TENNIS CHAMPIONSHIPS -- AND NOT JUST AMONG THE PLAYERS...
WHAT THE DEUCE?!?!
PLOP!
OOO, I SAY!
HA HA! I'D SAY THAT MAKES IT ADVANTAGE COLIN NETTO!
WALLACE'S
738
DON'T YOU WORRY: I'M SURE TO BOUNCE BACK!
NEW BALL, PLEASE!

Wallace & Gromit - First Come, First Served by Aardman & Titan Comics

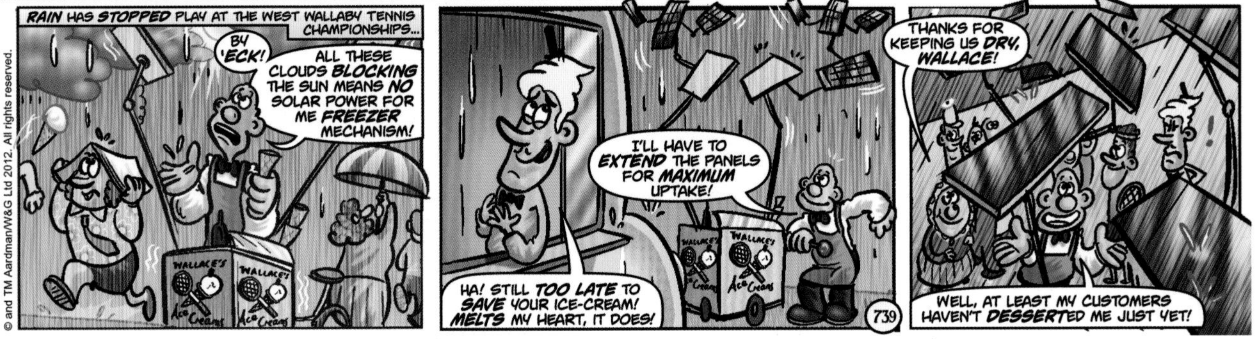

RAIN HAS STOPPED PLAY AT THE WEST WALLABY TENNIS CHAMPIONSHIPS...
BY 'ECK!
ALL THESE CLOUDS BLOCKING THE SUN MEANS NO SOLAR POWER FOR ME FREEZER MECHANISM!
WALLACE'S Ace Creams
I'LL HAVE TO EXTEND THE PANELS FOR MAXIMUM UPTAKE!
HA! STILL TOO LATE TO SAVE YOUR ICE-CREAM! MELTS MY HEART, IT DOES!
739
THANKS FOR KEEPING US DRY, WALLACE!
WELL, AT LEAST MY CUSTOMERS HAVEN'T DESSERTED ME JUST YET!

Wallace & Gromit - First Come, First Served by Aardman & Titan Comics

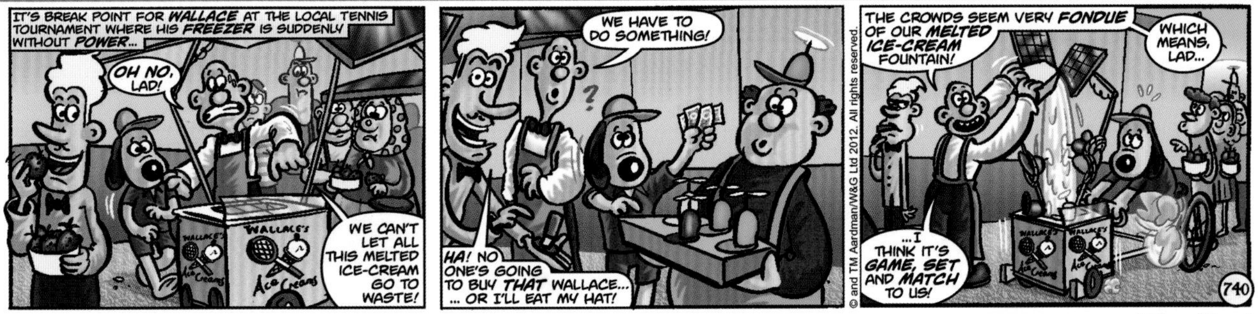

IT'S BREAK POINT FOR WALLACE AT THE LOCAL TENNIS TOURNAMENT WHERE HIS FREEZER IS SUDDENLY WITHOUT POWER...
OH NO, LAD!
WE CAN'T LET ALL THIS MELTED ICE-CREAM GO TO WASTE!
WALLACE'S Ace Creams
WE HAVE TO DO SOMETHING!
HA! NO ONE'S GOING TO BUY THAT WALLACE... ... OR I'LL EAT MY HAT!
THE CROWDS SEEM VERY FONDUE OF OUR MELTED ICE-CREAM FOUNTAIN!
WHICH MEANS, LAD...
...I THINK IT'S GAME, SET AND MATCH TO US!
740

The End

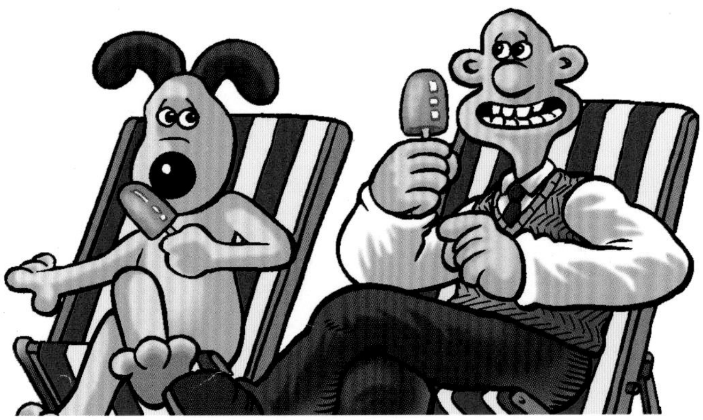

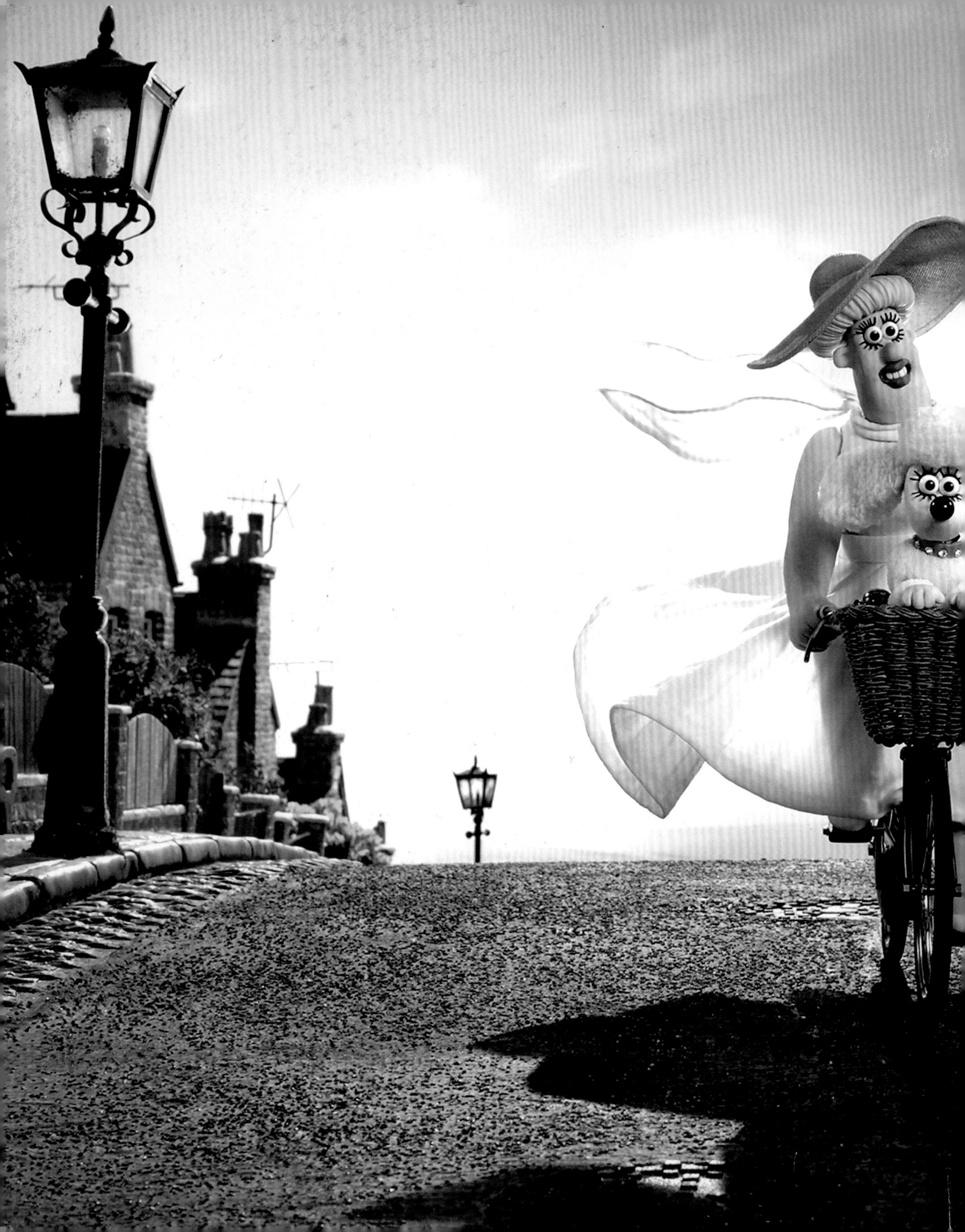

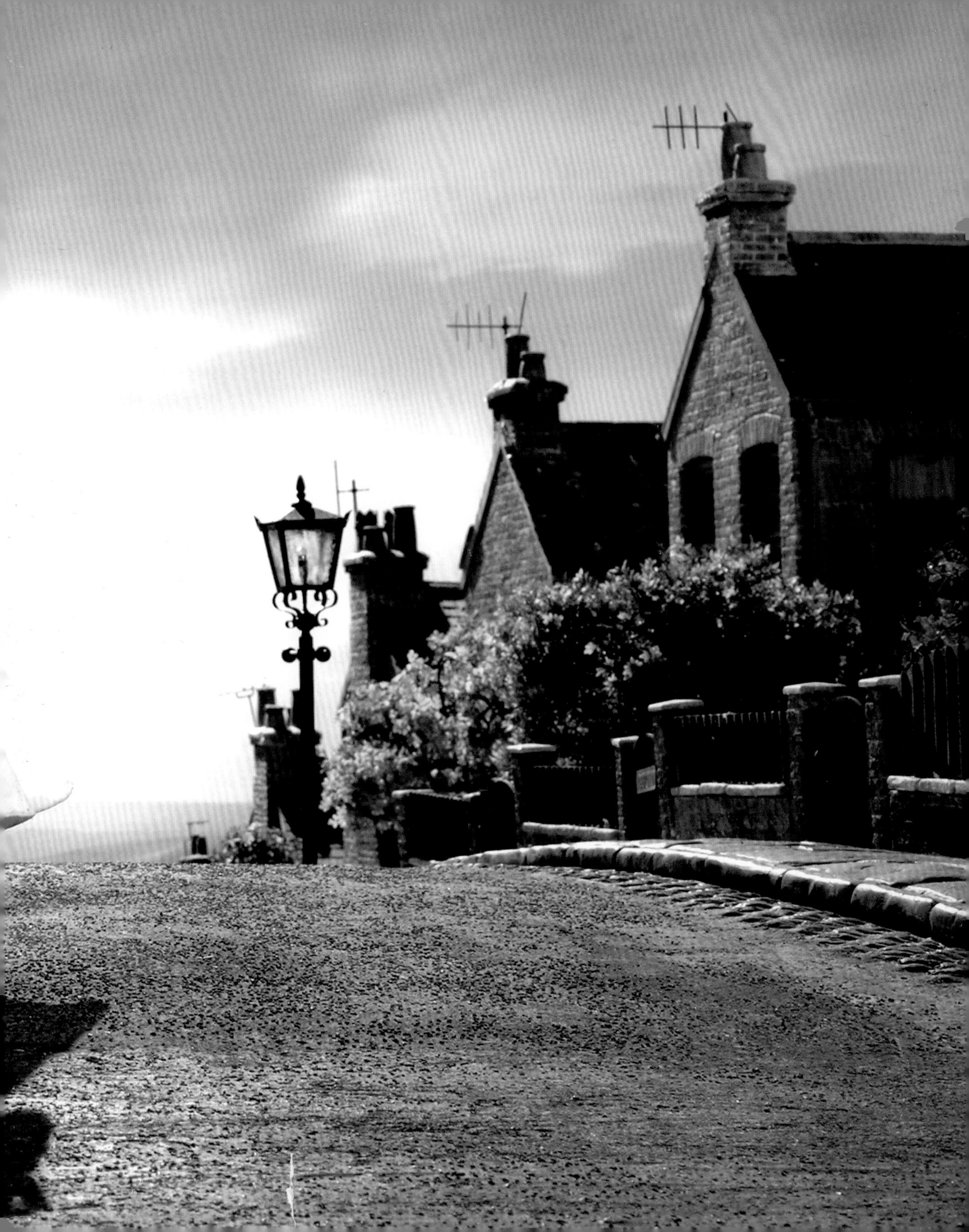

Wallace & Gromit - Go Fish

by Aardman & Titan Comics

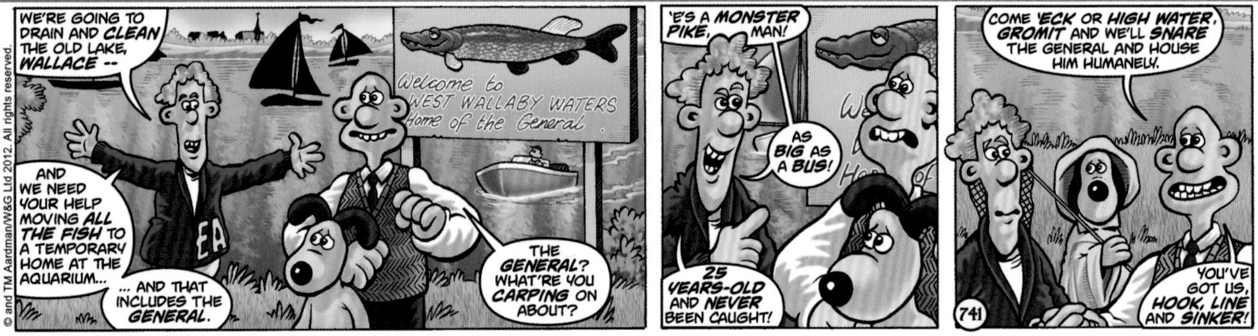

WE'RE GOING TO DRAIN AND CLEAN THE OLD LAKE, WALLACE --
AND WE NEED YOUR HELP MOVING ALL THE FISH TO A TEMPORARY HOME AT THE AQUARIUM...
... AND THAT INCLUDES THE GENERAL.
Welcome to WEST WALLABY WATERS Home of the General.
THE GENERAL? WHAT'RE YOU CARPING ON ABOUT?
'E'S A MONSTER PIKE, MAN!
AS BIG AS A BUS!
25 YEARS-OLD AND NEVER BEEN CAUGHT!
COME 'ECK OR HIGH WATER, GROMIT AND WE'LL SNARE THE GENERAL AND HOUSE HIM HUMANELY.
YOU'VE GOT US, HOOK, LINE AND SINKER!
741

Wallace & Gromit - Go Fish

by Aardman & Titan Comics

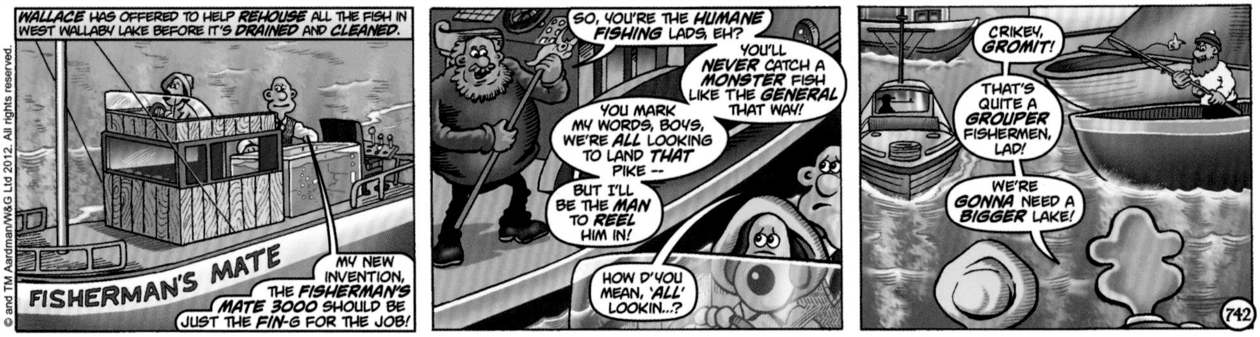

WALLACE HAS OFFERED TO HELP REHOUSE ALL THE FISH IN WEST WALLABY LAKE BEFORE IT'S DRAINED AND CLEANED.
FISHERMAN'S MATE
MY NEW INVENTION, THE FISHERMAN'S MATE 3000 SHOULD BE JUST THE FIN-G FOR THE JOB!
SO, YOU'RE THE HUMANE FISHING LADS, EH?
YOU'LL NEVER CATCH A MONSTER FISH LIKE THE GENERAL THAT WAY!
YOU MARK MY WORDS, BOYS, WE'RE ALL LOOKING TO LAND THAT PIKE --
BUT I'LL BE THE MAN TO REEL HIM IN!
HOW D'YOU MEAN, 'ALL' LOOKIN...?
CRIKEY, GROMIT!
THAT'S QUITE A GROUPER FISHERMEN, LAD!
WE'RE GONNA NEED A BIGGER LAKE!
742

Wallace & Gromit - Go Fish

by Aardman & Titan Comics

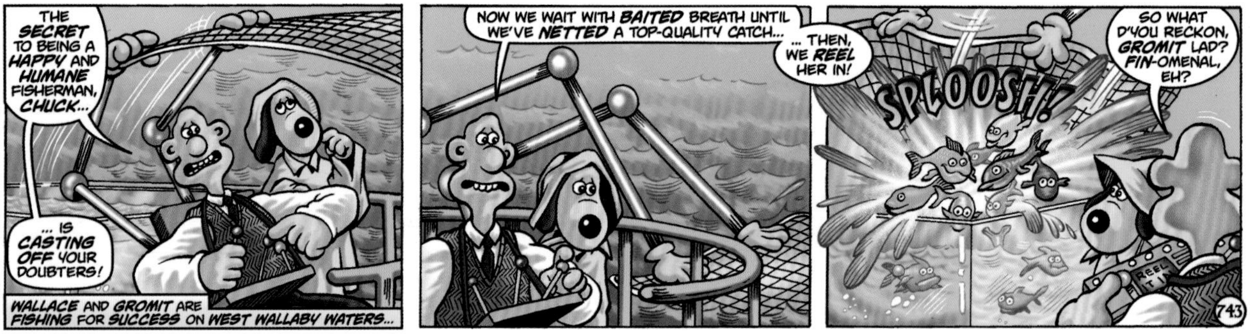

THE SECRET TO BEING A HAPPY AND HUMANE FISHERMAN, CHUCK...
... IS CASTING OFF YOUR DOUBTERS!
WALLACE AND GROMIT ARE FISHING FOR SUCCESS ON WEST WALLABY WATERS...
NOW WE WAIT WITH BAITED BREATH UNTIL WE'VE NETTED A TOP-QUALITY CATCH...
... THEN, WE REEL HER IN!
SPLOOSH!
SO WHAT D'YOU RECKON, GROMIT LAD? FIN-OMENAL, EH?
743

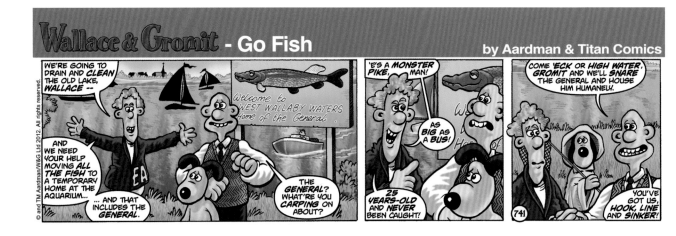

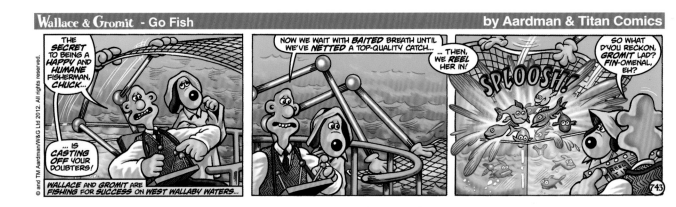

Wallace & Gromit - Go Fish
by Aardman & Titan Comics

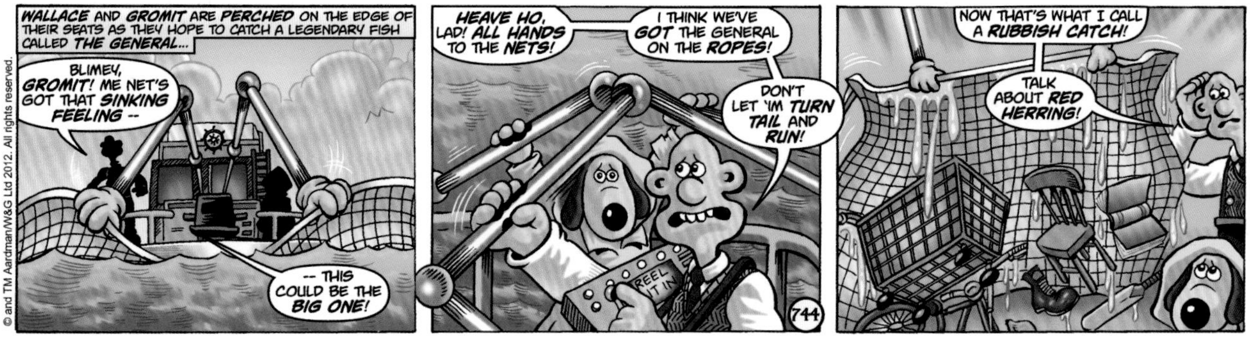
WALLACE AND GROMIT ARE PERCHED ON THE EDGE OF THEIR SEATS AS THEY HOPE TO CATCH A LEGENDARY FISH CALLED THE GENERAL...
BLIMEY, GROMIT! ME NET'S GOT THAT SINKING FEELING --
-- THIS COULD BE THE BIG ONE!
© and TM Aardman/W&G Ltd 2012. All rights reserved.
HEAVE HO, LAD! ALL HANDS TO THE NETS!
I THINK WE'VE GOT THE GENERAL ON THE ROPES!
DON'T LET 'IM TURN TAIL AND RUN!
REEL IT IN
744
NOW THAT'S WHAT I CALL A RUBBISH CATCH!
TALK ABOUT RED HERRING!

Wallace & Gromit - Go Fish
by Aardman & Titan Comics

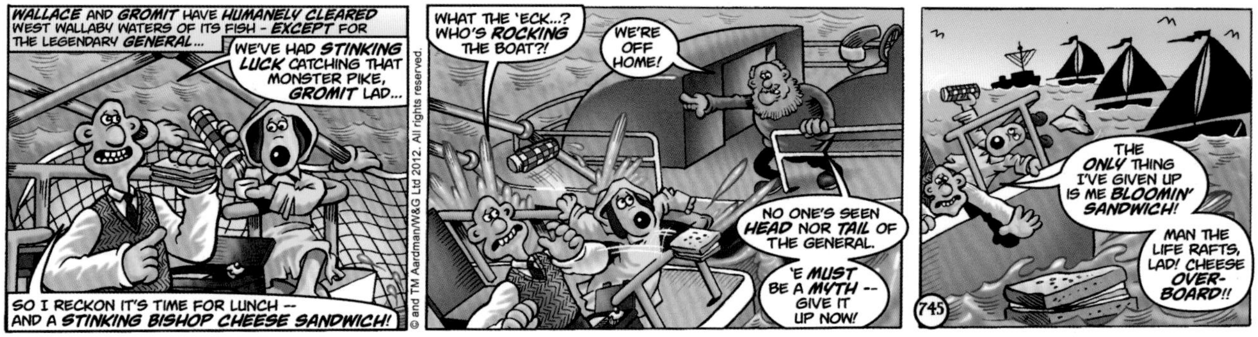
WALLACE AND GROMIT HAVE HUMANELY CLEARED WEST WALLABY WATERS OF ITS FISH - EXCEPT FOR THE LEGENDARY GENERAL...
WE'VE HAD STINKING LUCK CATCHING THAT MONSTER PIKE, GROMIT LAD...
SO I RECKON IT'S TIME FOR LUNCH -- AND A STINKING BISHOP CHEESE SANDWICH!
© and TM Aardman/W&G Ltd 2012. All rights reserved.
WHAT THE 'ECK...? WHO'S ROCKING THE BOAT?!
WE'RE OFF HOME!
NO ONE'S SEEN HEAD NOR TAIL OF THE GENERAL.
'E MUST BE A MYTH -- GIVE IT UP NOW!
THE ONLY THING I'VE GIVEN UP IS ME BLOOMIN' SANDWICH!
MAN THE LIFE RAFTS, LAD! CHEESE OVER-BOARD!!
745

Wallace & Gromit - Go Fish
by Aardman & Titan Comics

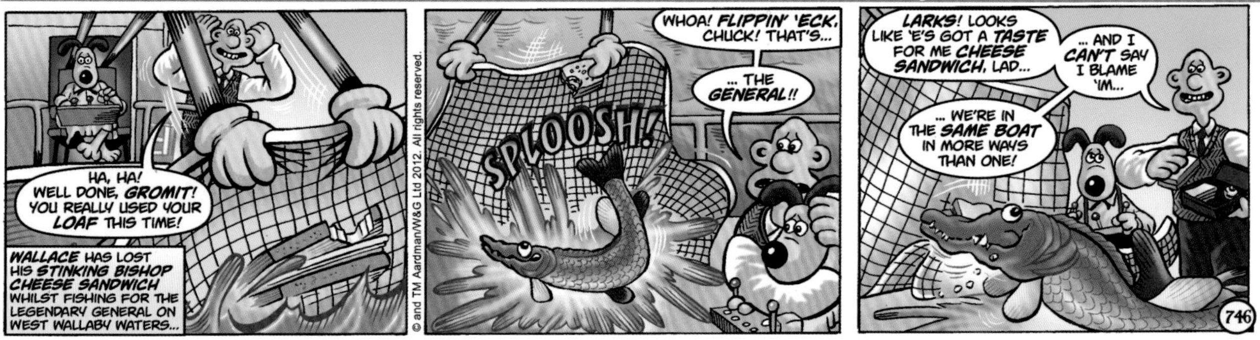
HA, HA! WELL DONE, GROMIT! YOU REALLY USED YOUR LOAF THIS TIME!
WALLACE HAS LOST HIS STINKING BISHOP CHEESE SANDWICH WHILST FISHING FOR THE LEGENDARY GENERAL ON WEST WALLABY WATERS...
© and TM Aardman/W&G Ltd 2012. All rights reserved.
WHOA! FLIPPIN' 'ECK, CHUCK! THAT'S...
... THE GENERAL!!
SPLOOSH!
LARKS! LOOKS LIKE 'E'S GOT A TASTE FOR ME CHEESE SANDWICH, LAD...
... AND I CAN'T SAY I BLAME 'IM...
... WE'RE IN THE SAME BOAT IN MORE WAYS THAN ONE!
746

Wallace & Gromit - Go Fish

by Aardman & Titan Comics

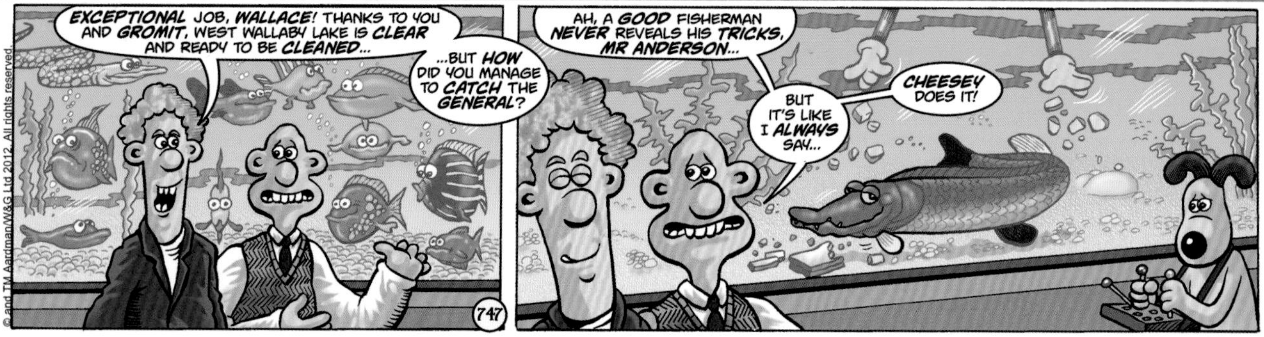
EXCEPTIONAL JOB, WALLACE! THANKS TO YOU AND GROMIT, WEST WALLABY LAKE IS CLEAR AND READY TO BE CLEANED...
...BUT HOW DID YOU MANAGE TO CATCH THE GENERAL?
747
AH, A GOOD FISHERMAN NEVER REVEALS HIS TRICKS, MR ANDERSON...
BUT IT'S LIKE I ALWAYS SAY...
CHEESEY DOES IT!

The End

Wallace & Gromit - The Dream Machine

by Aardman & Titan Comics

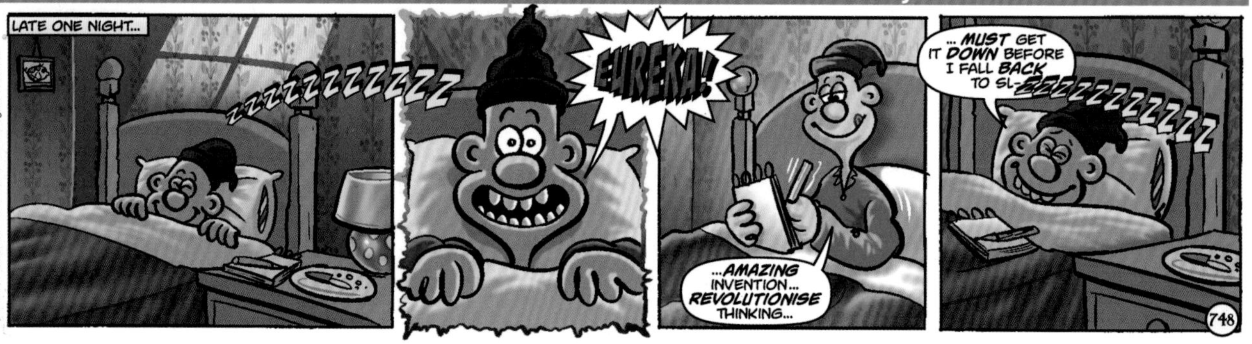
LATE ONE NIGHT...
ZZZZZZZZZZZZZ
EUREKA!
...AMAZING INVENTION... REVOLUTIONISE THINKING...
...MUST GET IT DOWN BEFORE I FALL BACK TO SL-ZZZZZZZZZZZ
748

Wallace & Gromit - The Dream Machine

by Aardman & Titan Comics

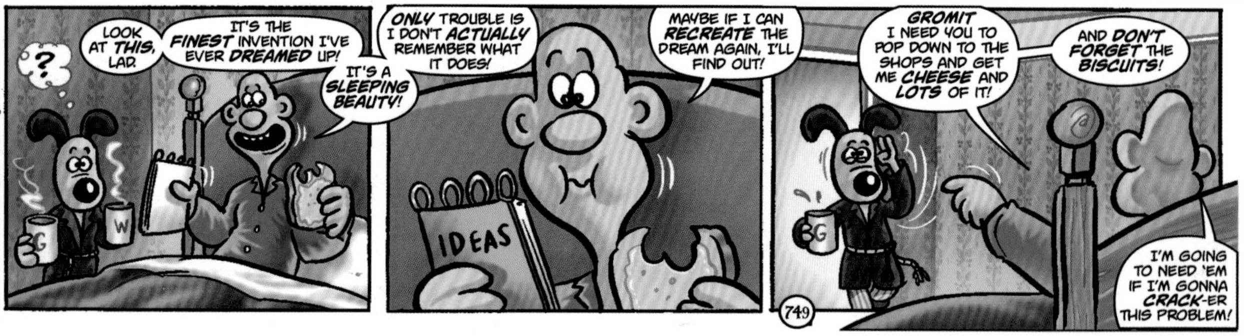
?
LOOK AT THIS, LAD.
IT'S THE FINEST INVENTION I'VE EVER DREAMED UP!
IT'S A SLEEPING BEAUTY!
ONLY TROUBLE IS I DON'T ACTUALLY REMEMBER WHAT IT DOES!
IDEAS
MAYBE IF I CAN RECREATE THE DREAM AGAIN, I'LL FIND OUT!
GROMIT I NEED YOU TO POP DOWN TO THE SHOPS AND GET ME CHEESE AND LOTS OF IT!
AND DON'T FORGET THE BISCUITS!
I'M GOING TO NEED 'EM IF I'M GONNA CRACK-ER THIS PROBLEM!
749

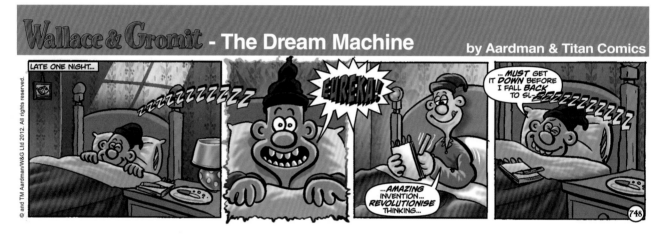

Wallace & Gromit - The Dream Machine by Aardman & Titan Comics

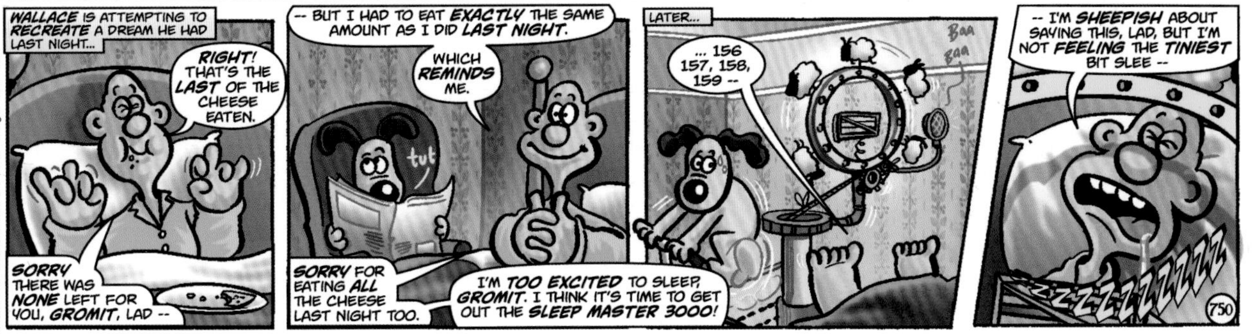
WALLACE IS ATTEMPTING TO RECREATE A DREAM HE HAD LAST NIGHT...
RIGHT! THAT'S THE LAST OF THE CHEESE EATEN.
SORRY THERE WAS NONE LEFT FOR YOU, GROMIT, LAD --
-- BUT I HAD TO EAT EXACTLY THE SAME AMOUNT AS I DID LAST NIGHT.
WHICH REMINDS ME.
tut
SORRY FOR EATING ALL THE CHEESE LAST NIGHT TOO.
I'M TOO EXCITED TO SLEEP, GROMIT. I THINK IT'S TIME TO GET OUT THE SLEEP MASTER 3000!
LATER...
... 156 157, 158, 159 --
Baa
Baa
-- I'M SHEEPISH ABOUT SAYING THIS, LAD, BUT I'M NOT FEELING THE TINIEST BIT SLEE --
ZZZZZZZZZZZZZ
750

Wallace & Gromit - The Dream Machine by Aardman & Titan Comics

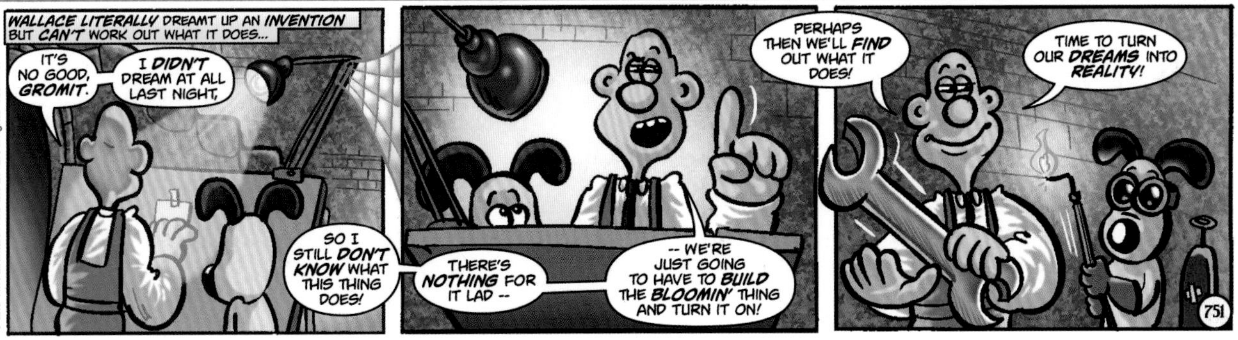
WALLACE LITERALLY DREAMT UP AN INVENTION BUT CAN'T WORK OUT WHAT IT DOES...
IT'S NO GOOD, GROMIT.
I DIDN'T DREAM AT ALL LAST NIGHT,
SO I STILL DON'T KNOW WHAT THIS THING DOES!
THERE'S NOTHING FOR IT LAD --
-- WE'RE JUST GOING TO HAVE TO BUILD THE BLOOMIN' THING AND TURN IT ON!
PERHAPS THEN WE'LL FIND OUT WHAT IT DOES!
TIME TO TURN OUR DREAMS INTO REALITY!
751

Wallace & Gromit - The Dream Machine by Aardman & Titan Comics

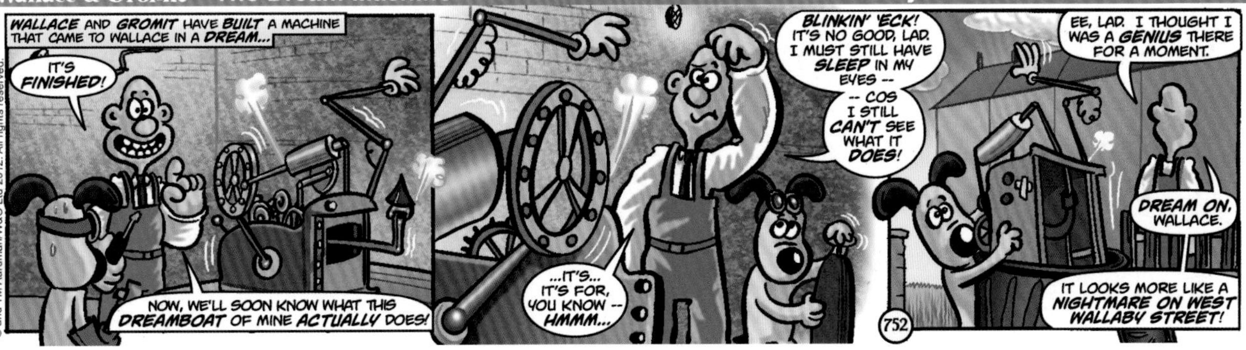
WALLACE AND GROMIT HAVE BUILT A MACHINE THAT CAME TO WALLACE IN A DREAM...
IT'S FINISHED!
NOW, WE'LL SOON KNOW WHAT THIS DREAMBOAT OF MINE ACTUALLY DOES!
BLINKIN' 'ECK! IT'S NO GOOD, LAD. I MUST STILL HAVE SLEEP IN MY EYES --
-- COS I STILL CAN'T SEE WHAT IT DOES!
...IT'S... IT'S FOR, YOU KNOW -- HMMM...
752
EE, LAD. I THOUGHT I WAS A GENIUS THERE FOR A MOMENT.
DREAM ON, WALLACE.
IT LOOKS MORE LIKE A NIGHTMARE ON WEST WALLABY STREET!

Wallace & Gromit - The Dream Machine

by Aardman & Titan Comics

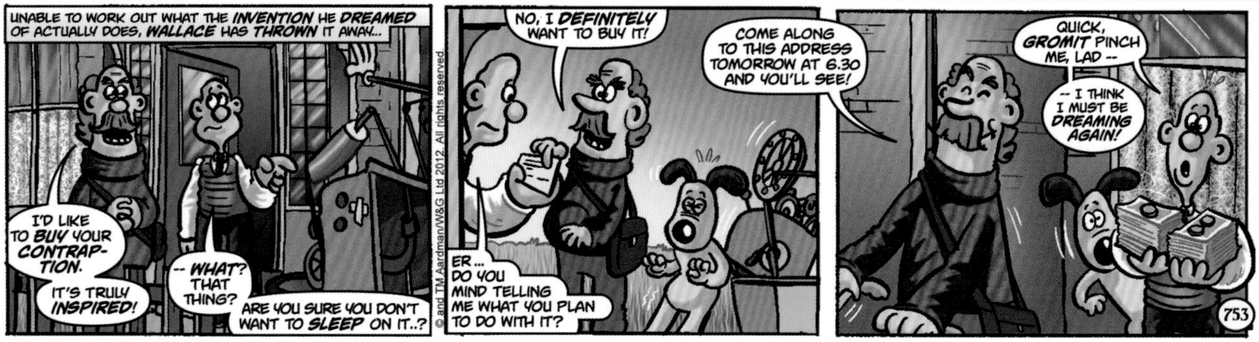

UNABLE TO WORK OUT WHAT THE INVENTION HE DREAMED OF ACTUALLY DOES, WALLACE HAS THROWN IT AWAY...
I'D LIKE TO BUY YOUR CONTRAP-TION.
IT'S TRULY INSPIRED!
-- WHAT? THAT THING?
ARE YOU SURE YOU DON'T WANT TO SLEEP ON IT..?
NO, I DEFINITELY WANT TO BUY IT!
ER... DO YOU MIND TELLING ME WHAT YOU PLAN TO DO WITH IT?
COME ALONG TO THIS ADDRESS TOMORROW AT 6.30 AND YOU'LL SEE!
QUICK, GROMIT PINCH ME, LAD --
-- I THINK I MUST BE DREAMING AGAIN!
753

Wallace & Gromit - The Dream Machine

by Aardman & Titan Comics

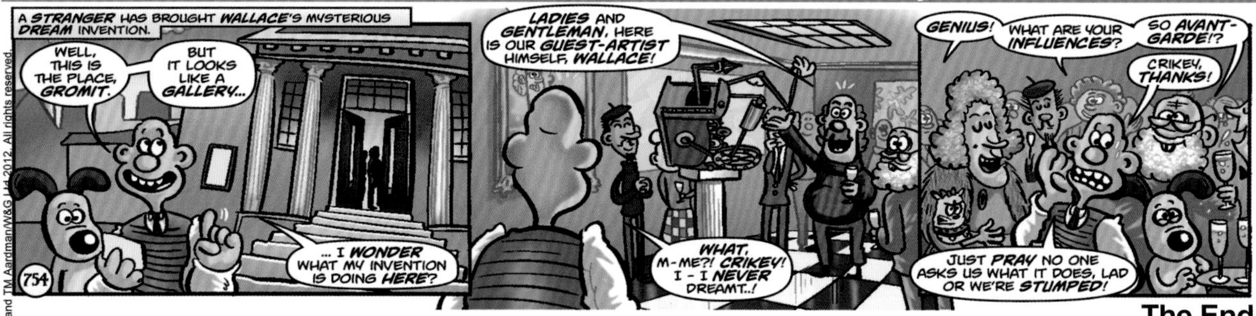

A STRANGER HAS BROUGHT WALLACE'S MYSTERIOUS DREAM INVENTION.
WELL, THIS IS THE PLACE, GROMIT.
BUT IT LOOKS LIKE A GALLERY...
... I WONDER WHAT MY INVENTION IS DOING HERE?
754
LADIES AND GENTLEMAN, HERE IS OUR GUEST-ARTIST HIMSELF, WALLACE!
WHAT, M-ME?! CRIKEY! I - I NEVER DREAMT..!
GENIUS!
WHAT ARE YOUR INFLUENCES?
SO AVANT-GARDE!?
CRIKEY, THANKS!
JUST PRAY NO ONE ASKS US WHAT IT DOES, LAD OR WE'RE STUMPED!

The End

Wallace & Gromit - Inventor's Block

by Aardman & Titan Comics

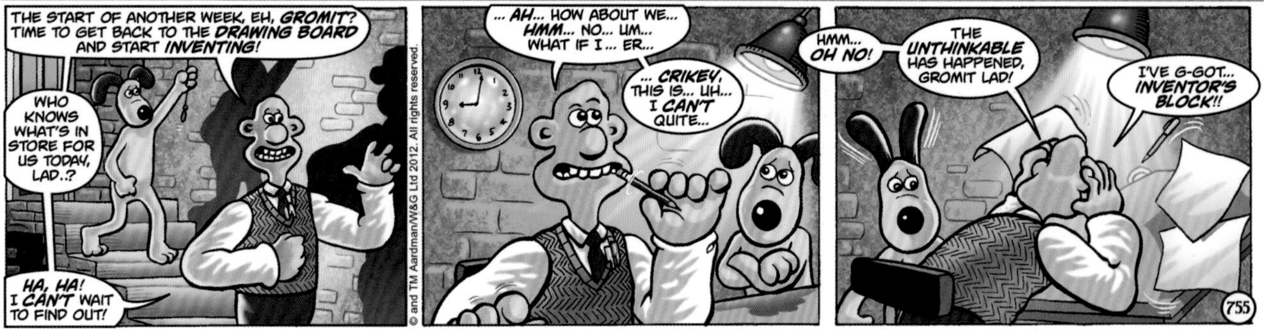

THE START OF ANOTHER WEEK, EH, GROMIT? TIME TO GET BACK TO THE DRAWING BOARD AND START INVENTING!
WHO KNOWS WHAT'S IN STORE FOR US TODAY, LAD..?
HA, HA! I CAN'T WAIT TO FIND OUT!
... AH... HOW ABOUT WE... HMM... NO... UM... WHAT IF I... ER...
... CRIKEY, THIS IS... UH... I CAN'T QUITE...
HMM... OH NO!
THE UNTHINKABLE HAS HAPPENED, GROMIT LAD!
I'VE G-GOT... INVENTOR'S BLOCK!!
755

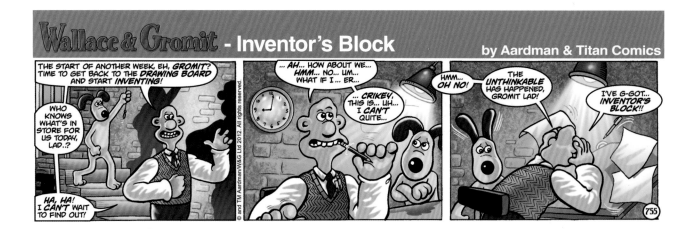

Wallace & Gromit - Inventor's Block by Aardman & Titan Comics

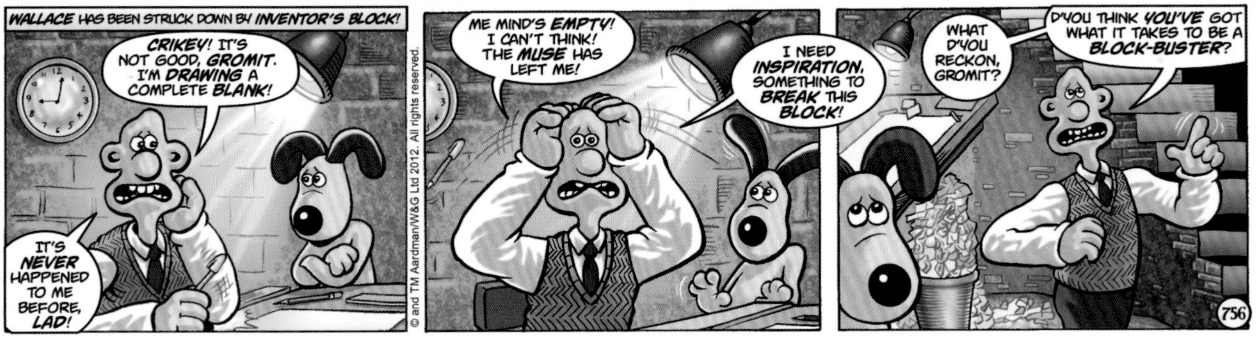
WALLACE HAS BEEN STRUCK DOWN BY INVENTOR'S BLOCK!
CRIKEY! IT'S NOT GOOD, GROMIT. I'M DRAWING A COMPLETE BLANK!
IT'S NEVER HAPPENED TO ME BEFORE, LAD!
© and TM Aardman/W&G Ltd 2012. All rights reserved.
ME MIND'S EMPTY! I CAN'T THINK! THE MUSE HAS LEFT ME!
I NEED INSPIRATION, SOMETHING TO BREAK THIS BLOCK!
WHAT D'YOU RECKON, GROMIT?
D'YOU THINK YOU'VE GOT WHAT IT TAKES TO BE A BLOCK-BUSTER?
756

Wallace & Gromit - Inventor's Block by Aardman & Titan Comics

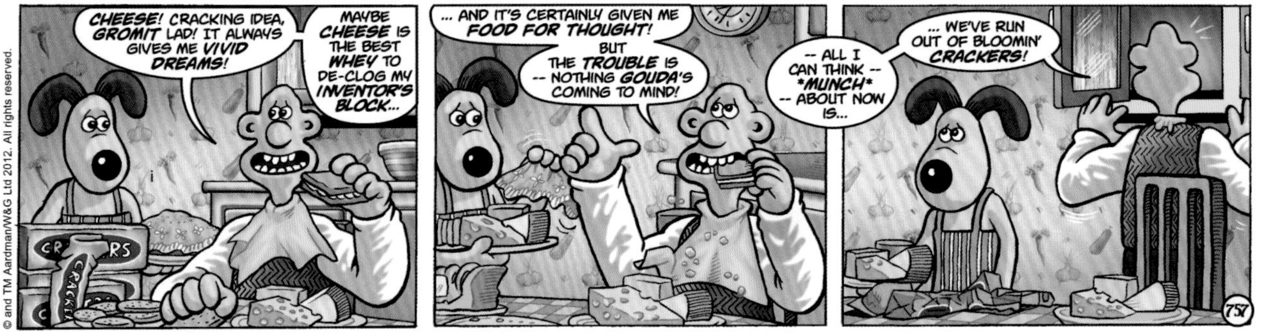
© and TM Aardman/W&G Ltd 2012. All rights reserved.
CHEESE! CRACKING IDEA, GROMIT LAD! IT ALWAYS GIVES ME VIVID DREAMS!
MAYBE CHEESE IS THE BEST WHEY TO DE-CLOG MY INVENTOR'S BLOCK...
CRACKERS
... AND IT'S CERTAINLY GIVEN ME FOOD FOR THOUGHT!
BUT THE TROUBLE IS -- NOTHING GOUDA'S COMING TO MIND!
-- ALL I CAN THINK -- *MUNCH* -- ABOUT NOW IS...
... WE'VE RUN OUT OF BLOOMIN' CRACKERS!
757

Wallace & Gromit - Inventor's Block by Aardman & Titan Comics

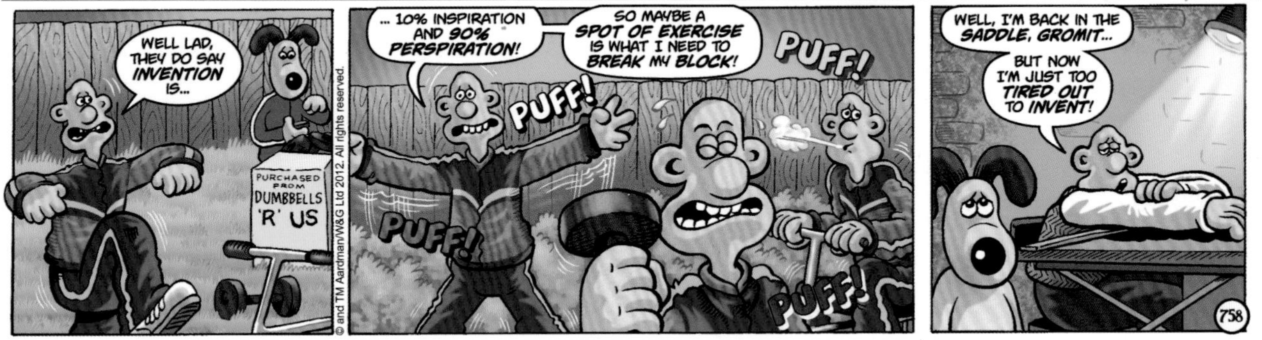
WELL LAD, THEY DO SAY INVENTION IS...
PURCHASED FROM DUMBBELLS 'R' US
© and TM Aardman/W&G Ltd 2012. All rights reserved.
... 10% INSPIRATION AND 90% PERSPIRATION!
SO MAYBE A SPOT OF EXERCISE IS WHAT I NEED TO BREAK MY BLOCK!
PUFF!
PUFF!
PUFF!
PUFF!
WELL, I'M BACK IN THE SADDLE, GROMIT...
BUT NOW I'M JUST TOO TIRED OUT TO INVENT!
758

Wallace & Gromit - Inventor's Block by Aardman & Titan Comics

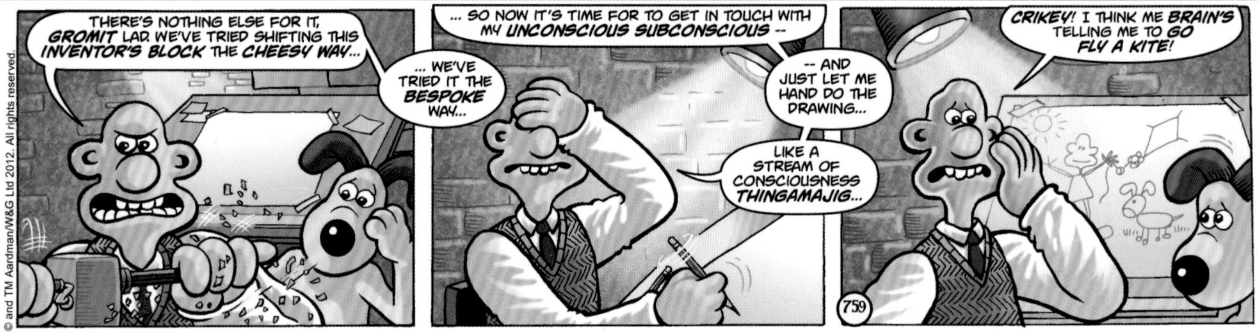

THERE'S NOTHING ELSE FOR IT, GROMIT LAD. WE'VE TRIED SHIFTING THIS INVENTOR'S BLOCK THE CHEESY WAY...
... WE'VE TRIED IT THE BESPOKE WAY...
... SO NOW IT'S TIME FOR TO GET IN TOUCH WITH MY UNCONSCIOUS SUBCONSCIOUS --
-- AND JUST LET ME HAND DO THE DRAWING...
LIKE A STREAM OF CONSCIOUSNESS THINGAMAJIG...
CRIKEY! I THINK ME BRAIN'S TELLING ME TO GO FLY A KITE!
759
© and TM Aardman/W&G Ltd 2012. All rights reserved.

Wallace & Gromit - Inventor's Block by Aardman & Titan Comics

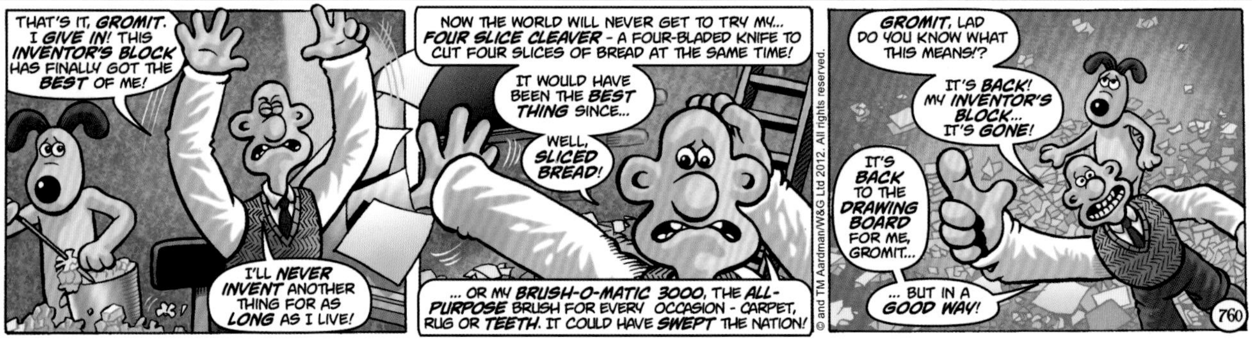

THAT'S IT, GROMIT. I GIVE IN! THIS INVENTOR'S BLOCK HAS FINALLY GOT THE BEST OF ME!
I'LL NEVER INVENT ANOTHER THING FOR AS LONG AS I LIVE!
NOW THE WORLD WILL NEVER GET TO TRY MY... FOUR SLICE CLEAVER - A FOUR-BLADED KNIFE TO CUT FOUR SLICES OF BREAD AT THE SAME TIME!
IT WOULD HAVE BEEN THE BEST THING SINCE...
WELL, SLICED BREAD!
... OR MY BRUSH-O-MATIC 3000, THE ALL-PURPOSE BRUSH FOR EVERY OCCASION - CARPET, RUG OR TEETH. IT COULD HAVE SWEPT THE NATION!
GROMIT, LAD DO YOU KNOW WHAT THIS MEANS!?
IT'S BACK! MY INVENTOR'S BLOCK... IT'S GONE!
IT'S BACK TO THE DRAWING BOARD FOR ME, GROMIT...
... BUT IN A GOOD WAY!
760
© and TM Aardman/W&G Ltd 2012. All rights reserved.

Wallace & Gromit - Inventor's Block by Aardman & Titan Comics

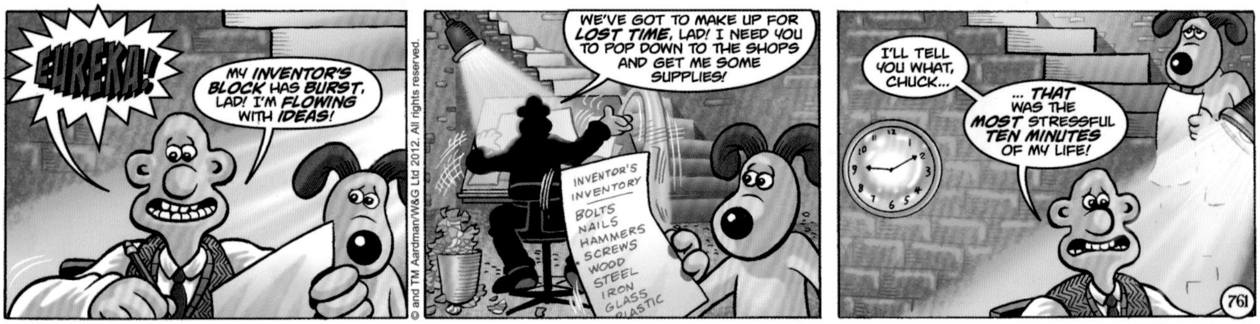

EUREKA!
MY INVENTOR'S BLOCK HAS BURST, LAD! I'M FLOWING WITH IDEAS!
WE'VE GOT TO MAKE UP FOR LOST TIME, LAD! I NEED YOU TO POP DOWN TO THE SHOPS AND GET ME SOME SUPPLIES!
INVENTOR'S INVENTORY
BOLTS
NAILS
HAMMERS
SCREWS
WOOD
STEEL
IRON
GLASS
I'LL TELL YOU WHAT, CHUCK...
... THAT WAS THE MOST STRESSFUL TEN MINUTES OF MY LIFE!
761
© and TM Aardman/W&G Ltd 2012. All rights reserved.

The End

Wallace & Gromit - Home from Home

by Aardman & Titan Comics

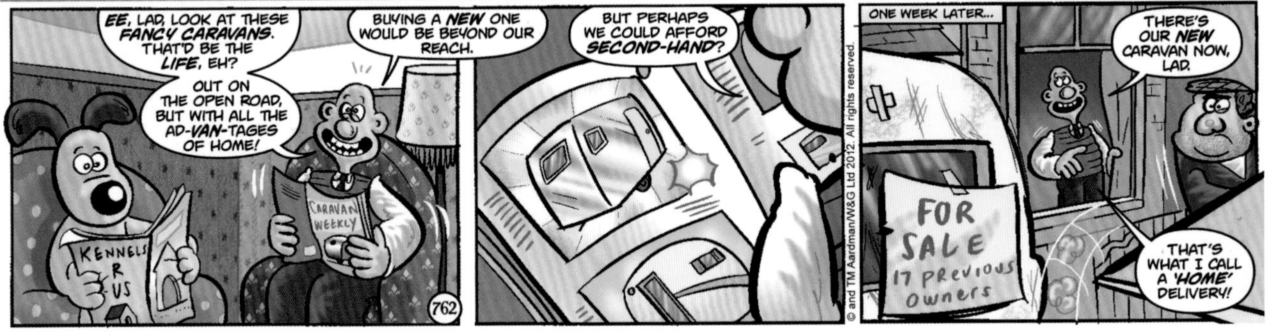

EE, LAD, LOOK AT THESE FANCY CARAVANS. THAT'D BE THE LIFE, EH?
OUT ON THE OPEN ROAD, BUT WITH ALL THE AD-VAN-TAGES OF HOME!
KENNELS R US
CARAVAN WEEKLY
BUYING A NEW ONE WOULD BE BEYOND OUR REACH.
762
BUT PERHAPS WE COULD AFFORD SECOND-HAND?
ONE WEEK LATER...
THERE'S OUR NEW CARAVAN NOW, LAD.
FOR SALE 17 PREVIOUS OWNERS
THAT'S WHAT I CALL A 'HOME' DELIVERY!

Wallace & Gromit - Home from Home

by Aardman & Titan Comics

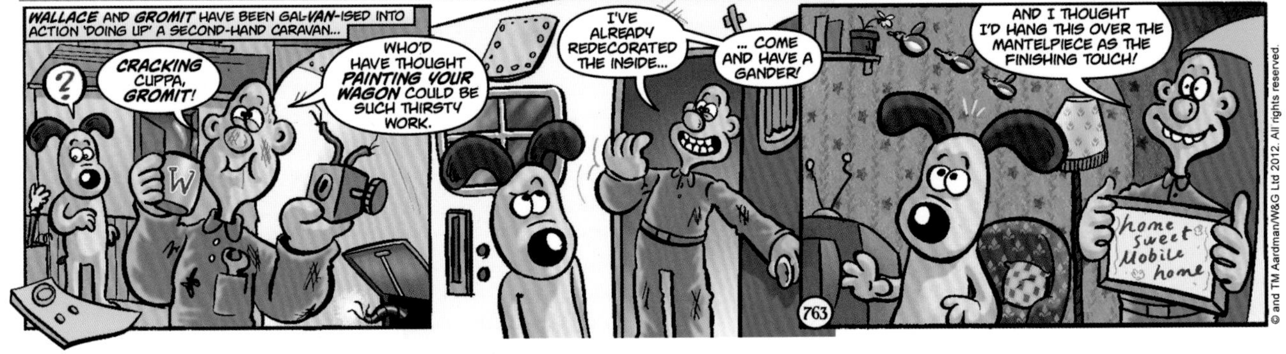

WALLACE AND GROMIT HAVE BEEN GAL-VAN-ISED INTO ACTION 'DOING UP' A SECOND-HAND CARAVAN...
?
CRACKING CUPPA, GROMIT!
W
WHO'D HAVE THOUGHT PAINTING YOUR WAGON COULD BE SUCH THIRSTY WORK.
I'VE ALREADY REDECORATED THE INSIDE...
... COME AND HAVE A GANDER!
763
AND I THOUGHT I'D HANG THIS OVER THE MANTELPIECE AS THE FINISHING TOUCH!
home sweet Mobile home

Wallace & Gromit - Home from Home

by Aardman & Titan Comics

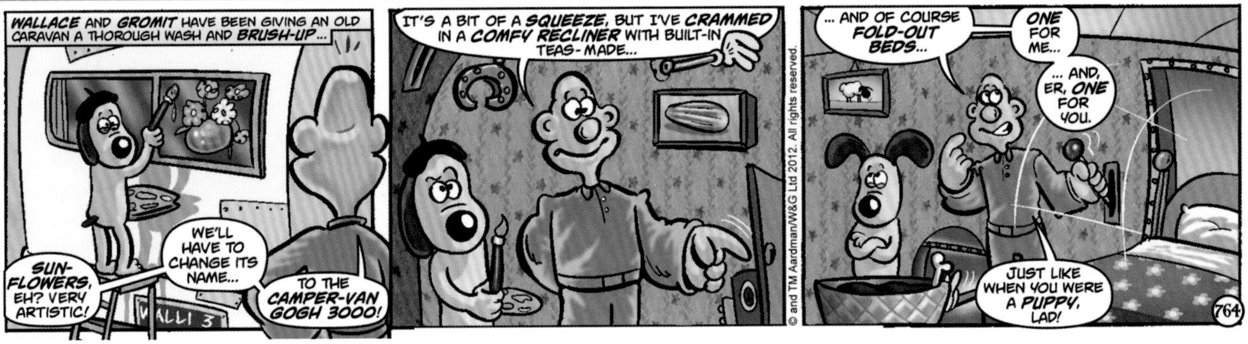

WALLACE AND GROMIT HAVE BEEN GIVING AN OLD CARAVAN A THOROUGH WASH AND BRUSH-UP...
SUN-FLOWERS, EH? VERY ARTISTIC!
WE'LL HAVE TO CHANGE ITS NAME...
TO THE CAMPER-VAN GOGH 3000!
IT'S A BIT OF A SQUEEZE, BUT I'VE CRAMMED IN A COMFY RECLINER WITH BUILT-IN TEAS-MADE...
... AND OF COURSE FOLD-OUT BEDS...
ONE FOR ME...
... AND, ER, ONE FOR YOU.
JUST LIKE WHEN YOU WERE A PUPPY, LAD!
764

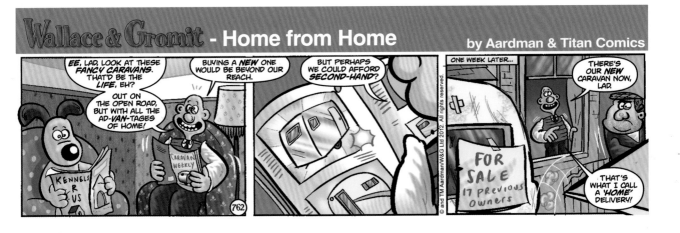

Wallace & Gromit - Home from Home by Aardman & Titan Comics

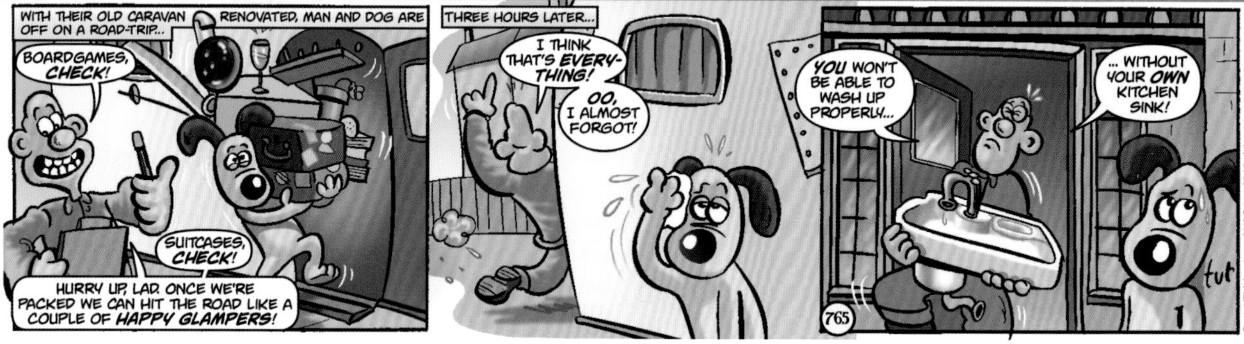
WITH THEIR OLD CARAVAN RENOVATED, MAN AND DOG ARE OFF ON A ROAD-TRIP...
BOARDGAMES, CHECK!
SUITCASES, CHECK!
HURRY UP, LAD. ONCE WE'RE PACKED WE CAN HIT THE ROAD LIKE A COUPLE OF HAPPY GLAMPERS!
THREE HOURS LATER...
I THINK THAT'S EVERY-THING!
OO, I ALMOST FORGOT!
YOU WON'T BE ABLE TO WASH UP PROPERLY...
... WITHOUT YOUR OWN KITCHEN SINK!
tut
765

Wallace & Gromit - Home from Home by Aardman & Titan Comics

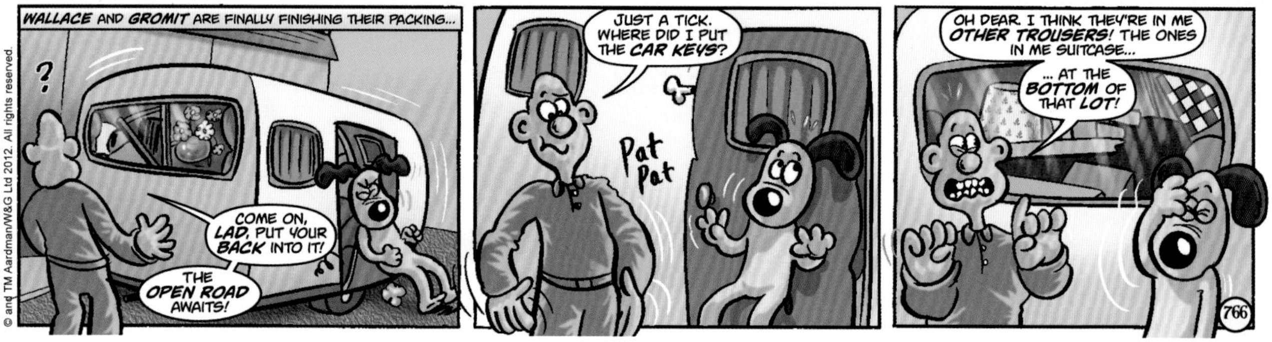
WALLACE AND GROMIT ARE FINALLY FINISHING THEIR PACKING...
?
COME ON, LAD, PUT YOUR BACK INTO IT!
THE OPEN ROAD AWAITS!
JUST A TICK. WHERE DID I PUT THE CAR KEYS?
Pat Pat
OH DEAR. I THINK THEY'RE IN ME OTHER TROUSERS! THE ONES IN ME SUITCASE...
... AT THE BOTTOM OF THAT LOT!
766

Wallace & Gromit - Home from Home by Aardman & Titan Comics

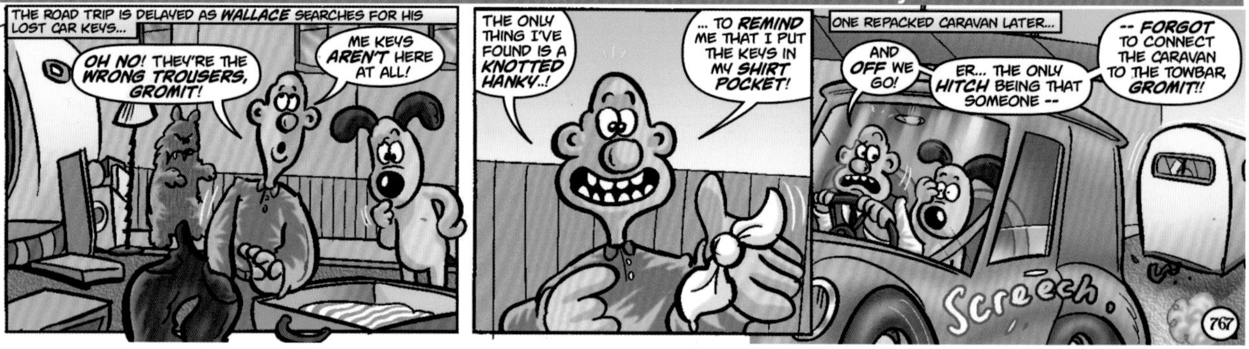
THE ROAD TRIP IS DELAYED AS WALLACE SEARCHES FOR HIS LOST CAR KEYS...
OH NO! THEY'RE THE WRONG TROUSERS, GROMIT!
ME KEYS AREN'T HERE AT ALL!
THE ONLY THING I'VE FOUND IS A KNOTTED HANKY..!
... TO REMIND ME THAT I PUT THE KEYS IN MY SHIRT POCKET!
ONE REPACKED CARAVAN LATER...
AND OFF WE GO!
ER... THE ONLY HITCH BEING THAT SOMEONE --
-- FORGOT TO CONNECT THE CARAVAN TO THE TOWBAR, GROMIT!!
Screech
767

Wallace & Gromit - Home from Home

by Aardman & Titan Comics

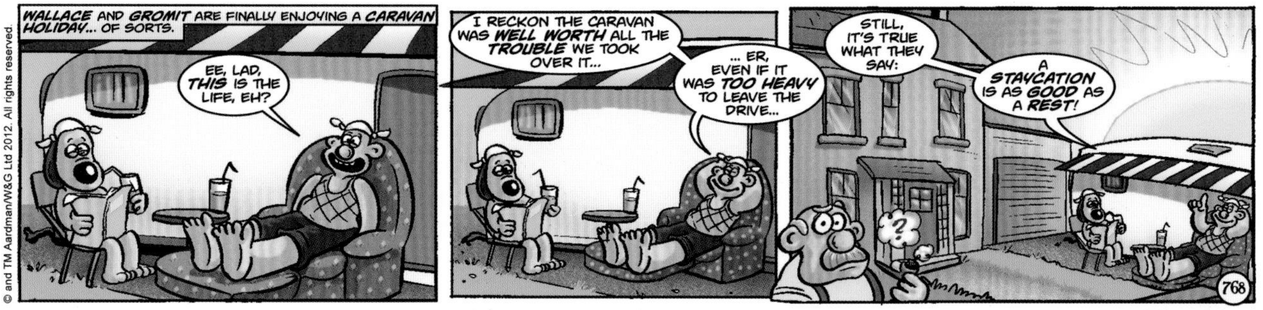
WALLACE AND GROMIT ARE FINALLY ENJOYING A CARAVAN HOLIDAY... OF SORTS.
EE, LAD, THIS IS THE LIFE, EH?
I RECKON THE CARAVAN WAS WELL WORTH ALL THE TROUBLE WE TOOK OVER IT...
... ER, EVEN IF IT WAS TOO HEAVY TO LEAVE THE DRIVE...
STILL, IT'S TRUE WHAT THEY SAY:
A STAYCATION IS AS GOOD AS A REST!
?
768

The End

Wallace & Gromit - Mecha-Wallace

by Aardman & Titan Comics

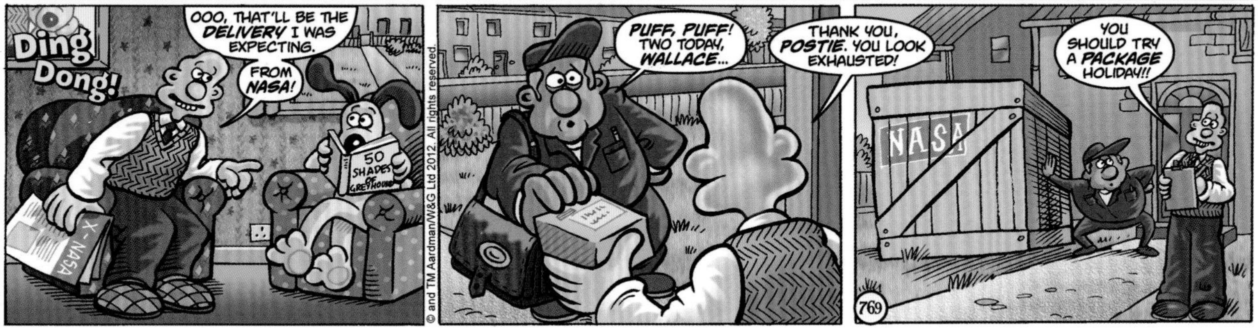
Ding Dong!
OOO, THAT'LL BE THE DELIVERY I WAS EXPECTING.
FROM NASA!
50 SHADES OF GREYHOUND
X-NASA
PUFF, PUFF! TWO TODAY, WALLACE...
THANK YOU, POSTIE. YOU LOOK EXHAUSTED!
YOU SHOULD TRY A PACKAGE HOLIDAY!!
NASA
769

Wallace & Gromit - Mecha-Wallace

by Aardman & Titan Comics

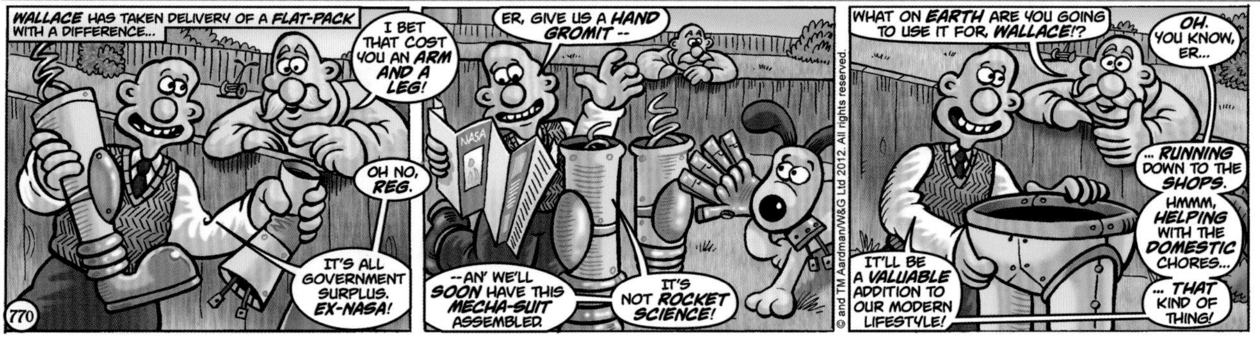
WALLACE HAS TAKEN DELIVERY OF A FLAT-PACK WITH A DIFFERENCE...
I BET THAT COST YOU AN ARM AND A LEG!
OH NO, REG.
IT'S ALL GOVERNMENT SURPLUS. EX-NASA!
770
ER, GIVE US A HAND GROMIT --
NASA
--AN' WE'LL SOON HAVE THIS MECHA-SUIT ASSEMBLED.
IT'S NOT ROCKET SCIENCE!
WHAT ON EARTH ARE YOU GOING TO USE IT FOR, WALLACE!?
IT'LL BE A VALUABLE ADDITION TO OUR MODERN LIFESTYLE!
OH. YOU KNOW, ER...
... RUNNING DOWN TO THE SHOPS.
HMMM, HELPING WITH THE DOMESTIC CHORES...
... THAT KIND OF THING!

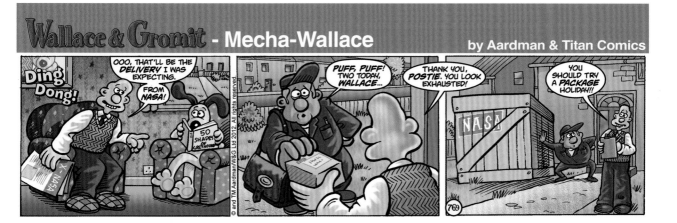

Wallace & Gromit - Mecha-Wallace by Aardman & Titan Comics

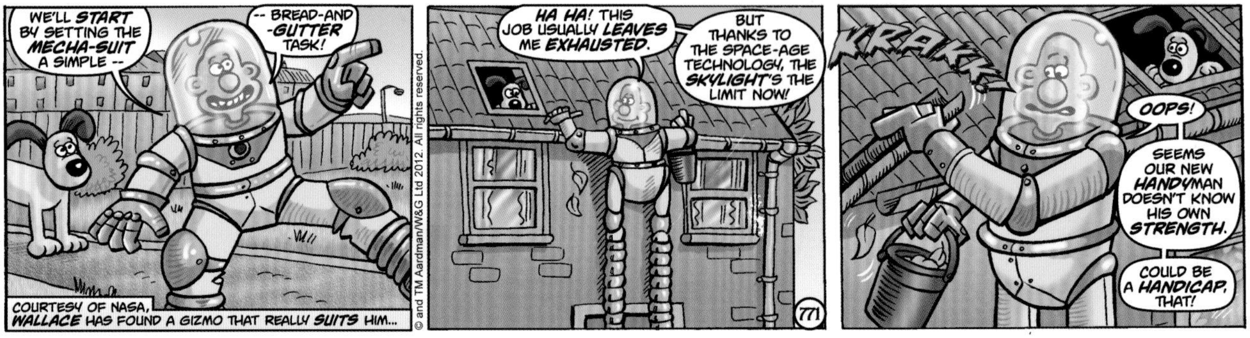

WE'LL START BY SETTING THE MECHA-SUIT A SIMPLE --
-- BREAD-AND -GUTTER TASK!
COURTESY OF NASA, WALLACE HAS FOUND A GIZMO THAT REALLY SUITS HIM...
HA HA! THIS JOB USUALLY LEAVES ME EXHAUSTED.
BUT THANKS TO THE SPACE-AGE TECHNOLOGY, THE SKYLIGHT'S THE LIMIT NOW!
771
KRAKK
OOPS!
SEEMS OUR NEW HANDYMAN DOESN'T KNOW HIS OWN STRENGTH.
COULD BE A HANDICAP, THAT!

Wallace & Gromit - Mecha-Wallace by Aardman & Titan Comics

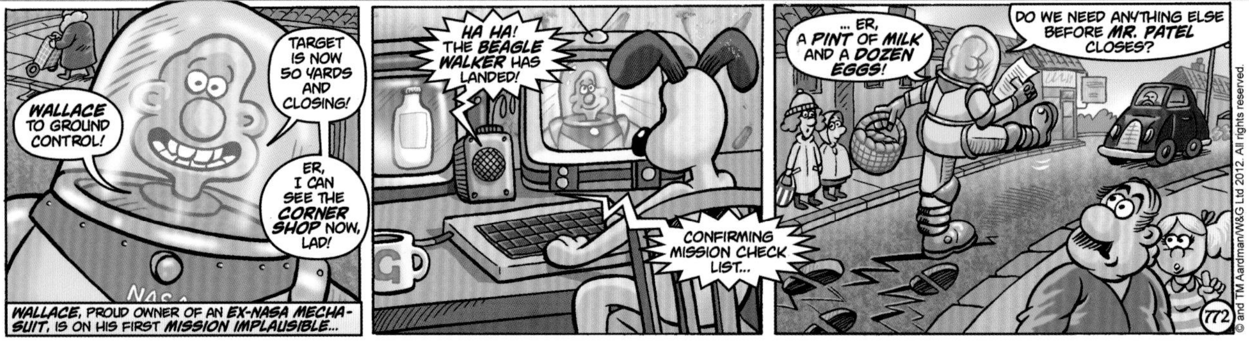

WALLACE TO GROUND CONTROL!
TARGET IS NOW 50 YARDS AND CLOSING!
ER, I CAN SEE THE CORNER SHOP NOW, LAD!
WALLACE, PROUD OWNER OF AN EX-NASA MECHA-SUIT, IS ON HIS FIRST MISSION IMPLAUSIBLE...
HA HA! THE BEAGLE WALKER HAS LANDED!
CONFIRMING MISSION CHECK LIST...
... ER, A PINT OF MILK AND A DOZEN EGGS!
DO WE NEED ANYTHING ELSE BEFORE MR. PATEL CLOSES?
772

Wallace & Gromit - Mecha-Wallace by Aardman & Titan Comics

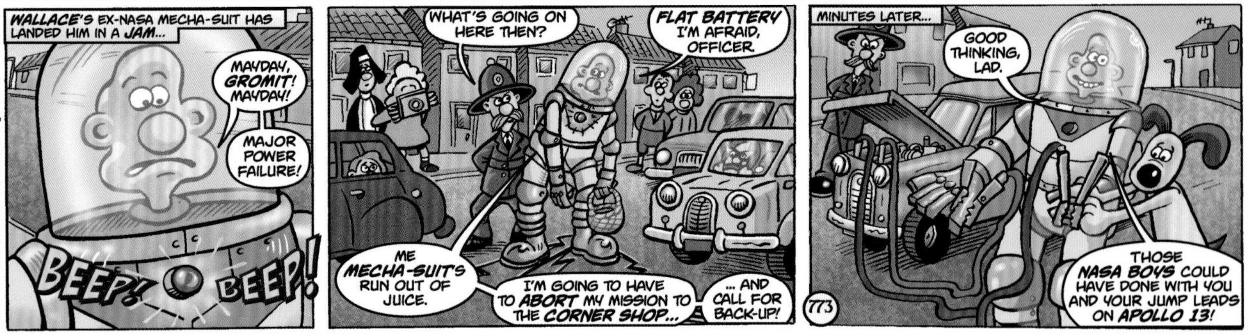

WALLACE'S EX-NASA MECHA-SUIT HAS LANDED HIM IN A JAM...
MAYDAY, GROMIT! MAYDAY!
MAJOR POWER FAILURE!
BEEP! BEEP!
WHAT'S GOING ON HERE THEN?
FLAT BATTERY I'M AFRAID, OFFICER.
ME MECHA-SUIT'S RUN OUT OF JUICE.
I'M GOING TO HAVE TO ABORT MY MISSION TO THE CORNER SHOP...
... AND CALL FOR BACK-UP!
773
MINUTES LATER...
GOOD THINKING, LAD.
THOSE NASA BOYS COULD HAVE DONE WITH YOU AND YOUR JUMP LEADS ON APOLLO 13!

Wallace & Gromit - Mecha-Wallace

by Aardman & Titan Comics

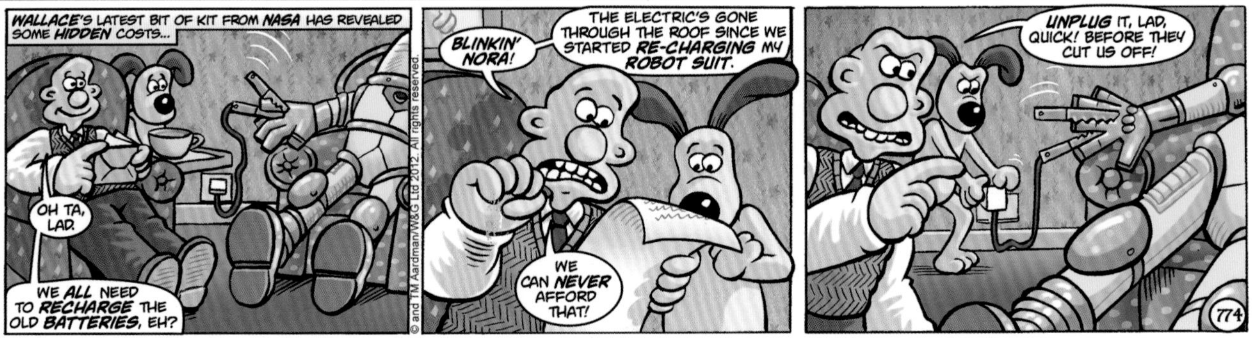

WALLACE'S LATEST BIT OF KIT FROM NASA HAS REVEALED SOME HIDDEN COSTS...
OH TA, LAD.
WE ALL NEED TO RECHARGE THE OLD BATTERIES, EH?
BLINKIN' NORA!
THE ELECTRIC'S GONE THROUGH THE ROOF SINCE WE STARTED RE-CHARGING MY ROBOT SUIT.
WE CAN NEVER AFFORD THAT!
UNPLUG IT, LAD, QUICK! BEFORE THEY CUT US OFF!
774

Wallace & Gromit - Mecha-Wallace

by Aardman & Titan Comics

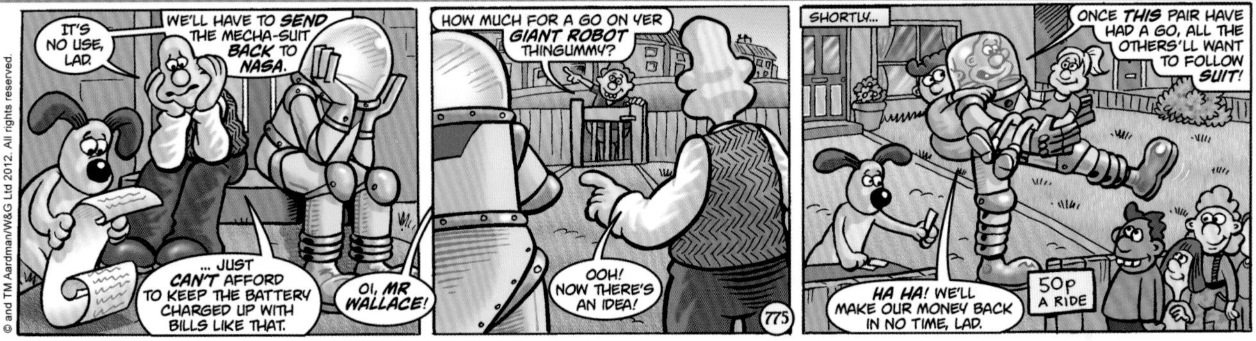

IT'S NO USE, LAD.
WE'LL HAVE TO SEND THE MECHA-SUIT BACK TO NASA.
... JUST CAN'T AFFORD TO KEEP THE BATTERY CHARGED UP WITH BILLS LIKE THAT.
OI, MR WALLACE!
HOW MUCH FOR A GO ON YER GIANT ROBOT THINGUMMY?
OOH! NOW THERE'S AN IDEA!
775
SHORTLY...
ONCE THIS PAIR HAVE HAD A GO, ALL THE OTHERS'LL WANT TO FOLLOW SUIT!
HA HA! WE'LL MAKE OUR MONEY BACK IN NO TIME, LAD.
50p A RIDE

The End

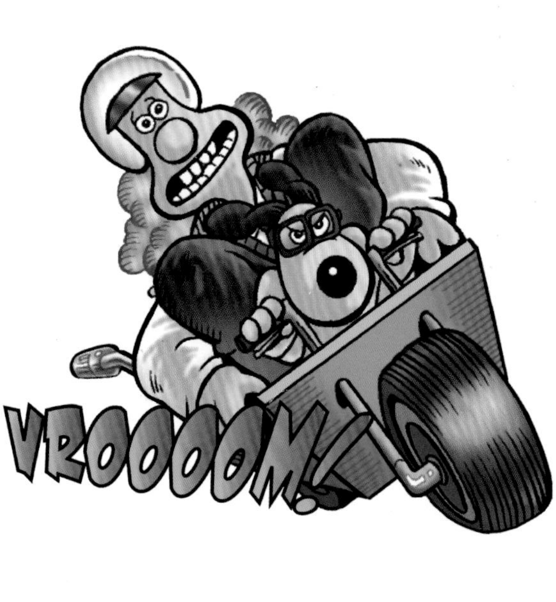

VROOOOOM!

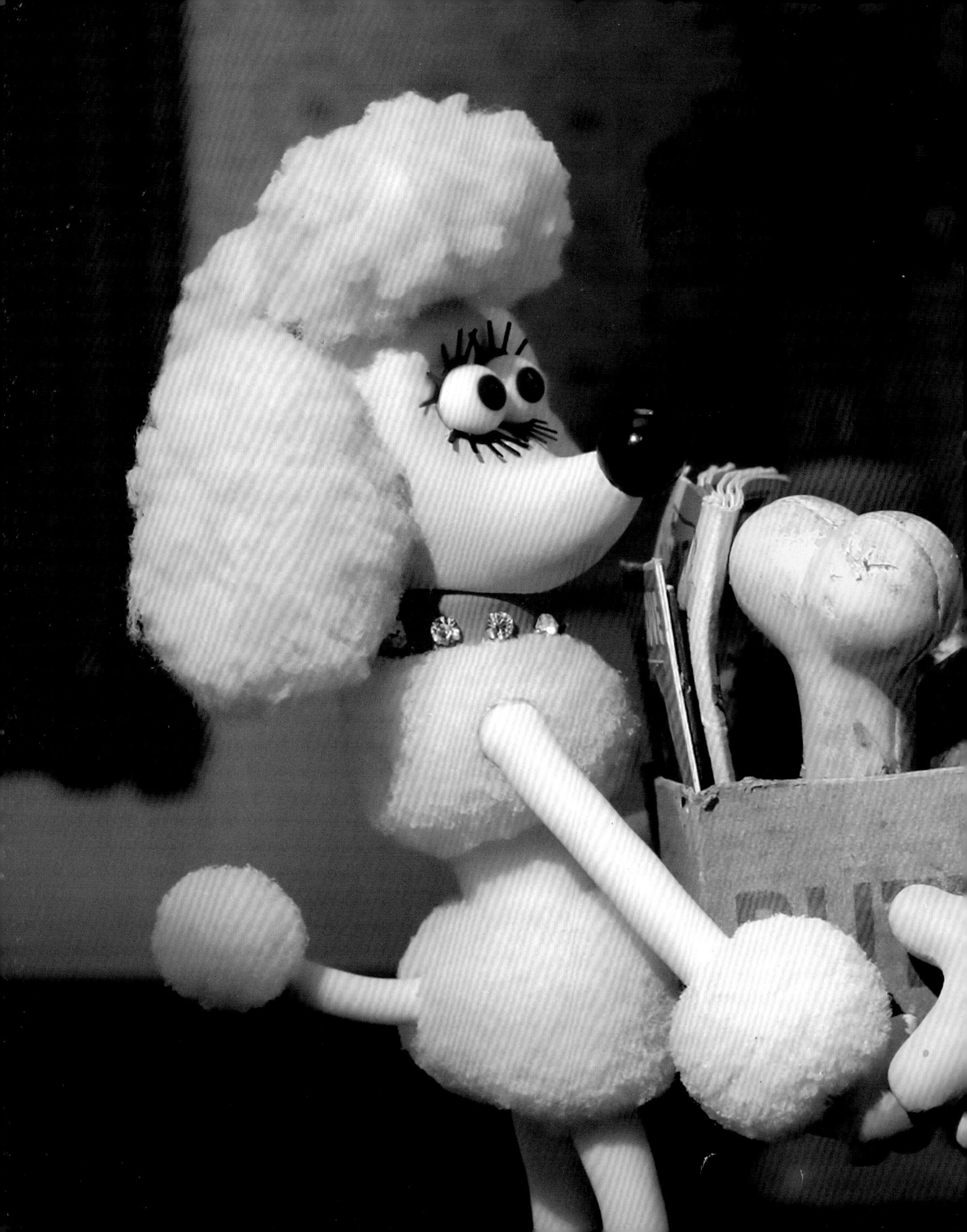

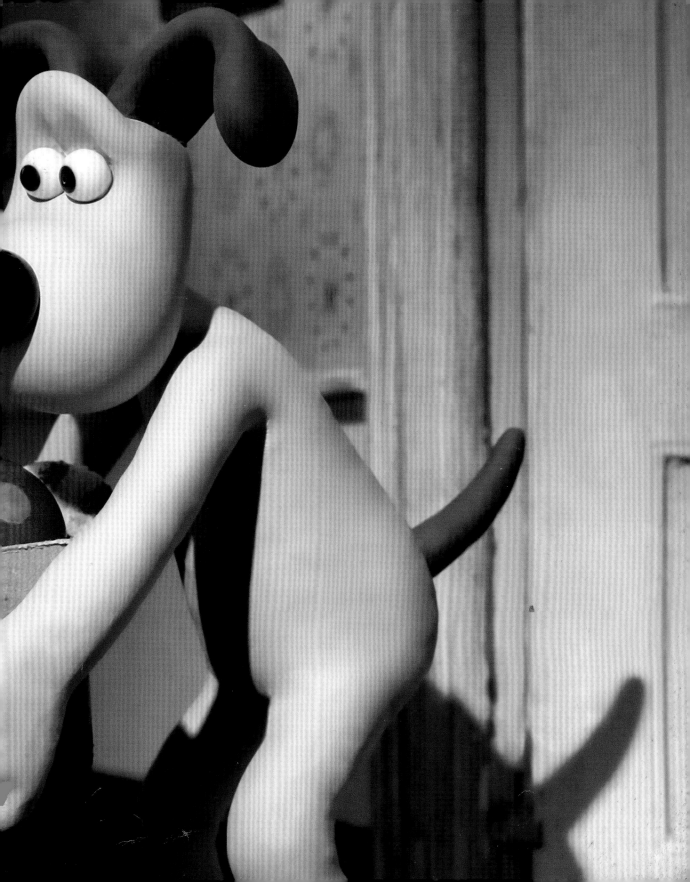

Wallace & Gromit - The Dinner Party
by Aardman & Titan Comics

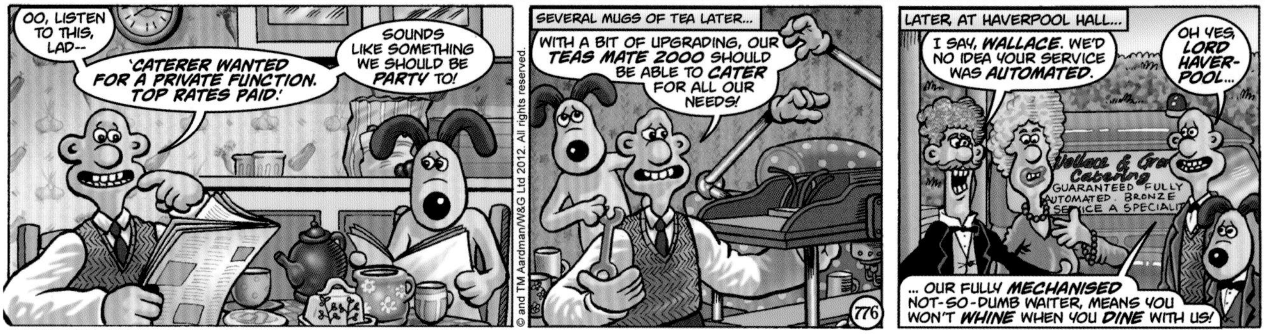

OO, LISTEN TO THIS, LAD--
'CATERER WANTED FOR A PRIVATE FUNCTION. TOP RATES PAID.'
SOUNDS LIKE SOMETHING WE SHOULD BE PARTY TO!
SEVERAL MUGS OF TEA LATER...
WITH A BIT OF UPGRADING, OUR TEAS MATE 2000 SHOULD BE ABLE TO CATER FOR ALL OUR NEEDS!
776
LATER, AT HAVERPOOL HALL...
I SAY, WALLACE. WE'D NO IDEA YOUR SERVICE WAS AUTOMATED.
OH YES, LORD HAVER-POOL...
... OUR FULLY MECHANISED NOT-SO-DUMB WAITER, MEANS YOU WON'T WHINE WHEN YOU DINE WITH US!

Wallace & Gromit - The Dinner Party
by Aardman & Titan Comics

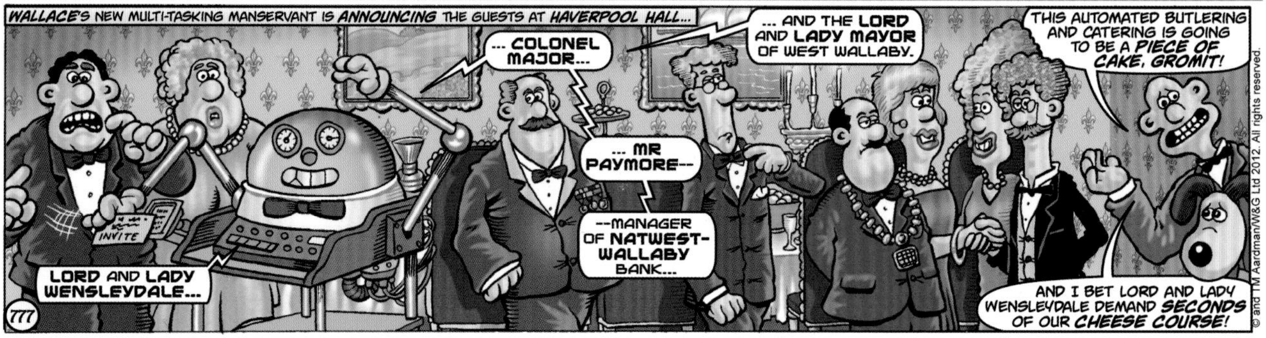

WALLACE'S NEW MULTI-TASKING MANSERVANT IS ANNOUNCING THE GUESTS AT HAVERPOOL HALL...
INVITE
LORD AND LADY WENSLEYDALE...
... COLONEL MAJOR...
... MR PAYMORE--
--MANAGER OF NATWEST-WALLABY BANK...
... AND THE LORD AND LADY MAYOR OF WEST WALLABY.
THIS AUTOMATED BUTLERING AND CATERING IS GOING TO BE A PIECE OF CAKE, GROMIT!
AND I BET LORD AND LADY WENSLEYDALE DEMAND SECONDS OF OUR CHEESE COURSE!
777

Wallace & Gromit - The Dinner Party
by Aardman & Titan Comics

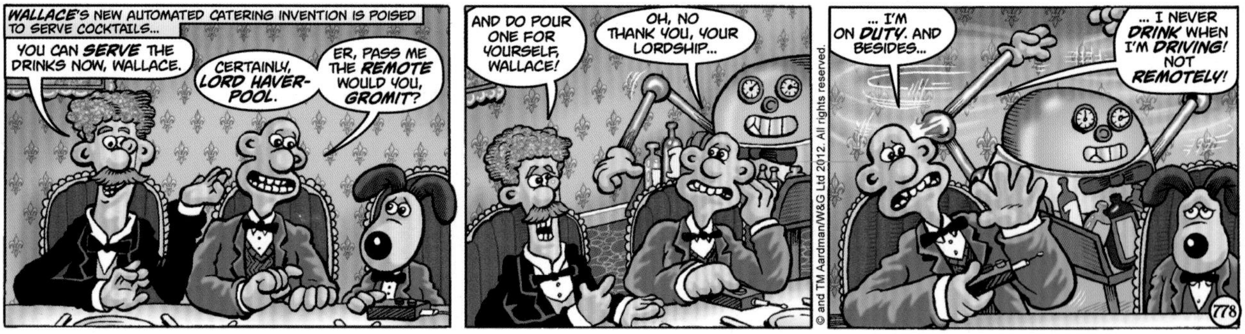

WALLACE'S NEW AUTOMATED CATERING INVENTION IS POISED TO SERVE COCKTAILS...
YOU CAN SERVE THE DRINKS NOW, WALLACE.
CERTAINLY, LORD HAVER-POOL.
ER, PASS ME THE REMOTE WOULD YOU, GROMIT?
AND DO POUR ONE FOR YOURSELF, WALLACE!
OH, NO THANK YOU, YOUR LORDSHIP...
... I'M ON DUTY. AND BESIDES...
... I NEVER DRINK WHEN I'M DRIVING! NOT REMOTELY!
778

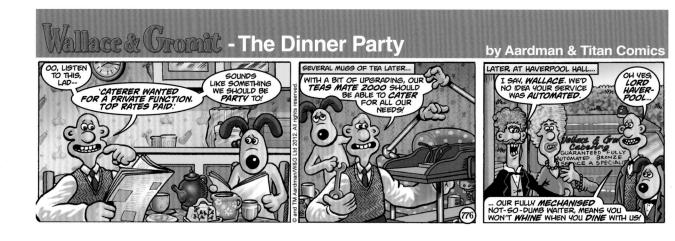

Wallace & Gromit - The Dinner Party by Aardman & Titan Comics

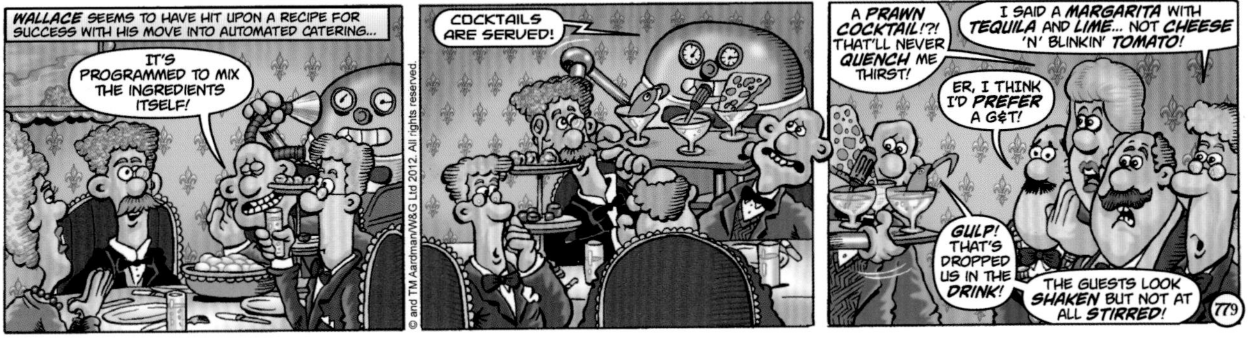
WALLACE SEEMS TO HAVE HIT UPON A RECIPE FOR SUCCESS WITH HIS MOVE INTO AUTOMATED CATERING...
IT'S PROGRAMMED TO MIX THE INGREDIENTS ITSELF!
COCKTAILS ARE SERVED!
A PRAWN COCKTAIL!?! THAT'LL NEVER QUENCH ME THIRST!
I SAID A MARGARITA WITH TEQUILA AND LIME... NOT CHEESE 'N' BLINKIN' TOMATO!
ER, I THINK I'D PREFER A G&T!
GULP! THAT'S DROPPED US IN THE DRINK!
THE GUESTS LOOK SHAKEN BUT NOT AT ALL STIRRED!
779

Wallace & Gromit - The Dinner Party by Aardman & Titan Comics

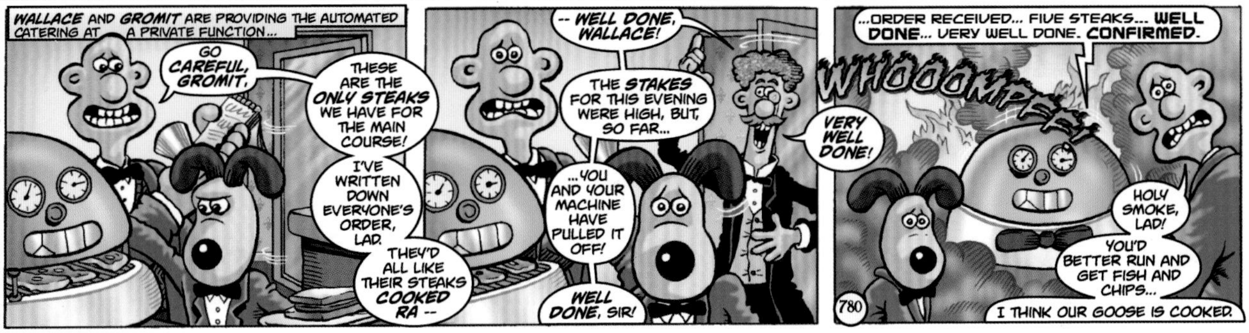
WALLACE AND GROMIT ARE PROVIDING THE AUTOMATED CATERING AT A PRIVATE FUNCTION...
GO CAREFUL, GROMIT,
THESE ARE THE ONLY STEAKS WE HAVE FOR THE MAIN COURSE!
I'VE WRITTEN DOWN EVERYONE'S ORDER, LAD.
THEY'D ALL LIKE THEIR STEAKS COOKED RA --
-- WELL DONE, WALLACE!
THE STAKES FOR THIS EVENING WERE HIGH, BUT, SO FAR...
...YOU AND YOUR MACHINE HAVE PULLED IT OFF!
VERY WELL DONE!
WELL DONE, SIR!
...ORDER RECEIVED... FIVE STEAKS... WELL DONE... VERY WELL DONE. CONFIRMED.
WHOOOOMPFF!
HOLY SMOKE, LAD!
YOU'D BETTER RUN AND GET FISH AND CHIPS...
780
I THINK OUR GOOSE IS COOKED.

Wallace & Gromit - The Dinner Party by Aardman & Titan Comics

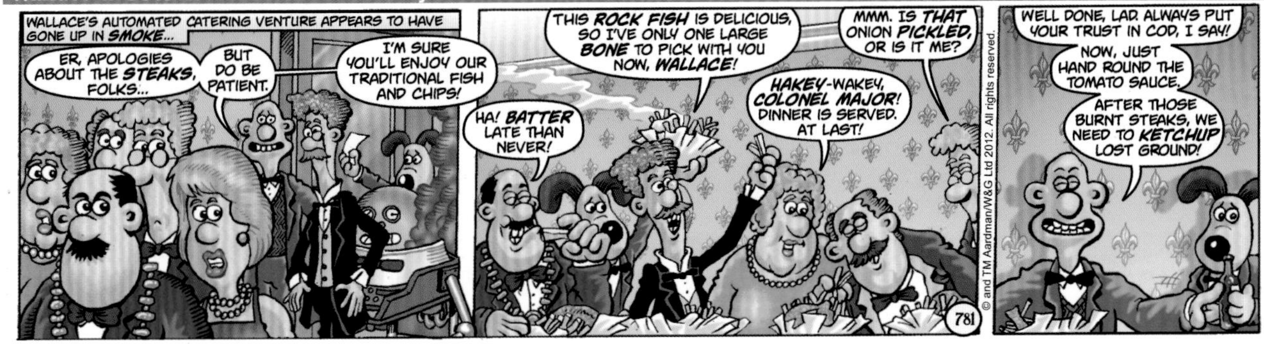
WALLACE'S AUTOMATED CATERING VENTURE APPEARS TO HAVE GONE UP IN SMOKE...
ER, APOLOGIES ABOUT THE STEAKS, FOLKS...
BUT DO BE PATIENT.
I'M SURE YOU'LL ENJOY OUR TRADITIONAL FISH AND CHIPS!
THIS ROCK FISH IS DELICIOUS, SO I'VE ONLY ONE LARGE BONE TO PICK WITH YOU NOW, WALLACE!
MMM. IS THAT ONION PICKLED, OR IS IT ME?
HA! BATTER LATE THAN NEVER!
HAKEY-WAKEY, COLONEL MAJOR! DINNER IS SERVED. AT LAST!
781
WELL DONE, LAD. ALWAYS PUT YOUR TRUST IN COD, I SAY!
NOW, JUST HAND ROUND THE TOMATO SAUCE.
AFTER THOSE BURNT STEAKS, WE NEED TO KETCHUP LOST GROUND!

Wallace & Gromit - The Dinner Party

by Aardman & Titan Comics

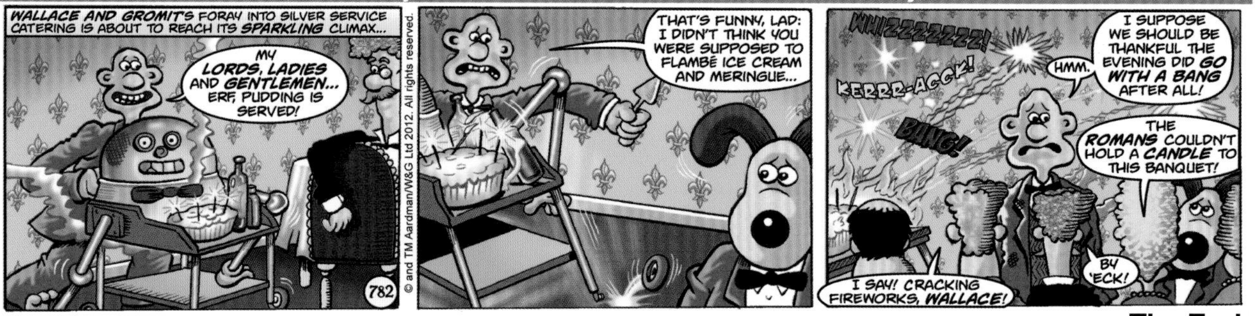
WALLACE AND GROMIT'S FORAY INTO SILVER SERVICE CATERING IS ABOUT TO REACH ITS SPARKLING CLIMAX...
MY LORDS, LADIES AND GENTLEMEN... ERF, PUDDING IS SERVED!
782
THAT'S FUNNY, LAD: I DIDN'T THINK YOU WERE SUPPOSED TO FLAMBÉ ICE CREAM AND MERINGUE...
WHIZZZZZZZZ!
KERRR-ACCK!
BANG!
HMM.
I SUPPOSE WE SHOULD BE THANKFUL THE EVENING DID GO WITH A BANG AFTER ALL!
THE ROMANS COULDN'T HOLD A CANDLE TO THIS BANQUET!
I SAY! CRACKING FIREWORKS, WALLACE!
BY 'ECK!

The End

Wallace & Gromit - Pane in the Glass

by Aardman & Titan Comics

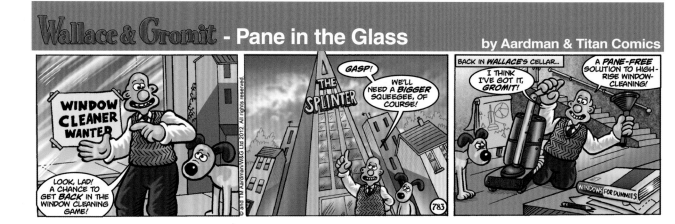

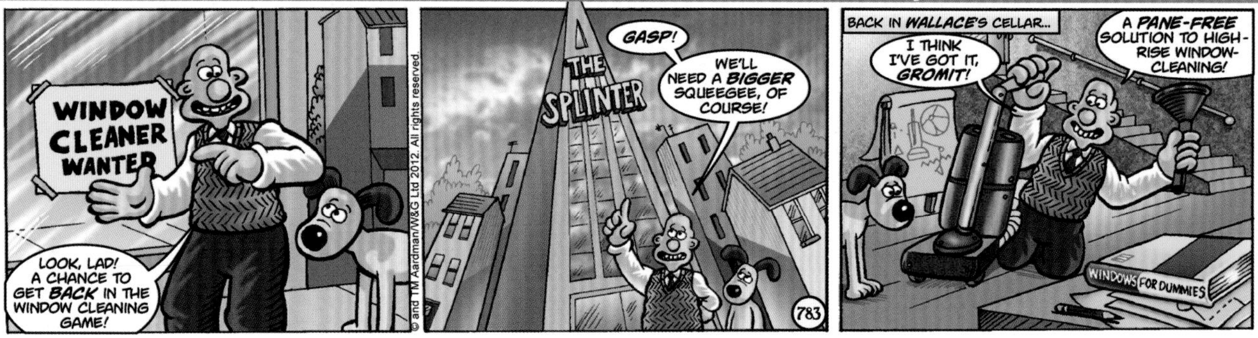
WINDOW CLEANER WANTED
LOOK, LAD! A CHANCE TO GET BACK IN THE WINDOW CLEANING GAME!
THE SPLINTER
GASP!
WE'LL NEED A BIGGER SQUEEGEE, OF COURSE!
783
BACK IN WALLACE'S CELLAR...
I THINK I'VE GOT IT, GROMIT!
A PANE-FREE SOLUTION TO HIGH-RISE WINDOW-CLEANING!
WINDOWS FOR DUMMIES

Wallace & Gromit - Pane in the Glass

by Aardman & Titan Comics

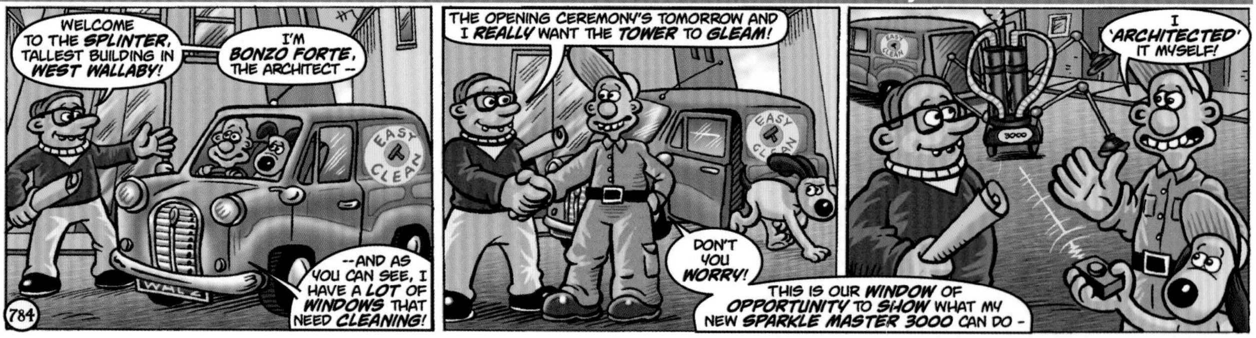
WELCOME TO THE SPLINTER, TALLEST BUILDING IN WEST WALLABY!
I'M BONZO FORTE, THE ARCHITECT --
EASY CLEAN
--AND AS YOU CAN SEE, I HAVE A LOT OF WINDOWS THAT NEED CLEANING!
784
THE OPENING CEREMONY'S TOMORROW AND I REALLY WANT THE TOWER TO GLEAM!
DON'T YOU WORRY!
THIS IS OUR WINDOW OF OPPORTUNITY TO SHOW WHAT MY NEW SPARKLE MASTER 3000 CAN DO -
I 'ARCHITECTED' IT MYSELF!
3000

Wallace & Gromit - Pane in the Glass   by Aardman & Titan Comics

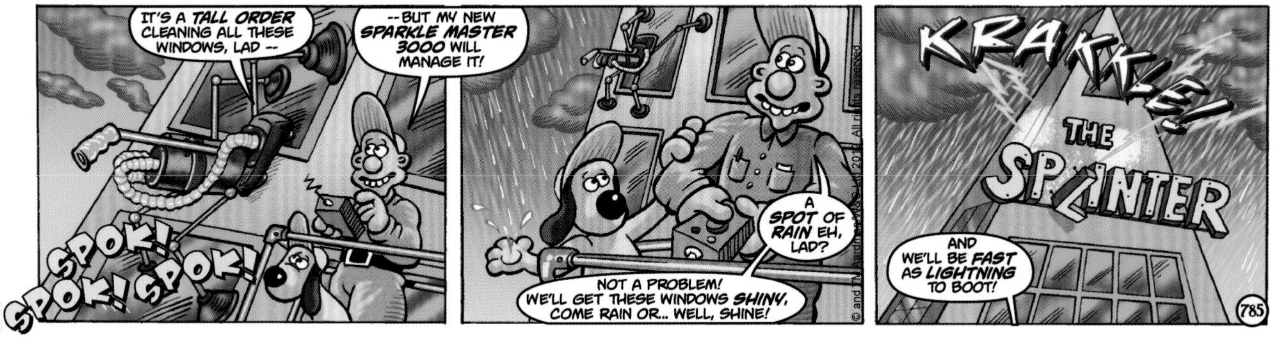

IT'S A TALL ORDER CLEANING ALL THESE WINDOWS, LAD --
--BUT MY NEW SPARKLE MASTER 3000 WILL MANAGE IT!
SPOK! SPOK! SPOK!
A SPOT OF RAIN EH, LAD?
NOT A PROBLEM! WE'LL GET THESE WINDOWS SHINY, COME RAIN OR.. WELL, SHINE!
KRAKKLE!
THE SPLINTER
AND WE'LL BE FAST AS LIGHTNING TO BOOT!
785

Wallace & Gromit - Pane in the Glass   by Aardman & Titan Comics

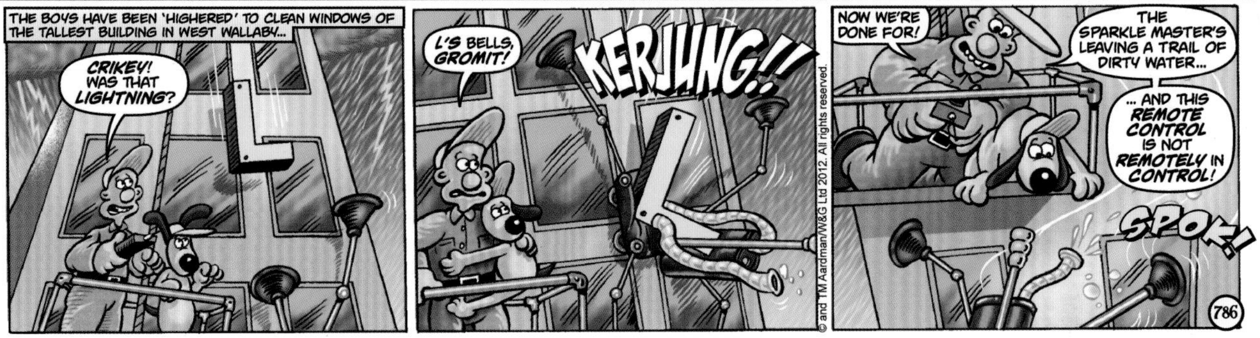

THE BOYS HAVE BEEN 'HIGHERED' TO CLEAN WINDOWS OF THE TALLEST BUILDING IN WEST WALLABY...
CRIKEY! WAS THAT LIGHTNING?
L'S BELLS, GROMIT!
KERJUNG!!
NOW WE'RE DONE FOR!
THE SPARKLE MASTER'S LEAVING A TRAIL OF DIRTY WATER...
... AND THIS REMOTE CONTROL IS NOT REMOTELY IN CONTROL!
SPOK!
786

Wallace & Gromit - Pane in the Glass   by Aardman & Titan Comics

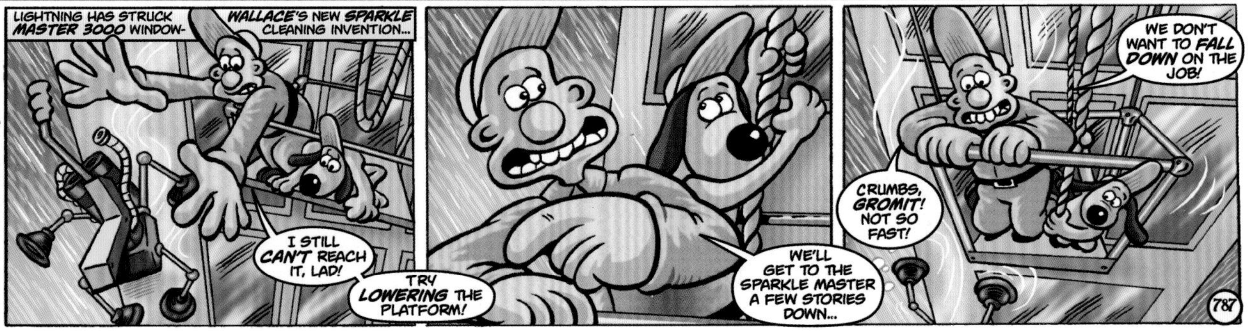

LIGHTNING HAS STRUCK WALLACE'S NEW SPARKLE MASTER 3000 WINDOW-CLEANING INVENTION...
I STILL CAN'T REACH IT, LAD!
TRY LOWERING THE PLATFORM!
WE'LL GET TO THE SPARKLE MASTER A FEW STORIES DOWN...
WE DON'T WANT TO FALL DOWN ON THE JOB!
CRUMBS, GROMIT! NOT SO FAST!
787

Wallace & Gromit - Pane in the Glass by Aardman & Titan Comics

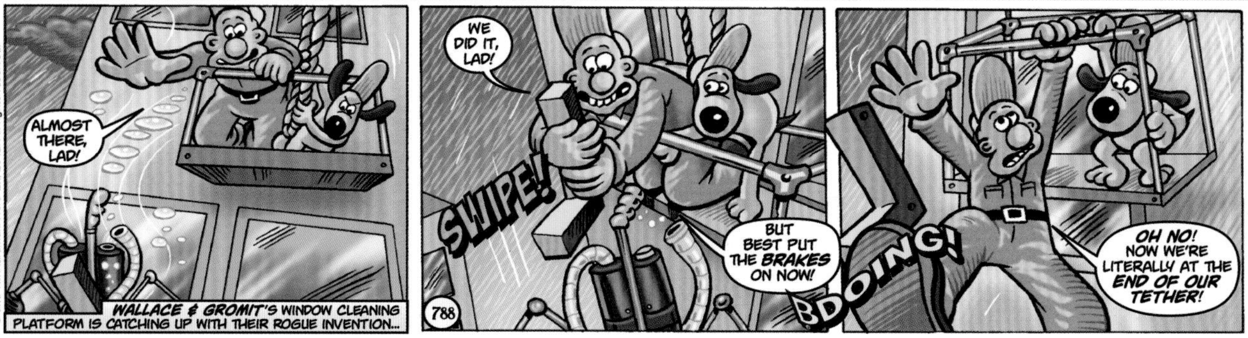
ALMOST THERE, LAD!
WALLACE & GROMIT'S WINDOW CLEANING PLATFORM IS CATCHING UP WITH THEIR ROGUE INVENTION...
WE DID IT, LAD!
SWIPE!
BUT BEST PUT THE BRAKES ON NOW!
788
BDOING!
OH NO! NOW WE'RE LITERALLY AT THE END OF OUR TETHER!

Wallace & Gromit - Pane in the Glass by Aardman & Titan Comics

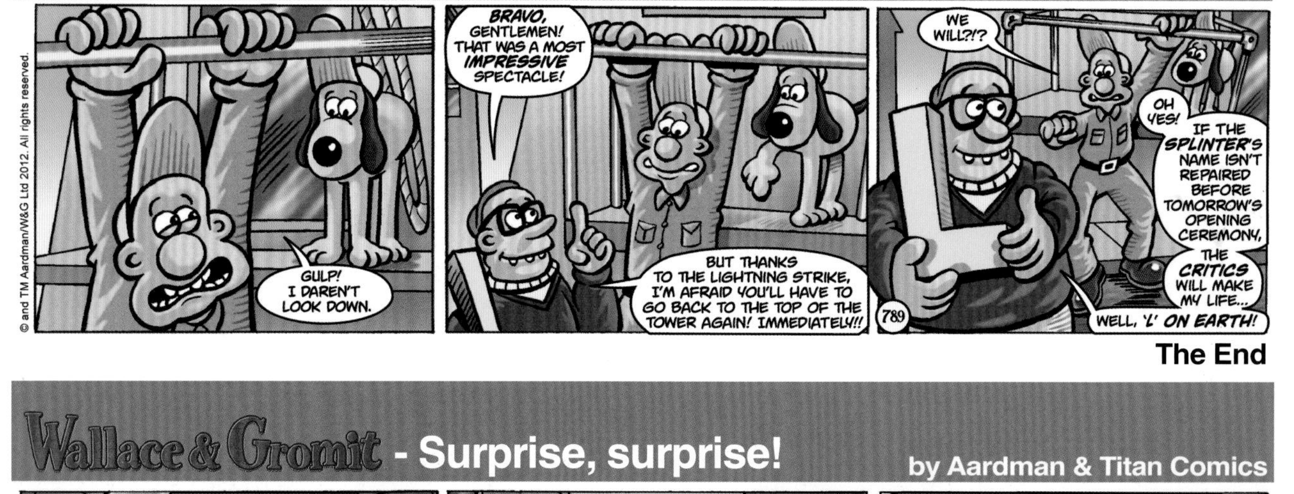
GULP! I DAREN'T LOOK DOWN.
BRAVO, GENTLEMEN! THAT WAS A MOST IMPRESSIVE SPECTACLE!
BUT THANKS TO THE LIGHTNING STRIKE, I'M AFRAID YOU'LL HAVE TO GO BACK TO THE TOP OF THE TOWER AGAIN! IMMEDIATELY!!!
WE WILL?!?
OH YES!
IF THE SPLINTER'S NAME ISN'T REPAIRED BEFORE TOMORROW'S OPENING CEREMONY, THE CRITICS WILL MAKE MY LIFE...
WELL, 'L' ON EARTH!
789

© and TM Aardman/W&G Ltd 2012. All rights reserved.

The End

Wallace & Gromit - Surprise, surprise!

by Aardman & Titan Comics

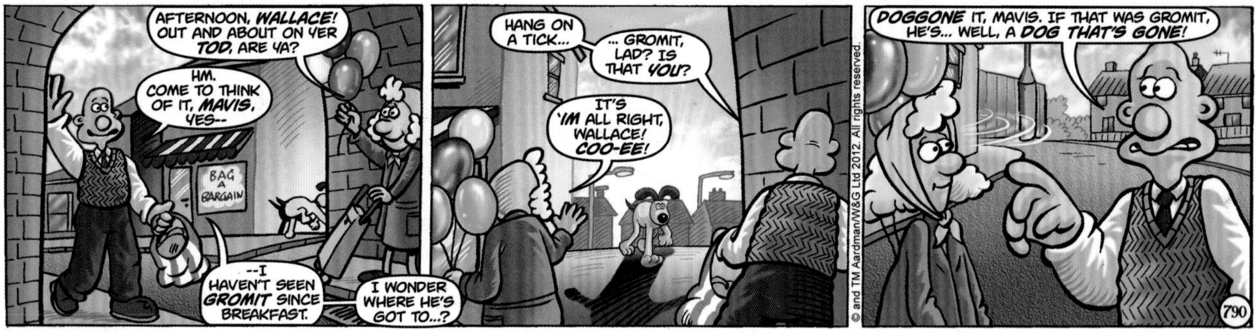
AFTERNOON, WALLACE! OUT AND ABOUT ON YER TOD, ARE YA?
HM. COME TO THINK OF IT, MAVIS, YES--
BAG A BARGAIN
--I HAVEN'T SEEN GROMIT SINCE BREAKFAST.
I WONDER WHERE HE'S GOT TO...?
HANG ON A TICK...
... GROMIT, LAD? IS THAT YOU?
IT'S 'IM ALL RIGHT, WALLACE! COO-EE!
DOGGONE IT, MAVIS. IF THAT WAS GROMIT, HE'S... WELL, A DOG THAT'S GONE!
790

© and TM Aardman/W&G Ltd 2012. All rights reserved.

Wallace & Gromit - Surprise, surprise! by Aardman & Titan Comics

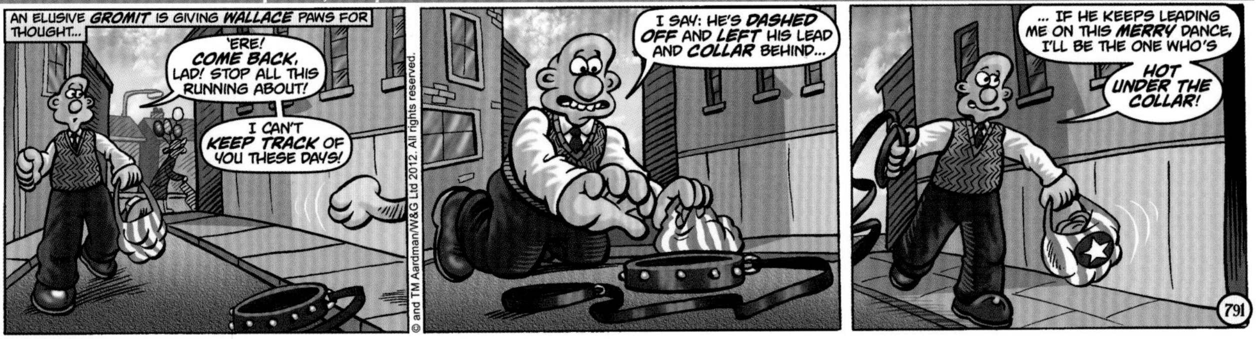

AN ELUSIVE GROMIT IS GIVING WALLACE PAWS FOR THOUGHT...
'ERE! COME BACK, LAD! STOP ALL THIS RUNNING ABOUT!
I CAN'T KEEP TRACK OF YOU THESE DAYS!
I SAY: HE'S DASHED OFF AND LEFT HIS LEAD AND COLLAR BEHIND...
... IF HE KEEPS LEADING ME ON THIS MERRY DANCE, I'LL BE THE ONE WHO'S HOT UNDER THE COLLAR!
791
© and TM Aardman/W&G Ltd 2012. All rights reserved.

Wallace & Gromit - Surprise, surprise! by Aardman & Titan Comics

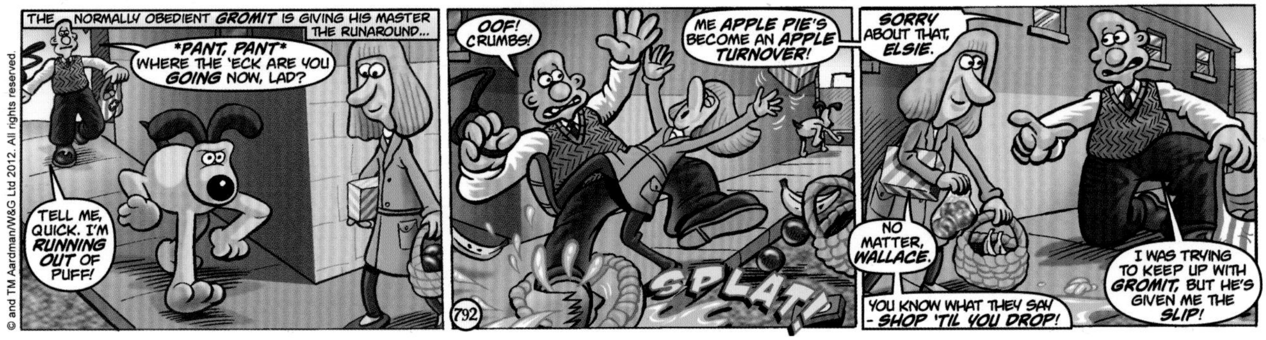

THE NORMALLY OBEDIENT GROMIT IS GIVING HIS MASTER THE RUNAROUND...
PANT, PANT WHERE THE 'ECK ARE YOU GOING NOW, LAD?
TELL ME, QUICK. I'M RUNNING OUT OF PUFF!
792
OOF! CRUMBS!
ME APPLE PIE'S BECOME AN APPLE TURNOVER!
SPLAT!
SORRY ABOUT THAT, ELSIE.
NO MATTER, WALLACE.
YOU KNOW WHAT THEY SAY - SHOP 'TIL YOU DROP!
I WAS TRYING TO KEEP UP WITH GROMIT, BUT HE'S GIVEN ME THE SLIP!
© and TM Aardman/W&G Ltd 2012. All rights reserved.

Wallace & Gromit - Surprise, surprise! by Aardman & Titan Comics

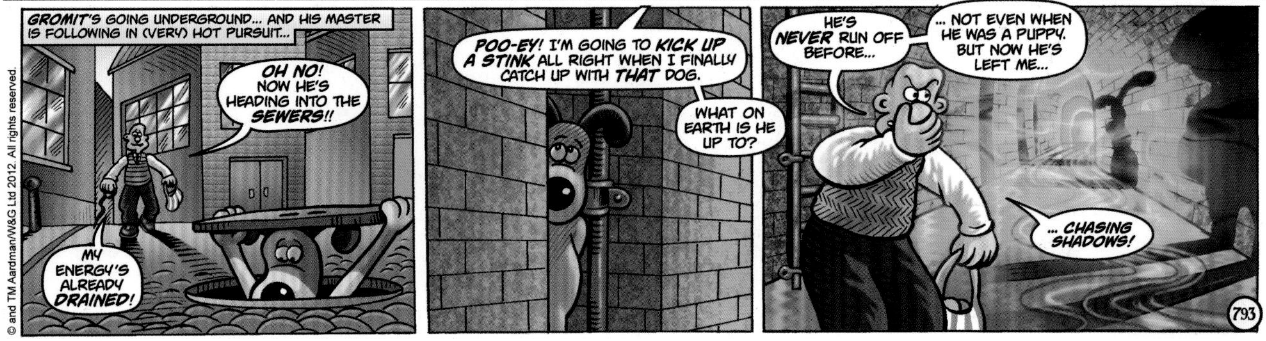

GROMIT'S GOING UNDERGROUND... AND HIS MASTER IS FOLLOWING IN (VERY) HOT PURSUIT...
OH NO! NOW HE'S HEADING INTO THE SEWERS!!
MY ENERGY'S ALREADY DRAINED!
POO-EY! I'M GOING TO KICK UP A STINK ALL RIGHT WHEN I FINALLY CATCH UP WITH THAT DOG.
WHAT ON EARTH IS HE UP TO?
HE'S NEVER RUN OFF BEFORE...
... NOT EVEN WHEN HE WAS A PUPPY. BUT NOW HE'S LEFT ME...
... CHASING SHADOWS!
793
© and TM Aardman/W&G Ltd 2012. All rights reserved.

Wallace & Gromit - Surprise, surprise! by Aardman & Titan Comics

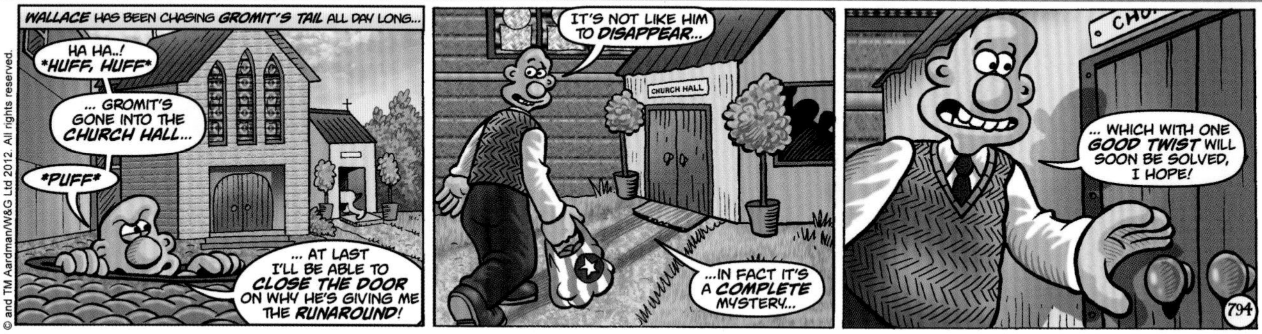
WALLACE HAS BEEN CHASING GROMIT'S TAIL ALL DAY LONG...
HA HA..! *HUFF, HUFF*
... GROMIT'S GONE INTO THE CHURCH HALL...
PUFF
... AT LAST I'LL BE ABLE TO CLOSE THE DOOR ON WHY HE'S GIVING ME THE RUNAROUND!
IT'S NOT LIKE HIM TO DISAPPEAR...
CHURCH HALL
...IN FACT IT'S A COMPLETE MYSTERY...
... WHICH WITH ONE GOOD TWIST WILL SOON BE SOLVED, I HOPE!
794

Wallace & Gromit - Surprise, surprise! by Aardman & Titan Comics

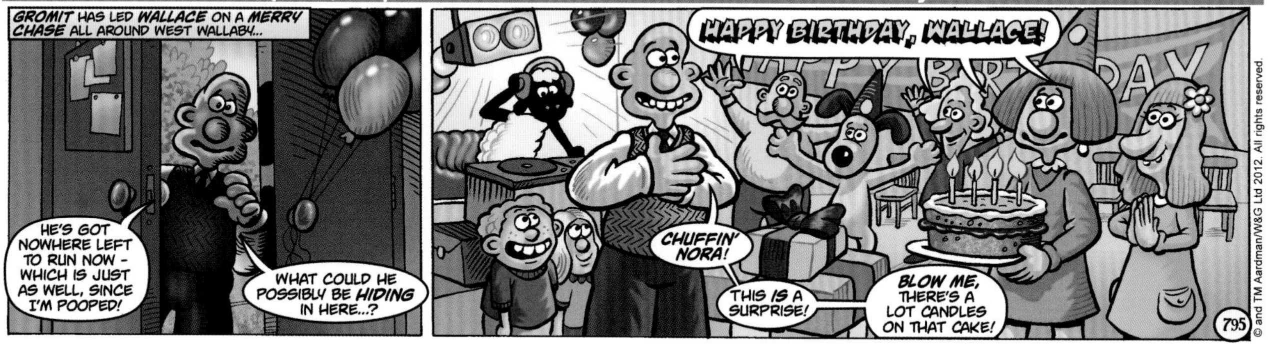
GROMIT HAS LED WALLACE ON A MERRY CHASE ALL AROUND WEST WALLABY...
HE'S GOT NOWHERE LEFT TO RUN NOW - WHICH IS JUST AS WELL, SINCE I'M POOPED!
WHAT COULD HE POSSIBLY BE HIDING IN HERE...?
HAPPY BIRTHDAY, WALLACE!
CHUFFIN' NORA!
THIS IS A SURPRISE!
BLOW ME, THERE'S A LOT CANDLES ON THAT CAKE!
795

Wallace & Gromit - Surprise, surprise! by Aardman & Titan Comics

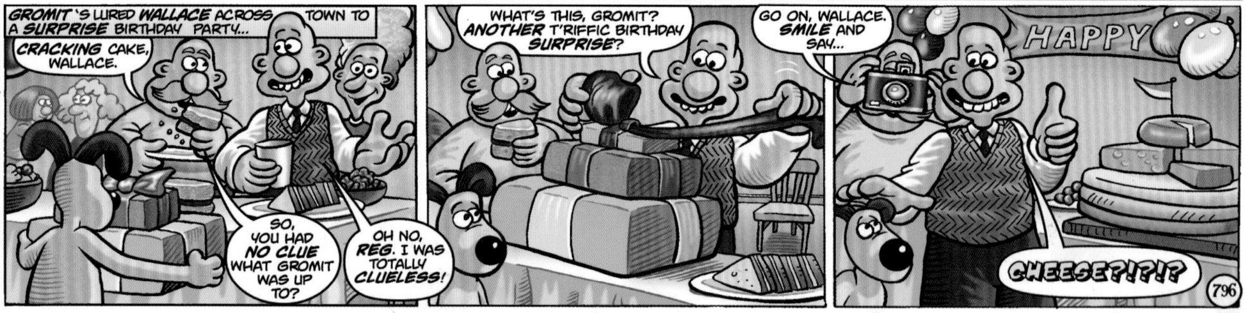
GROMIT 'S LURED WALLACE ACROSS TOWN TO A SURPRISE BIRTHDAY PARTY...
CRACKING CAKE, WALLACE.
SO, YOU HAD NO CLUE WHAT GROMIT WAS UP TO?
OH NO, REG. I WAS TOTALLY CLUELESS!
WHAT'S THIS, GROMIT? ANOTHER T'RIFFIC BIRTHDAY SURPRISE?
GO ON, WALLACE. SMILE AND SAY...
HAPPY
CHEESE?!?!?
796

The End

Wallace & Gromit - A Near Cat-astrophe

by Aardman & Titan Comics

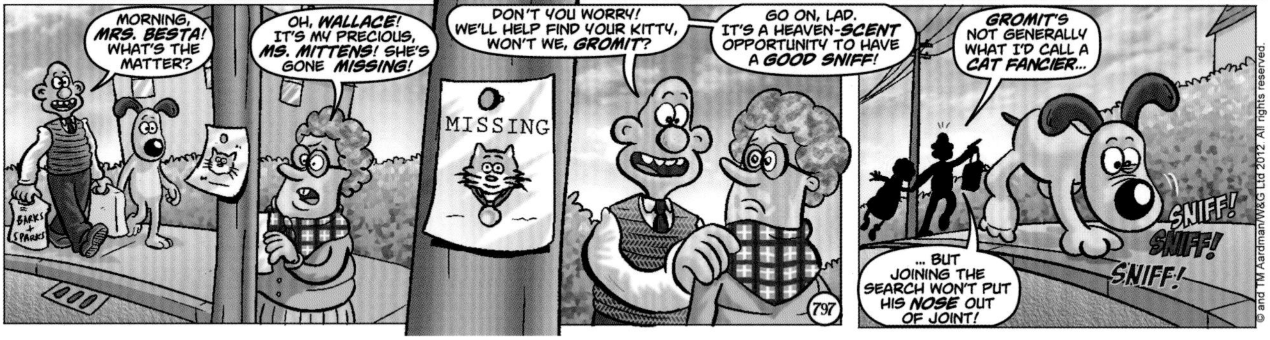
MORNING, MRS. BESTA! WHAT'S THE MATTER?
BARKS + SPARKS
OH, WALLACE! IT'S MY PRECIOUS, MS. MITTENS! SHE'S GONE MISSING!
MISSING
DON'T YOU WORRY! WE'LL HELP FIND YOUR KITTY, WON'T WE, GROMIT?
GO ON, LAD. IT'S A HEAVEN-SCENT OPPORTUNITY TO HAVE A GOOD SNIFF!
797
GROMIT'S NOT GENERALLY WHAT I'D CALL A CAT FANCIER...
... BUT JOINING THE SEARCH WON'T PUT HIS NOSE OUT OF JOINT!
SNIFF! SNIFF! SNIFF!

Wallace & Gromit - A Near Cat-astrophe!

by Aardman & Titan Comics

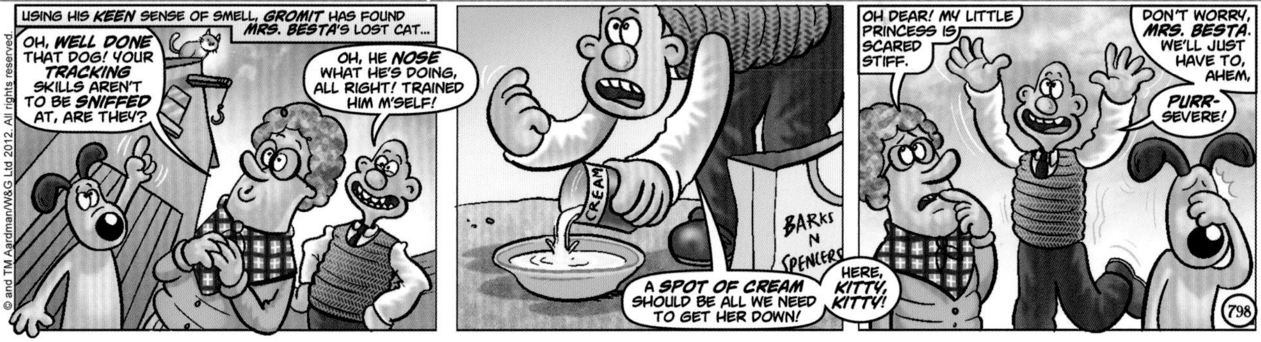
USING HIS KEEN SENSE OF SMELL, GROMIT HAS FOUND MRS. BESTA'S LOST CAT...
OH, WELL DONE THAT DOG! YOUR TRACKING SKILLS AREN'T TO BE SNIFFED AT, ARE THEY?
OH, HE NOSE WHAT HE'S DOING, ALL RIGHT! TRAINED HIM M'SELF!
CREAM
BARKS N SPENCERS
A SPOT OF CREAM SHOULD BE ALL WE NEED TO GET HER DOWN!
HERE, KITTY, KITTY!
OH DEAR! MY LITTLE PRINCESS IS SCARED STIFF.
DON'T WORRY, MRS. BESTA. WE'LL JUST HAVE TO, AHEM,
PURR-SEVERE!
798

Wallace & Gromit - A Near Cat-astrophe!

by Aardman & Titan Comics

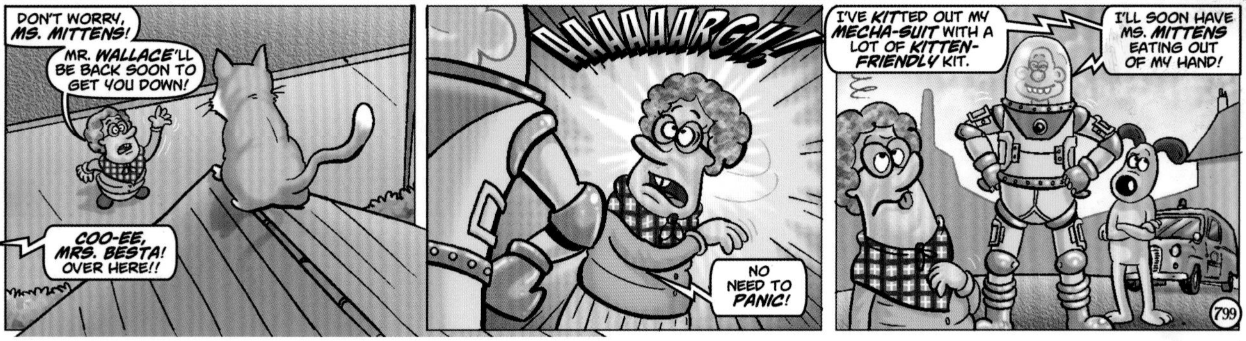
DON'T WORRY, MS. MITTENS!
MR. WALLACE'LL BE BACK SOON TO GET YOU DOWN!
COO-EE, MRS. BESTA! OVER HERE!!
AAAAAARGH!
NO NEED TO PANIC!
I'VE KITTED OUT MY MECHA-SUIT WITH A LOT OF KITTEN-FRIENDLY KIT.
I'LL SOON HAVE MS. MITTENS EATING OUT OF MY HAND!
799

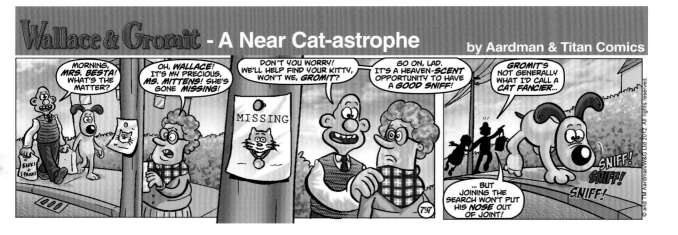

Wallace & Gromit - A Near Cat-astrophe! by Aardman & Titan Comics

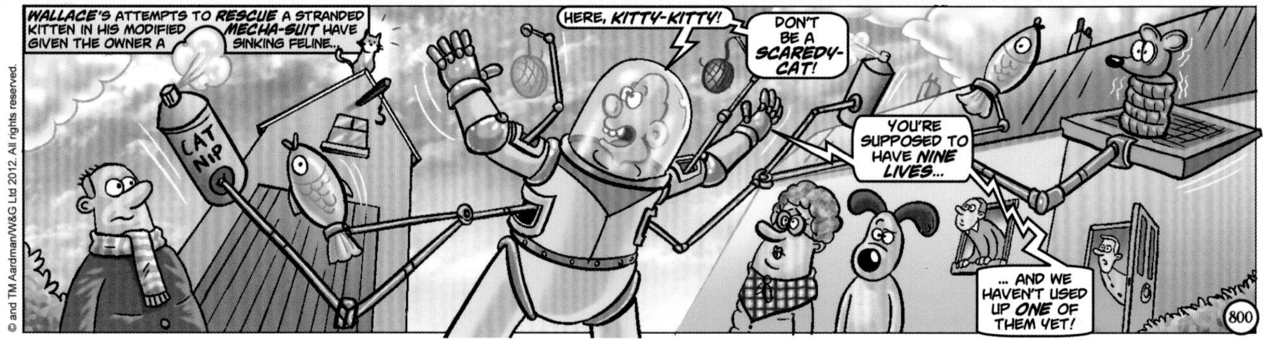

WALLACE'S ATTEMPTS TO RESCUE A STRANDED KITTEN IN HIS MODIFIED MECHA-SUIT HAVE GIVEN THE OWNER A SINKING FELINE...
CAT NIP
HERE, KITTY-KITTY!
DON'T BE A SCAREDY-CAT!
YOU'RE SUPPOSED TO HAVE NINE LIVES...
... AND WE HAVEN'T USED UP ONE OF THEM YET!
800

Wallace & Gromit - A Near Cat-astrophe! by Aardman & Titan Comics

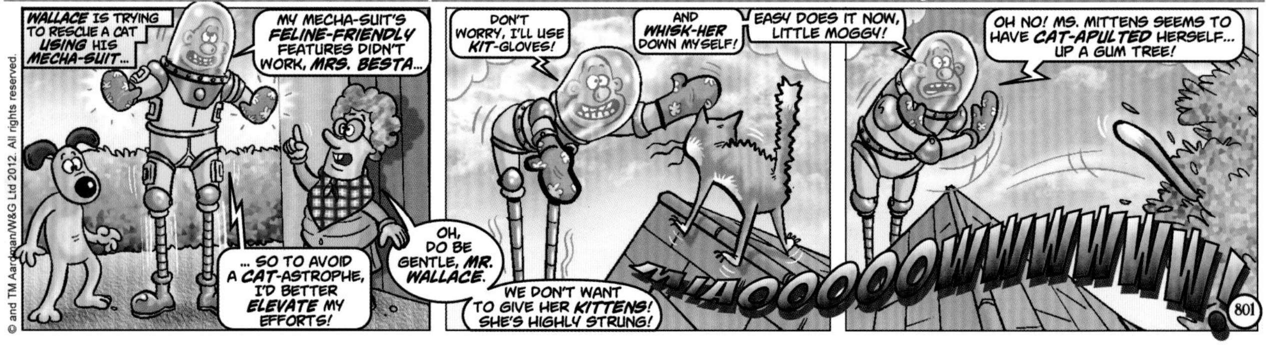

WALLACE IS TRYING TO RESCUE A CAT USING HIS MECHA-SUIT...
MY MECHA-SUIT'S FELINE-FRIENDLY FEATURES DIDN'T WORK, MRS. BESTA...
... SO TO AVOID A CAT-ASTROPHE, I'D BETTER ELEVATE MY EFFORTS!
OH, DO BE GENTLE, MR. WALLACE.
WE DON'T WANT TO GIVE HER KITTENS! SHE'S HIGHLY STRUNG!
DON'T WORRY, I'LL USE KIT-GLOVES!
AND WHISK-HER DOWN MYSELF!
EASY DOES IT NOW, LITTLE MOGGY!
MIAOOOOOOWWWWWWWW!
OH NO! MS. MITTENS SEEMS TO HAVE CAT-APULTED HERSELF... UP A GUM TREE!
801

Wallace & Gromit - A Near Cat-astrophe! by Aardman & Titan Comics

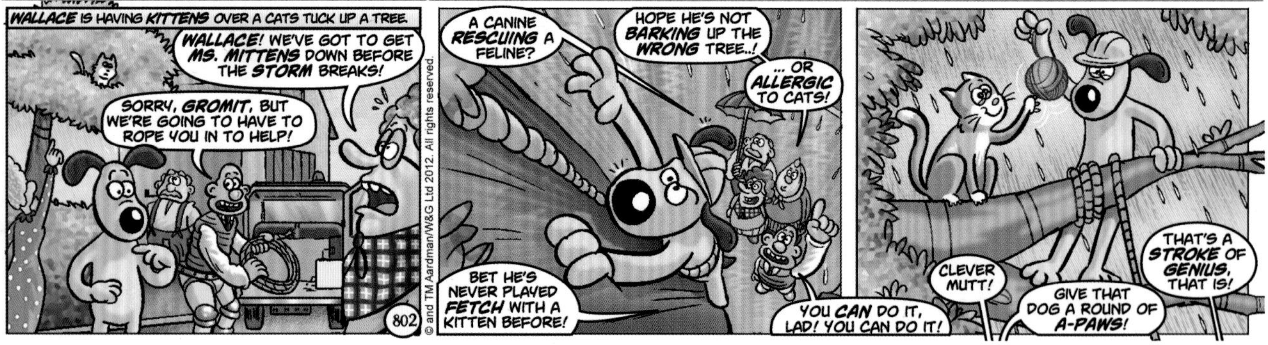

WALLACE IS HAVING KITTENS OVER A CATS TUCK UP A TREE.
WALLACE! WE'VE GOT TO GET MS. MITTENS DOWN BEFORE THE STORM BREAKS!
SORRY, GROMIT, BUT WE'RE GOING TO HAVE TO ROPE YOU IN TO HELP!
802
A CANINE RESCUING A FELINE?
HOPE HE'S NOT BARKING UP THE WRONG TREE..!
... OR ALLERGIC TO CATS!
BET HE'S NEVER PLAYED FETCH WITH A KITTEN BEFORE!
YOU CAN DO IT, LAD! YOU CAN DO IT!
CLEVER MUTT!
GIVE THAT DOG A ROUND OF A-PAWS!
THAT'S A STROKE OF GENIUS, THAT IS!

Wallace & Gromit - A Near Cat-astrophe!

by Aardman & Titan Comics

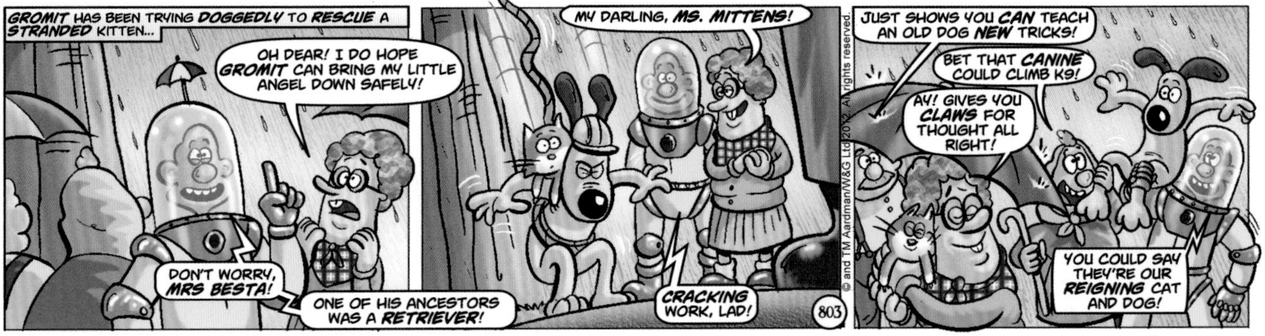

GROMIT HAS BEEN TRYING DOGGEDLY TO RESCUE A STRANDED KITTEN...
OH DEAR! I DO HOPE GROMIT CAN BRING MY LITTLE ANGEL DOWN SAFELY!
DON'T WORRY, MRS BESTA!
ONE OF HIS ANCESTORS WAS A RETRIEVER!
MY DARLING, MS. MITTENS!
CRACKING WORK, LAD!
803
JUST SHOWS YOU CAN TEACH AN OLD DOG NEW TRICKS!
BET THAT CANINE COULD CLIMB K9!
AY! GIVES YOU CLAWS FOR THOUGHT ALL RIGHT!
YOU COULD SAY THEY'RE OUR REIGNING CAT AND DOG!

The End

Wallace & Gromit - A Very British Coo!

by Aardman & Titan Comics

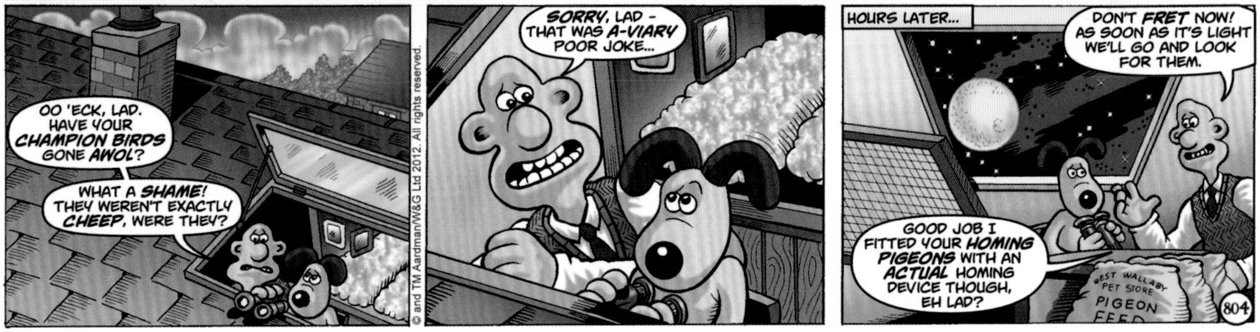

OO 'ECK, LAD. HAVE YOUR CHAMPION BIRDS GONE AWOL?
WHAT A SHAME! THEY WEREN'T EXACTLY CHEEP, WERE THEY?
SORRY, LAD - THAT WAS A-VIARY POOR JOKE...
HOURS LATER...
DON'T FRET NOW! AS SOON AS IT'S LIGHT WE'LL GO AND LOOK FOR THEM.
GOOD JOB I FITTED YOUR HOMING PIGEONS WITH AN ACTUAL HOMING DEVICE THOUGH, EH LAD?
WEST WALLABY PET STORE
PIGEON FEED
804

Wallace & Gromit - A Very British Coo!

by Aardman & Titan Comics

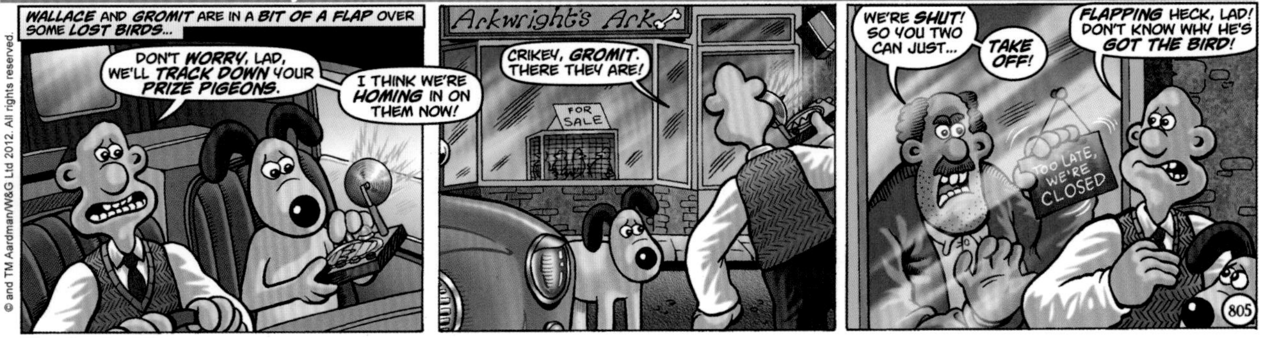

WALLACE AND GROMIT ARE IN A BIT OF A FLAP OVER SOME LOST BIRDS...
DON'T WORRY, LAD, WE'LL TRACK DOWN YOUR PRIZE PIGEONS.
I THINK WE'RE HOMING IN ON THEM NOW!
Arkwright's Ark
CRIKEY, GROMIT. THERE THEY ARE!
FOR SALE
WE'RE SHUT! SO YOU TWO CAN JUST...
TAKE OFF!
TOO LATE, WE'RE CLOSED
FLAPPING HECK, LAD! DON'T KNOW WHY HE'S GOT THE BIRD!
805

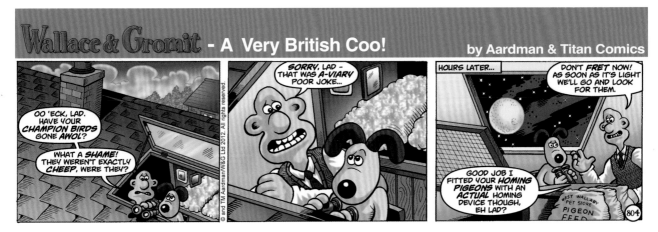

Wallace & Gromit - A Very British Coo! by Aardman & Titan Comics

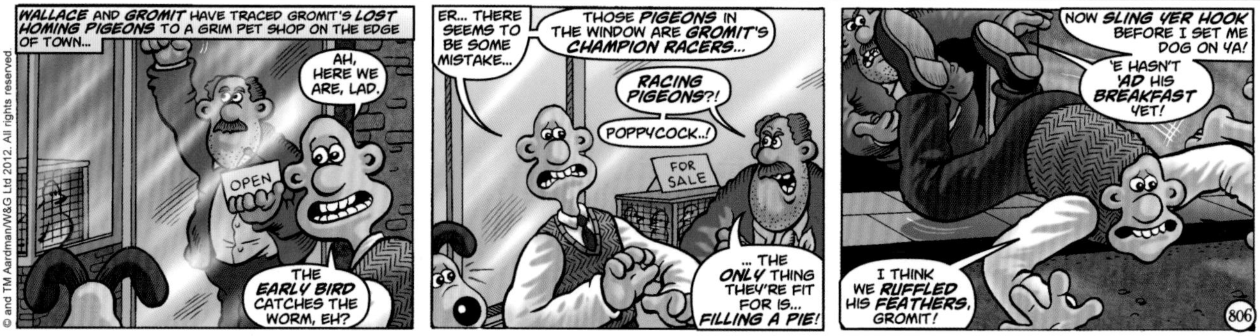
WALLACE AND GROMIT HAVE TRACED GROMIT'S LOST HOMING PIGEONS TO A GRIM PET SHOP ON THE EDGE OF TOWN...
AH, HERE WE ARE, LAD.
OPEN
THE EARLY BIRD CATCHES THE WORM, EH?
ER... THERE SEEMS TO BE SOME MISTAKE...
THOSE PIGEONS IN THE WINDOW ARE GROMIT'S CHAMPION RACERS...
RACING PIGEONS?!
POPPYCOCK..!
FOR SALE
... THE ONLY THING THEY'RE FIT FOR IS... FILLING A PIE!
NOW SLING YER HOOK BEFORE I SET ME DOG ON YA!
'E HASN'T 'AD HIS BREAKFAST YET!
I THINK WE RUFFLED HIS FEATHERS, GROMIT!
806

Wallace & Gromit - A Very British Coo! by Aardman & Titan Comics

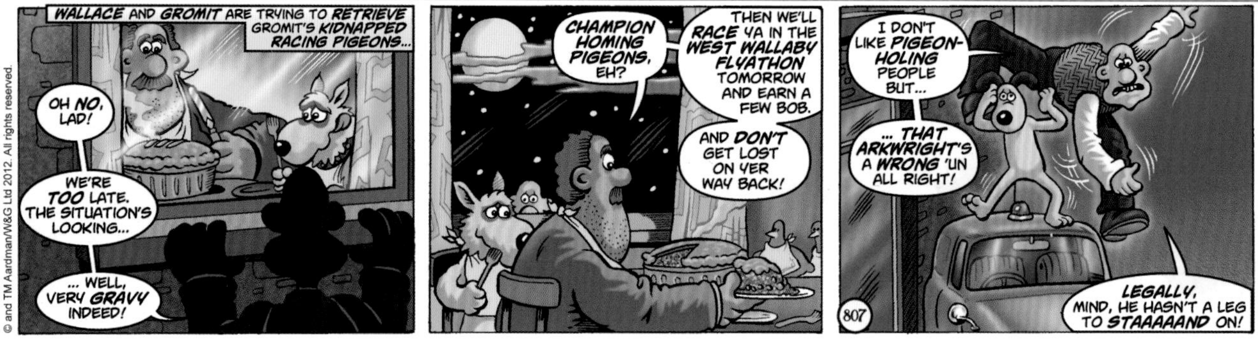
WALLACE AND GROMIT ARE TRYING TO RETRIEVE GROMIT'S KIDNAPPED RACING PIGEONS...
OH NO, LAD!
WE'RE TOO LATE. THE SITUATION'S LOOKING...
... WELL, VERY GRAVY INDEED!
CHAMPION HOMING PIGEONS, EH?
THEN WE'LL RACE YA IN THE WEST WALLABY FLYATHON TOMORROW AND EARN A FEW BOB.
AND DON'T GET LOST ON YER WAY BACK!
I DON'T LIKE PIGEON-HOLING PEOPLE BUT...
... THAT ARKWRIGHT'S A WRONG 'UN ALL RIGHT!
807
LEGALLY, MIND, HE HASN'T A LEG TO STAAAAAND ON!

Wallace & Gromit - A Very British Coo! by Aardman & Titan Comics

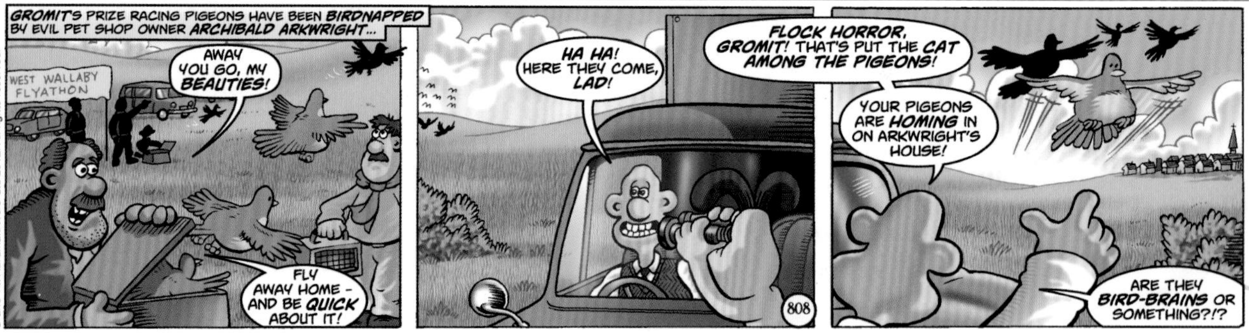
GROMIT'S PRIZE RACING PIGEONS HAVE BEEN BIRDNAPPED BY EVIL PET SHOP OWNER ARCHIBALD ARKWRIGHT...
WEST WALLABY FLYATHON
AWAY YOU GO, MY BEAUTIES!
FLY AWAY HOME - AND BE QUICK ABOUT IT!
HA HA! HERE THEY COME, LAD!
808
FLOCK HORROR, GROMIT! THAT'S PUT THE CAT AMONG THE PIGEONS!
YOUR PIGEONS ARE HOMING IN ON ARKWRIGHT'S HOUSE!
ARE THEY BIRD-BRAINS OR SOMETHING?!?

Wallace & Gromit - A Very British Coo! by Aardman & Titan Comics

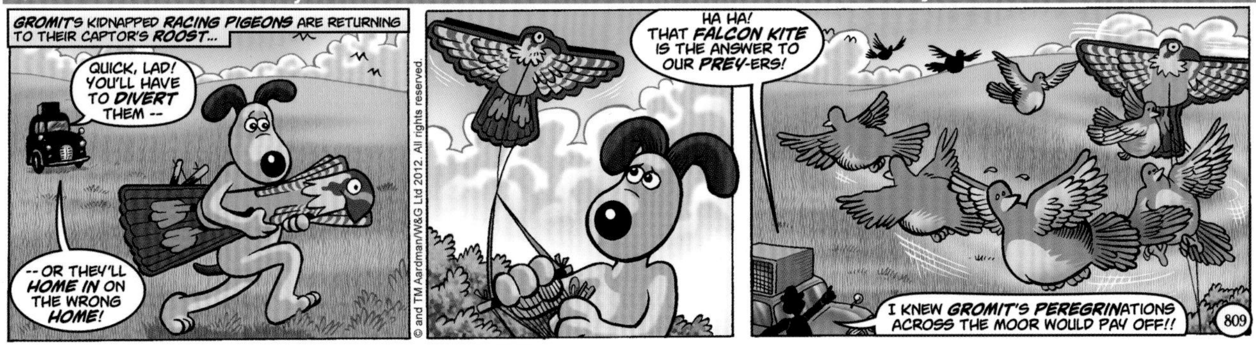

GROMIT'S KIDNAPPED RACING PIGEONS ARE RETURNING TO THEIR CAPTOR'S ROOST...
QUICK, LAD! YOU'LL HAVE TO DIVERT THEM --
-- OR THEY'LL HOME IN ON THE WRONG HOME!
© and TM Aardman/W&G 2012. All rights reserved.
HA HA! THAT FALCON KITE IS THE ANSWER TO OUR PREY-ERS!
I KNEW GROMIT'S PEREGRINATIONS ACROSS THE MOOR WOULD PAY OFF!!
809

Wallace & Gromit - A Very British Coo! by Aardman & Titan Comics

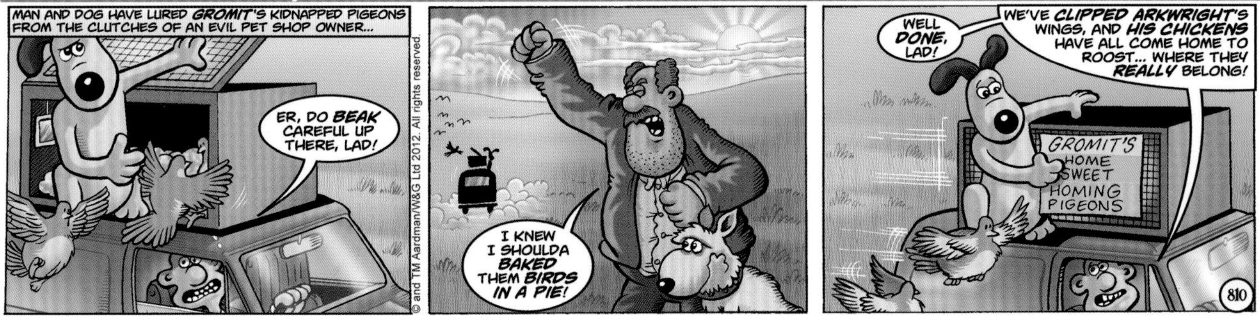

MAN AND DOG HAVE LURED GROMIT'S KIDNAPPED PIGEONS FROM THE CLUTCHES OF AN EVIL PET SHOP OWNER...
ER, DO BEAK CAREFUL UP THERE, LAD!
© and TM Aardman/W&G Ltd 2012. All rights reserved.
I KNEW I SHOULDA BAKED THEM BIRDS IN A PIE!
WELL DONE, LAD!
WE'VE CLIPPED ARKWRIGHT'S WINGS, AND HIS CHICKENS HAVE ALL COME HOME TO ROOST... WHERE THEY REALLY BELONG!
GROMIT'S HOME SWEET HOMING PIGEONS
810

The End

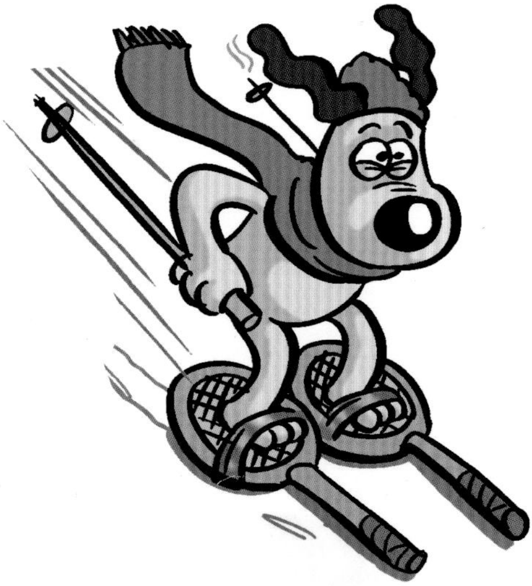

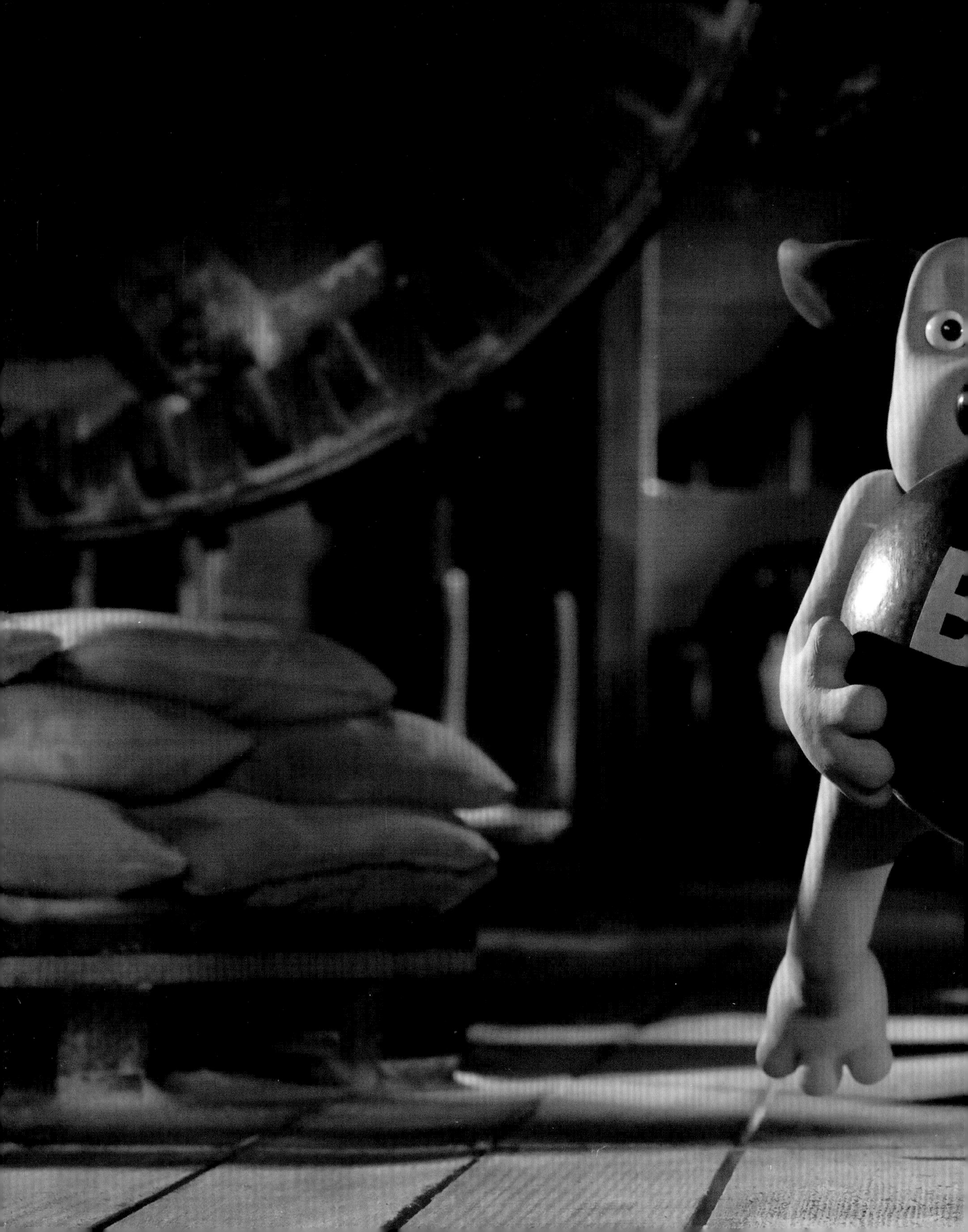

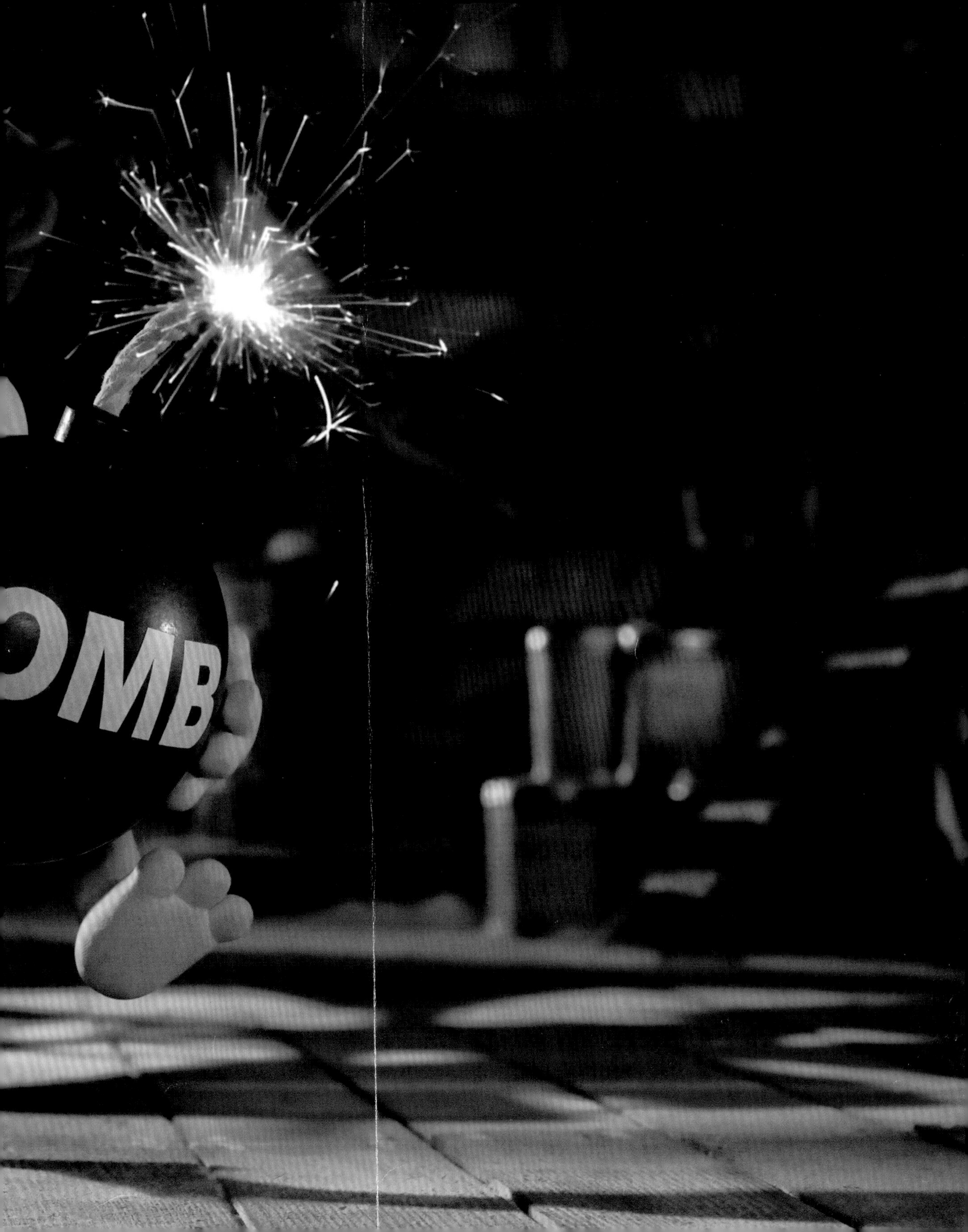
OMB

Wallace & Gromit - The Spider Who Came in from the Cold by Aardman & Titan Comics

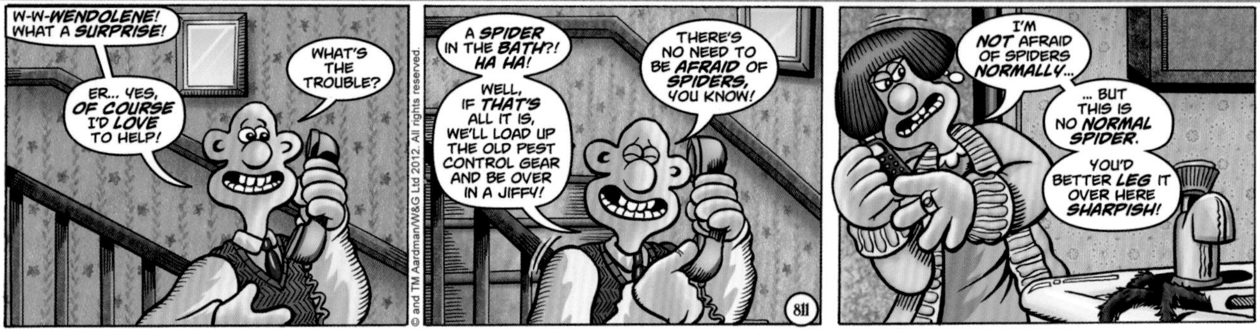

W-W-WENDOLENE! WHAT A SURPRISE!
ER... YES, OF COURSE I'D LOVE TO HELP!
WHAT'S THE TROUBLE?
A SPIDER IN THE BATH?! HA HA!
WELL, IF THAT'S ALL IT IS, WE'LL LOAD UP THE OLD PEST CONTROL GEAR AND BE OVER IN A JIFFY!
THERE'S NO NEED TO BE AFRAID OF SPIDERS, YOU KNOW!
I'M NOT AFRAID OF SPIDERS NORMALLY...
... BUT THIS IS NO NORMAL SPIDER.
YOU'D BETTER LEG IT OVER HERE SHARPISH!
811

Wallace & Gromit - The Spider Who Came in from the Cold by Aardman & Titan Comics

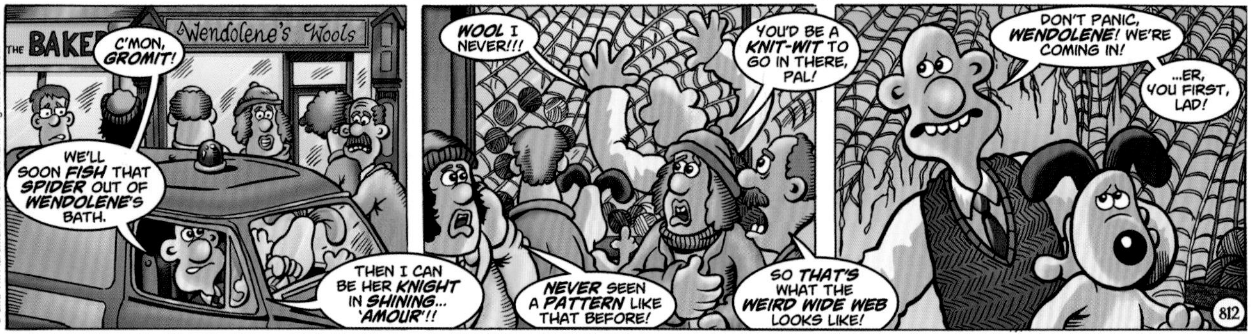

THE BAKER
Wendolene's Wools
C'MON, GROMIT!
WE'LL SOON FISH THAT SPIDER OUT OF WENDOLENE'S BATH.
THEN I CAN BE HER KNIGHT IN SHINING... 'AMOUR'!!
WOOL I NEVER!!!
YOU'D BE A KNIT-WIT TO GO IN THERE, PAL!
NEVER SEEN A PATTERN LIKE THAT BEFORE!
SO THAT'S WHAT THE WEIRD WIDE WEB LOOKS LIKE!
DON'T PANIC, WENDOLENE! WE'RE COMING IN!
...ER, YOU FIRST, LAD!
812

Wallace & Gromit - The Spider Who Came in from the Cold by Aardman & Titan Comics

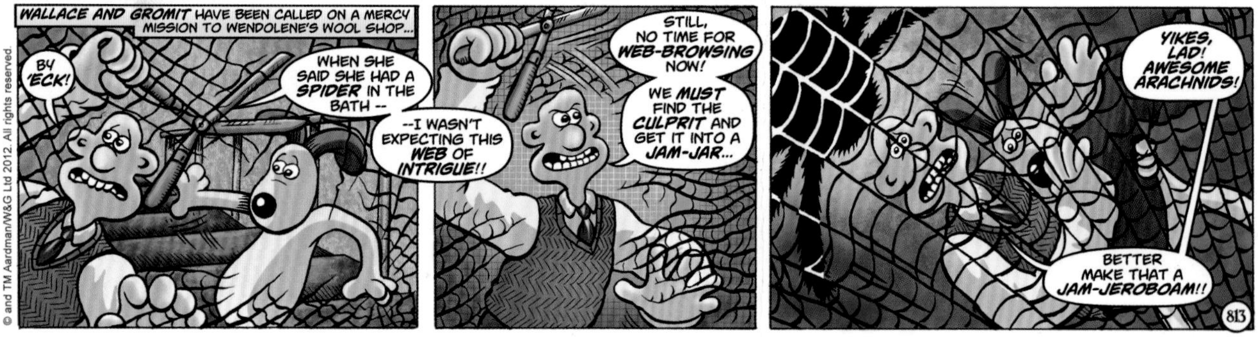

WALLACE AND GROMIT HAVE BEEN CALLED ON A MERCY MISSION TO WENDOLENE'S WOOL SHOP...
BY 'ECK!
WHEN SHE SAID SHE HAD A SPIDER IN THE BATH --
--I WASN'T EXPECTING THIS WEB OF INTRIGUE!!
STILL, NO TIME FOR WEB-BROWSING NOW!
WE MUST FIND THE CULPRIT AND GET IT INTO A JAM-JAR...
YIKES, LAD! AWESOME ARACHNIDS!
BETTER MAKE THAT A JAM-JEROBOAM!!
813

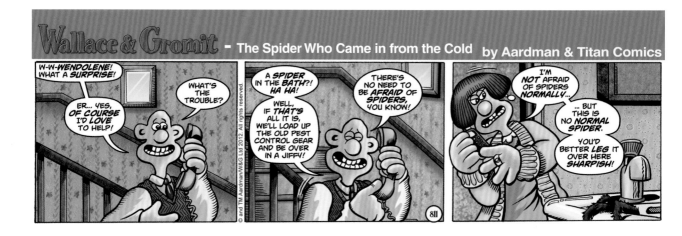

Wallace & Gromit - The Spider Who Came in from the Cold by Aardman & Titan Comics

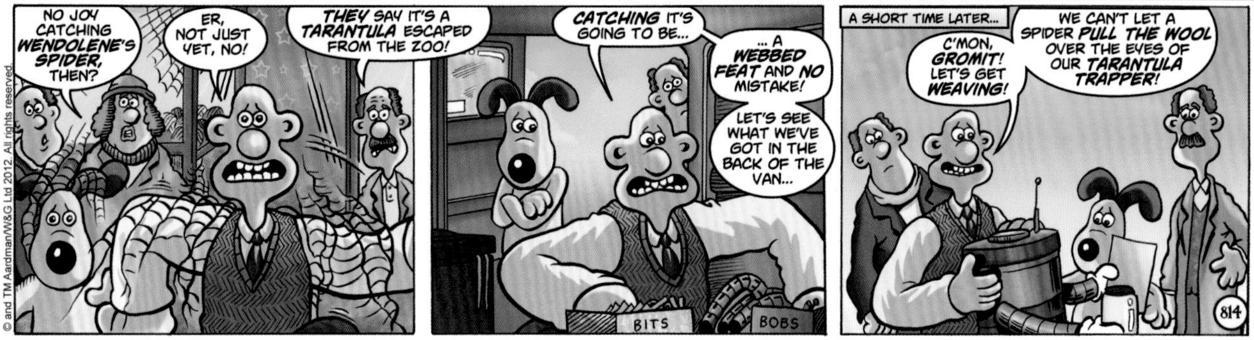

NO JOY CATCHING WENDOLENE'S SPIDER, THEN?
ER, NOT JUST YET, NO!
THEY SAY IT'S A TARANTULA ESCAPED FROM THE ZOO!
© and TM Aardman/W&G Ltd 2012. All rights reserved.
CATCHING IT'S GOING TO BE...
... A WEBBED FEAT AND NO MISTAKE!
LET'S SEE WHAT WE'VE GOT IN THE BACK OF THE VAN...
BITS
BOBS
A SHORT TIME LATER...
C'MON, GROMIT! LET'S GET WEAVING!
WE CAN'T LET A SPIDER PULL THE WOOL OVER THE EYES OF OUR TARANTULA TRAPPER!
814

Wallace & Gromit - The Spider Who Came in from the Cold by Aardman & Titan Comics

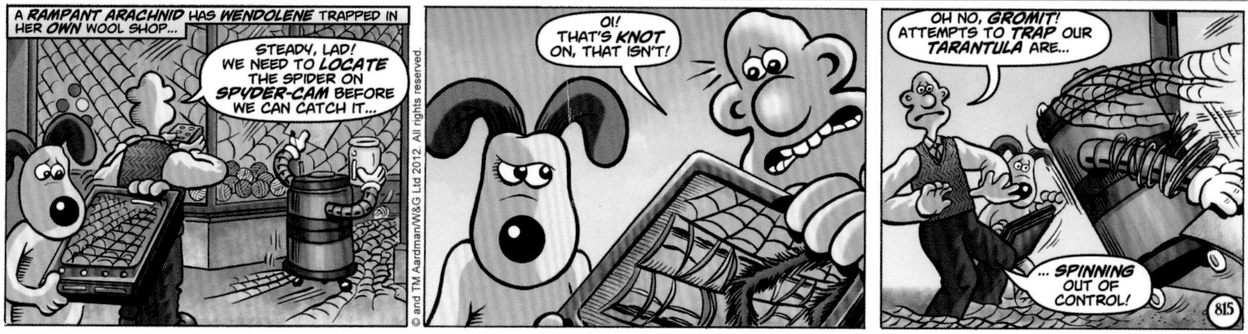

A RAMPANT ARACHNID HAS WENDOLENE TRAPPED IN HER OWN WOOL SHOP...
STEADY, LAD! WE NEED TO LOCATE THE SPIDER ON SPYDER-CAM BEFORE WE CAN CATCH IT...
© and TM Aardman/W&G Ltd 2012. All rights reserved.
OI! THAT'S KNOT ON, THAT ISN'T!
OH NO, GROMIT! ATTEMPTS TO TRAP OUR TARANTULA ARE...
... SPINNING OUT OF CONTROL!
815

Wallace & Gromit - The Spider Who Came in from the Cold by Aardman & Titan Comics

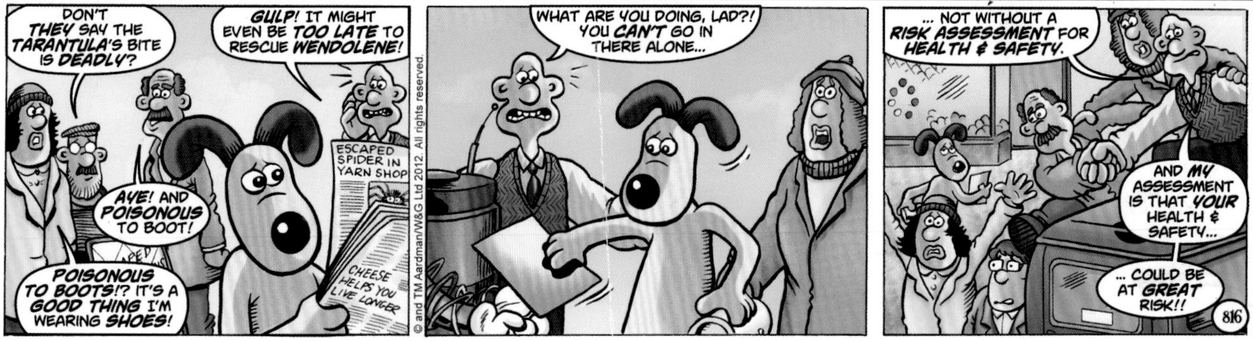

DON'T THEY SAY THE TARANTULA'S BITE IS DEADLY?
GULP! IT MIGHT EVEN BE TOO LATE TO RESCUE WENDOLENE!
ESCAPED SPIDER IN YARN SHOP
AYE! AND POISONOUS TO BOOT!
POISONOUS TO BOOTS!? IT'S A GOOD THING I'M WEARING SHOES!
CHEESE HELPS YOU LIVE LONGER
© and TM Aardman/W&G Ltd 2012. All rights reserved.
WHAT ARE YOU DOING, LAD?! YOU CAN'T GO IN THERE ALONE...
... NOT WITHOUT A RISK ASSESSMENT FOR HEALTH & SAFETY.
AND MY ASSESSMENT IS THAT YOUR HEALTH & SAFETY...
... COULD BE AT GREAT RISK!!
816

Wallace & Gromit - The Spider Who Came in from the Cold
by Aardman & Titan Comics

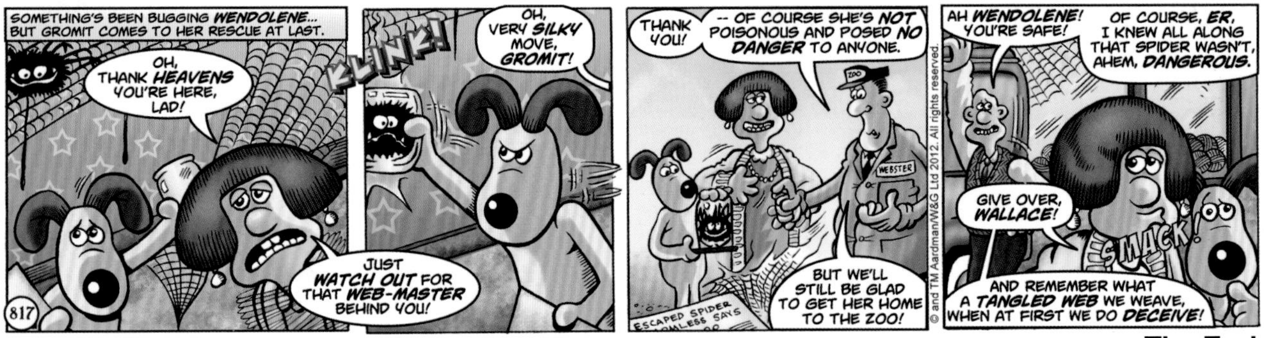
SOMETHING'S BEEN BUGGING WENDOLENE... BUT GROMIT COMES TO HER RESCUE AT LAST.
OH, THANK HEAVENS YOU'RE HERE, LAD!
JUST WATCH OUT FOR THAT WEB-MASTER BEHIND YOU!
817
KLINK!
OH, VERY SILKY MOVE, GROMIT!
THANK YOU!
-- OF COURSE SHE'S NOT POISONOUS AND POSED NO DANGER TO ANYONE.
BUT WE'LL STILL BE GLAD TO GET HER HOME TO THE ZOO!
ZOO
WEBSTER
ESCAPED SPIDER ...MLESS SAYS
AH WENDOLENE! YOU'RE SAFE!
OF COURSE, ER, I KNEW ALL ALONG THAT SPIDER WASN'T, AHEM, DANGEROUS.
GIVE OVER, WALLACE!
SMACK!
AND REMEMBER WHAT A TANGLED WEB WE WEAVE, WHEN AT FIRST WE DO DECEIVE!
© and TM Aardman/W&G Ltd 2012. All rights reserved.

The End

Wallace & Gromit - It's Snow Joke!
by Aardman & Titan Comics

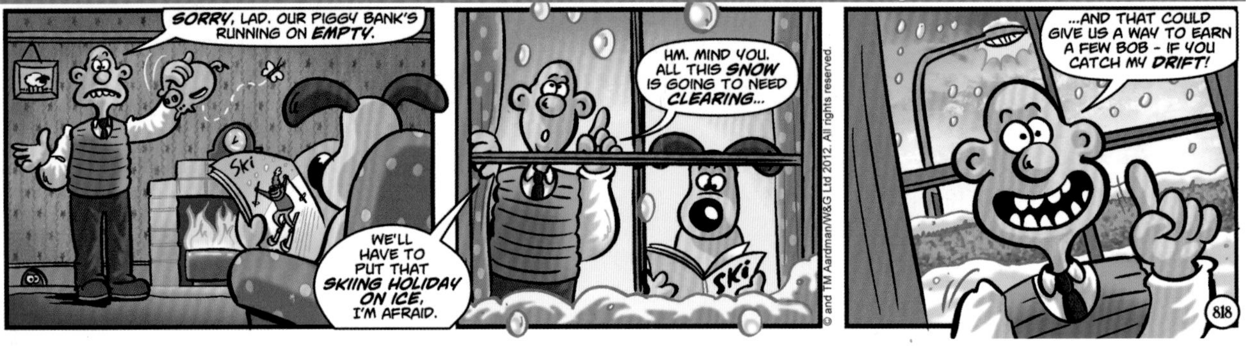
SORRY, LAD. OUR PIGGY BANK'S RUNNING ON EMPTY.
SKI
WE'LL HAVE TO PUT THAT SKIING HOLIDAY ON ICE, I'M AFRAID.
HM. MIND YOU. ALL THIS SNOW IS GOING TO NEED CLEARING...
SKI
...AND THAT COULD GIVE US A WAY TO EARN A FEW BOB - IF YOU CATCH MY DRIFT!
818
© and TM Aardman/W&G Ltd 2012. All rights reserved.

Wallace & Gromit - It's Snow Joke!
by Aardman & Titan Comics

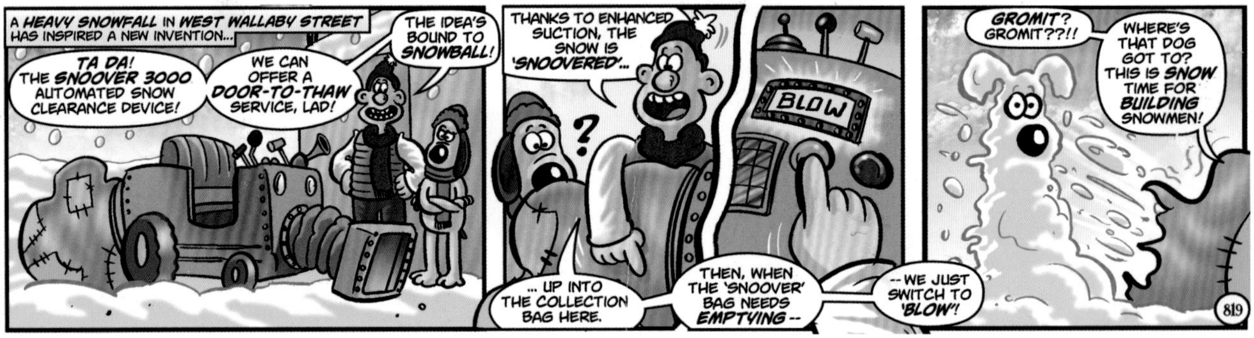
A HEAVY SNOWFALL IN WEST WALLABY STREET HAS INSPIRED A NEW INVENTION...
TA DA! THE SNOOVER 3000 AUTOMATED SNOW CLEARANCE DEVICE!
WE CAN OFFER A DOOR-TO-THAW SERVICE, LAD!
THE IDEA'S BOUND TO SNOWBALL!
THANKS TO ENHANCED SUCTION, THE SNOW IS 'SNOOVERED'...
?
... UP INTO THE COLLECTION BAG HERE.
BLOW
THEN, WHEN THE 'SNOOVER' BAG NEEDS EMPTYING --
-- WE JUST SWITCH TO 'BLOW'!
GROMIT? GROMIT??!!
WHERE'S THAT DOG GOT TO? THIS IS SNOW TIME FOR BUILDING SNOWMEN!
819

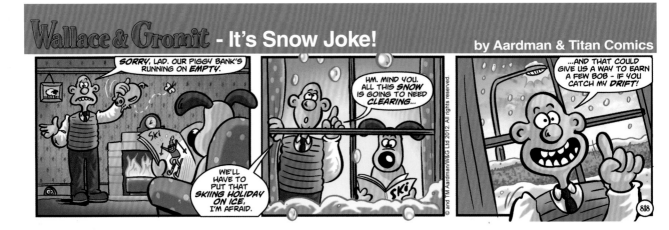

Wallace & Gromit - It's Snow Joke! by Aardman & Titan Comics

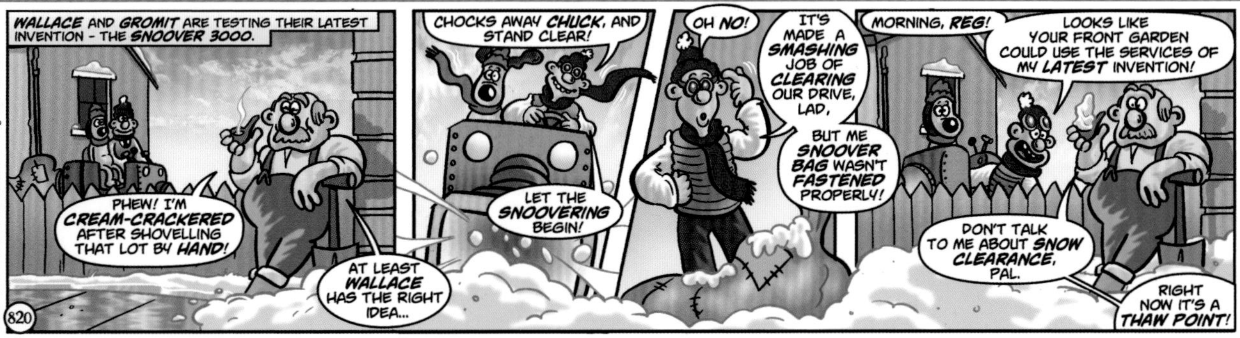
WALLACE AND GROMIT ARE TESTING THEIR LATEST INVENTION - THE SNOOVER 3000.
PHEW! I'M CREAM-CRACKERED AFTER SHOVELLING THAT LOT BY HAND!
AT LEAST WALLACE HAS THE RIGHT IDEA...
CHOCKS AWAY CHUCK, AND STAND CLEAR!
LET THE SNOOVERING BEGIN!
OH NO!
IT'S MADE A SMASHING JOB OF CLEARING OUR DRIVE, LAD,
BUT ME SNOOVER BAG WASN'T FASTENED PROPERLY!
MORNING, REG!
LOOKS LIKE YOUR FRONT GARDEN COULD USE THE SERVICES OF MY LATEST INVENTION!
DON'T TALK TO ME ABOUT SNOW CLEARANCE, PAL.
RIGHT NOW IT'S A THAW POINT!
820

Wallace & Gromit - It's Snow Joke! by Aardman & Titan Comics

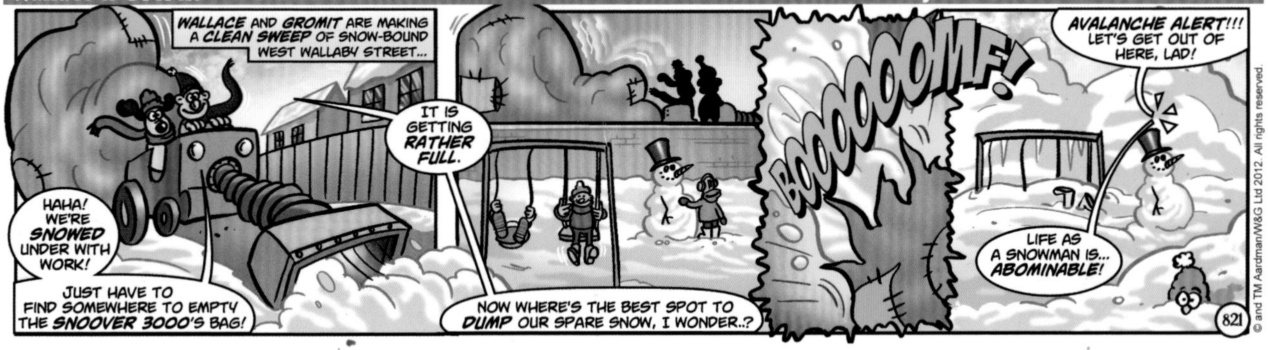
WALLACE AND GROMIT ARE MAKING A CLEAN SWEEP OF SNOW-BOUND WEST WALLABY STREET...
HAHA! WE'RE SNOWED UNDER WITH WORK!
JUST HAVE TO FIND SOMEWHERE TO EMPTY THE SNOOVER 3000's BAG!
IT IS GETTING RATHER FULL.
NOW WHERE'S THE BEST SPOT TO DUMP OUR SPARE SNOW, I WONDER..?
BOOOOOOOMF!
AVALANCHE ALERT!!! LET'S GET OUT OF HERE, LAD!
LIFE AS A SNOWMAN IS... ABOMINABLE!
821

Wallace & Gromit - It's Snow Joke! by Aardman & Titan Comics

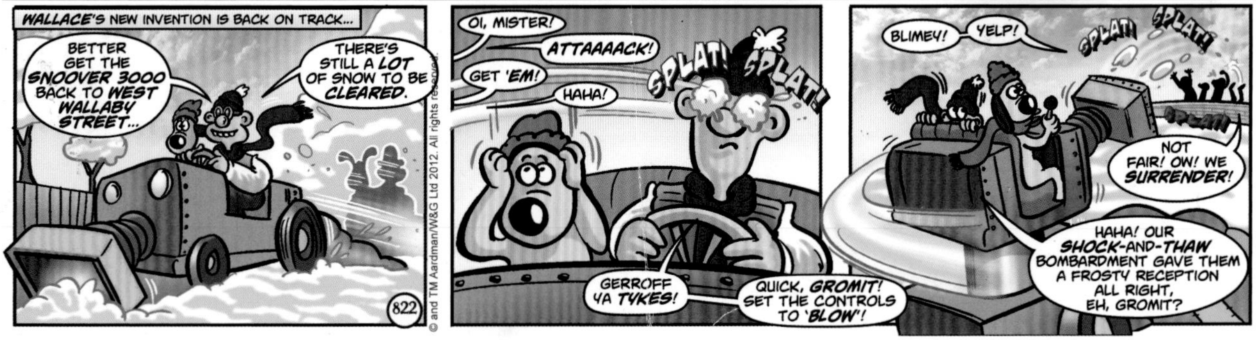
WALLACE'S NEW INVENTION IS BACK ON TRACK...
BETTER GET THE SNOOVER 3000 BACK TO WEST WALLABY STREET...
THERE'S STILL A LOT OF SNOW TO BE CLEARED.
822
OI, MISTER!
ATTAAAACK!
GET 'EM!
HAHA!
SPLAT! SPLAT!
GERROFF YA TYKES!
QUICK, GROMIT! SET THE CONTROLS TO 'BLOW'!
BLIMEY!
YELP!
SPLAT! SPLAT!
NOT FAIR! OW! WE SURRENDER!
HAHA! OUR SHOCK-AND-THAW BOMBARDMENT GAVE THEM A FROSTY RECEPTION ALL RIGHT, EH, GROMIT?

Wallace & Gromit - It's Snow Joke!

by Aardman & Titan Comics

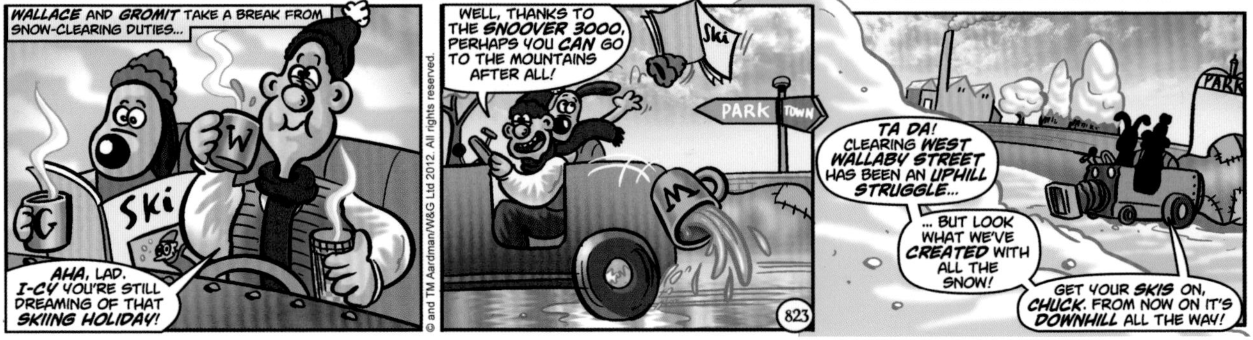

WALLACE AND GROMIT TAKE A BREAK FROM SNOW-CLEARING DUTIES...
AHA, LAD. I-CY YOU'RE STILL DREAMING OF THAT SKIING HOLIDAY!
SKI
WELL, THANKS TO THE SNOOVER 3000, PERHAPS YOU CAN GO TO THE MOUNTAINS AFTER ALL!
PARK
TOWN
TA DA! CLEARING WEST WALLABY STREET HAS BEEN AN UPHILL STRUGGLE...
... BUT LOOK WHAT WE'VE CREATED WITH ALL THE SNOW!
GET YOUR SKIS ON, CHUCK. FROM NOW ON IT'S DOWNHILL ALL THE WAY!
823

Wallace & Gromit - It's Snow Joke!

by Aardman & Titan Comics

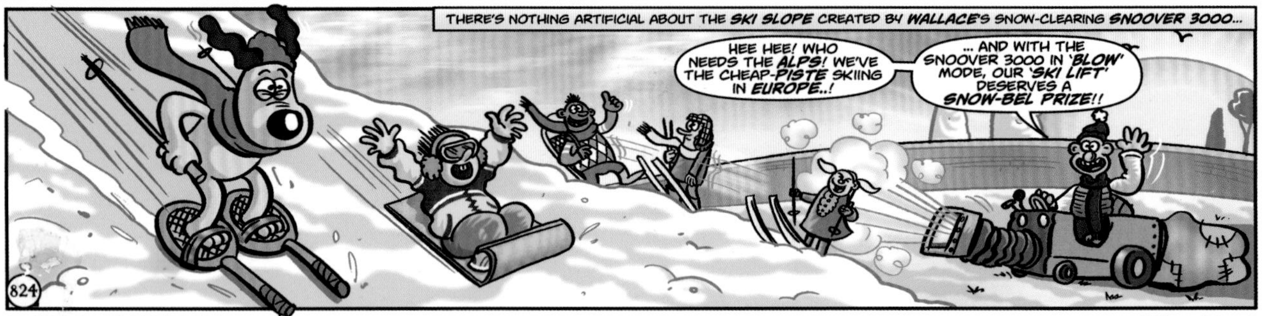

THERE'S NOTHING ARTIFICIAL ABOUT THE SKI SLOPE CREATED BY WALLACE'S SNOW-CLEARING SNOOVER 3000...
HEE HEE! WHO NEEDS THE ALPS! WE'VE THE CHEAP-PISTE SKIING IN EUROPE..!
... AND WITH THE SNOOVER 3000 IN 'BLOW' MODE, OUR 'SKI LIFT' DESERVES A SNOW-BEL PRIZE!!
824

The End

Wallace & Gromit - Cream Crackered!

by Aardman & Titan Comics

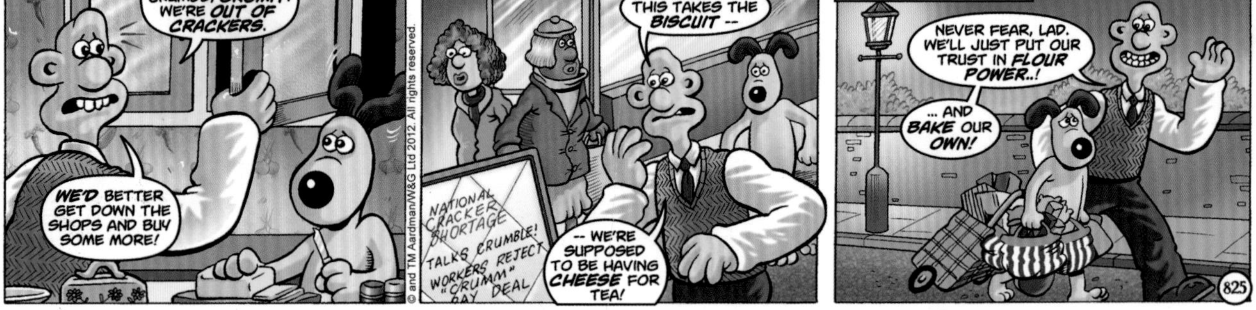

CRUMBS, GROMIT! WE'RE OUT OF CRACKERS.
WE'D BETTER GET DOWN THE SHOPS AND BUY SOME MORE!
OH, NO! THIS TAKES THE BISCUIT --
NATIONAL CRACKER SHORTAGE
TALKS CRUMBLE! WORKERS REJECT "CRUMM" PAY DEAL
-- WE'RE SUPPOSED TO BE HAVING CHEESE FOR TEA!
ONE PANIC-BUY LATER...
NEVER FEAR, LAD. WE'LL JUST PUT OUR TRUST IN FLOUR POWER..!
... AND BAKE OUR OWN!
825

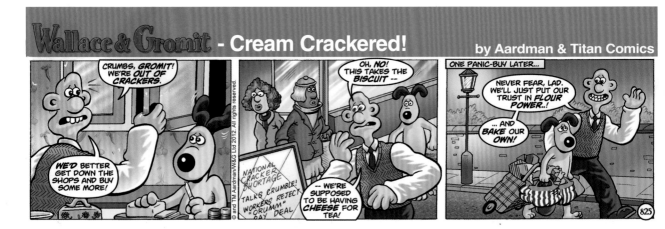

Wallace & Gromit - Cream Crackered! by Aardman & Titan Comics

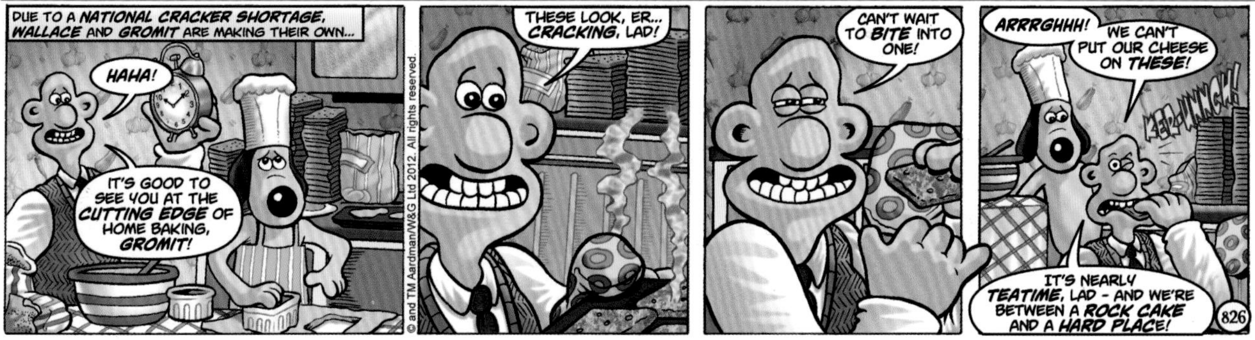

DUE TO A NATIONAL CRACKER SHORTAGE, WALLACE AND GROMIT ARE MAKING THEIR OWN...
HAHA!
IT'S GOOD TO SEE YOU AT THE CUTTING EDGE OF HOME BAKING, GROMIT!
THESE LOOK, ER... CRACKING, LAD!
CAN'T WAIT TO BITE INTO ONE!
ARRRGHHH!
WE CAN'T PUT OUR CHEESE ON THESE!
IT'S NEARLY TEATIME, LAD - AND WE'RE BETWEEN A ROCK CAKE AND A HARD PLACE!
826
© and TM Aardman/W&G Ltd 2012. All rights reserved.

Wallace & Gromit - Cream Crackered! by Aardman & Titan Comics

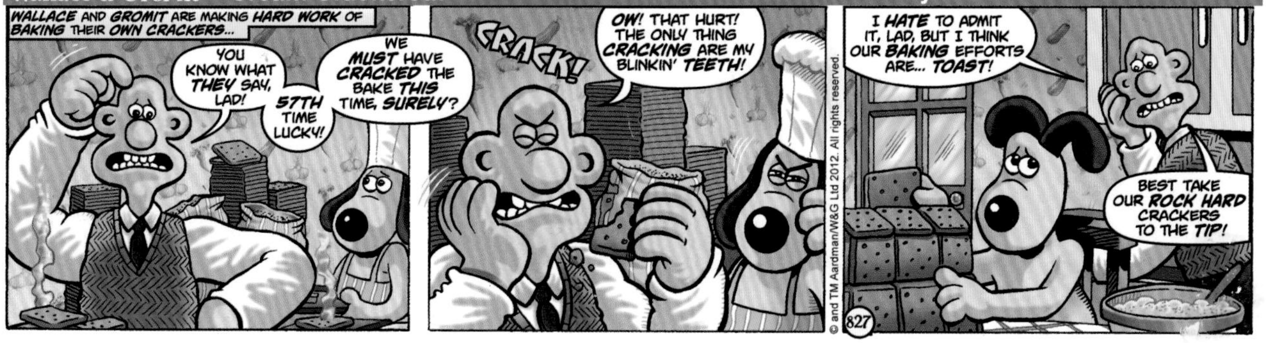

WALLACE AND GROMIT ARE MAKING HARD WORK OF BAKING THEIR OWN CRACKERS...
YOU KNOW WHAT THEY SAY, LAD!
57TH TIME LUCKY!
WE MUST HAVE CRACKED THE BAKE THIS TIME, SURELY?
CRACK!
OW! THAT HURT! THE ONLY THING CRACKING ARE MY BLINKIN' TEETH!
I HATE TO ADMIT IT, LAD, BUT I THINK OUR BAKING EFFORTS ARE... TOAST!
BEST TAKE OUR ROCK HARD CRACKERS TO THE TIP!
827
© and TM Aardman/W&G Ltd 2012. All rights reserved.

Wallace & Gromit - Cream Crackered! by Aardman & Titan Comics

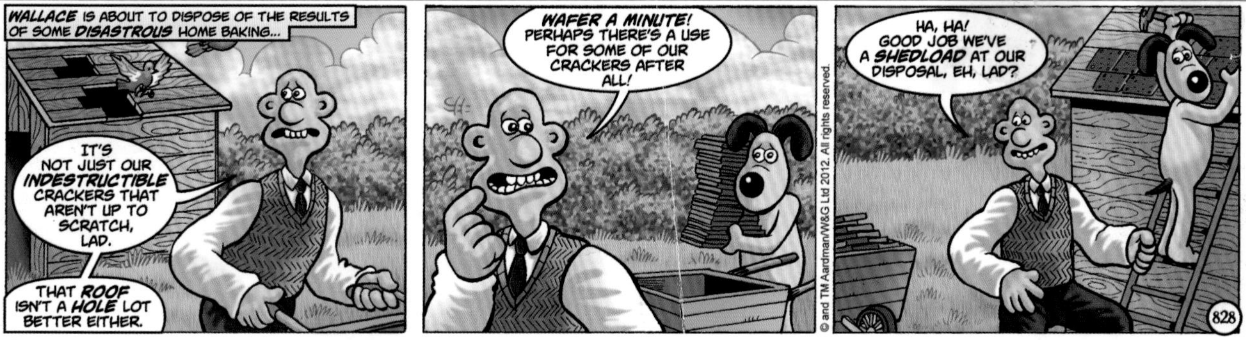

WALLACE IS ABOUT TO DISPOSE OF THE RESULTS OF SOME DISASTROUS HOME BAKING...
IT'S NOT JUST OUR INDESTRUCTIBLE CRACKERS THAT AREN'T UP TO SCRATCH, LAD.
THAT ROOF ISN'T A HOLE LOT BETTER EITHER.
WAFER A MINUTE! PERHAPS THERE'S A USE FOR SOME OF OUR CRACKERS AFTER ALL!
HA, HA! GOOD JOB WE'VE A SHEDLOAD AT OUR DISPOSAL, EH, LAD?
828
© and TM Aardman/W&G Ltd 2012. All rights reserved.

Wallace & Gromit - Cream Crackered! by Aardman & Titan Comics

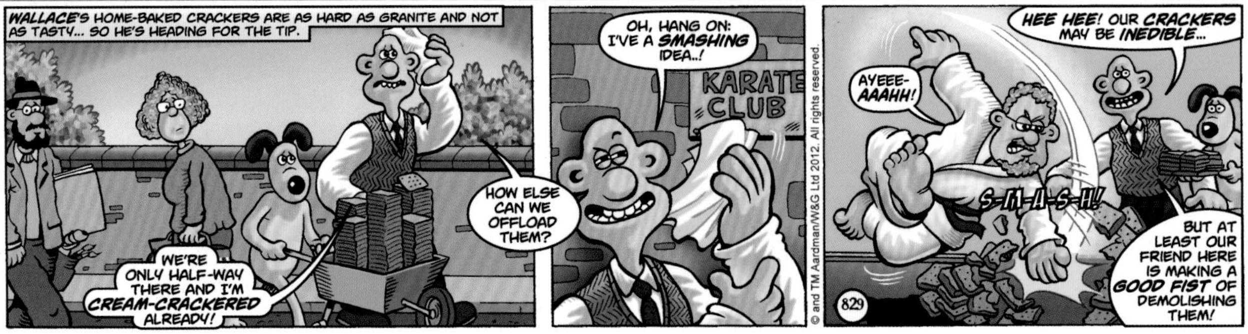

WALLACE'S HOME-BAKED CRACKERS ARE AS HARD AS GRANITE AND NOT AS TASTY... SO HE'S HEADING FOR THE TIP.
WE'RE ONLY HALF-WAY THERE AND I'M CREAM-CRACKERED ALREADY!
HOW ELSE CAN WE OFFLOAD THEM?
OH, HANG ON: I'VE A SMASHING IDEA..!
KARATE CLUB
AYEEE-AAAHH!
HEE HEE! OUR CRACKERS MAY BE INEDIBLE...
S-M-A-S-H!
BUT AT LEAST OUR FRIEND HERE IS MAKING A GOOD FIST OF DEMOLISHING THEM!
829

Wallace & Gromit - Cream Crackered! by Aardman & Titan Comics

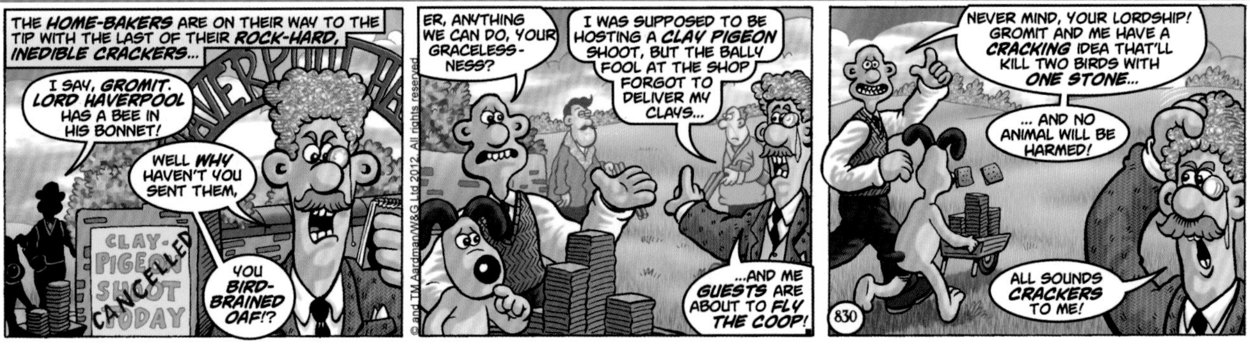

THE HOME-BAKERS ARE ON THEIR WAY TO THE TIP WITH THE LAST OF THEIR ROCK-HARD, INEDIBLE CRACKERS...
I SAY, GROMIT. LORD HAVERPOOL HAS A BEE IN HIS BONNET!
WELL WHY HAVEN'T YOU SENT THEM,
YOU BIRD-BRAINED OAF!?
CLAY-PIGEON SHOOT TODAY
CANCELLED
ER, ANYTHING WE CAN DO, YOUR GRACELESS-NESS?
I WAS SUPPOSED TO BE HOSTING A CLAY PIGEON SHOOT, BUT THE BALLY FOOL AT THE SHOP FORGOT TO DELIVER MY CLAYS...
...AND ME GUESTS ARE ABOUT TO FLY THE COOP!
NEVER MIND, YOUR LORDSHIP! GROMIT AND ME HAVE A CRACKING IDEA THAT'LL KILL TWO BIRDS WITH ONE STONE...
... AND NO ANIMAL WILL BE HARMED!
ALL SOUNDS CRACKERS TO ME!
830

Wallace & Gromit - Cream Crackered! by Aardman & Titan Comics

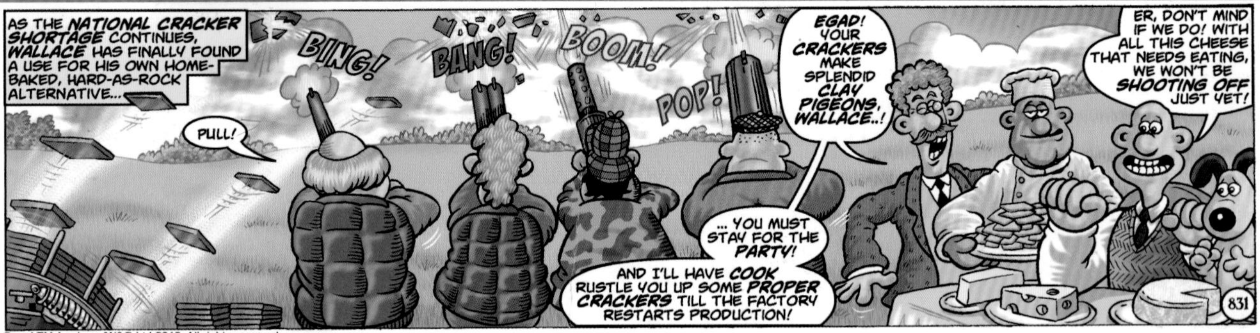

AS THE NATIONAL CRACKER SHORTAGE CONTINUES, WALLACE HAS FINALLY FOUND A USE FOR HIS OWN HOME-BAKED, HARD-AS-ROCK ALTERNATIVE...
PULL!
BING!
BANG!
BOOM!
POP!
EGAD! YOUR CRACKERS MAKE SPLENDID CLAY PIGEONS, WALLACE..!
... YOU MUST STAY FOR THE PARTY!
AND I'LL HAVE COOK RUSTLE YOU UP SOME PROPER CRACKERS TILL THE FACTORY RESTARTS PRODUCTION!
ER, DON'T MIND IF WE DO! WITH ALL THIS CHEESE THAT NEEDS EATING, WE WON'T BE SHOOTING OFF JUST YET!
831

The End

Wallace & Gromit - Great Minds

by Aardman & Titan Comics

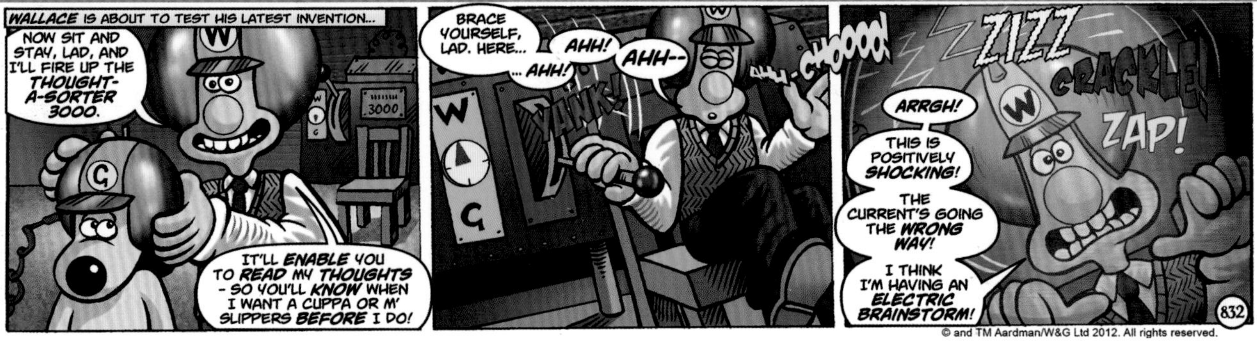
WALLACE IS ABOUT TO TEST HIS LATEST INVENTION...
NOW SIT AND STAY, LAD, AND I'LL FIRE UP THE THOUGHT-A-SORTER 3000.
IT'LL ENABLE YOU TO READ MY THOUGHTS - SO YOU'LL KNOW WHEN I WANT A CUPPA OR M' SLIPPERS BEFORE I DO!
3000
BRACE YOURSELF, LAD. HERE...
...AHH!
AHH!
AHH--
YANK!
-CHOOOO!
ZIZZ
CRACKLE!
ZAP!
ARRGH!
THIS IS POSITIVELY SHOCKING!
THE CURRENT'S GOING THE WRONG WAY!
I THINK I'M HAVING AN ELECTRIC BRAINSTORM!
832

Wallace & Gromit - Great Minds

by Aardman & Titan Comics

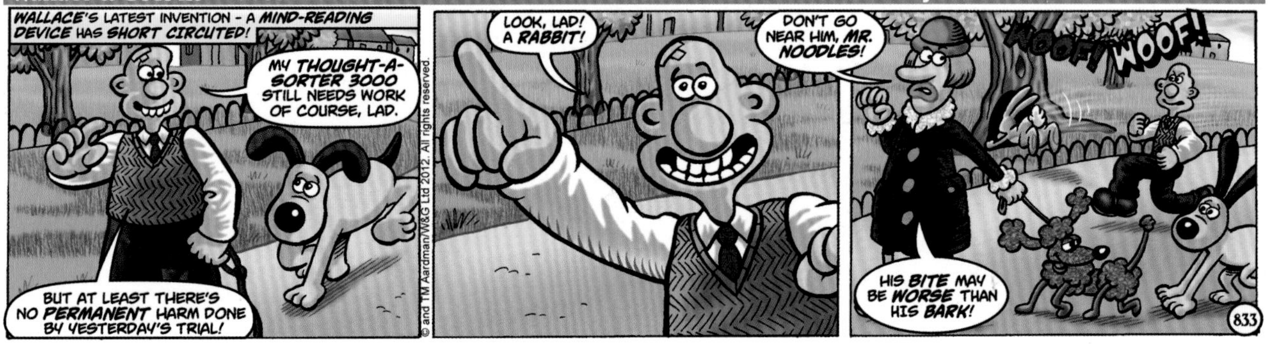
WALLACE'S LATEST INVENTION - A MIND-READING DEVICE HAS SHORT CIRCUITED!
MY THOUGHT-A-SORTER 3000 STILL NEEDS WORK OF COURSE, LAD.
BUT AT LEAST THERE'S NO PERMANENT HARM DONE BY YESTERDAY'S TRIAL!
LOOK, LAD! A RABBIT!
DON'T GO NEAR HIM, MR. NOODLES!
WOOF! WOOF!
HIS BITE MAY BE WORSE THAN HIS BARK!
833

Wallace & Gromit - Great Minds

by Aardman & Titan Comics

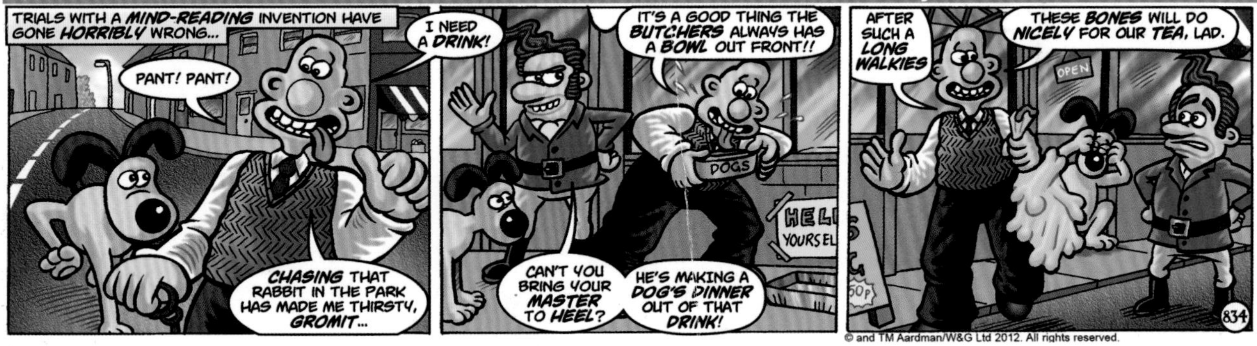
TRIALS WITH A MIND-READING INVENTION HAVE GONE HORRIBLY WRONG...
PANT! PANT!
I NEED A DRINK!
CHASING THAT RABBIT IN THE PARK HAS MADE ME THIRSTY, GROMIT...
IT'S A GOOD THING THE BUTCHERS ALWAYS HAS A BOWL OUT FRONT!!
DOGS
HEL
YOURSEL
CAN'T YOU BRING YOUR MASTER TO HEEL?
HE'S MAKING A DOG'S DINNER OUT OF THAT DRINK!
AFTER SUCH A LONG WALKIES
THESE BONES WILL DO NICELY FOR OUR TEA, LAD.
OPEN
834

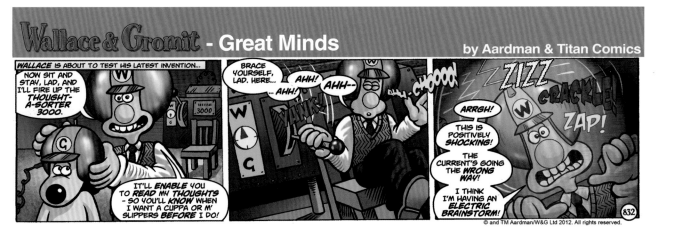

Wallace & Gromit - Great Minds by Aardman & Titan Comics

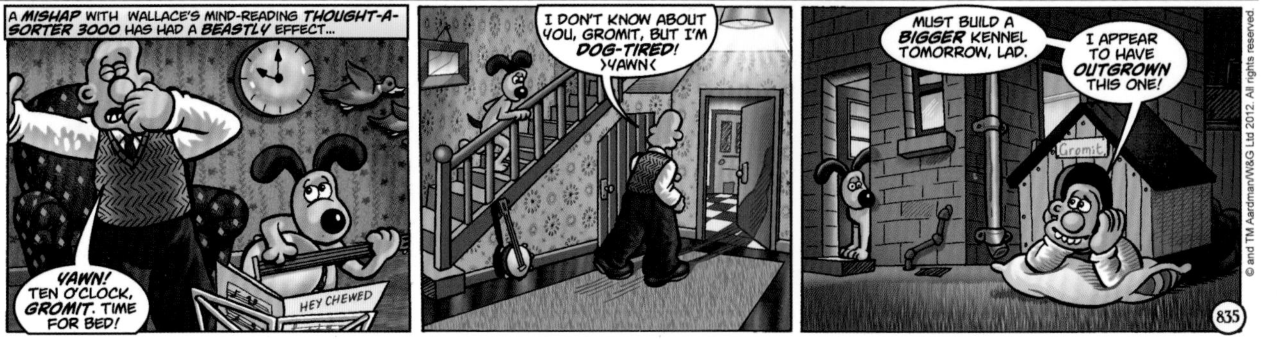
A MISHAP WITH WALLACE'S MIND-READING THOUGHT-A-SORTER 3000 HAS HAD A BEASTLY EFFECT...
YAWN! TEN O'CLOCK, GROMIT. TIME FOR BED!
HEY CHEWED
I DON'T KNOW ABOUT YOU, GROMIT, BUT I'M DOG-TIRED! ›YAWN‹
MUST BUILD A BIGGER KENNEL TOMORROW, LAD.
I APPEAR TO HAVE OUTGROWN THIS ONE!
Gromit
835
© and TM Aardman/W&G Ltd 2012. All rights reserved.

Wallace & Gromit - Great Minds by Aardman & Titan Comics

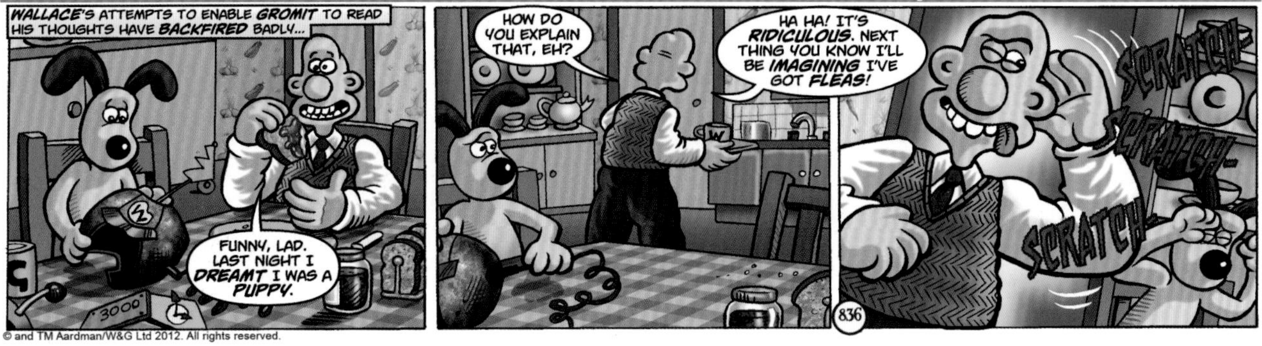
WALLACE'S ATTEMPTS TO ENABLE GROMIT TO READ HIS THOUGHTS HAVE BACKFIRED BADLY...
FUNNY, LAD. LAST NIGHT I DREAMT I WAS A PUPPY.
3000
HOW DO YOU EXPLAIN THAT, EH?
HA HA! IT'S RIDICULOUS. NEXT THING YOU KNOW I'LL BE IMAGINING I'VE GOT FLEAS!
836
SCRATCH
SCRATCH...
SCRATCH...

Wallace & Gromit - Great Minds by Aardman & Titan Comics

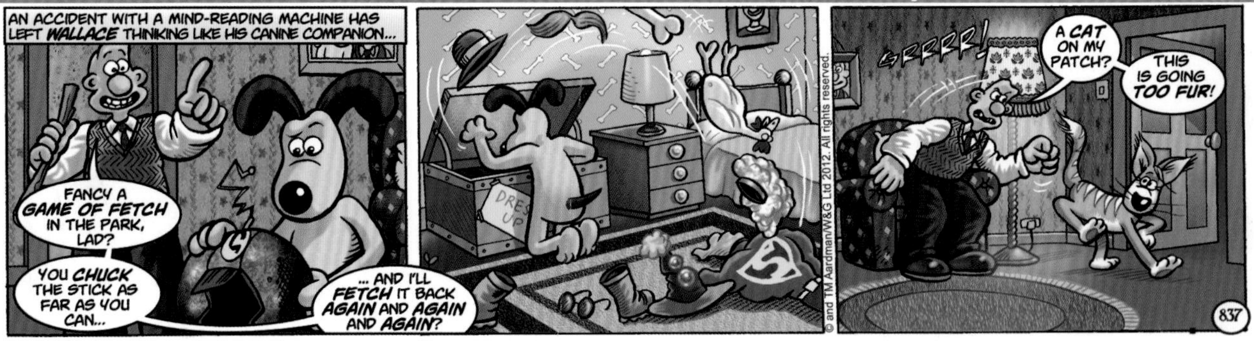
AN ACCIDENT WITH A MIND-READING MACHINE HAS LEFT WALLACE THINKING LIKE HIS CANINE COMPANION...
FANCY A GAME OF FETCH IN THE PARK, LAD?
YOU CHUCK THE STICK AS FAR AS YOU CAN...
... AND I'LL FETCH IT BACK AGAIN AND AGAIN AND AGAIN?
© and TM Aardman/W&G Ltd 2012. All rights reserved.
GRRRR!
A CAT ON MY PATCH?
THIS IS GOING TOO FUR!
837

Wallace & Gromit - Great Minds

by Aardman & Titan Comics

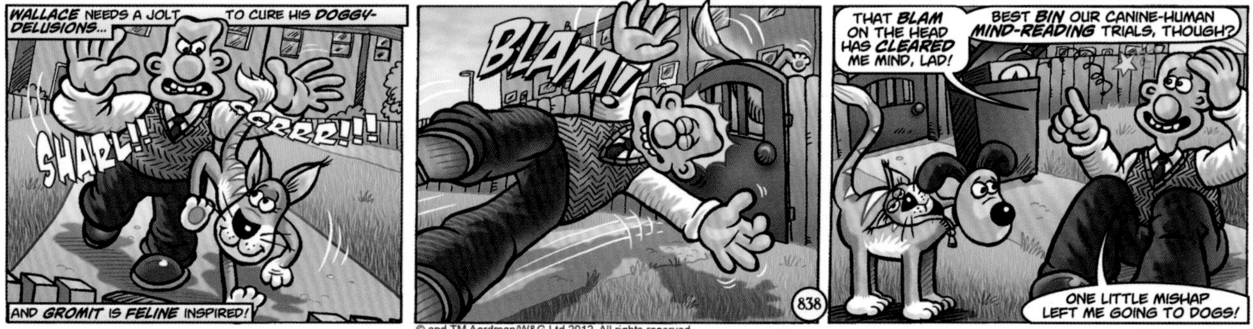

WALLACE NEEDS A JOLT TO CURE HIS DOGGY-DELUSIONS...
SHARL!!
GRRRR!!!
AND GROMIT IS FELINE INSPIRED!
BLAM!
838
THAT BLAM ON THE HEAD HAS CLEARED ME MIND, LAD!
BEST BIN OUR CANINE-HUMAN MIND-READING TRIALS, THOUGH?
ONE LITTLE MISHAP LEFT ME GOING TO DOGS!

The End

Wallace & Gromit - The Trouble with Truffles

by Aardman & Titan Comics

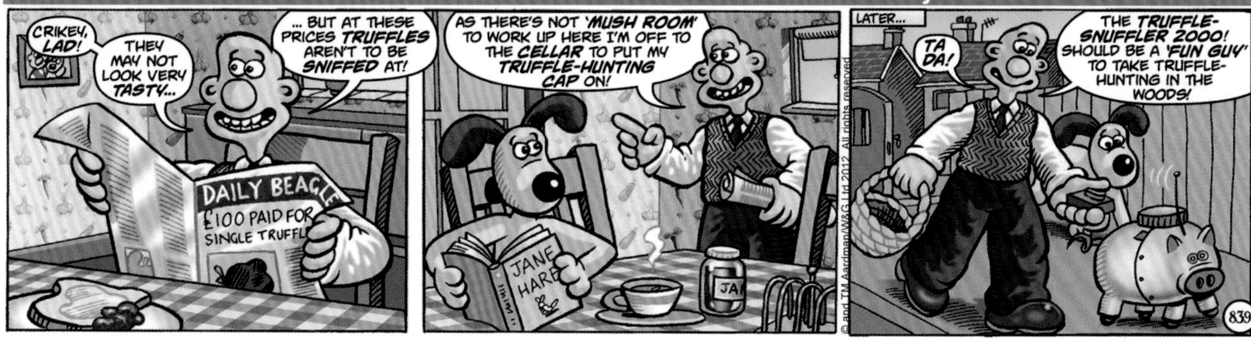

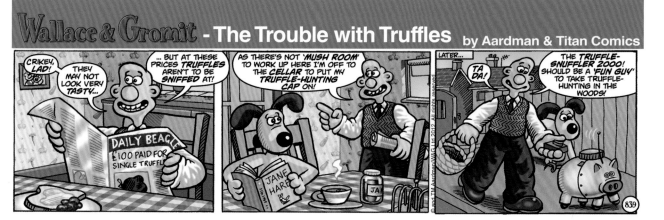

CRIKEY, LAD!
THEY MAY NOT LOOK VERY TASTY...
... BUT AT THESE PRICES TRUFFLES AREN'T TO BE SNIFFED AT!
DAILY BEAGLE
£100 PAID FOR SINGLE TRUFFL
AS THERE'S NOT 'MUSH ROOM' TO WORK UP HERE I'M OFF TO THE CELLAR TO PUT MY TRUFFLE-HUNTING CAP ON!
JANE HARE
LATER...
TA DA!
THE TRUFFLE-SNUFFLER 2000! SHOULD BE A 'FUN GUY' TO TAKE TRUFFLE-HUNTING IN THE WOODS!
839

© and TM Aardman/W&G Ltd 2012. All rights reserved.

Wallace & Gromit - The Trouble with Truffles

by Aardman & Titan Comics

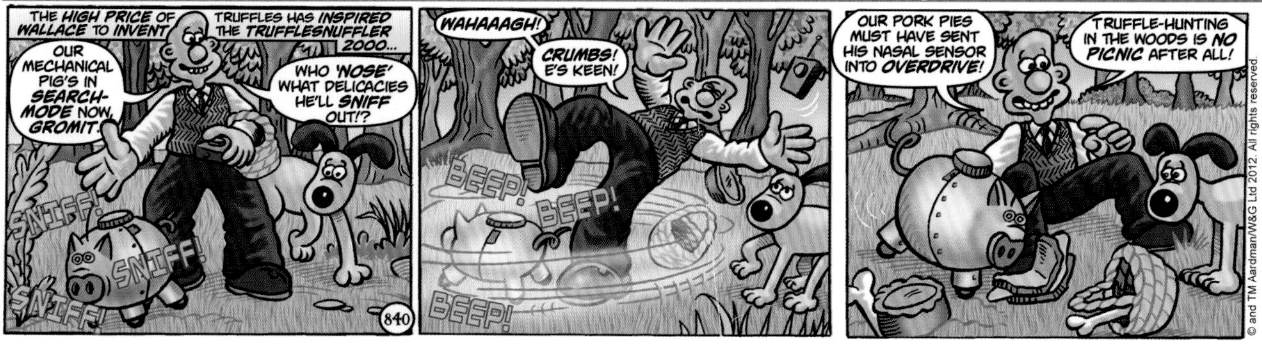

THE HIGH PRICE OF WALLACE TO INVENT
TRUFFLES HAS INSPIRED THE TRUFFLESNUFFLER 2000...
OUR MECHANICAL PIG'S IN SEARCH-MODE NOW, GROMIT.
WHO 'NOSE' WHAT DELICACIES HE'LL SNIFF OUT!?
SNIFF!
SNIFF!
SNIFF!
840
WAHAAAGH!
CRUMBS! 'E'S KEEN!
BEEP!
BEEP!
BEEP!
OUR PORK PIES MUST HAVE SENT HIS NASAL SENSOR INTO OVERDRIVE!
TRUFFLE-HUNTING IN THE WOODS IS NO PICNIC AFTER ALL!

© and TM Aardman/W&G Ltd 2012. All rights reserved.

Wallace & Gromit - The Trouble with Truffles
by Aardman & Titan Comics

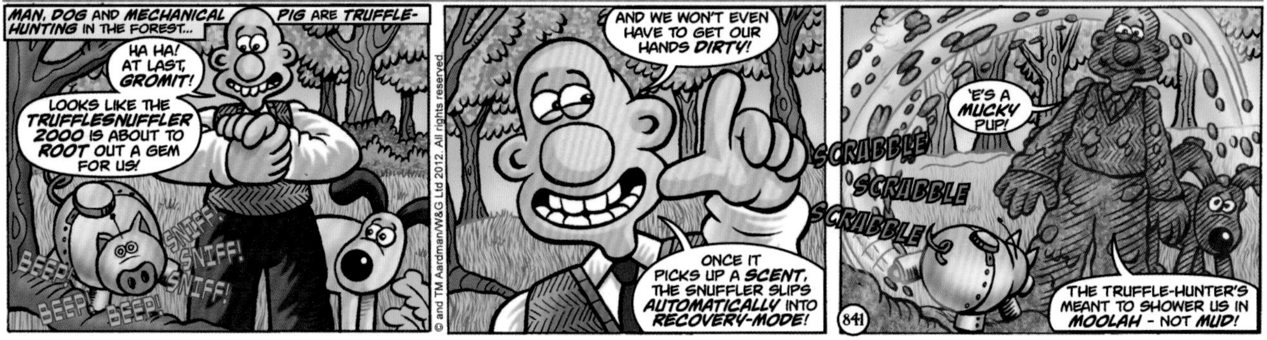

MAN, DOG AND MECHANICAL PIG ARE TRUFFLE-HUNTING IN THE FOREST...
HA HA! AT LAST, GROMIT!
LOOKS LIKE THE TRUFFLESNUFFLER 2000 IS ABOUT TO ROOT OUT A GEM FOR US!
SNIFF! SNIFF! SNIFF!
BEEP! BEEP! BEEP!
AND WE WON'T EVEN HAVE TO GET OUR HANDS DIRTY!
ONCE IT PICKS UP A SCENT, THE SNUFFLER SLIPS AUTOMATICALLY INTO RECOVERY-MODE!
SCRABBLE SCRABBLE SCRABBLE
'E'S A MUCKY PUP!
THE TRUFFLE-HUNTER'S MEANT TO SHOWER US IN MOOLAH - NOT MUD!
841
© and TM Aardman/W&G Ltd 2012. All rights reserved.

Wallace & Gromit - The Trouble with Truffles
by Aardman & Titan Comics

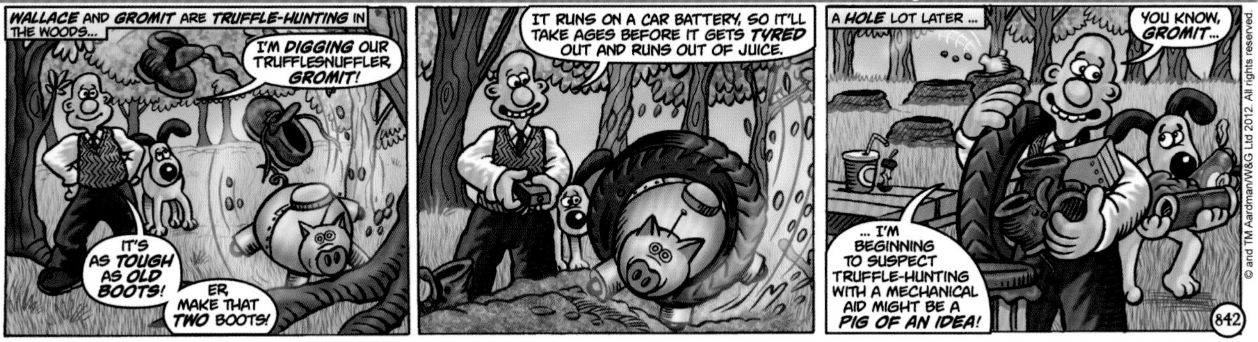

WALLACE AND GROMIT ARE TRUFFLE-HUNTING IN THE WOODS...
I'M DIGGING OUR TRUFFLESNUFFLER, GROMIT!
IT'S AS TOUGH AS OLD BOOTS!
ER, MAKE THAT TWO BOOTS!
IT RUNS ON A CAR BATTERY, SO IT'LL TAKE AGES BEFORE IT GETS TYRED OUT AND RUNS OUT OF JUICE.
A HOLE LOT LATER ...
YOU KNOW, GROMIT...
... I'M BEGINNING TO SUSPECT TRUFFLE-HUNTING WITH A MECHANICAL AID MIGHT BE A PIG OF AN IDEA!
842
© and TM Aardman/W&G Ltd 2012. All rights reserved.

Wallace & Gromit - The Trouble with Truffles
by Aardman & Titan Comics

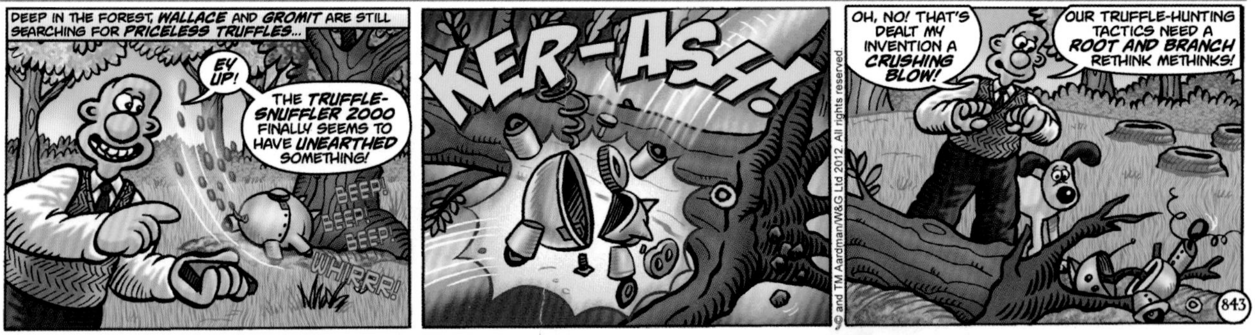

DEEP IN THE FOREST, WALLACE AND GROMIT ARE STILL SEARCHING FOR PRICELESS TRUFFLES...
EY UP!
THE TRUFFLE-SNUFFLER 2000 FINALLY SEEMS TO HAVE UNEARTHED SOMETHING!
BEEP! BEEP! BEEP!
WHIRRR!
KER-ASH!
OH, NO! THAT'S DEALT MY INVENTION A CRUSHING BLOW!
OUR TRUFFLE-HUNTING TACTICS NEED A ROOT AND BRANCH RETHINK METHINKS!
843
© and TM Aardman/W&G Ltd 2012. All rights reserved.

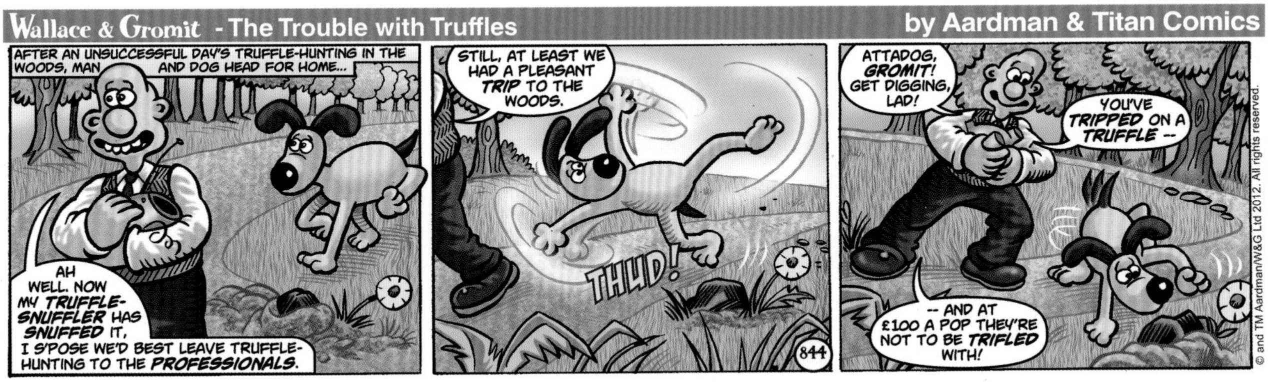
Wallace & Gromit - The Trouble with Truffles
by Aardman & Titan Comics
AFTER AN UNSUCCESSFUL DAY'S TRUFFLE-HUNTING IN THE WOODS, MAN AND DOG HEAD FOR HOME...
AH WELL. NOW MY TRUFFLE-SNUFFLER HAS SNUFFED IT, I S'POSE WE'D BEST LEAVE TRUFFLE-HUNTING TO THE PROFESSIONALS.
STILL, AT LEAST WE HAD A PLEASANT TRIP TO THE WOODS.
THUD!
844
ATTADOG, GROMIT! GET DIGGING, LAD!
YOU'VE TRIPPED ON A TRUFFLE --
-- AND AT £100 A POP THEY'RE NOT TO BE TRIFLED WITH!
© and TM Aardman/W&G Ltd 2012. All rights reserved.

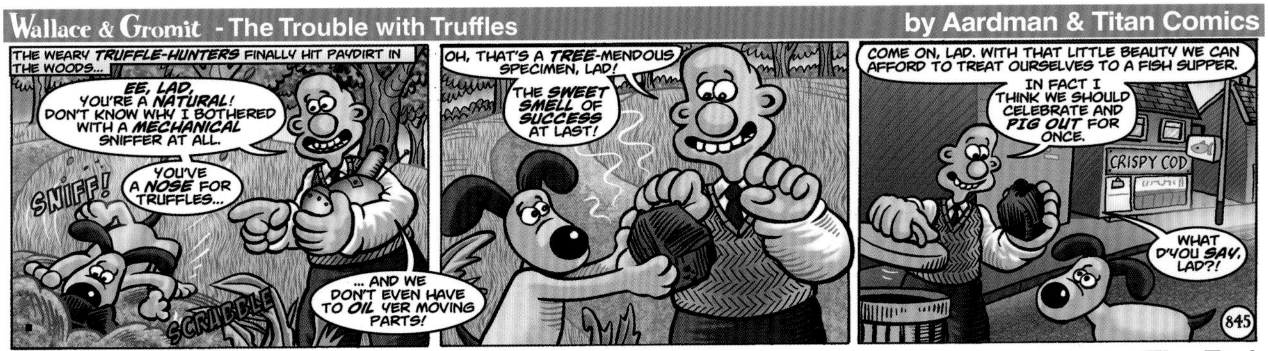
Wallace & Gromit - The Trouble with Truffles
by Aardman & Titan Comics
THE WEARY TRUFFLE-HUNTERS FINALLY HIT PAYDIRT IN THE WOODS...
EE, LAD, YOU'RE A NATURAL! DON'T KNOW WHY I BOTHERED WITH A MECHANICAL SNIFFER AT ALL.
YOU'VE A NOSE FOR TRUFFLES...
SNIFF!
SCRIBBLE
... AND WE DON'T EVEN HAVE TO OIL YER MOVING PARTS!
OH, THAT'S A TREE-MENDOUS SPECIMEN, LAD!
THE SWEET SMELL OF SUCCESS AT LAST!
COME ON, LAD. WITH THAT LITTLE BEAUTY WE CAN AFFORD TO TREAT OURSELVES TO A FISH SUPPER.
IN FACT I THINK WE SHOULD CELEBRATE AND PIG OUT FOR ONCE.
CRISPY COD
WHAT D'YOU SAY, LAD?!
845

The End

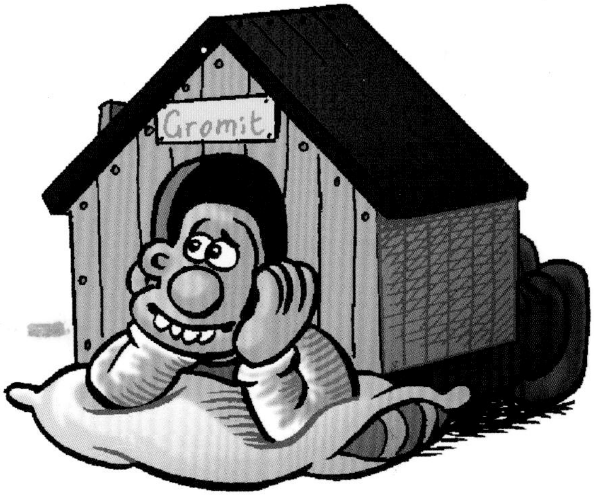
Gromit

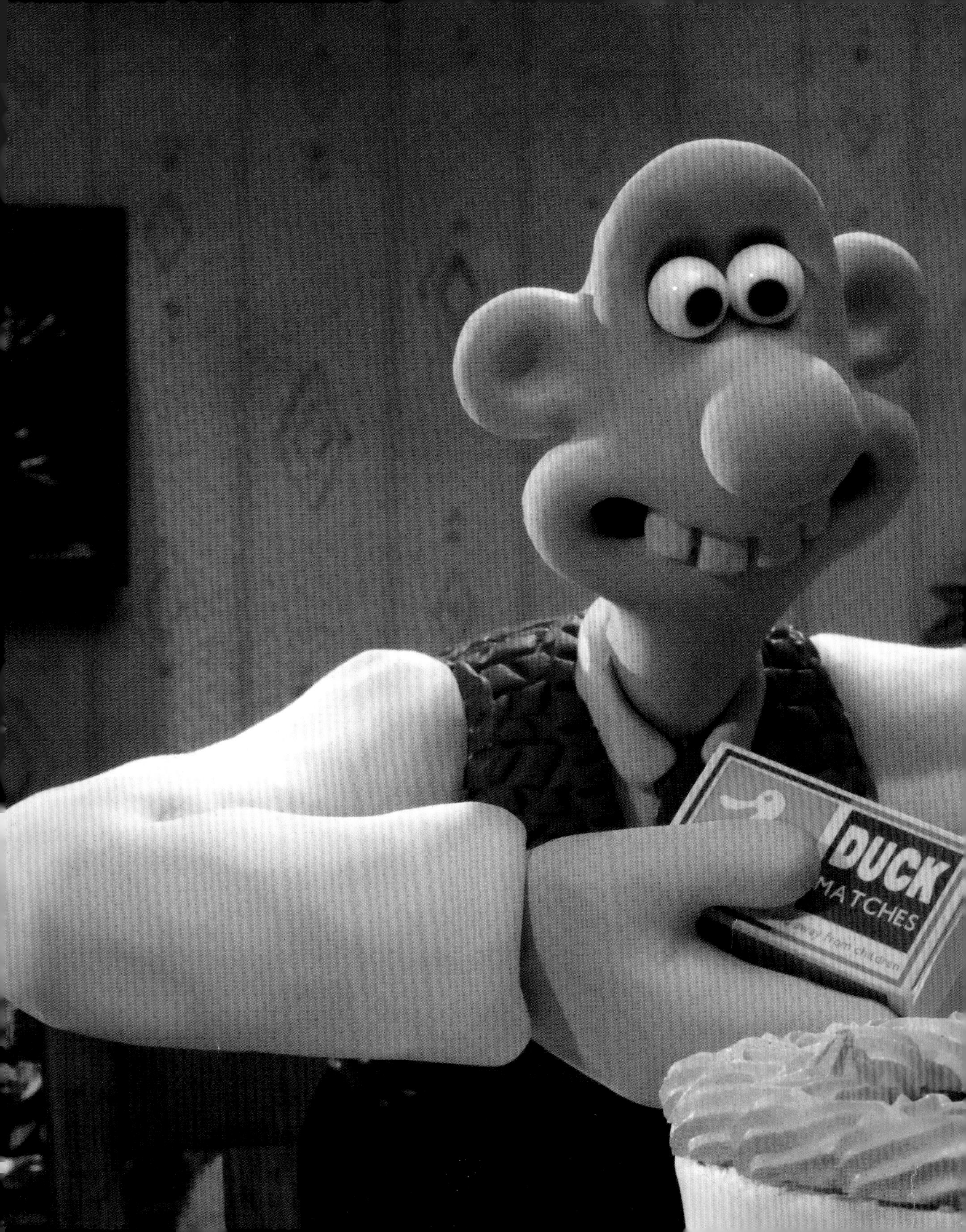
DUCK
MATCHES

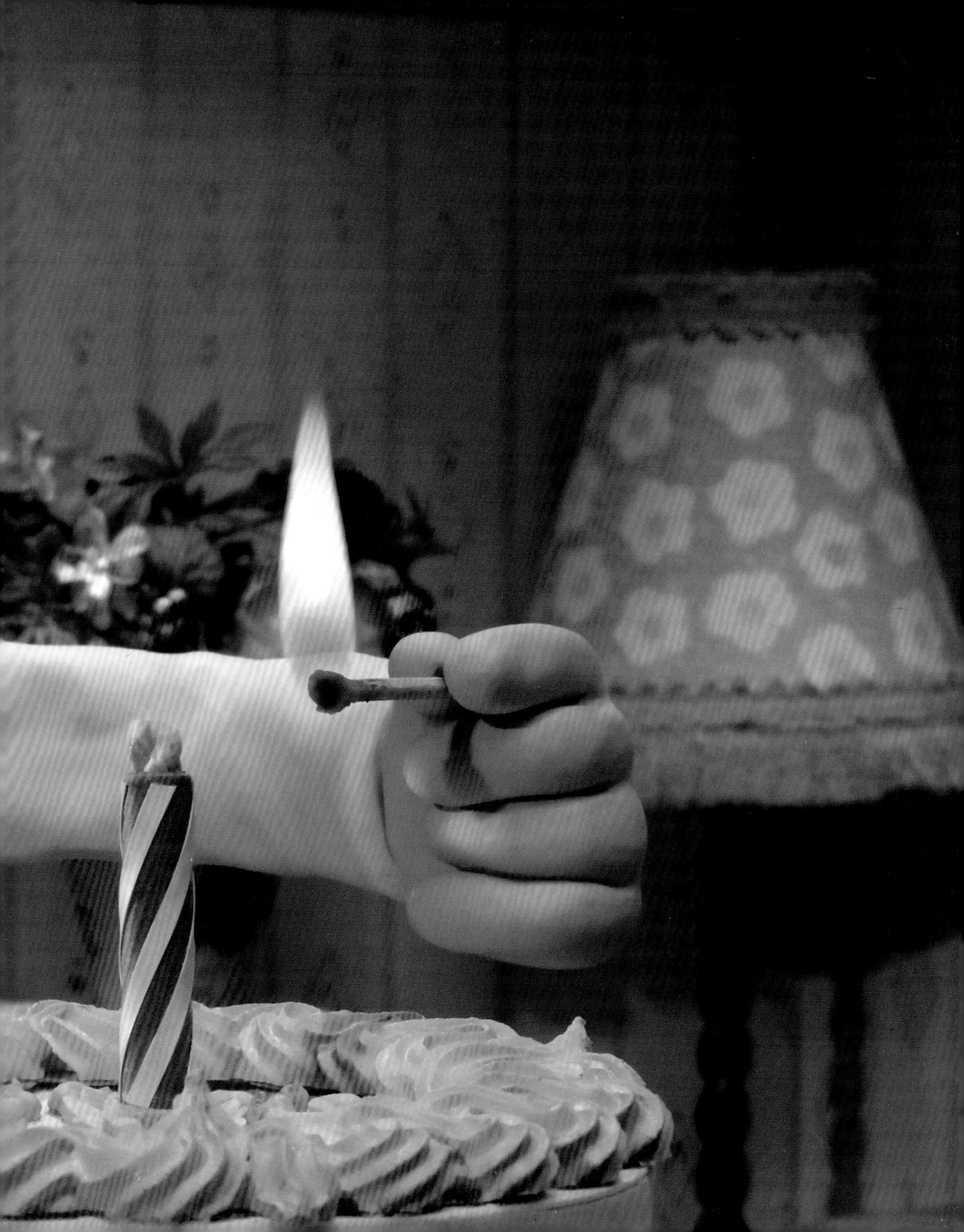

Wallace & Gromit - Presents of Mind

by Aardman & Titan Comics

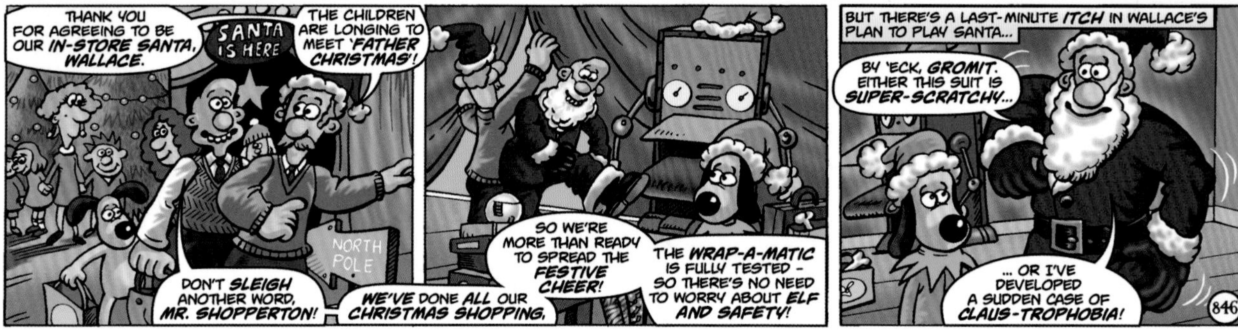
THANK YOU FOR AGREEING TO BE OUR IN-STORE SANTA, WALLACE.
SANTA IS HERE
THE CHILDREN ARE LONGING TO MEET 'FATHER CHRISTMAS'!
NORTH POLE
DON'T SLEIGH ANOTHER WORD, MR. SHOPPERTON!
WE'VE DONE ALL OUR CHRISTMAS SHOPPING,
SO WE'RE MORE THAN READY TO SPREAD THE FESTIVE CHEER!
THE WRAP-A-MATIC IS FULLY TESTED - SO THERE'S NO NEED TO WORRY ABOUT ELF AND SAFETY!
BUT THERE'S A LAST-MINUTE ITCH IN WALLACE'S PLAN TO PLAY SANTA...
BY 'ECK, GROMIT. EITHER THIS SUIT IS SUPER-SCRATCHY...
... OR I'VE DEVELOPED A SUDDEN CASE OF CLAUS-TROPHOBIA!
846

Wallace & Gromit - Presents of Mind

by Aardman & Titan Comics

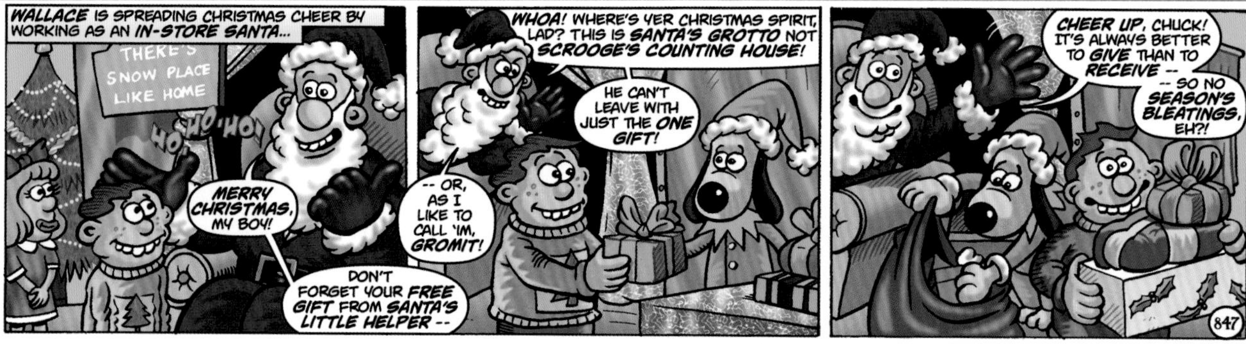
WALLACE IS SPREADING CHRISTMAS CHEER BY WORKING AS AN IN-STORE SANTA...
THERE'S SNOW PLACE LIKE HOME
HO HO HO
MERRY CHRISTMAS, MY BOY!
DON'T FORGET YOUR FREE GIFT FROM SANTA'S LITTLE HELPER --
-- OR, AS I LIKE TO CALL 'IM, GROMIT!
WHOA! WHERE'S YER CHRISTMAS SPIRIT, LAD? THIS IS SANTA'S GROTTO NOT SCROOGE'S COUNTING HOUSE!
HE CAN'T LEAVE WITH JUST THE ONE GIFT!
CHEER UP, CHUCK! IT'S ALWAYS BETTER TO GIVE THAN TO RECEIVE --
-- SO NO SEASON'S BLEATINGS, EH?!
847

Wallace & Gromit - Presents of Mind

by Aardman & Titan Comics

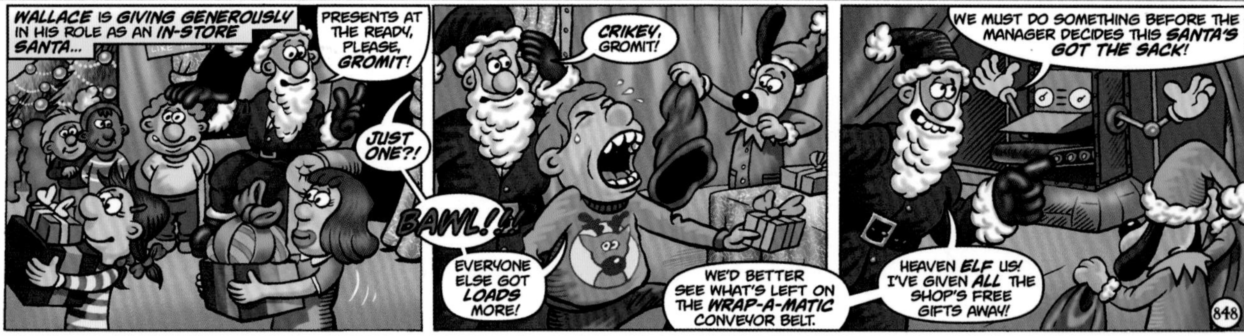
WALLACE IS GIVING GENEROUSLY IN HIS ROLE AS AN IN-STORE SANTA...
PRESENTS AT THE READY, PLEASE, GROMIT!
JUST ONE?!
BAWL!
EVERYONE ELSE GOT LOADS MORE!
CRIKEY, GROMIT!
WE'D BETTER SEE WHAT'S LEFT ON THE WRAP-A-MATIC CONVEYOR BELT.
WE MUST DO SOMETHING BEFORE THE MANAGER DECIDES THIS SANTA'S GOT THE SACK!
HEAVEN ELF US! I'VE GIVEN ALL THE SHOP'S FREE GIFTS AWAY!
848

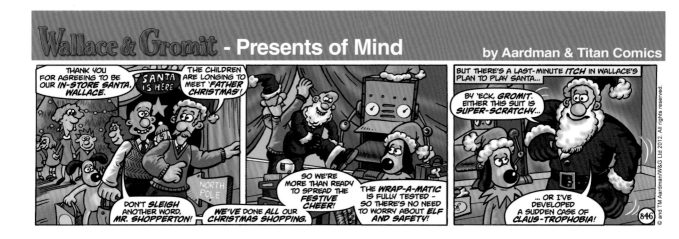

Wallace & Gromit - Presents of Mind
by Aardman & Titan Comics

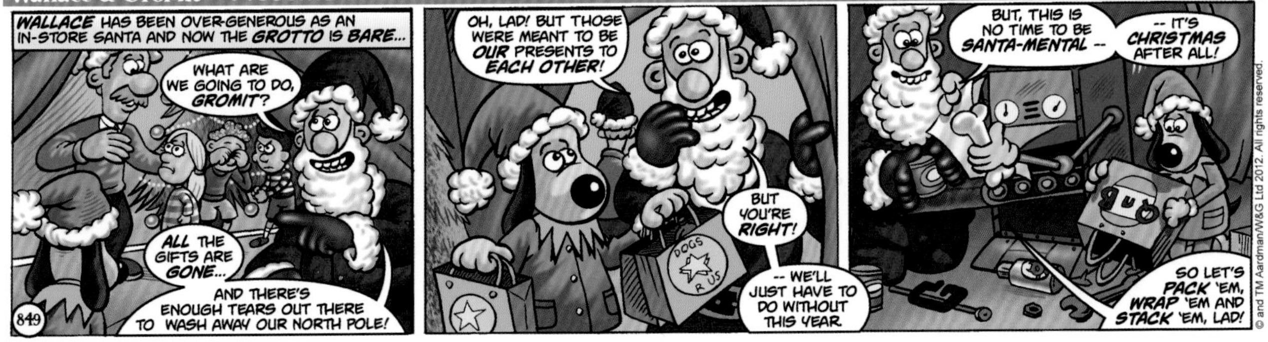
WALLACE HAS BEEN OVER-GENEROUS AS AN IN-STORE SANTA AND NOW THE GROTTO IS BARE...
WHAT ARE WE GOING TO DO, GROMIT?
ALL THE GIFTS ARE GONE...
AND THERE'S ENOUGH TEARS OUT THERE TO WASH AWAY OUR NORTH POLE!
849
OH, LAD! BUT THOSE WERE MEANT TO BE OUR PRESENTS TO EACH OTHER!
BUT YOU'RE RIGHT!
-- WE'LL JUST HAVE TO DO WITHOUT THIS YEAR.
DOGS R US
BUT, THIS IS NO TIME TO BE SANTA-MENTAL --
-- IT'S CHRISTMAS AFTER ALL!
SO LET'S PACK 'EM, WRAP 'EM AND STACK 'EM, LAD!

Wallace & Gromit - Presents of Mind
by Aardman & Titan Comics

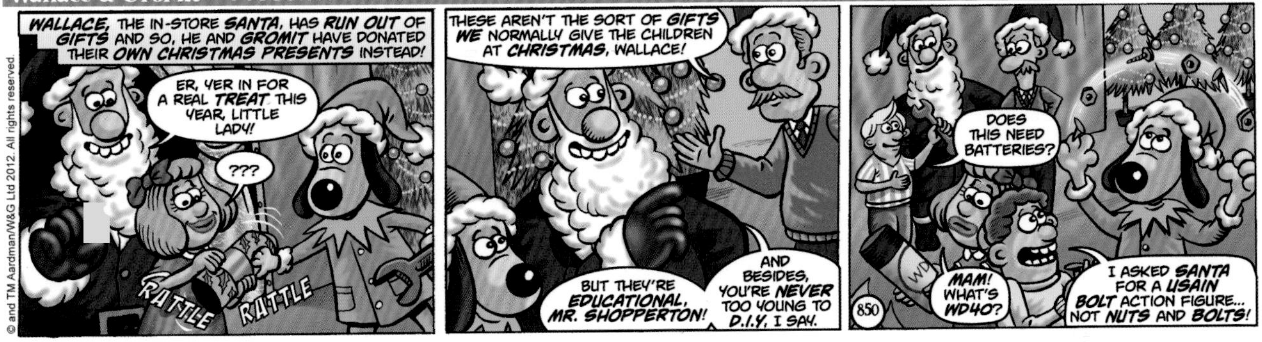
WALLACE, THE IN-STORE SANTA, HAS RUN OUT OF GIFTS AND SO, HE AND GROMIT HAVE DONATED THEIR OWN CHRISTMAS PRESENTS INSTEAD!
ER, YER IN FOR A REAL TREAT THIS YEAR, LITTLE LADY!
???
RATTLE
RATTLE
THESE AREN'T THE SORT OF GIFTS WE NORMALLY GIVE THE CHILDREN AT CHRISTMAS, WALLACE!
BUT THEY'RE EDUCATIONAL, MR. SHOPPERTON!
AND BESIDES, YOU'RE NEVER TOO YOUNG TO D.I.Y, I SAY.
DOES THIS NEED BATTERIES?
MAM! WHAT'S WD40?
I ASKED SANTA FOR A USAIN BOLT ACTION FIGURE... NOT NUTS AND BOLTS!
850

Wallace & Gromit - Presents of Mind
by Aardman & Titan Comics

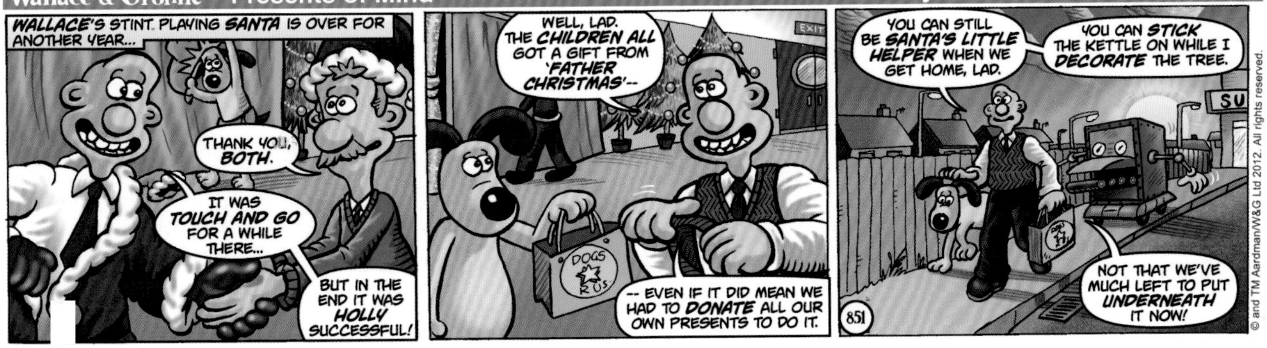
WALLACE'S STINT PLAYING SANTA IS OVER FOR ANOTHER YEAR...
THANK YOU, BOTH.
IT WAS TOUCH AND GO FOR A WHILE THERE...
BUT IN THE END IT WAS HOLLY SUCCESSFUL!
EXIT
WELL, LAD. THE CHILDREN ALL GOT A GIFT FROM 'FATHER CHRISTMAS'--
DOGS R US
-- EVEN IF IT DID MEAN WE HAD TO DONATE ALL OUR OWN PRESENTS TO DO IT.
851
YOU CAN STILL BE SANTA'S LITTLE HELPER WHEN WE GET HOME, LAD.
YOU CAN STICK THE KETTLE ON WHILE I DECORATE THE TREE.
NOT THAT WE'VE MUCH LEFT TO PUT UNDERNEATH IT NOW!

Wallace & Gromit - Presents of Mind by Aardman & Titan Comics

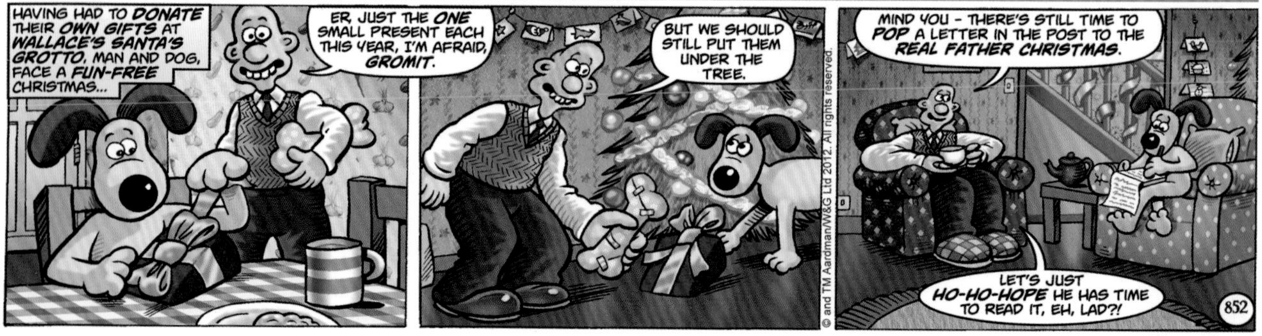
HAVING HAD TO DONATE THEIR OWN GIFTS AT WALLACE'S SANTA'S GROTTO, MAN AND DOG, FACE A FUN-FREE CHRISTMAS...
ER, JUST THE ONE SMALL PRESENT EACH THIS YEAR, I'M AFRAID, GROMIT.
BUT WE SHOULD STILL PUT THEM UNDER THE TREE.
© and TM Aardman/W&G Ltd 2012. All rights reserved.
MIND YOU - THERE'S STILL TIME TO POP A LETTER IN THE POST TO THE REAL FATHER CHRISTMAS.
LET'S JUST HO-HO-HOPE HE HAS TIME TO READ IT, EH, LAD?!
852

The End

Wallace & Gromit - 'Twas (Another) Night Before Christmas by Aardman & Titan Comics

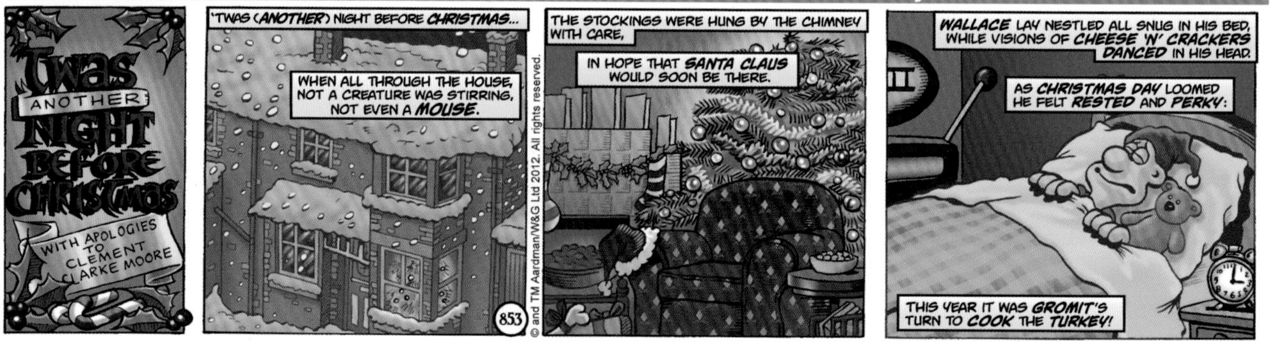
'TWAS ANOTHER NIGHT BEFORE CHRISTMAS
WITH APOLOGIES TO CLEMENT CLARKE MOORE
'TWAS (ANOTHER) NIGHT BEFORE CHRISTMAS...
WHEN ALL THROUGH THE HOUSE, NOT A CREATURE WAS STIRRING, NOT EVEN A MOUSE.
853
© and TM Aardman/W&G Ltd 2012. All rights reserved.
THE STOCKINGS WERE HUNG BY THE CHIMNEY WITH CARE,
IN HOPE THAT SANTA CLAUS WOULD SOON BE THERE.
WALLACE LAY NESTLED ALL SNUG IN HIS BED, WHILE VISIONS OF CHEESE 'N' CRACKERS DANCED IN HIS HEAD.
AS CHRISTMAS DAY LOOMED HE FELT RESTED AND PERKY:
THIS YEAR IT WAS GROMIT'S TURN TO COOK THE TURKEY!

Wallace & Gromit - 'Twas (Another) Night Before Christmas by Aardman & Titan Comics

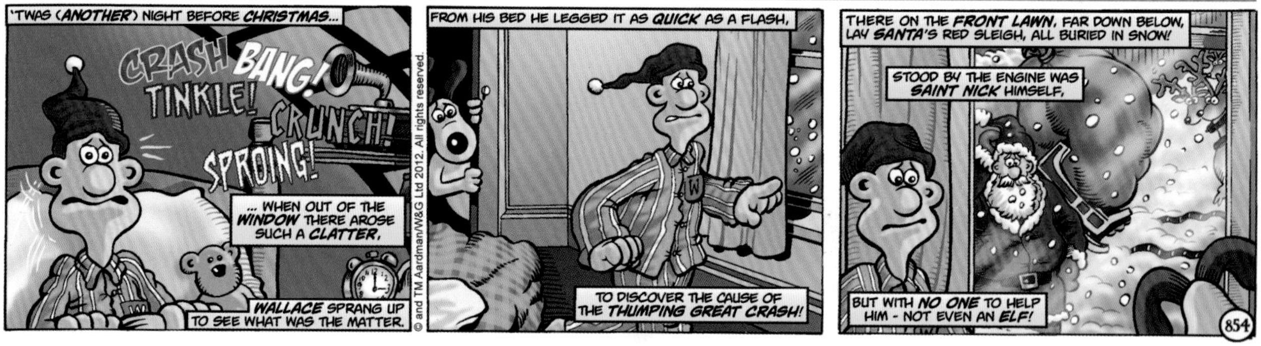
'TWAS (ANOTHER) NIGHT BEFORE CHRISTMAS...
CRASH BANG! TINKLE! CRUNCH! SPROING!
... WHEN OUT OF THE WINDOW THERE AROSE SUCH A CLATTER,
WALLACE SPRANG UP TO SEE WHAT WAS THE MATTER.
© and TM Aardman/W&G Ltd 2012. All rights reserved.
FROM HIS BED HE LEGGED IT AS QUICK AS A FLASH,
TO DISCOVER THE CAUSE OF THE THUMPING GREAT CRASH!
THERE ON THE FRONT LAWN, FAR DOWN BELOW, LAY SANTA'S RED SLEIGH, ALL BURIED IN SNOW!
STOOD BY THE ENGINE WAS SAINT NICK HIMSELF,
BUT WITH NO ONE TO HELP HIM - NOT EVEN AN ELF!
854

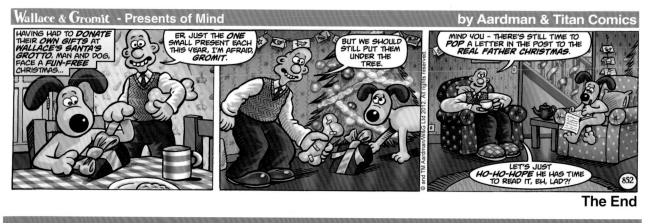

Wallace & Gromit - 'Twas (Another) Night Before Christmas by Aardman & Titan Comics

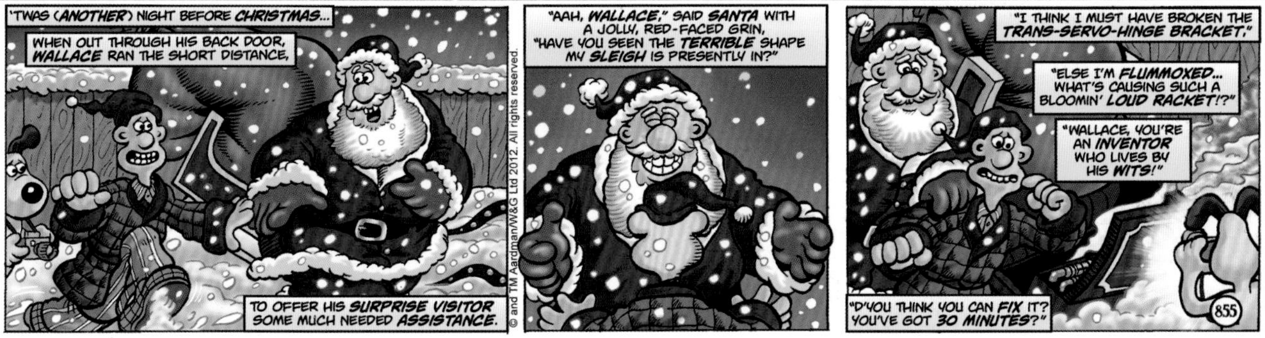
'TWAS (ANOTHER) NIGHT BEFORE CHRISTMAS...
WHEN OUT THROUGH HIS BACK DOOR, WALLACE RAN THE SHORT DISTANCE,
TO OFFER HIS SURPRISE VISITOR SOME MUCH NEEDED ASSISTANCE.
© and TM Aardman/W&G Ltd 2012. All rights reserved.
"AAH, WALLACE," SAID SANTA WITH A JOLLY, RED-FACED GRIN,
"HAVE YOU SEEN THE TERRIBLE SHAPE MY SLEIGH IS PRESENTLY IN?"
"I THINK I MUST HAVE BROKEN THE TRANS-SERVO-HINGE BRACKET."
"ELSE I'M FLUMMOXED... WHAT'S CAUSING SUCH A BLOOMIN' LOUD RACKET!?"
"WALLACE, YOU'RE AN INVENTOR WHO LIVES BY HIS WITS!"
"D'YOU THINK YOU CAN FIX IT? YOU'VE GOT 30 MINUTES?"
855

Wallace & Gromit - 'Twas (Another) Night Before Christmas by Aardman & Titan Comics

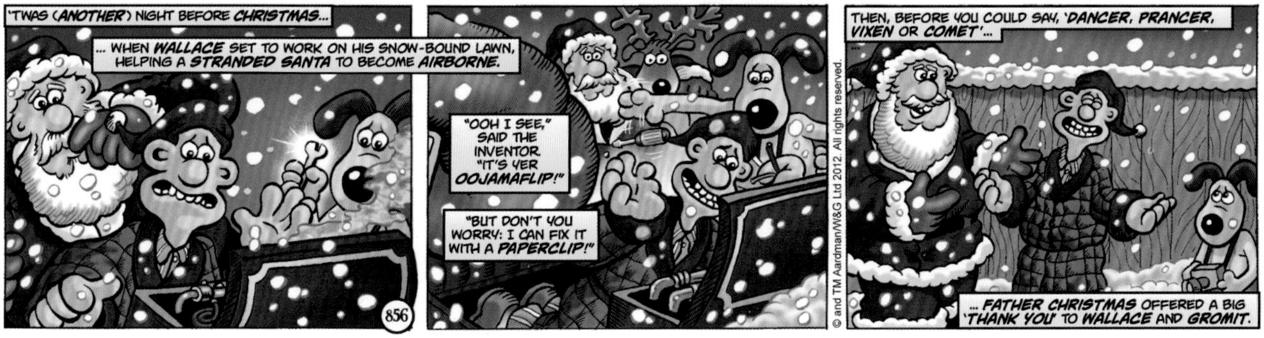
'TWAS (ANOTHER) NIGHT BEFORE CHRISTMAS...
... WHEN WALLACE SET TO WORK ON HIS SNOW-BOUND LAWN, HELPING A STRANDED SANTA TO BECOME AIRBORNE.
856
"OOH I SEE," SAID THE INVENTOR "IT'S YER OOJAMAFLIP!"
"BUT DON'T YOU WORRY: I CAN FIX IT WITH A PAPERCLIP!"
© and TM Aardman/W&G Ltd 2012. All rights reserved.
THEN, BEFORE YOU COULD SAY, 'DANCER, PRANCER, VIXEN OR COMET'...
... FATHER CHRISTMAS OFFERED A BIG 'THANK YOU' TO WALLACE AND GROMIT.

Wallace & Gromit - 'Twas (Another) Night Before Christmas by Aardman & Titan Comics

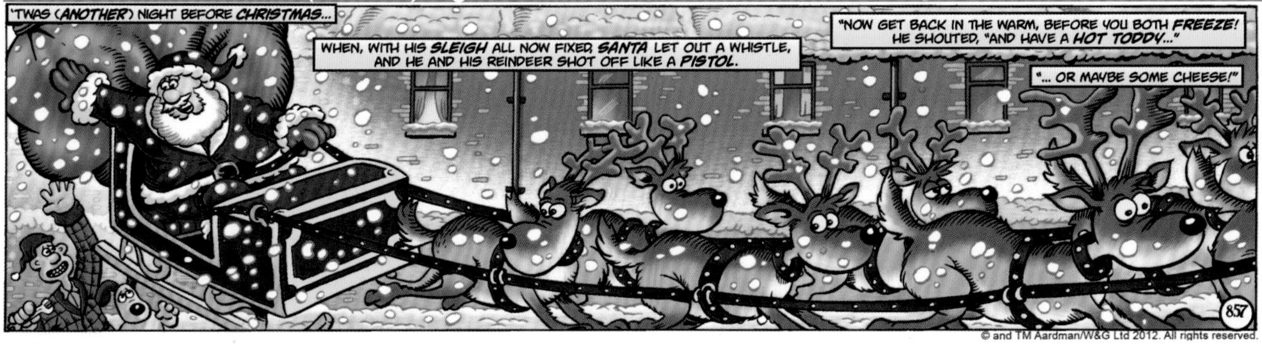
'TWAS (ANOTHER) NIGHT BEFORE CHRISTMAS...
WHEN, WITH HIS SLEIGH ALL NOW FIXED, SANTA LET OUT A WHISTLE, AND HE AND HIS REINDEER SHOT OFF LIKE A PISTOL.
"NOW GET BACK IN THE WARM, BEFORE YOU BOTH FREEZE! HE SHOUTED, "AND HAVE A HOT TODDY..."
"... OR MAYBE SOME CHEESE!"
857

Wallace & Gromit - 'Twas (Another) Night Before Christmas

by Aardman & Titan Comics

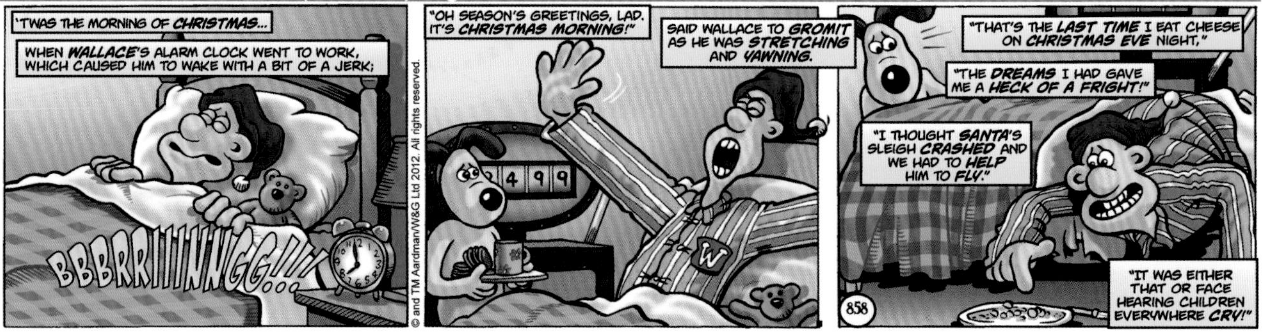
'TWAS THE MORNING OF CHRISTMAS...
WHEN WALLACE'S ALARM CLOCK WENT TO WORK, WHICH CAUSED HIM TO WAKE WITH A BIT OF A JERK;
BBBRRIIIINNGG!!!...
"OH SEASON'S GREETINGS, LAD. IT'S CHRISTMAS MORNING!"
SAID WALLACE TO GROMIT AS HE WAS STRETCHING AND YAWNING.
"THAT'S THE LAST TIME I EAT CHEESE ON CHRISTMAS EVE NIGHT,"
"THE DREAMS I HAD GAVE ME A HECK OF A FRIGHT!"
"I THOUGHT SANTA'S SLEIGH CRASHED AND WE HAD TO HELP HIM TO FLY."
"IT WAS EITHER THAT OR FACE HEARING CHILDREN EVERYWHERE CRY!"
858

Wallace & Gromit - 'Twas (Another) Night Before Christmas

by Aardman & Titan Comics

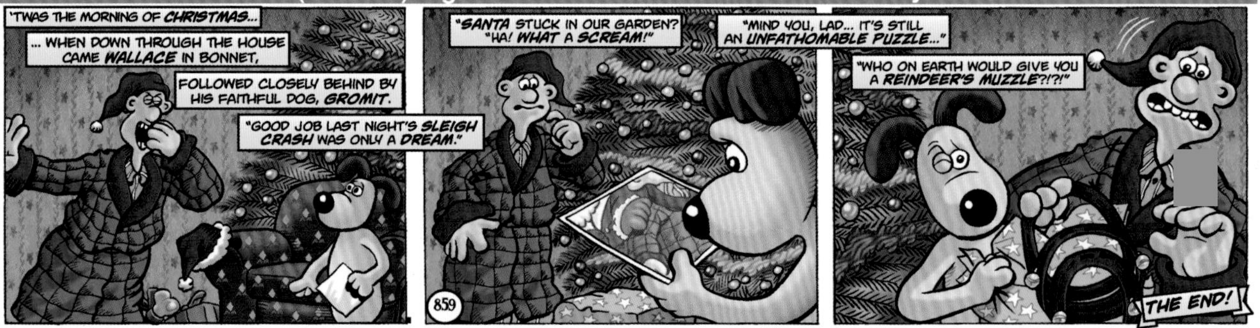
'TWAS THE MORNING OF CHRISTMAS...
... WHEN DOWN THROUGH THE HOUSE CAME WALLACE IN BONNET,
FOLLOWED CLOSELY BEHIND BY HIS FAITHFUL DOG, GROMIT.
"GOOD JOB LAST NIGHT'S SLEIGH CRASH WAS ONLY A DREAM."
"SANTA STUCK IN OUR GARDEN?" "HA! WHAT A SCREAM!"
859
"MIND YOU, LAD... IT'S STILL AN UNFATHOMABLE PUZZLE..."
"WHO ON EARTH WOULD GIVE YOU A REINDEER'S MUZZLE?!?!"
THE END!

The End

Wallace & Gromit - Dance Resolution

by Aardman & Titan Comics

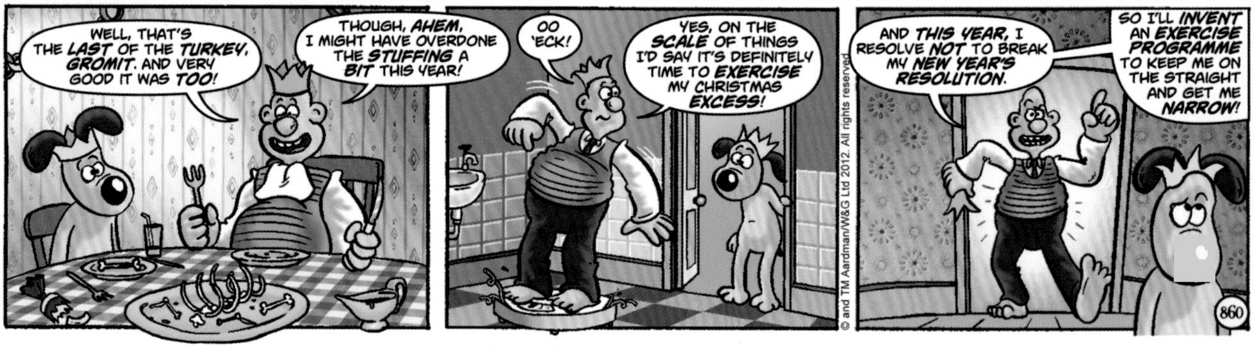
WELL, THAT'S THE LAST OF THE TURKEY, GROMIT. AND VERY GOOD IT WAS TOO!
THOUGH, AHEM, I MIGHT HAVE OVERDONE THE STUFFING A BIT THIS YEAR!
OO 'ECK!
YES, ON THE SCALE OF THINGS I'D SAY IT'S DEFINITELY TIME TO EXERCISE MY CHRISTMAS EXCESS!
AND THIS YEAR, I RESOLVE NOT TO BREAK MY NEW YEAR'S RESOLUTION.
SO I'LL INVENT AN EXERCISE PROGRAMME TO KEEP ME ON THE STRAIGHT AND GET ME NARROW!
860

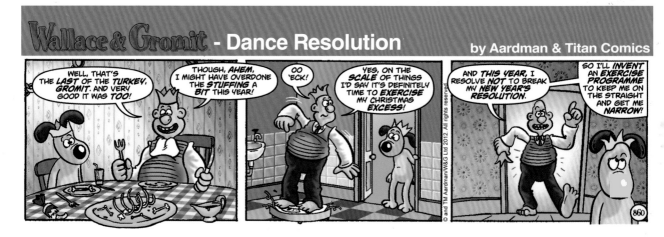

Wallace & Gromit - Dance Resolution by Aardman & Titan Comics

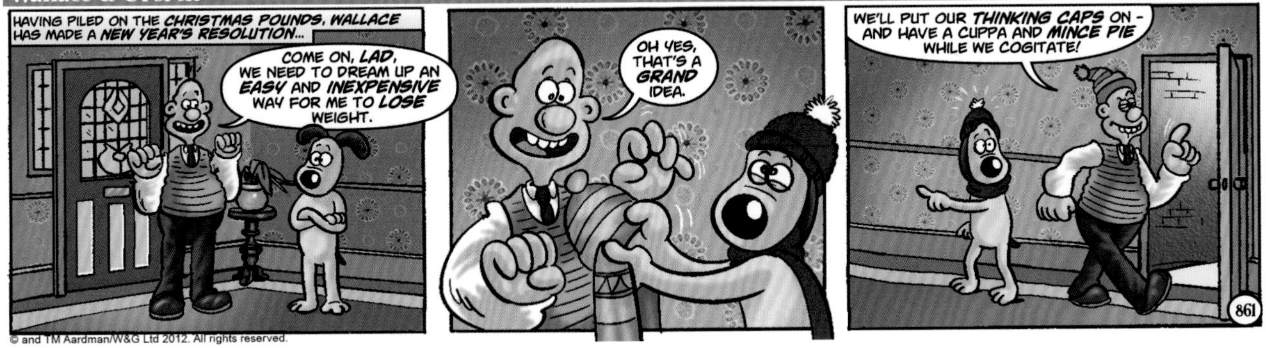
HAVING PILED ON THE CHRISTMAS POUNDS, WALLACE HAS MADE A NEW YEAR'S RESOLUTION...
COME ON, LAD, WE NEED TO DREAM UP AN EASY AND INEXPENSIVE WAY FOR ME TO LOSE WEIGHT.
OH YES, THAT'S A GRAND IDEA.
WE'LL PUT OUR THINKING CAPS ON - AND HAVE A CUPPA AND MINCE PIE WHILE WE COGITATE!
861

Wallace & Gromit - Dance Resolution by Aardman & Titan Comics

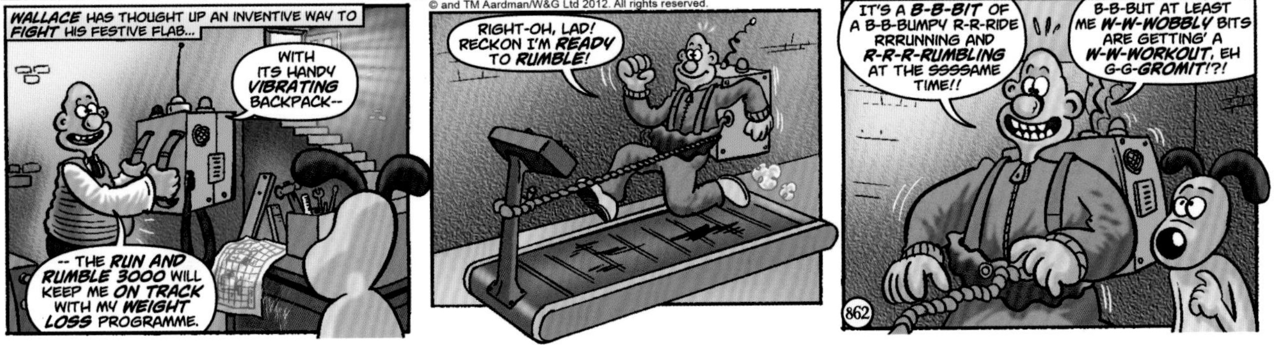
WALLACE HAS THOUGHT UP AN INVENTIVE WAY TO FIGHT HIS FESTIVE FLAB...
WITH ITS HANDY VIBRATING BACKPACK--
-- THE RUN AND RUMBLE 3000 WILL KEEP ME ON TRACK WITH MY WEIGHT LOSS PROGRAMME.
RIGHT-OH, LAD! RECKON I'M READY TO RUMBLE!
IT'S A B-B-BIT OF A B-B-BUMPY R-R-RIDE RRRUNNING AND R-R-R-RUMBLING AT THE SSSSAME TIME!!
B-B-BUT AT LEAST ME W-W-WOBBLY BITS ARE GETTING' A W-W-WORKOUT, EH G-G-GROMIT!?!
862

Wallace & Gromit - Dance Resolution by Aardman & Titan Comics

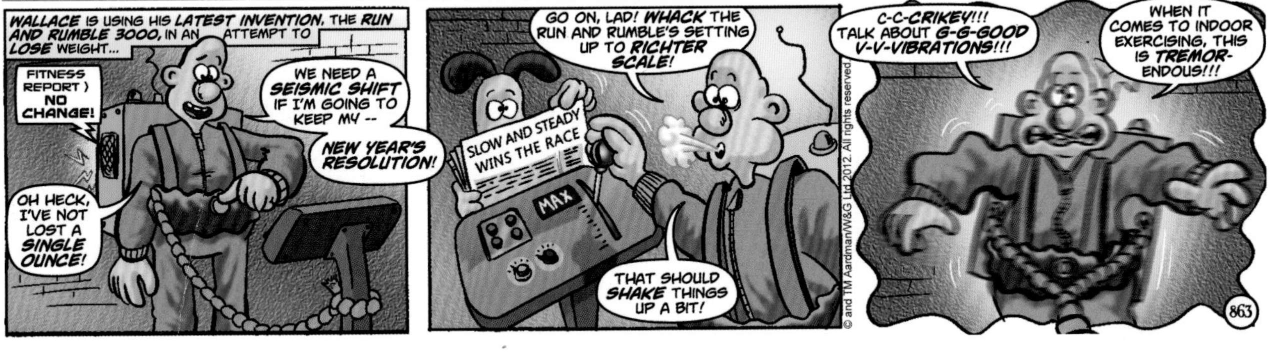
WALLACE IS USING HIS LATEST INVENTION, THE RUN AND RUMBLE 3000, IN AN ATTEMPT TO LOSE WEIGHT...
FITNESS REPORT) NO CHANGE!
WE NEED A SEISMIC SHIFT IF I'M GOING TO KEEP MY --
NEW YEAR'S RESOLUTION!
OH HECK, I'VE NOT LOST A SINGLE OUNCE!
GO ON, LAD! WHACK THE RUN AND RUMBLE'S SETTING UP TO RICHTER SCALE!
SLOW AND STEADY WINS THE RACE
MAX
THAT SHOULD SHAKE THINGS UP A BIT!
C-C-CRIKEY!!! TALK ABOUT G-G-GOOD V-V-VIBRATIONS!!!
WHEN IT COMES TO INDOOR EXERCISING, THIS IS TREMOR-ENDOUS!!!
863

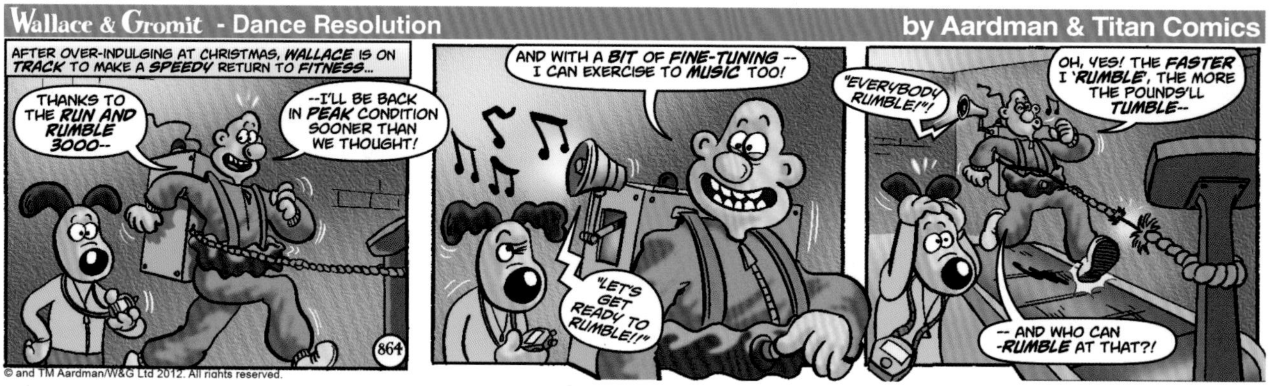
Wallace & Gromit - Dance Resolution
by Aardman & Titan Comics
AFTER OVER-INDULGING AT CHRISTMAS, WALLACE IS ON TRACK TO MAKE A SPEEDY RETURN TO FITNESS...
THANKS TO THE RUN AND RUMBLE 3000--
--I'LL BE BACK IN PEAK CONDITION SOONER THAN WE THOUGHT!
864
AND WITH A BIT OF FINE-TUNING -- I CAN EXERCISE TO MUSIC TOO!
"LET'S GET READY TO RUMBLE!!"
"EVERYBODY RUMBLE!"!
OH, YES! THE FASTER I 'RUMBLE', THE MORE THE POUNDS'LL TUMBLE--
-- AND WHO CAN -RUMBLE AT THAT?!

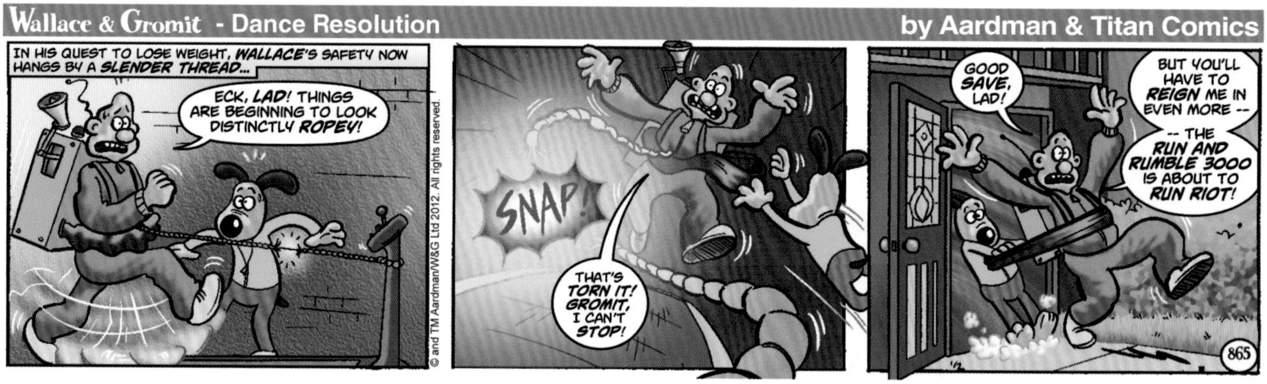
Wallace & Gromit - Dance Resolution
by Aardman & Titan Comics
IN HIS QUEST TO LOSE WEIGHT, WALLACE'S SAFETY NOW HANGS BY A SLENDER THREAD...
ECK, LAD! THINGS ARE BEGINNING TO LOOK DISTINCTLY ROPEY!
SNAP!
THAT'S TORN IT! GROMIT, I CAN'T STOP!
GOOD SAVE, LAD!
BUT YOU'LL HAVE TO REIGN ME IN EVEN MORE --
-- THE RUN AND RUMBLE 3000 IS ABOUT TO RUN RIOT!
865

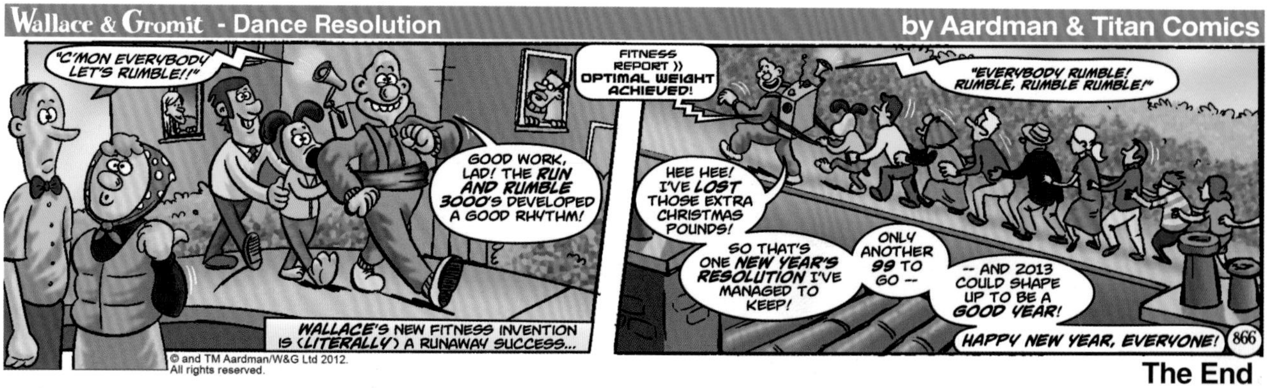
Wallace & Gromit - Dance Resolution
by Aardman & Titan Comics
"C'MON EVERYBODY LET'S RUMBLE!!"
GOOD WORK, LAD! THE RUN AND RUMBLE 3000'S DEVELOPED A GOOD RHYTHM!
WALLACE'S NEW FITNESS INVENTION IS (LITERALLY) A RUNAWAY SUCCESS...
FITNESS REPORT)) OPTIMAL WEIGHT ACHIEVED!
"EVERYBODY RUMBLE! RUMBLE, RUMBLE RUMBLE!"
HEE HEE! I'VE LOST THOSE EXTRA CHRISTMAS POUNDS!
SO THAT'S ONE NEW YEAR'S RESOLUTION I'VE MANAGED TO KEEP!
ONLY ANOTHER 99 TO GO --
-- AND 2013 COULD SHAPE UP TO BE A GOOD YEAR!
HAPPY NEW YEAR, EVERYONE!
866

The End

Wallace & Gromit - Daily Funnies

by Aardman & Titan Comics

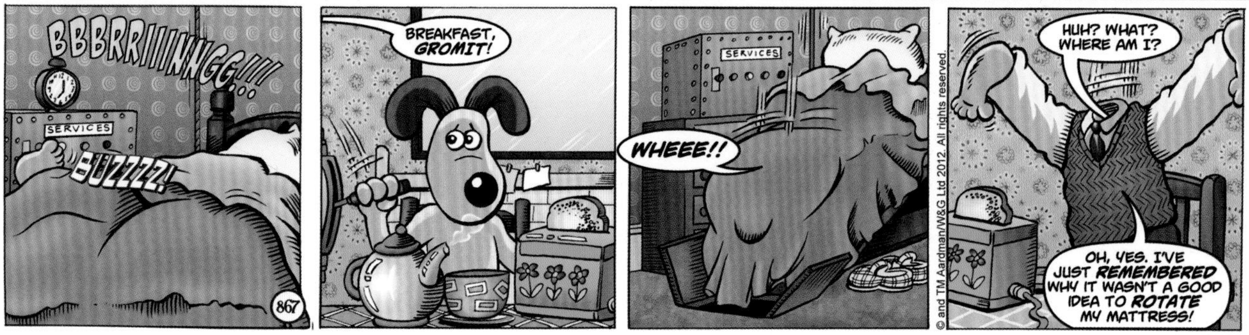

BBBRRIIINNGG!!!
SERVICES
BUZZZZ!
867
BREAKFAST, GROMIT!
SERVICES
WHEEE!!
HUH? WHAT? WHERE AM I?
OH, YES. I'VE JUST REMEMBERED WHY IT WASN'T A GOOD IDEA TO ROTATE MY MATTRESS!
© and TM Aardman/W&G Ltd 2012. All rights reserved.

Wallace & Gromit - Daily Funnies

by Aardman & Titan Comics

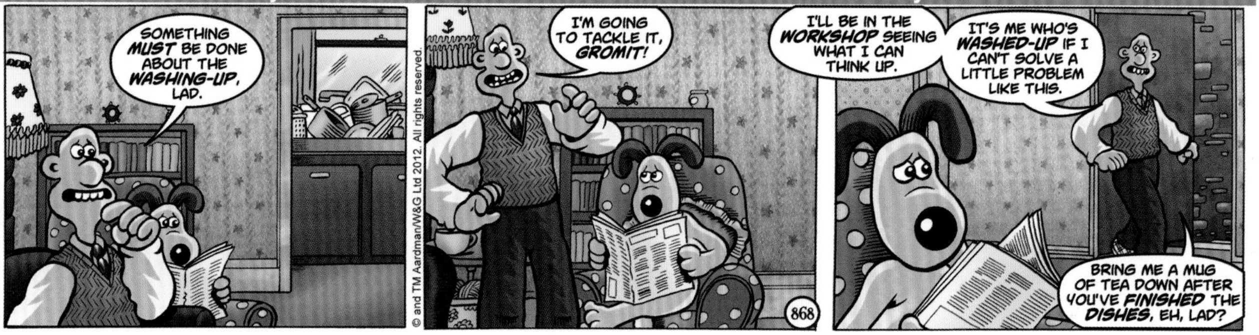

SOMETHING MUST BE DONE ABOUT THE WASHING-UP, LAD.
© and TM Aardman/W&G Ltd 2012. All rights reserved.
I'M GOING TO TACKLE IT, GROMIT!
868
I'LL BE IN THE WORKSHOP SEEING WHAT I CAN THINK UP.
IT'S ME WHO'S WASHED-UP IF I CAN'T SOLVE A LITTLE PROBLEM LIKE THIS.
BRING ME A MUG OF TEA DOWN AFTER YOU'VE FINISHED THE DISHES, EH, LAD?

Wallace & Gromit - Daily Funnies

by Aardman & Titan Comics

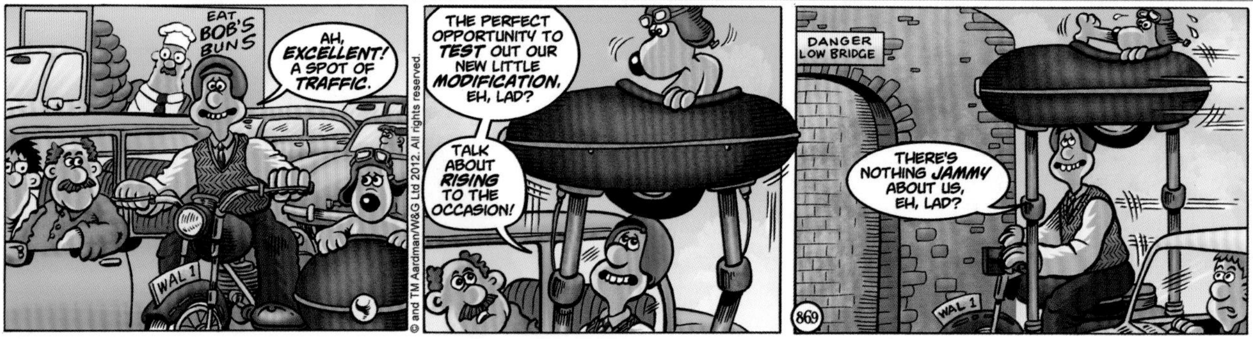

EAT BOB'S BUNS
AH, EXCELLENT! A SPOT OF TRAFFIC.
WAL 1
© and TM Aardman/W&G Ltd 2012. All rights reserved.
THE PERFECT OPPORTUNITY TO TEST OUT OUR NEW LITTLE MODIFICATION, EH, LAD?
TALK ABOUT RISING TO THE OCCASION!
DANGER LOW BRIDGE
THERE'S NOTHING JAMMY ABOUT US, EH, LAD?
WAL 1
869

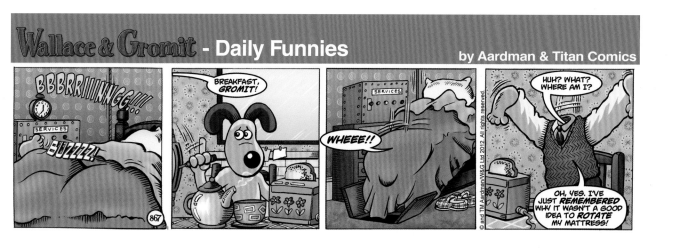

Wallace & Gromit - Daily Funnies

by Aardman & Titan Comics

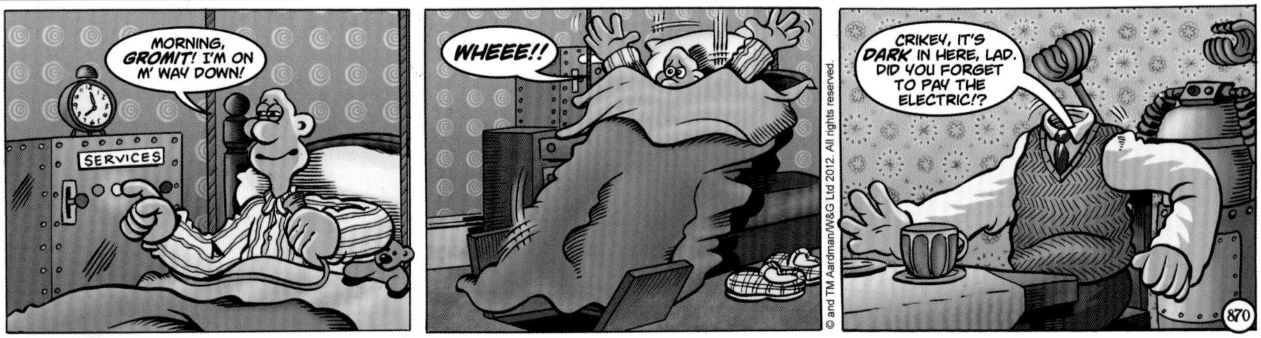

MORNING, GROMIT! I'M ON M' WAY DOWN!
SERVICES
WHEEE!!
CRIKEY, IT'S DARK IN HERE, LAD. DID YOU FORGET TO PAY THE ELECTRIC!?
870

Wallace & Gromit - Daily Funnies

by Aardman & Titan Comics

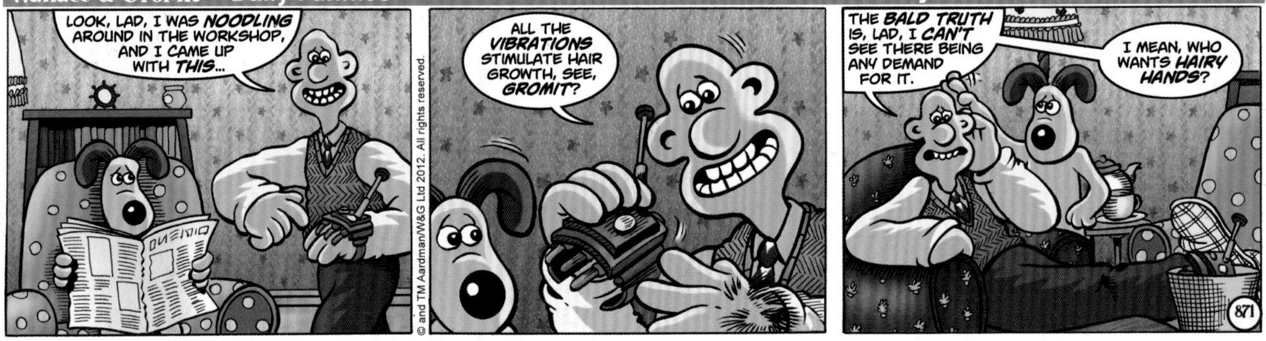

LOOK, LAD, I WAS NOODLING AROUND IN THE WORKSHOP, AND I CAME UP WITH THIS...
ALL THE VIBRATIONS STIMULATE HAIR GROWTH, SEE, GROMIT?
THE BALD TRUTH IS, LAD, I CAN'T SEE THERE BEING ANY DEMAND FOR IT.
I MEAN, WHO WANTS HAIRY HANDS?
871

Wallace & Gromit - Daily Funnies

by Aardman & Titan Comics

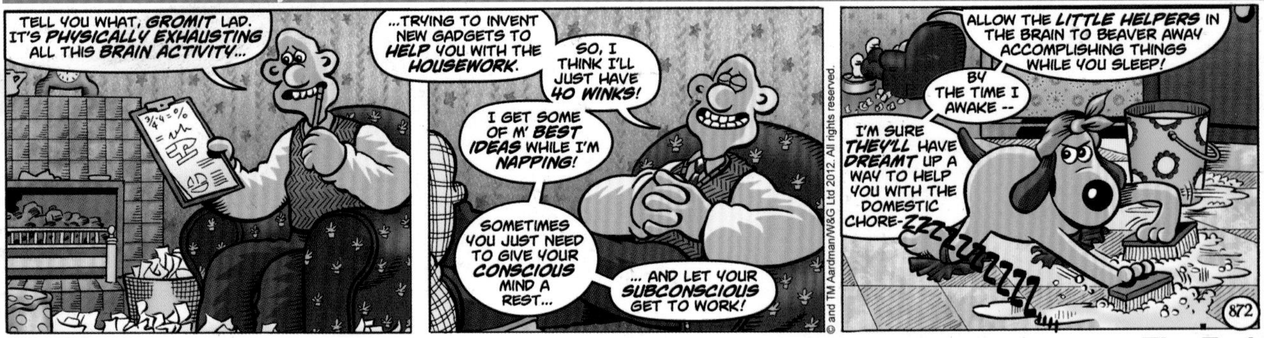

TELL YOU WHAT, GROMIT LAD. IT'S PHYSICALLY EXHAUSTING ALL THIS BRAIN ACTIVITY...
...TRYING TO INVENT NEW GADGETS TO HELP YOU WITH THE HOUSEWORK.
SO, I THINK I'LL JUST HAVE 40 WINKS!
I GET SOME OF M' BEST IDEAS WHILE I'M NAPPING!
SOMETIMES YOU JUST NEED TO GIVE YOUR CONSCIOUS MIND A REST...
... AND LET YOUR SUBCONSCIOUS GET TO WORK!
ALLOW THE LITTLE HELPERS IN THE BRAIN TO BEAVER AWAY ACCOMPLISHING THINGS WHILE YOU SLEEP!
BY THE TIME I AWAKE --
I'M SURE THEY'LL HAVE DREAMT UP A WAY TO HELP YOU WITH THE DOMESTIC CHORE-ZZZZZZZZZZZ
872

The End

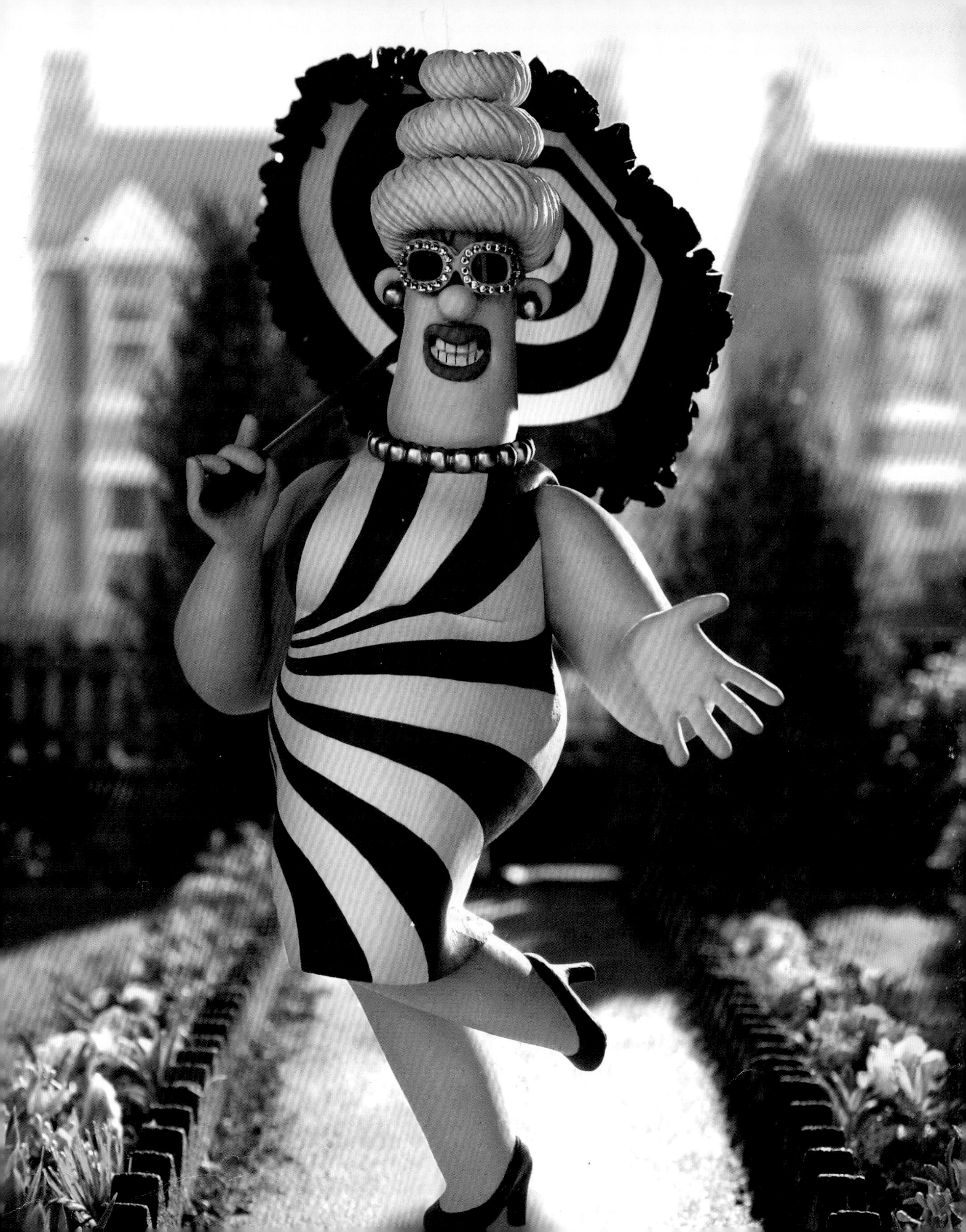

Wallace & Gromit - Family Tree

by Aardman & Titan Comics

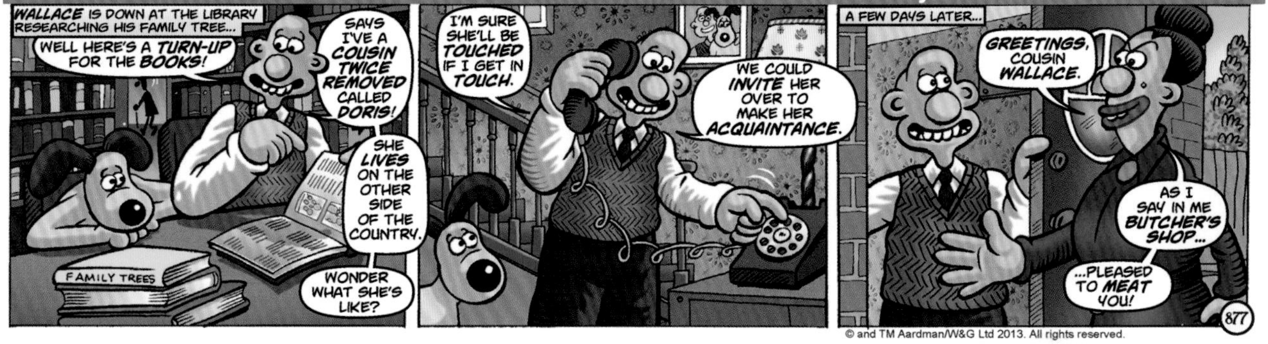
WALLACE IS DOWN AT THE LIBRARY RESEARCHING HIS FAMILY TREE...
WELL HERE'S A TURN-UP FOR THE BOOKS!
SAYS I'VE A COUSIN TWICE REMOVED CALLED DORIS!
SHE LIVES ON THE OTHER SIDE OF THE COUNTRY.
WONDER WHAT SHE'S LIKE?
FAMILY TREES
I'M SURE SHE'LL BE TOUCHED IF I GET IN TOUCH.
WE COULD INVITE HER OVER TO MAKE HER ACQUAINTANCE.
A FEW DAYS LATER...
GREETINGS, COUSIN WALLACE.
AS I SAY IN ME BUTCHER'S SHOP...
...PLEASED TO MEAT YOU!
877

Wallace & Gromit - Family Tree

by Aardman & Titan Comics

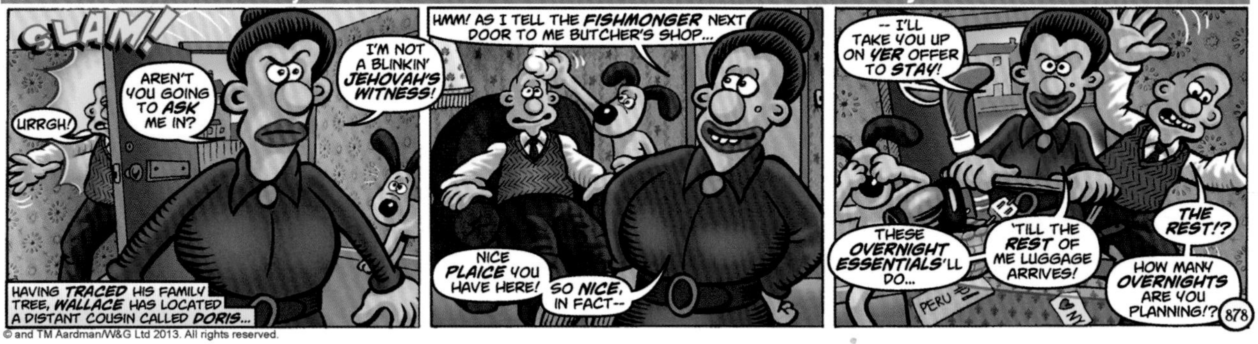
SLAM!
URRGH!
AREN'T YOU GOING TO ASK ME IN?
I'M NOT A BLINKIN' JEHOVAH'S WITNESS!
HAVING TRACED HIS FAMILY TREE, WALLACE HAS LOCATED A DISTANT COUSIN CALLED DORIS...
HMM! AS I TELL THE FISHMONGER NEXT DOOR TO ME BUTCHER'S SHOP...
NICE PLAICE YOU HAVE HERE!
SO NICE, IN FACT--
-- I'LL TAKE YOU UP ON YER OFFER TO STAY!
THESE OVERNIGHT ESSENTIALS'LL DO...
'TILL THE REST OF ME LUGGAGE ARRIVES!
THE REST!?
HOW MANY OVERNIGHTS ARE YOU PLANNING!?
PERU
878

Wallace & Gromit - Family Tree

by Aardman & Titan Comics

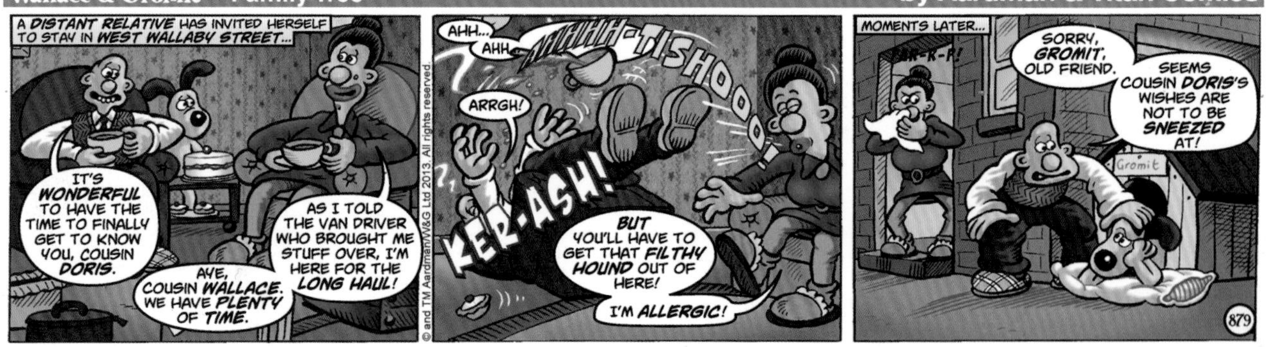
A DISTANT RELATIVE HAS INVITED HERSELF TO STAY IN WEST WALLABY STREET...
IT'S WONDERFUL TO HAVE THE TIME TO FINALLY GET TO KNOW YOU, COUSIN DORIS.
AYE, COUSIN WALLACE. WE HAVE PLENTY OF TIME.
AS I TOLD THE VAN DRIVER WHO BROUGHT ME STUFF OVER, I'M HERE FOR THE LONG HAUL!
AHH...
AHH...
AHHHH-TISHOOO
ARRGH!
KER-ASH!
BUT YOU'LL HAVE TO GET THAT FILTHY HOUND OUT OF HERE!
I'M ALLERGIC!
MOMENTS LATER...
SORRY, GROMIT, OLD FRIEND.
SEEMS COUSIN DORIS'S WISHES ARE NOT TO BE SNEEZED AT!
Gromit
879

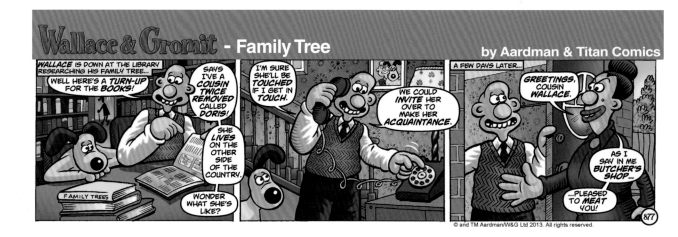

Wallace & Gromit - Family Tree

by Aardman & Titan Comics

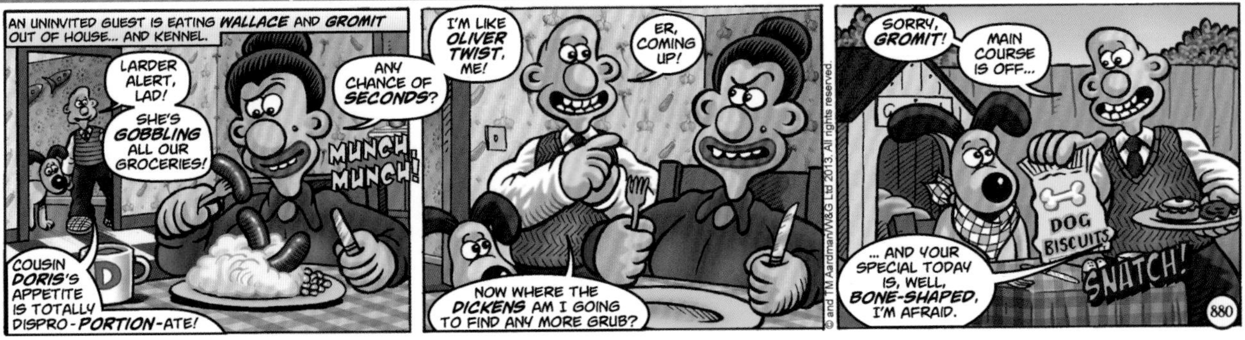

AN UNINVITED GUEST IS EATING WALLACE AND GROMIT OUT OF HOUSE... AND KENNEL.
LARDER ALERT, LAD!
SHE'S GOBBLING ALL OUR GROCERIES!
ANY CHANCE OF SECONDS?
MUNCH, MUNCH!
COUSIN DORIS'S APPETITE IS TOTALLY DISPRO-PORTION-ATE!
I'M LIKE OLIVER TWIST, ME!
ER, COMING UP!
NOW WHERE THE DICKENS AM I GOING TO FIND ANY MORE GRUB?
SORRY, GROMIT!
MAIN COURSE IS OFF...
DOG BISCUITS
... AND YOUR SPECIAL TODAY IS, WELL, BONE-SHAPED, I'M AFRAID.
SNATCH!
880

Wallace & Gromit - Family Tree

by Aardman & Titan Comics

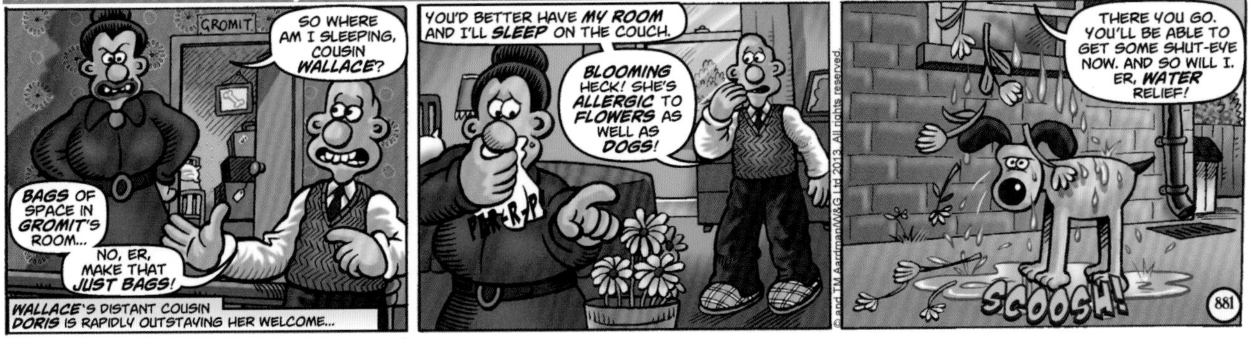

GROMIT
SO WHERE AM I SLEEPING, COUSIN WALLACE?
BAGS OF SPACE IN GROMIT'S ROOM...
NO, ER, MAKE THAT JUST BAGS!
WALLACE'S DISTANT COUSIN DORIS IS RAPIDLY OUTSTAYING HER WELCOME...
YOU'D BETTER HAVE MY ROOM AND I'LL SLEEP ON THE COUCH.
BLOOMING HECK! SHE'S ALLERGIC TO FLOWERS AS WELL AS DOGS!
PHRR-R-P!
THERE YOU GO. YOU'LL BE ABLE TO GET SOME SHUT-EYE NOW. AND SO WILL I. ER, WATER RELIEF!
SCOOSH!
881

Wallace & Gromit - Family Tree

by Aardman & Titan Comics

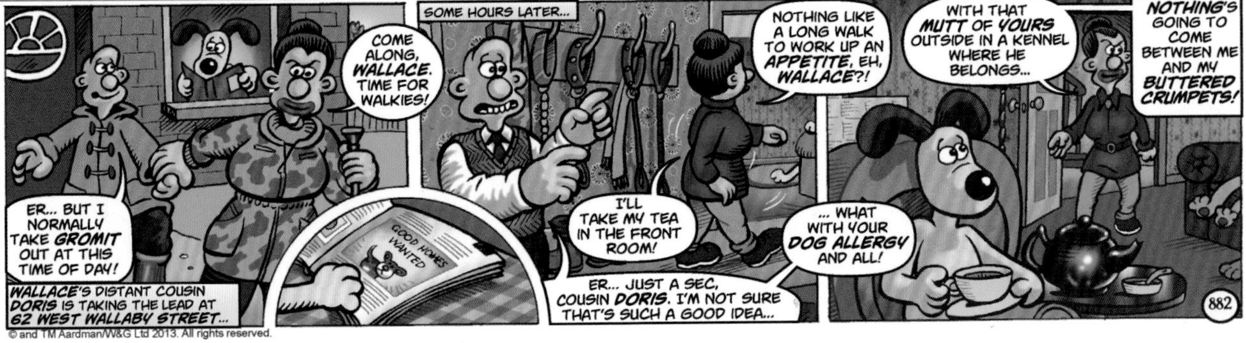

COME ALONG, WALLACE. TIME FOR WALKIES!
ER... BUT I NORMALLY TAKE GROMIT OUT AT THIS TIME OF DAY!
WALLACE'S DISTANT COUSIN DORIS IS TAKING THE LEAD AT 62 WEST WALLABY STREET...
GOOD HOMES WANTED
SOME HOURS LATER...
NOTHING LIKE A LONG WALK TO WORK UP AN APPETITE, EH, WALLACE?!
I'LL TAKE MY TEA IN THE FRONT ROOM!
ER... JUST A SEC, COUSIN DORIS. I'M NOT SURE THAT'S SUCH A GOOD IDEA...
WITH THAT MUTT OF YOURS OUTSIDE IN A KENNEL WHERE HE BELONGS...
... WHAT WITH YOUR DOG ALLERGY AND ALL!
NOTHING'S GOING TO COME BETWEEN ME AND MY BUTTERED CRUMPETS!
882

Wallace & Gromit - Family Tree

by Aardman & Titan Comics

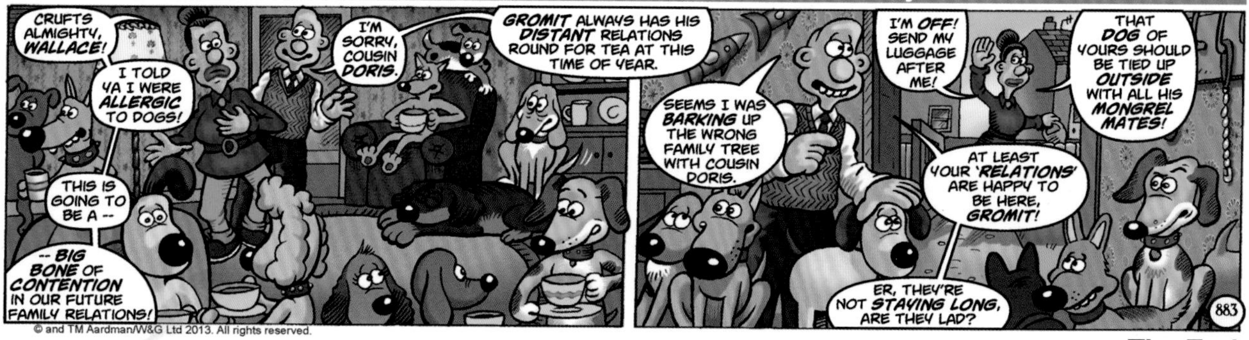

CRUFTS ALMIGHTY, WALLACE!
I TOLD YA I WERE ALLERGIC TO DOGS!
THIS IS GOING TO BE A --
-- BIG BONE OF CONTENTION IN OUR FUTURE FAMILY RELATIONS!
I'M SORRY, COUSIN DORIS.
GROMIT ALWAYS HAS HIS DISTANT RELATIONS ROUND FOR TEA AT THIS TIME OF YEAR.
SEEMS I WAS BARKING UP THE WRONG FAMILY TREE WITH COUSIN DORIS.
I'M OFF! SEND MY LUGGAGE AFTER ME!
THAT DOG OF YOURS SHOULD BE TIED UP OUTSIDE WITH ALL HIS MONGREL MATES!
AT LEAST YOUR 'RELATIONS' ARE HAPPY TO BE HERE, GROMIT!
ER, THEY'RE NOT STAYING LONG, ARE THEY LAD?
883

The End

Wallace & Gromit - A Mole Lot of Trouble

by Aardman & Titan Comics

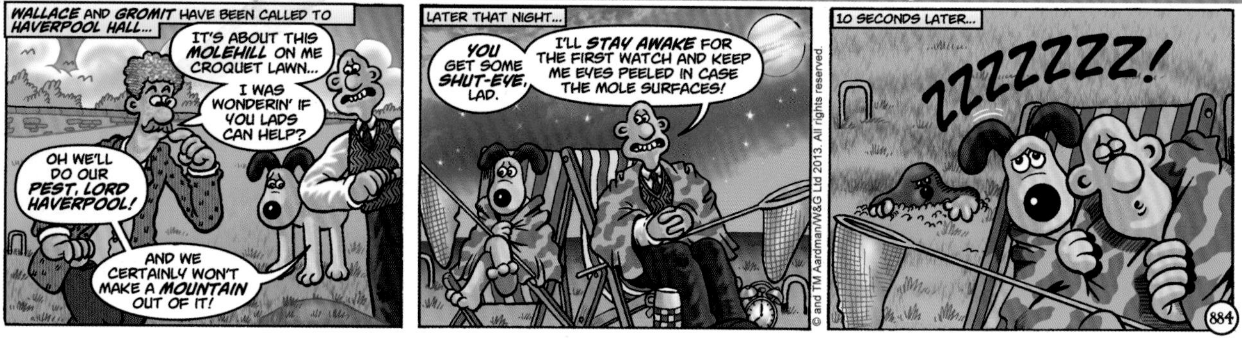

WALLACE AND GROMIT HAVE BEEN CALLED TO HAVERPOOL HALL...
IT'S ABOUT THIS MOLEHILL ON ME CROQUET LAWN...
I WAS WONDERIN' IF YOU LADS CAN HELP?
OH WE'LL DO OUR PEST, LORD HAVERPOOL!
AND WE CERTAINLY WON'T MAKE A MOUNTAIN OUT OF IT!
LATER THAT NIGHT...
YOU GET SOME SHUT-EYE, LAD.
I'LL STAY AWAKE FOR THE FIRST WATCH AND KEEP ME EYES PEELED IN CASE THE MOLE SURFACES!
© and TM Aardman/W&G Ltd 2013. All rights reserved.
10 SECONDS LATER...
ZZZZZZZ!
884

Wallace & Gromit - A Mole Lot of Trouble

by Aardman & Titan Comics

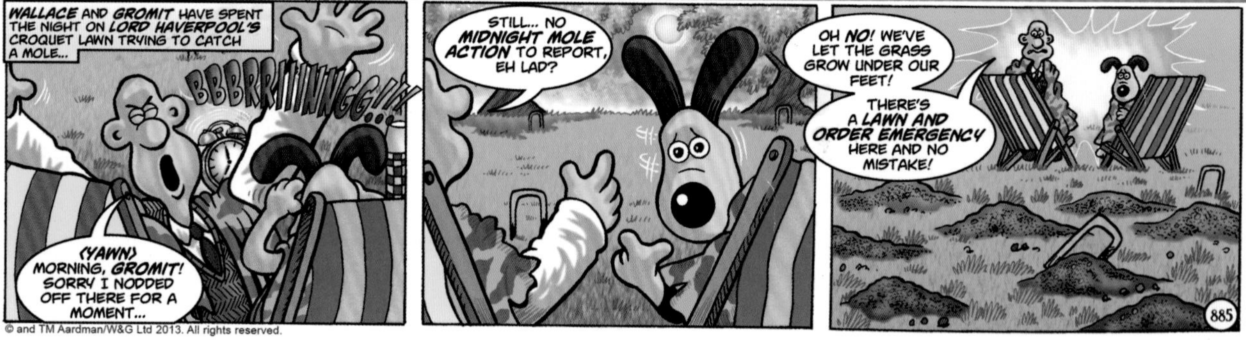

WALLACE AND GROMIT HAVE SPENT THE NIGHT ON LORD HAVERPOOL'S CROQUET LAWN TRYING TO CATCH A MOLE...
BBBBRRIIINNGG!!!
(YAWN) MORNING, GROMIT! SORRY I NODDED OFF THERE FOR A MOMENT...
STILL... NO MIDNIGHT MOLE ACTION TO REPORT, EH LAD?
OH NO! WE'VE LET THE GRASS GROW UNDER OUR FEET!
THERE'S A LAWN AND ORDER EMERGENCY HERE AND NO MISTAKE!
885

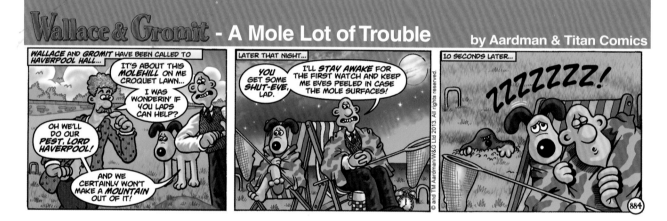

Wallace & Gromit - A Mole Lot of Trouble by Aardman & Titan Comics

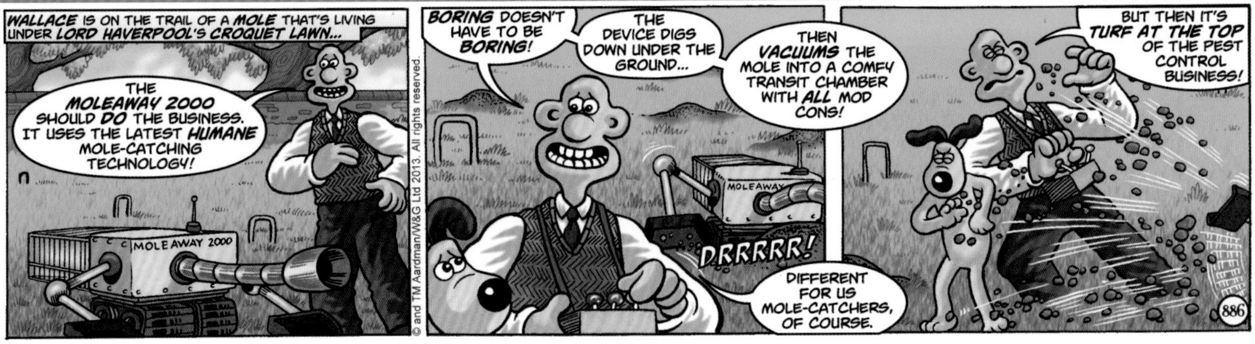
WALLACE IS ON THE TRAIL OF A MOLE THAT'S LIVING UNDER LORD HAVERPOOL'S CROQUET LAWN...
THE MOLEAWAY 2000 SHOULD DO THE BUSINESS. IT USES THE LATEST HUMANE MOLE-CATCHING TECHNOLOGY!
MOLEAWAY 2000
© and TM Aardman/W&G Ltd 2013. All rights reserved.
BORING DOESN'T HAVE TO BE BORING!
THE DEVICE DIGS DOWN UNDER THE GROUND...
THEN VACUUMS THE MOLE INTO A COMFY TRANSIT CHAMBER WITH ALL MOD CONS!
MOLEAWAY
DRRRRR!
DIFFERENT FOR US MOLE-CATCHERS, OF COURSE.
BUT THEN IT'S TURF AT THE TOP OF THE PEST CONTROL BUSINESS!
886

Wallace & Gromit - A Mole Lot of Trouble by Aardman & Titan Comics

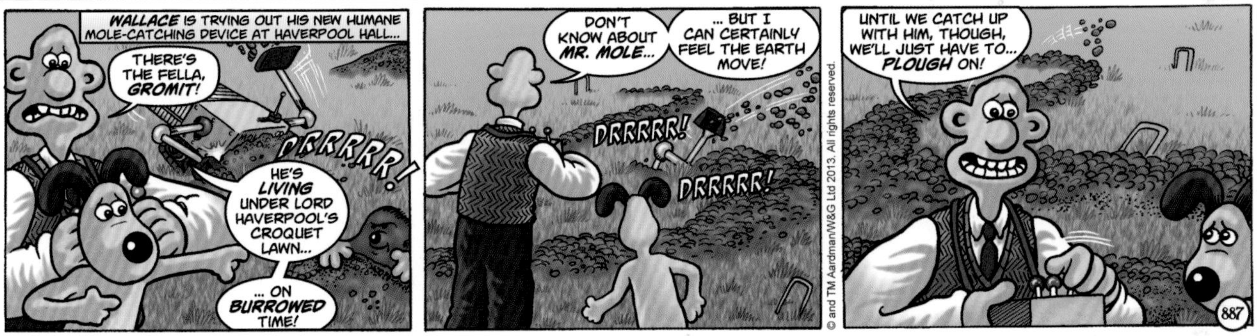
WALLACE IS TRYING OUT HIS NEW HUMANE MOLE-CATCHING DEVICE AT HAVERPOOL HALL...
THERE'S THE FELLA, GROMIT!
DRRRRRR!
HE'S LIVING UNDER LORD HAVERPOOL'S CROQUET LAWN...
... ON BURROWED TIME!
DON'T KNOW ABOUT MR. MOLE...
... BUT I CAN CERTAINLY FEEL THE EARTH MOVE!
DRRRRRR!
DRRRRRR!
© and TM Aardman/W&G Ltd 2013. All rights reserved.
UNTIL WE CATCH UP WITH HIM, THOUGH, WE'LL JUST HAVE TO... PLOUGH ON!
887

Wallace & Gromit - A Mole Lot of Trouble by Aardman & Titan Comics

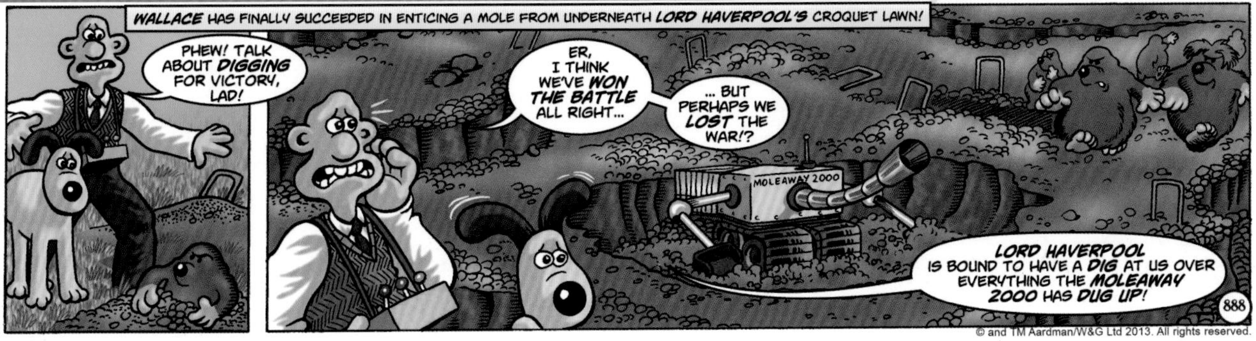
WALLACE HAS FINALLY SUCCEEDED IN ENTICING A MOLE FROM UNDERNEATH LORD HAVERPOOL'S CROQUET LAWN!
PHEW! TALK ABOUT DIGGING FOR VICTORY, LAD!
ER, I THINK WE'VE WON THE BATTLE ALL RIGHT...
... BUT PERHAPS WE LOST THE WAR!?
MOLEAWAY 2000
LORD HAVERPOOL IS BOUND TO HAVE A DIG AT US OVER EVERYTHING THE MOLEAWAY 2000 HAS DUG UP!
888

Wallace & Gromit - A Mole Lot of Trouble

by Aardman & Titan Comics

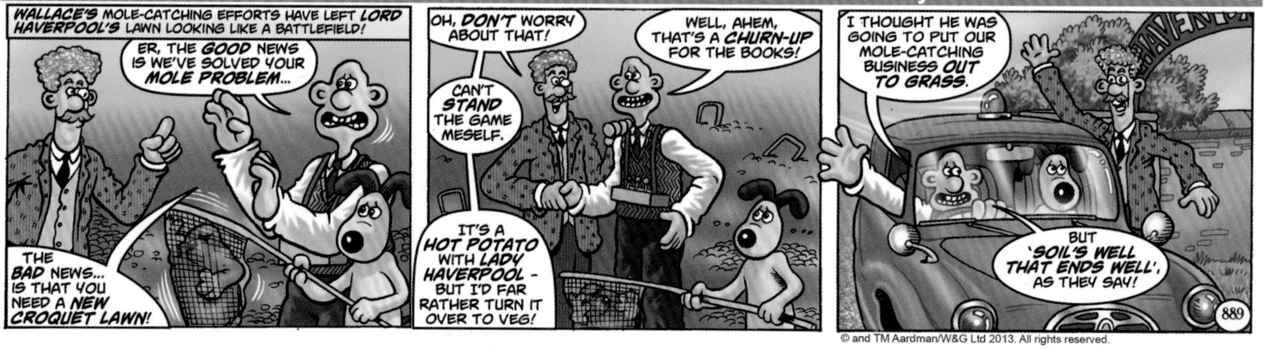

WALLACE'S MOLE-CATCHING EFFORTS HAVE LEFT LORD HAVERPOOL'S LAWN LOOKING LIKE A BATTLEFIELD!
ER, THE GOOD NEWS IS WE'VE SOLVED YOUR MOLE PROBLEM...
THE BAD NEWS... IS THAT YOU NEED A NEW CROQUET LAWN!
OH, DON'T WORRY ABOUT THAT!
WELL, AHEM, THAT'S A CHURN-UP FOR THE BOOKS!
CAN'T STAND THE GAME MESELF.
IT'S A HOT POTATO WITH LADY HAVERPOOL - BUT I'D FAR RATHER TURN IT OVER TO VEG!
I THOUGHT HE WAS GOING TO PUT OUR MOLE-CATCHING BUSINESS OUT TO GRASS.
BUT 'SOIL'S WELL THAT ENDS WELL', AS THEY SAY!
889

Wallace & Gromit - A Mole Lot of Trouble

by Aardman & Titan Comics

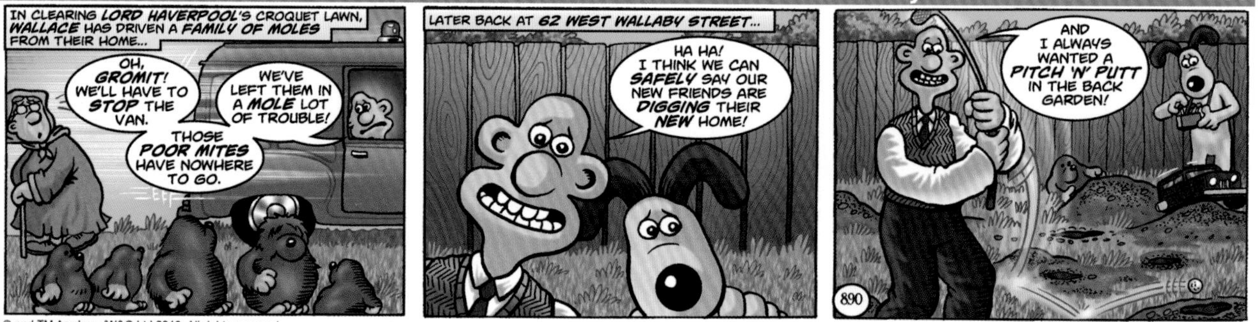

IN CLEARING LORD HAVERPOOL'S CROQUET LAWN, WALLACE HAS DRIVEN A FAMILY OF MOLES FROM THEIR HOME...
OH, GROMIT! WE'LL HAVE TO STOP THE VAN.
WE'VE LEFT THEM IN A MOLE LOT OF TROUBLE!
THOSE POOR MITES HAVE NOWHERE TO GO.
LATER BACK AT 62 WEST WALLABY STREET...
HA HA! I THINK WE CAN SAFELY SAY OUR NEW FRIENDS ARE DIGGING THEIR NEW HOME!
AND I ALWAYS WANTED A PITCH 'N' PUTT IN THE BACK GARDEN!
890

The End

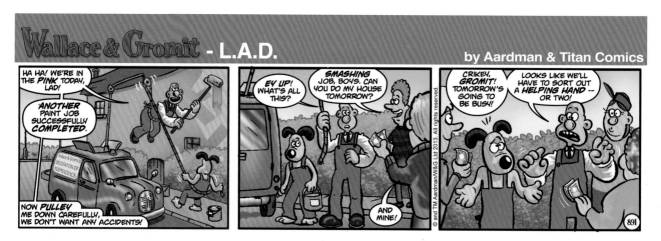

Wallace & Gromit - L.A.D.

by Aardman & Titan Comics

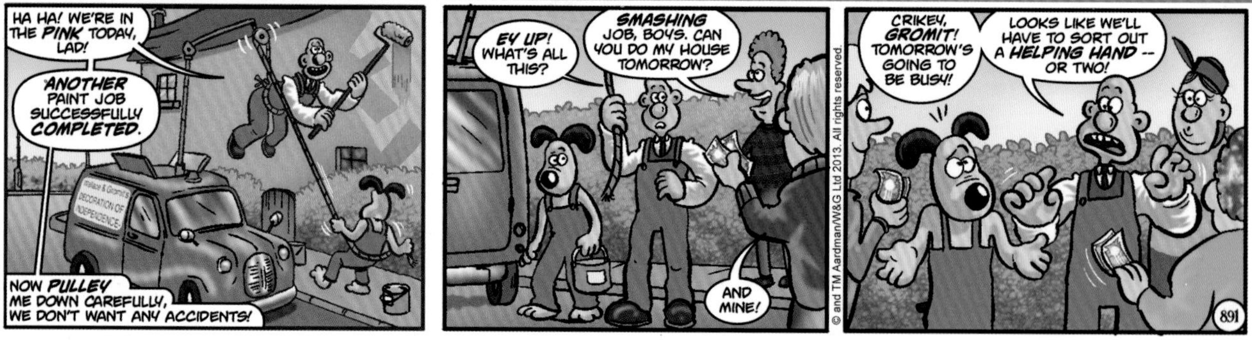

HA HA! WE'RE IN THE PINK TODAY, LAD!
ANOTHER PAINT JOB SUCCESSFULLY COMPLETED.
NOW PULLEY ME DOWN CAREFULLY, WE DON'T WANT ANY ACCIDENTS!
EY UP! WHAT'S ALL THIS?
SMASHING JOB, BOYS. CAN YOU DO MY HOUSE TOMORROW?
AND MINE!
CRIKEY, GROMIT! TOMORROW'S GOING TO BE BUSY!
LOOKS LIKE WE'LL HAVE TO SORT OUT A HELPING HAND -- OR TWO!
891

Wallace & Gromit - L.A.D. — by Aardman & Titan Comics

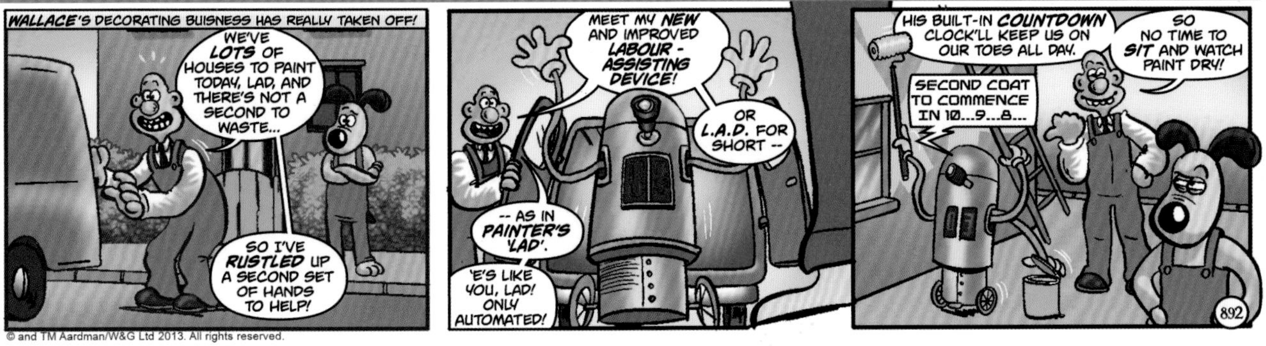

WALLACE'S DECORATING BUISNESS HAS REALLY TAKEN OFF!
WE'VE LOTS OF HOUSES TO PAINT TODAY, LAD, AND THERE'S NOT A SECOND TO WASTE...
SO I'VE RUSTLED UP A SECOND SET OF HANDS TO HELP!
MEET MY NEW AND IMPROVED LABOUR - ASSISTING DEVICE!
OR L.A.D. FOR SHORT --
-- AS IN PAINTER'S 'LAD'.
'E'S LIKE YOU, LAD! ONLY AUTOMATED!
HIS BUILT-IN COUNTDOWN CLOCK'LL KEEP US ON OUR TOES ALL DAY.
SO NO TIME TO SIT AND WATCH PAINT DRY!
SECOND COAT TO COMMENCE IN 10...9...8...
892

Wallace & Gromit - L.A.D. — by Aardman & Titan Comics

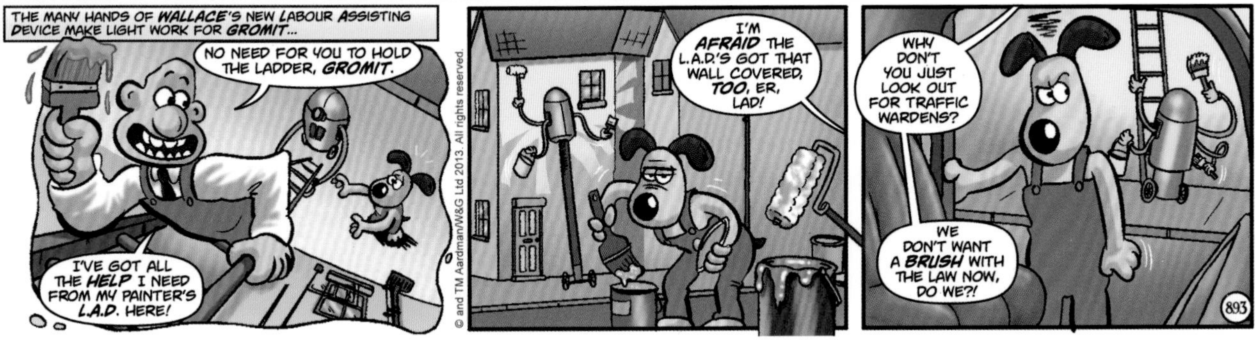

THE MANY HANDS OF WALLACE'S NEW LABOUR ASSISTING DEVICE MAKE LIGHT WORK FOR GROMIT...
NO NEED FOR YOU TO HOLD THE LADDER, GROMIT.
I'VE GOT ALL THE HELP I NEED FROM MY PAINTER'S L.A.D. HERE!
© and TM Aardman/W&G Ltd 2013. All rights reserved.
I'M AFRAID THE L.A.D.'S GOT THAT WALL COVERED, TOO, ER, LAD!
WHY DON'T YOU JUST LOOK OUT FOR TRAFFIC WARDENS?
WE DON'T WANT A BRUSH WITH THE LAW NOW, DO WE?!
893

Wallace & Gromit - L.A.D. — by Aardman & Titan Comics

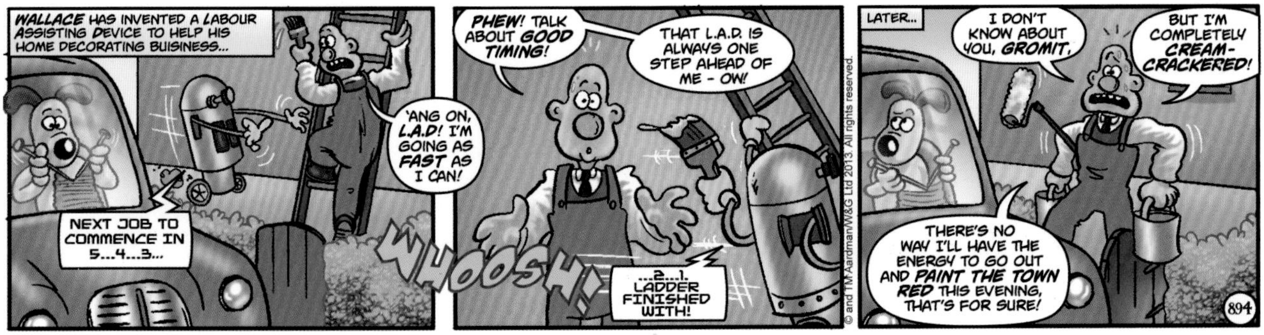

WALLACE HAS INVENTED A LABOUR ASSISTING DEVICE TO HELP HIS HOME DECORATING BUISINESS...
'ANG ON, L.A.D! I'M GOING AS FAST AS I CAN!
NEXT JOB TO COMMENCE IN 5...4...3...
WHOOSH!
PHEW! TALK ABOUT GOOD TIMING!
THAT L.A.D. IS ALWAYS ONE STEP AHEAD OF ME - OW!
...2...1. LADDER FINISHED WITH!
© and TM Aardman/W&G Ltd 2013. All rights reserved.
LATER...
I DON'T KNOW ABOUT YOU, GROMIT,
BUT I'M COMPLETELY CREAM-CRACKERED!
THERE'S NO WAY I'LL HAVE THE ENERGY TO GO OUT AND PAINT THE TOWN RED THIS EVENING, THAT'S FOR SURE!
894

Wallace & Gromit - L.A.D. by Aardman & Titan Comics

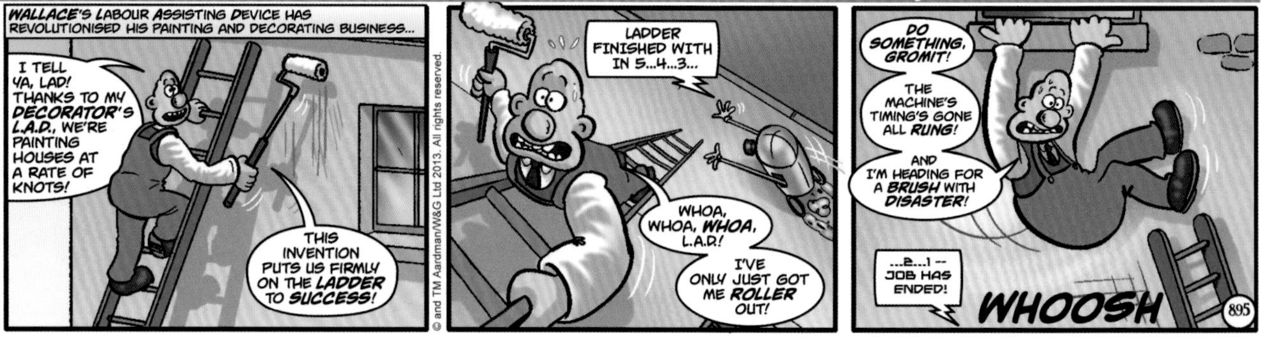
WALLACE'S LABOUR ASSISTING DEVICE HAS REVOLUTIONISED HIS PAINTING AND DECORATING BUSINESS...
I TELL YA, LAD! THANKS TO MY DECORATOR'S L.A.D., WE'RE PAINTING HOUSES AT A RATE OF KNOTS!
THIS INVENTION PUTS US FIRMLY ON THE LADDER TO SUCCESS!
LADDER FINISHED WITH IN 5...4...3...
WHOA, WHOA, WHOA, L.A.D.!
I'VE ONLY JUST GOT ME ROLLER OUT!
DO SOMETHING, GROMIT!
THE MACHINE'S TIMING'S GONE ALL RUNG!
AND I'M HEADING FOR A BRUSH WITH DISASTER!
...2...1 -- JOB HAS ENDED!
WHOOSH
895

Wallace & Gromit - L.A.D. by Aardman & Titan Comics

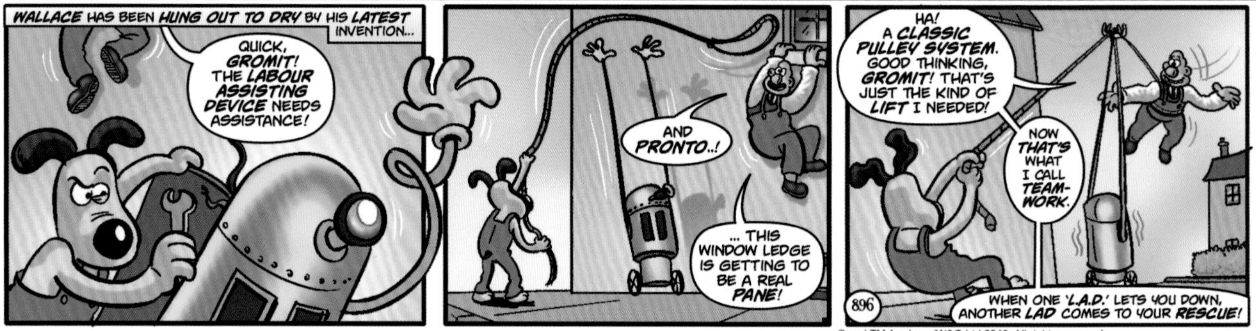
WALLACE HAS BEEN HUNG OUT TO DRY BY HIS LATEST INVENTION...
QUICK, GROMIT! THE LABOUR ASSISTING DEVICE NEEDS ASSISTANCE!
AND PRONTO..!
... THIS WINDOW LEDGE IS GETTING TO BE A REAL PANE!
HA! A CLASSIC PULLEY SYSTEM. GOOD THINKING, GROMIT! THAT'S JUST THE KIND OF LIFT I NEEDED!
NOW THAT'S WHAT I CALL TEAM-WORK.
896
WHEN ONE 'L.A.D.' LETS YOU DOWN, ANOTHER LAD COMES TO YOUR RESCUE!

Wallace & Gromit - L.A.D. by Aardman & Titan Comics

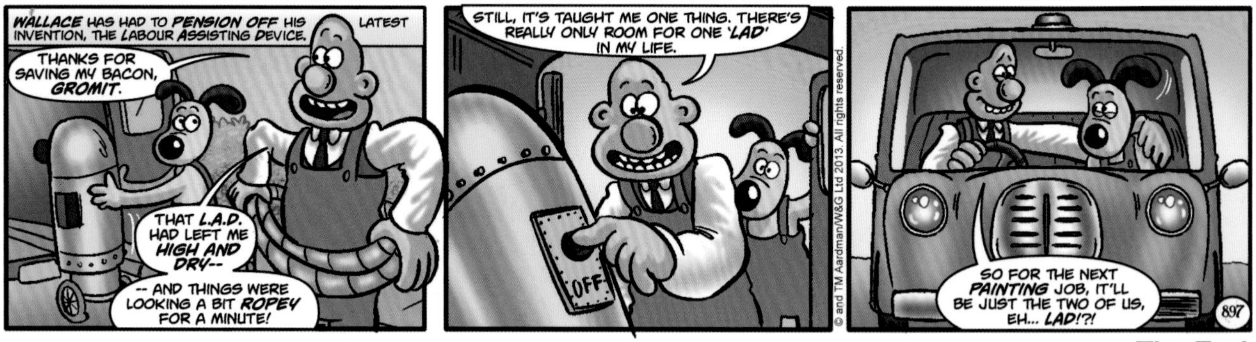
WALLACE HAS HAD TO PENSION OFF HIS LATEST INVENTION, THE LABOUR ASSISTING DEVICE.
THANKS FOR SAVING MY BACON, GROMIT.
THAT L.A.D. HAD LEFT ME HIGH AND DRY--
-- AND THINGS WERE LOOKING A BIT ROPEY FOR A MINUTE!
STILL, IT'S TAUGHT ME ONE THING. THERE'S REALLY ONLY ROOM FOR ONE 'LAD' IN MY LIFE.
OFF
SO FOR THE NEXT PAINTING JOB, IT'LL BE JUST THE TWO OF US, EH... LAD!?!
897

The End

Wallace & Gromit - A Bit of a Flap

by Aardman & Titan Comics

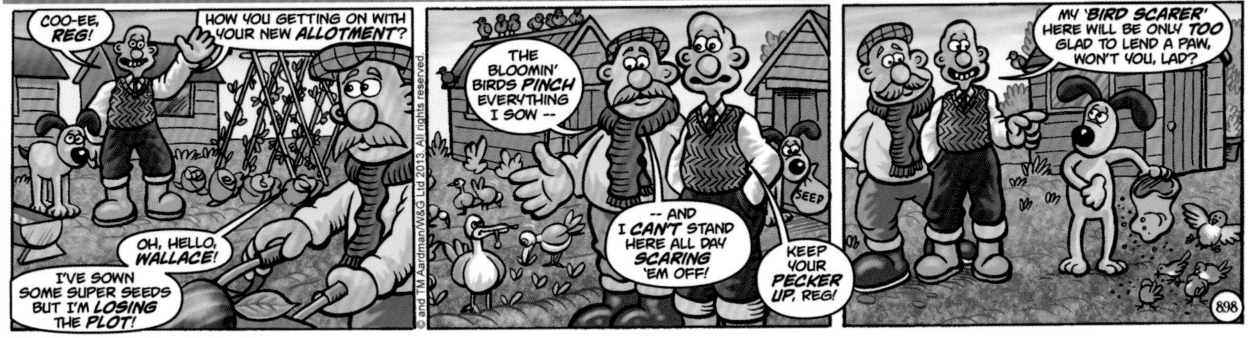

COO-EE, REG!
HOW YOU GETTING ON WITH YOUR NEW ALLOTMENT?
OH, HELLO, WALLACE!
I'VE SOWN SOME SUPER SEEDS BUT I'M LOSING THE PLOT!
THE BLOOMIN' BIRDS PINCH EVERYTHING I SOW --
-- AND I CAN'T STAND HERE ALL DAY SCARING 'EM OFF!
KEEP YOUR PECKER UP, REG!
SEED
MY 'BIRD SCARER' HERE WILL BE ONLY TOO GLAD TO LEND A PAW, WON'T YOU, LAD?
898

Wallace & Gromit - A Bit of a Flap

by Aardman & Titan Comics

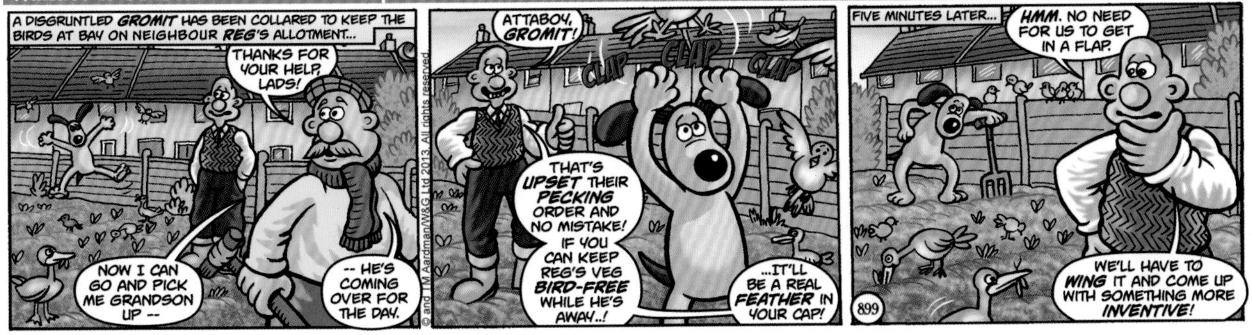

A DISGRUNTLED GROMIT HAS BEEN COLLARED TO KEEP THE BIRDS AT BAY ON NEIGHBOUR REG'S ALLOTMENT...
THANKS FOR YOUR HELP, LADS!
NOW I CAN GO AND PICK ME GRANDSON UP --
-- HE'S COMING OVER FOR THE DAY.
ATTABOY, GROMIT!
CLAP
CLAP
CLAP
THAT'S UPSET THEIR PECKING ORDER AND NO MISTAKE! IF YOU CAN KEEP REG'S VEG BIRD-FREE WHILE HE'S AWAY..!
...IT'LL BE A REAL FEATHER IN YOUR CAP!
FIVE MINUTES LATER...
HMM. NO NEED FOR US TO GET IN A FLAP.
WE'LL HAVE TO WING IT AND COME UP WITH SOMETHING MORE INVENTIVE!
899

Wallace & Gromit - A Bit of a Flap

by Aardman & Titan Comics

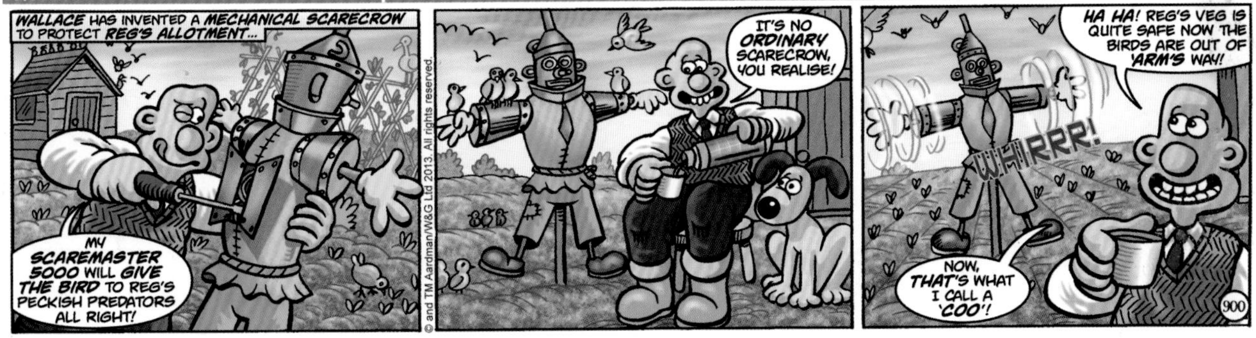

WALLACE HAS INVENTED A MECHANICAL SCARECROW TO PROTECT REG'S ALLOTMENT...
MY SCAREMASTER 5000 WILL GIVE THE BIRD TO REG'S PECKISH PREDATORS ALL RIGHT!
IT'S NO ORDINARY SCARECROW, YOU REALISE!
HA HA! REG'S VEG IS QUITE SAFE NOW THE BIRDS ARE OUT OF 'ARM'S WAY!
WHIRRR!
NOW, THAT'S WHAT I CALL A 'COO'!
900

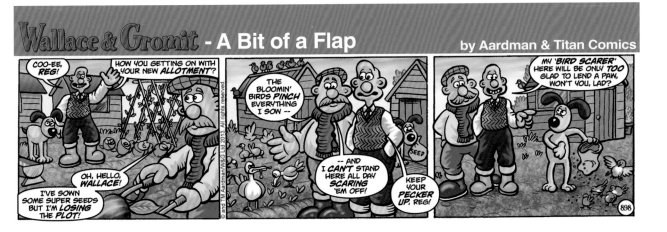

Wallace & Gromit - A Bit of a Flap by Aardman & Titan Comics

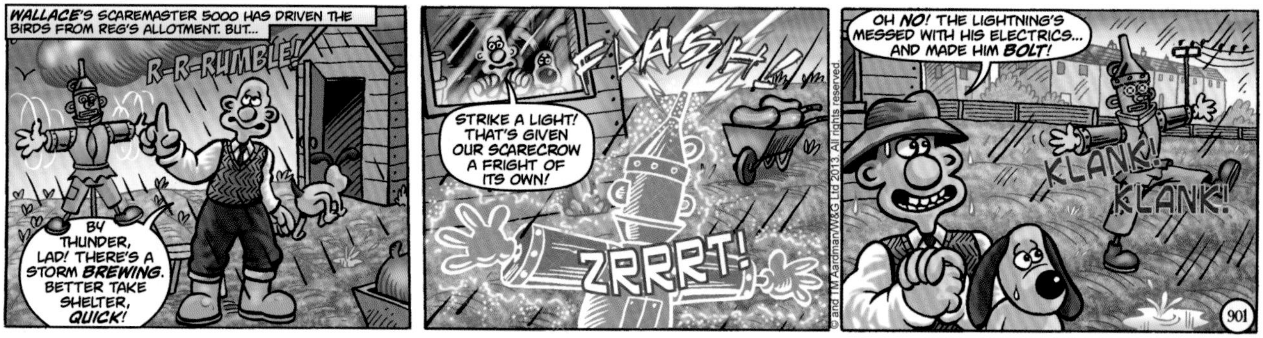

WALLACE'S SCAREMASTER 5000 HAS DRIVEN THE BIRDS FROM REG'S ALLOTMENT. BUT...
R-R-RUMBLE!
BY THUNDER, LAD! THERE'S A STORM BREWING. BETTER TAKE SHELTER, QUICK!
FLASH!
STRIKE A LIGHT! THAT'S GIVEN OUR SCARECROW A FRIGHT OF ITS OWN!
ZRRRT!
© and TM Aardman/W&G Ltd 2013. All rights reserved.
OH NO! THE LIGHTNING'S MESSED WITH HIS ELECTRICS... AND MADE HIM BOLT!
KLANK! KLANK!
901

Wallace & Gromit - A Bit of a Flap by Aardman & Titan Comics

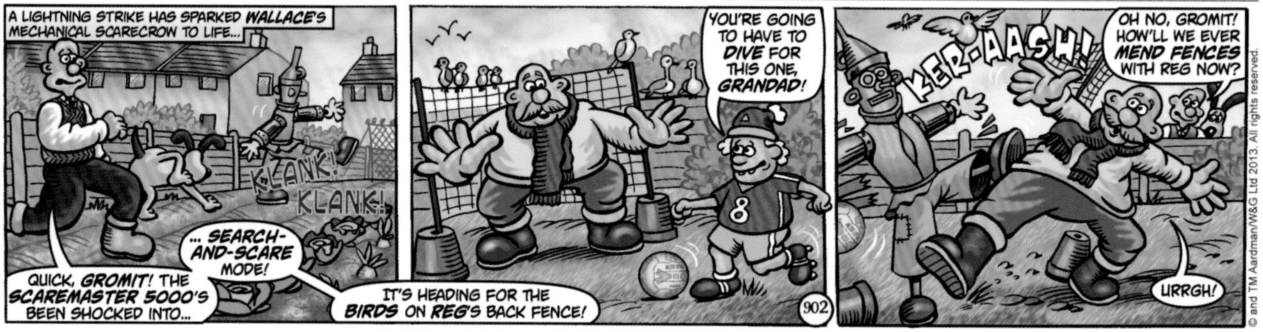

A LIGHTNING STRIKE HAS SPARKED WALLACE'S MECHANICAL SCARECROW TO LIFE...
KLANK! KLANK!
QUICK, GROMIT! THE SCAREMASTER 5000'S BEEN SHOCKED INTO...
... SEARCH-AND-SCARE MODE!
IT'S HEADING FOR THE BIRDS ON REG'S BACK FENCE!
YOU'RE GOING TO HAVE TO DIVE FOR THIS ONE, GRANDAD!
902
KER-AASH!
OH NO, GROMIT! HOW'LL WE EVER MEND FENCES WITH REG NOW?
URRGH!
© and TM Aardman/W&G Ltd 2013. All rights reserved.

Wallace & Gromit - A Bit of a Flap by Aardman & Titan Comics

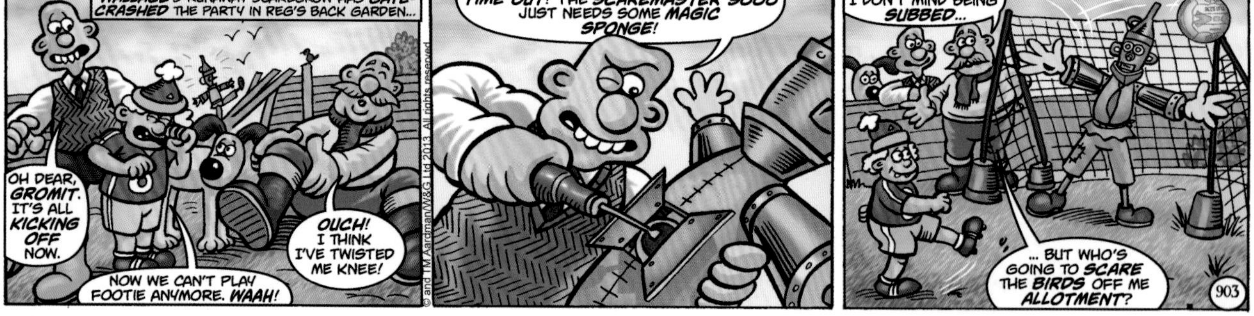

WALLACE'S RUNAWAY SCARECROW HAS GATE-CRASHED THE PARTY IN REG'S BACK GARDEN...
OH DEAR, GROMIT. IT'S ALL KICKING OFF NOW.
NOW WE CAN'T PLAY FOOTIE ANYMORE. WAAH!
OUCH! I THINK I'VE TWISTED ME KNEE!
© and TM Aardman/W&G Ltd 2013. All rights reserved.
TIME OUT! THE SCAREMASTER 5000 JUST NEEDS SOME MAGIC SPONGE!
I DON'T MIND BEING SUBBED...
... BUT WHO'S GOING TO SCARE THE BIRDS OFF ME ALLOTMENT?
903

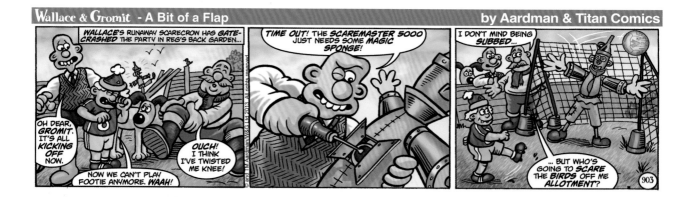

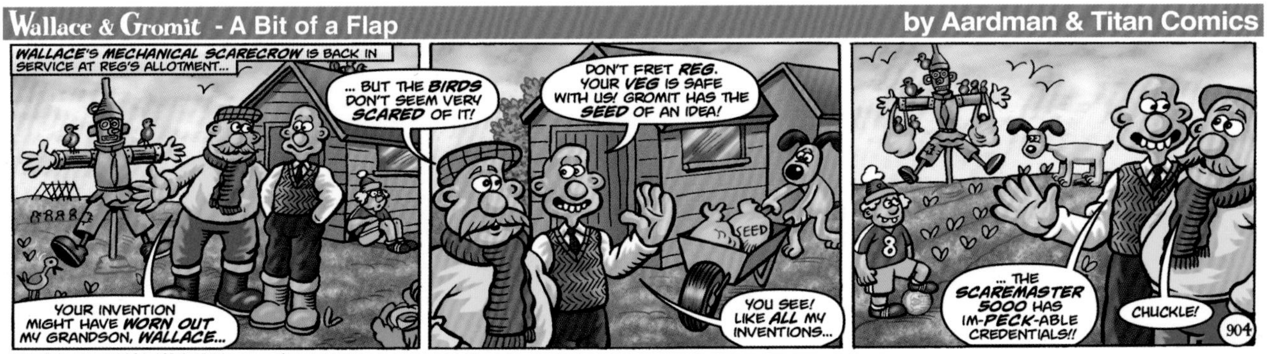
Wallace & Gromit - A Bit of a Flap
by Aardman & Titan Comics
WALLACE'S MECHANICAL SCARECROW IS BACK IN SERVICE AT REG'S ALLOTMENT...
YOUR INVENTION MIGHT HAVE WORN OUT MY GRANDSON, WALLACE...
... BUT THE BIRDS DON'T SEEM VERY SCARED OF IT!
DON'T FRET REG. YOUR VEG IS SAFE WITH US! GROMIT HAS THE SEED OF AN IDEA!
SEED
YOU SEE! LIKE ALL MY INVENTIONS...
... THE SCAREMASTER 5000 HAS IM-PECK-ABLE CREDENTIALS!!
CHUCKLE!
904

The End

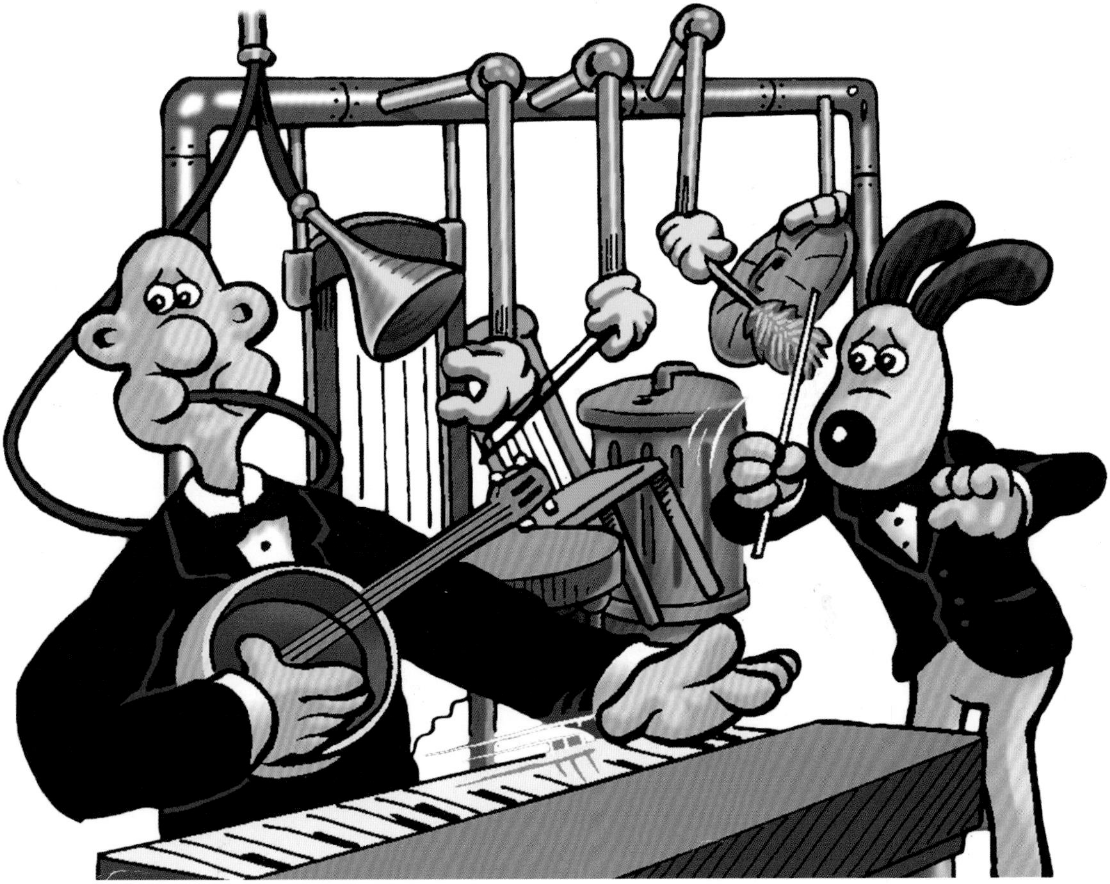

Tomb of the unknown artist.

Once again, we pay our respects to the various men and women who have all contributed to the creation of the comic strips featured in this book, from the writers to the pencillers, inkers, colourists and letterers without whom none of this would have been possible.

However, many of the writers listed below have made it known that they cannot be held responsible for any injuries resulting from the terrible puns found in this collection and indeed state that when they handed in their scripts, they were, on the whole, relatively pun free.

They lay the blame for the sheer number of the puns in this volume firmly at the feet of the editor who, they claim, demanded that the strips include as many of them as was humanly possible, and even went as far as to insert his own into the scripts once they were written.

Naturally, the editor vehemently denies such a heinous practice and suggested it must have been the work of the letterer! However, all attempts to contact the letterer, known only as DML have failed and the truth behind the inclusion of so many bad puns may now never be known.

STRIP CREDITS:
Writers: Richy K. Chandler, Mike Garley, Luke Paton, Gordon Volke and David Leach
Artists: Mychailo Kazybird, Sylvia Bull and Jay Clarke
Inker: Bambos & Jay Clarke **Colourist:** John Burns
Editor: David Manley-Leach
Letterer: DML
Book cover: David Manley-Leach, **concept**. Jay Clarke, **artist**.
John Burns, **colourist**.

And special thanks to Aardman and Nick Park.

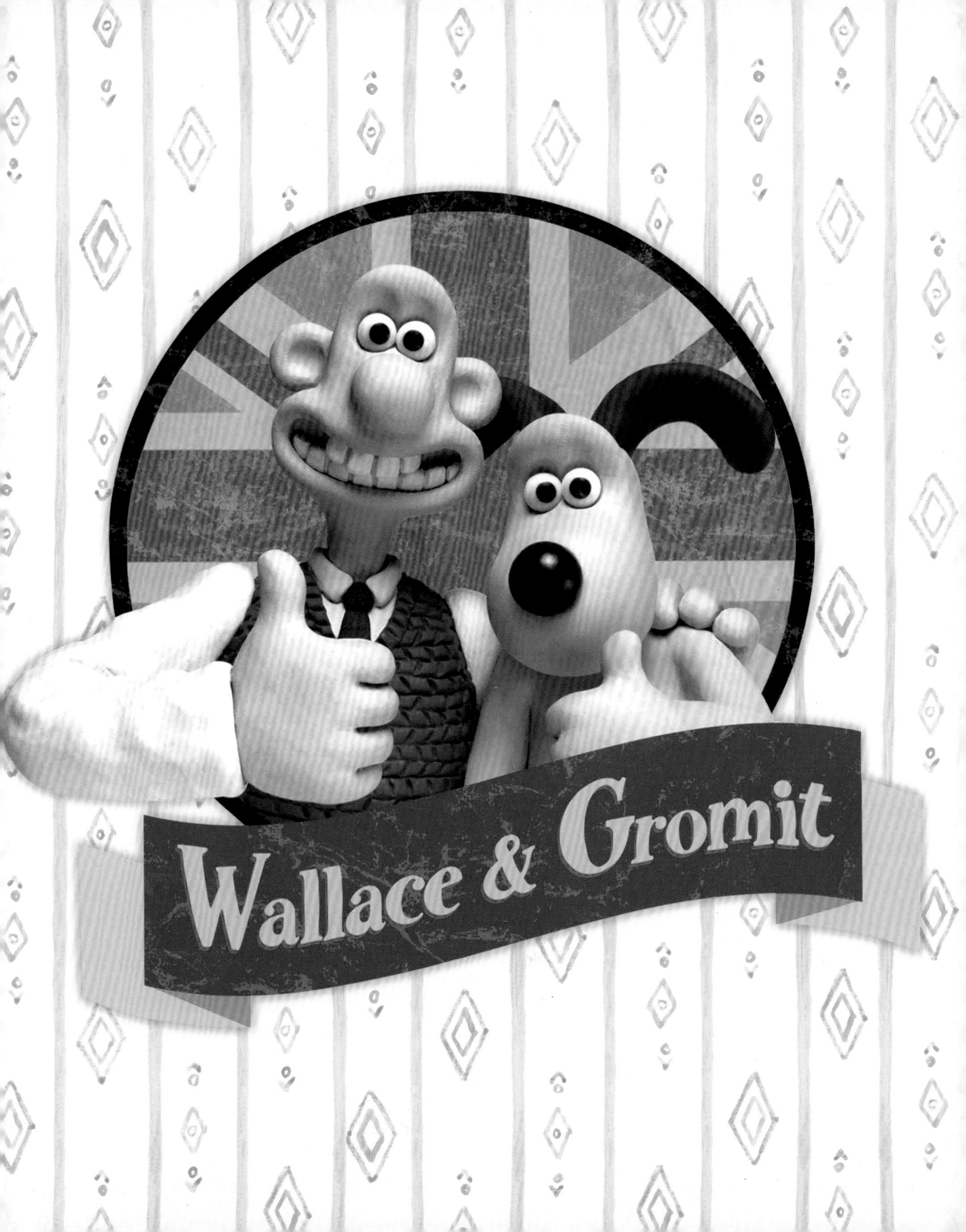
Wallace & Gromit

Also Available

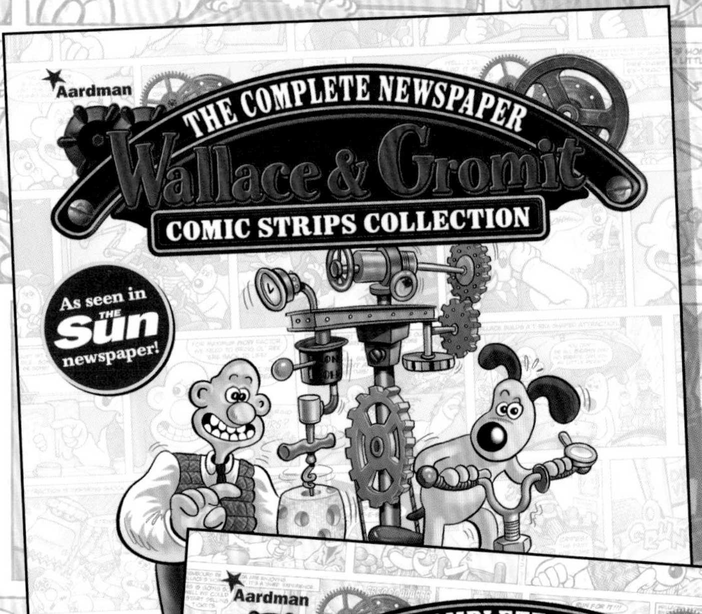

Aardman
THE COMPLETE NEWSPAPER
Wallace & Gromit
COMIC STRIPS COLLECTION
As seen in THE Sun newspaper!

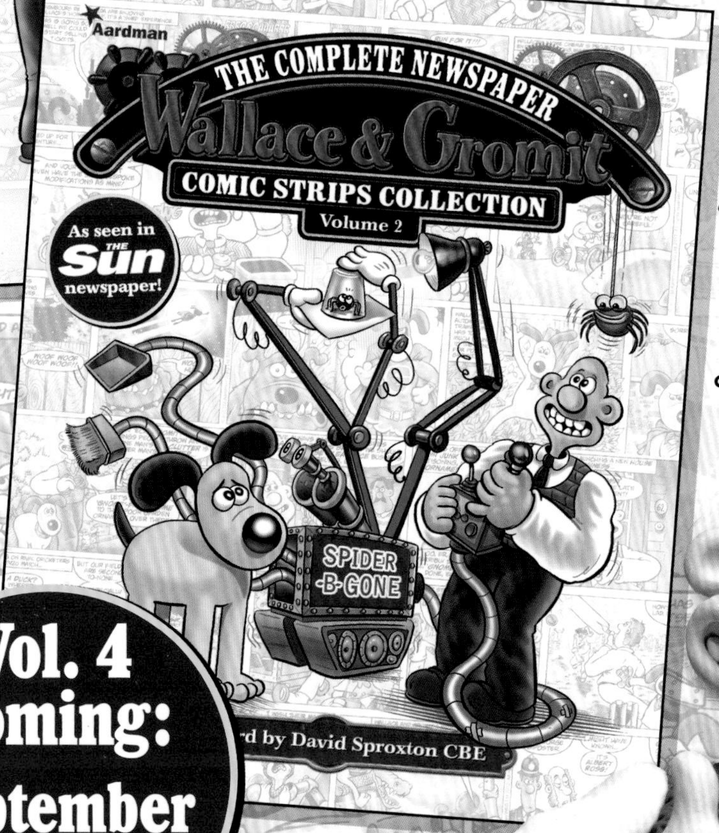

Aardman
THE COMPLETE NEWSPAPER
Wallace & Gromit
COMIC STRIPS COLLECTION
Volume 2
As seen in THE Sun newspaper!
SPIDER-B-GONE
by David Sproxton CBE

"If you're a Wallace & Gromit fan at all, this is definitely a must-have for your collection."
- Trash Mutant

'Kitschy and adorable.'
- The Geek Girl Project

'A solid collection of Wallace & Gromit hi-jinx and gags.'
- Retrenders

'If you're unafraid of groan-inducing puns that still manage to put a smile on your face or you're a big W&G fan...I can safely say you'll get a kick out of this book.'
- City of Films

'A fun romp through the daily adventures of Wallace and Gromit.'
- Culture Mass

'If you're a die-hard Wallace & Gromit fan, these are not to be missed.'
- Geek Dad

'Charming and funny, this is a cracking collection. Perfect for readers young and old.'
- Bookshelf Butterfly

Vol. 4 Coming: September 15th 2015

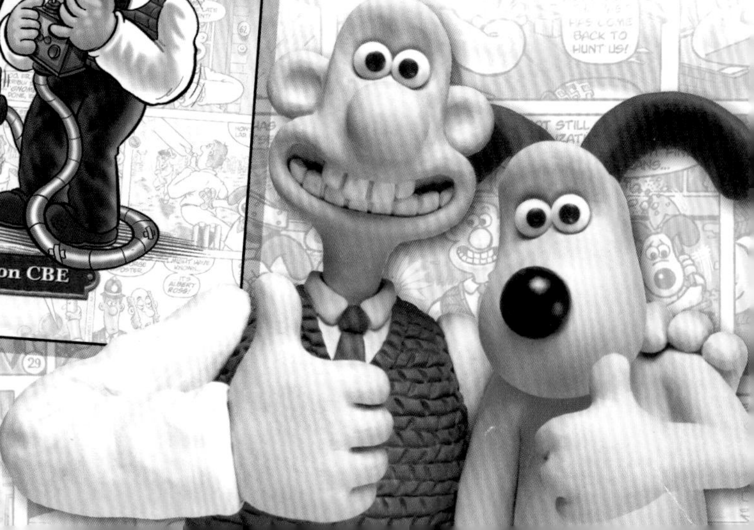

Aardman

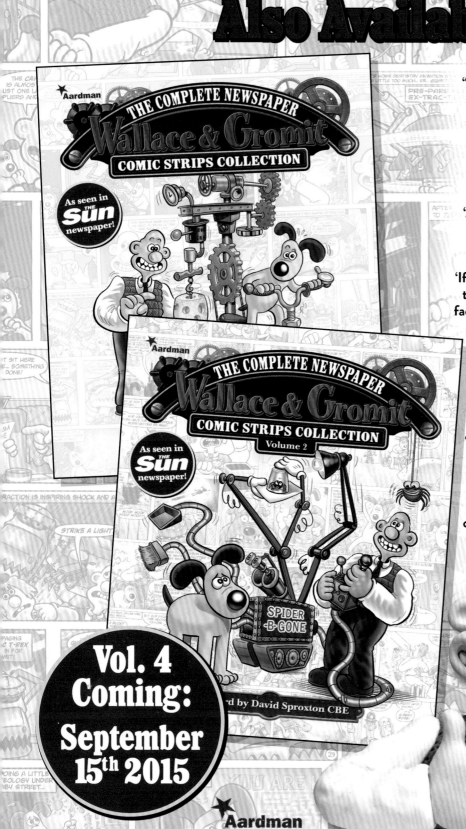